WALES AND THE FRENCH REVOLUTION

General Editors: Mary-Ann Constantine and Dafydd Johnston

D1610590

'A Fishguard Fencible', 1797, artist unknown

'Footsteps of Liberty and Revolt'

Essays on Wales and the French Revolution

edited by

MARY-ANN CONSTANTINE

AND

DAFYDD JOHNSTON

UNIVERSITY OF WALES PRESS
CARDIFF
2013

www.uwp.co.uk

British Library Cataloguing-in-Publication Data
A catalogue record for this book is available from the British Library.

ISBN   978-0-7083-2590-2
e-ISBN 978-0-7083-2591-9

Typeset in Wales by Eira Fenn Gaunt, Cardiff
Printed by CPI Antony Rowe, Chippenham, Wiltshire

'We are generally dismissed with loud applause and with the cry of "Vive la Nation. Toujours le tiers État!" . . . We were stop'd by similar inquiries, and as we travers'd along we found that we did not outrun the footsteps of Liberty and Revolt.'

George Cadogan Morgan, France, July 1789

WALES AND THE FRENCH REVOLUTION

The French Revolution of 1789 was perhaps the defining event of the Romantic period in Europe. It unsettled not only the ordering of society but language and thought itself: its effects were profoundly cultural, and they were long-lasting. The last twenty years have radically altered our understanding of the impact of the Revolution and its aftermath on British culture. In literature, as critical attention has shifted from a handful of major poets to the non-canonical edges, we can now see how the works of women writers, self-educated authors, radical pamphleteers, prophets and loyalist propagandists both shaped and were shaped by the language and ideas of the period. Yet surprising gaps remain, and even recent studies of the 'British' reaction to the Revolution remain poorly informed about responses from the regions. In literary and historical discussions of the so-called 'four nations' of Britain, Wales has been virtually invisible; many researchers working in this period are unaware of the kinds of sources available for comparative study.

The Wales and the French Revolution Series is the product of a four-year project funded by the AHRC and the University of Wales at the Centre for Advanced Welsh and Celtic Studies. It makes available a wide range of Welsh material from the decades spanning the Revolution and the subsequent wars with France. Each volume, edited by an expert in the field, presents a collection of texts (including, where relevant, translations) from a particular genre with a critical essay situating the material in its historical and literary context. A great deal of material is published here for the first time, and all kinds of genres are explored. From ballads and pamphlets to personal letters and prize-winning poems, essays, journals, sermons, songs and satires, the range of texts covered by this series is a stimulating reflection of the political and cultural complexity of the time. We hope these volumes will encourage scholars and students of Welsh history and literature to rediscover this fascinating period, and will offer ample comparative scope for those working further afield.

Mary-Ann Constantine and Dafydd Johnston
General Editors

Contents

Figures

Contributors

Dr Cathryn A. Charnell-White, Research Fellow, University of Wales Centre for Advanced Welsh and Celtic Studies

Dr Mary-Ann Constantine, Senior Research Fellow, University of Wales Centre for Advanced Welsh and Celtic Studies

Dr Hywel M. Davies, Director of Recruitment and Admissions, Aberystwyth University

Dr Elizabeth Edwards, Research Fellow, University of Wales Centre for Advanced Welsh and Celtic Studies

Mr Paul Frame, Independent Researcher, Swansea

Professor Caroline Franklin, Professor of English Literature, Swansea University

Professor Geraint H. Jenkins, Emeritus Professor and Former Director, University of Wales Centre for Advanced Welsh and Celtic Studies

Professor Dafydd Johnston, Director, University of Wales Centre for Advanced Welsh and Celtic Studies

Dr Ffion Mair Jones, Research Fellow, University of Wales Centre for Advanced Welsh and Celtic Studies

Dr Marion Löffler, Research Fellow, University of Wales Centre for Advanced Welsh and Celtic Studies

Professor Jon Mee, Professor of Romanticism Studies, University of Warwick

Professor Murray Pittock, Bradley Professor of English Literature and Vice-Principal, University of Glasgow

Mr Geoffrey W. Powell, Formerly Lecturer in Education, Keele University, and Tutor in Philosophy, Coleg Harlech

Dr Stephen K. Roberts, Editor, House of Commons 1640–1660, History of Parliament Trust, London

Dr Heather Williams, Research Fellow, University of Wales Centre for Advanced Welsh and Celtic Studies

Preface

This collection of essays comes out of a four-year research project at the University of Wales Centre for Advanced Welsh and Celtic Studies, which set out to explore the impact of the French Revolution and the subsequent wars with France on the culture of Wales. A range of fascinating texts is being published as part of the Wales and the French Revolution Series, which is discussed further in the Introduction below. This volume, however, is devoted to consideration of some of the broader themes of the period, and to many of the extraordinary people who played their part in shaping perceptions of Wales's place within Britain, Europe and the wider world.

The image on the cover of the volume is a water-colour study made by the twenty-three year old J. M. W. Turner on a seven-week tour of north Wales in 1798. From its alarming, weirdly lit mass of shapes and colours emerge, with a little concentration, the bulk of Caernarfon castle, troubling symbol of defence (against whom?) in times of war, and the skewed masts of ships, linking Wales to the conflict on the seas. The pull of the picture is both back into history and outwards into current affairs: both past and present are challenging and bloody. That complex pulling and meshing of different loyalties with and against new and inherited identities (Welsh, British, 'Citizen of the World', republican, Dissenter, loyalist, Volunteer) is explored, in a variety of different contexts, in the contributions published here.

We are hugely grateful to all our authors, therefore, and to the people and institutions that have made the work possible. The AHRC and the University of Wales have between them funded four years of intense research; the National Library of Wales, repository of many of the period's most interesting texts, has been a pleasant second home to many of us. We are especially grateful to the Library for the use of several images in this volume, and to Tom Lloyd and Martin Crampin for the delightful 'Fishguard Fencible' who guards the entrance to this book. Thanks go also to the director and staff of the University of Wales Press for their enthusiasm and practical support for this project from the very beginning. Members of our Advisory Panel have been generous with time and ideas – some have contributed essays here – and it has been a real pleasure to work with them. Nia Davies, Angharad Elias and Annie Carruthers, our administrative staff in the Centre, have all made the load lighter on many occasions. Most of all, we would like to thank our immediate colleagues on the project for their work and commitment over the last four years: Cathryn Charnell-White, Elizabeth Edwards, Ffion Mair Jones, Marion Löffler, Heather Williams – and our heroic copy editor, Gwen Gruffudd.

February 2013   Mary-Ann Constantine and Dafydd Johnston

Acknowledgements

Martin Crampin and Tom Lloyd: Frontispiece

The National Library of Wales: Figs. 1, 2, 4, 6, 8

David Parsons: Fig. 3

The British Library: Fig. 5

Stephen K. Roberts: Fig. 10

Abbreviations

BBCS	*Bulletin of the Board of Celtic Studies*
BL	British Library
BM	British Museum
Cardiff	Cardiff Central Library
CIM	Geraint H. Jenkins, Ffion Mair Jones and David Ceri Jones (eds.), *The Correspondence of Iolo Morganwg* (3 vols., Cardiff, 2007)
DNB	*The Dictionary of National Biography* (37 vols., London, 1885–1990)
DWB	*Dictionary of Welsh Biography down to 1940* (London, 1959)
HHSC	R. T. Jenkins and Helen M. Ramage, *A History of the Honourable Society of Cymmrodorion and of the Gwyneddigion and Cymreigyddion Societies (1751–1951)* (London, 1951)
JWBS	*Journal of the Welsh Bibliographical Society*
LlC	*Llên Cymru*
MC	*Montgomeryshire Collections*
NLW	National Library of Wales
NLWJ	*National Library of Wales Journal*
ODNB	*Oxford Dictionary of National Biography* at *http://www.oxforddnb.com*
TDHS	*Transactions of the Denbighshire Historical Society*
THSC	*Transactions of the Honourable Society of Cymmrodorion*
WHR	*Welsh History Review*

Introduction:
Writing the Revolution in Wales

MARY-ANN CONSTANTINE AND DAFYDD JOHNSTON

Glimpsed briefly in the vast crowd of characters with walk-on parts in Simon Schama's epic account of the French Revolution, we find:

> fashionable orators and writers like the ecumenical vegetarian Robert Pigott (who extended the message of fraternity into the animal kingdom) and the Quaker David Williams, both English pilgrims at the holy place of Liberty.[1]

These are, implies Schama, minor oddities, amusing marginals, their expressions of faith in the fraternal and internationalizing ideals of the early years of the revolution ('civic sentimentalism', he calls it) part and parcel of their eccentricity. Quakers! Vegetarians! The lofty ideals of the French Revolution have had some curious adherents indeed. But eccentricity – off-centredness – depends a great deal on where you are standing in the first place. While it is true that Robert Pigott (brother of the better-known Charles Pigott, author of the contentious *Political Dictionary* (1795)) was hardly a major player in the revolutionary drama, his particular 'eccentricity' has at least formed a continuous discrete strand within radical thinking since at least the Civil War.[2] And as for the second character – if he is indeed the David Williams most obviously present in Paris in the 1790s – then he was neither English nor a Quaker, but a renowned political and religious theorist and educationalist, born near Caerphilly and resident in London; the author of *Letters on Political Liberty* (1782) and of a deist liturgy welcomed by Voltaire and Rousseau, and the founder of the Literary Fund which bailed out 'Men of Genius and Learning in Distress', among them the newly married Coleridge, George Dyer and Iolo Morganwg.[3]

The shrinking and distorting of David Williams in this particular historical narrative is not surprising. *Citizens* has a cast of thousands and is laudably Francocentric – neither Thomas Paine nor even Edmund Burke receive a great deal of attention either. But this jolting moment of recognition is an extreme example of a relatively common occurrence to anyone working on Welsh culture – people and texts that seem central, canonical, mainstream in Wales appear as if viewed through the wrong end of a telescope, terribly distant and indistinct; or in a circus mirror, made ridiculous. Often they are 'present' as a glaring absence. This is, to some extent, both inevitable and necessary; it is how human and cultural relations work, and not everyone starts from the same centre. One of the great achievements of Romantic-era literary criticism over the last two decades has been the revelation of very different perspectives on the same historical events through studying a much richer, much more diverse range of texts. Thanks to digital tools, such as Eighteenth Century Collections Online, and thanks to armies of scholars working to publish texts from the edges of the traditional literary canon – letters, pamphlets, diaries, marginalia – we also have a finer sense of how ideas and opinions rippled through the networks and groupings of the period, of who knew whom, who read whom, and when. The importance of an author has come to depend, at least to some extent, on one's own centre of gravity at any time.

And centres of gravity have shifted. Another achievement in the last twenty years has been the evolution of devolution, of 'four nations' or 'archipelagic' criticism, which offers multiple perspectives on the period informed by the cultural differences of England, Ireland, Scotland and Wales.[4] This school has been responsible for a surge of writing on literature from Scotland and Ireland in particular, much of it testing the possibilities for national identities, and even national Romanticisms, as they were played out within the comparatively new political entity of Britain.[5] Of the four, Wales has been the Cinderella nation, misrepresented and overlooked. The reasons for this neglect are complex. In the late eighteenth century itself, as a result of its early union with England, Wales barely registers as a separate culture within certain types of legal and political discourse: as Rémy Duthille has noted, the language of those seeking parliamentary reform within Britain takes little account of the regions, even of Scotland, and virtually none at all of Wales.[6] And although by this period many of the London Welsh were demonstrating their cultural confidence through what Murray Pittock terms 'the performance of the self in diaspora',[7] some of the most influential Welsh voices on the wider international stage (notably Richard Price and David Williams, both discussed in this volume) express little interest in 'Welshness' in their public (or even their private) writings. There are, then, areas of discourse within the period where Welshness simply does not show up. On the other hand, as recent work has demonstrated again and again, the idea of Wales loomed large in the Romantic imagination:[8] Coleridge, Wordsworth, Southey, Blake, Bloomfield, the Shelleys, De Quincey, all have significant encounters with Welsh culture or the Welsh landscape. Essays in this volume by Caroline Franklin and Jon Mee remind us that Wales also informed the work of Godwin, Piozzi, Wollstonecraft and Seward. And there is, of course, no shortage of material from Wales itself.

At a practical level, it seems that the relative invisibility of Wales in modern critical writing is a problem of our own creating: many researchers working in this period are simply unaware of the kinds of sources available for comparative study. In the bicentenary year of the French Revolution – the year *Citizens* was published – the Welsh historian Gwyn Alf Williams had had enough:

> In 1968, I wrote: 'French historians of these islands nearly always use Welsh evidence, English historians hardly ever; I find this eccentric.' I no longer find it eccentric; I find it intolerable.[9]

'Almost nothing', noted one historian in 2000, 'is known of Welsh loyalism during the 1790s and 1800s'.[10] Not known by whom, one wonders? There are, after all, Welsh ballads to the Duke of York and Nelson, and Welsh eisteddfodic odes praising George III; there are anxious letters to the press by Dissenters protesting loyalty to the Crown in troubled times; published reports of loyalist meetings in small Welsh towns; patriotic songs to the local militia, and Tom Paine burned in effigy in Cardiff. These have not gone unnoticed by Welsh historians. It seems, at times, that Romantic-era Wales is caught in a double bind: largely Protestant, and largely loyal, it appears less foreign, and less troubling, in matters of politics and religion than do Scotland or Ireland, and is more likely to be overlooked. And yet (although much eighteenth-century writing from Wales is in fact in English) it is also more foreign in its actual text production – and so even more likely to be overlooked. Here be dragons indeed; from a critical perspective, Welsh culture is still, all too often, off the map.

In order that more than lip service is paid to the notion of four-nations criticism, then, some heed must be given to Welsh sources in both languages. One major aim of the recent AHRC-funded project on 'Wales and the French Revolution' has been to make this task easier for literary critics and historians of the period who are unlikely ever to read Welsh for themselves. A series of volumes, of which this book is one, presents a range of material reflecting responses to the events of the period. Most are anthologies, each taking a different genre – poetry in Welsh or English, printed ballads, journals and newspapers, letters and pamphlets – and providing a generous sample of texts, with translations; others have focused on a single author and an entire text (a journal, a travel diary) or explored an artistic oeuvre. Each volume offers close readings of the material, and maps the interplay of specific historical events with the times and places and people who produced it.[11]

The impact of the Age of Revolutions on the culture of Wales is not a new topic. In the 1920s David Davies and J. J. Evans published discursive accounts (in English and Welsh respectively) of the effect of events in France on Welsh lives and letters.[12] Both laid much of the groundwork for future research, locating Welsh texts from the period in manuscript collections, or in the rare surviving copies of printed journals, and weaving them into a narrative set against the backdrop of events in Britain and France. Though the thrust of both books was essentially literary – that is, their focus was on texts in their historical moment – it is striking how little interest this material has elicited in nearly a century of subsequent literary studies: the Welsh-literature university syllabus has been reluctant to stray from a focus on the 1760s and 1770s, with a Classical or Augustan period (exemplified by the poetry of Goronwy Owen) played off contrapuntally against a more emotional Methodism (the hymns of Williams Pantycelyn and Ann Griffiths). The more miscellaneous – and politically unsettling – literature of the 1790s and early 1800s has effectively dropped from sight.

Just as Welsh material has been missing from English/British accounts of the period, so, conversely, has new critical thinking about the Romantic period been relatively slow in permeating Welsh scholarship. Indeed, as an entertaining essay by Gwyn Alf Williams showed many years ago, the whole concept of Romanticism has had a tricky time of it in Wales.[13] But as Romantic-period criticism now inhabits a far more interdisciplinary space, where literature *is* history, and history becomes infinitely more nuanced by precise attention to language, all that is changing. Indeed, a wealth of the kind of marginal, non-canonical texts that used to disqualify Wales from 'real' Romanticism – pamphlets and sermons, letters and printed ballads – now make Welsh literature of the 1790s and early 1800s prime Romantic-period territory. The recent major research project focused on the manifold writings of the stonemason bard Edward Williams (Iolo Morganwg; 1747–1826) shows just how much can be done with the archive of a single (albeit extraordinary) author.[14]

Romantic Wales has been better served by its historians, both between the covers of the big general histories of Wales, and at local level in the myriad thriving county journals, where so much of the coal-face historical research takes place.[15] During the 1970s and 1980s the historian Gwyn Alf

Williams became the period's most passionate spokesman, with his energetic narratives packed with extraordinary characters, from the young adventurer John Evans, hunting for Welsh-speaking American Indians in the upper reaches of the Missouri, to the Millenarian preacher Morgan John Rhys, founder of a brave, if short-lived, radical Welsh-language journal in the mid-1790s and an even braver colony of Welsh settlers in Ohio.[16] Williams's Romantic Wales fizzes with lives lived against the huge political and social upheavals of industrialization, war, shifts in language and power, and mass emigration. His natural sympathies are with the 'organic intellectuals': the self-taught artisans, like Tomos Glyn Cothi and Iolo Morganwg or the tenant farmer William Jones (discussed by Geraint H. Jenkins in this volume), avid readers, sharp thinkers, men (they are inevitably men) of strong convictions and opinions. His enthusiasm, like theirs, is irresistible, and he cannot help but let them punch above their weight, leaving, one suspects, an abiding impression of the period as more radical than it really was. Like others who have followed him, his historian's instinct is biographical, and he is a master of a kind of indirect personal narrative, rich in quotation, which draws the reader in to the life of his characters with something of the novelist's flair.

But however immersed in their words, however sensitive to their personalities, the historian's ventriloquizing of these characters is still not the same as hearing their actual, unmediated, voices. Rather than write a narrative of the period, the aim of this series has been to return the focus to texts and sources, opening up new kinds of approaches and making it possible to ask different questions.[17] This volume of essays, besides offering new light on the period, acts as an interpretive companion to the series as a whole: its aim is to explore contexts, pick out themes, and give more life to some of the authors.

The study of literary responses to the French Revolution in Wales has long been hindered by academic structures which place our two languages in quite separate departments and disciplines. In recent years there have been moves to break down these divisions, primarily in twentieth-century literature, and to a lesser extent in eighteenth-century studies. The 'Wales and the French Revolution' project has engaged fully with writing in both languages, and that synthetic approach was dictated by the nature of the material. Although some individual writers had worked in both Welsh and English in earlier periods, most notably Morgan Llwyd in another Age of Revolution in the seventeenth century,[18] it is not until the 1790s that a whole generation of writers is seen to be operating bilingually. The causes and motivations of that bilingualism were multiple, including the influence of the periodical press and (as discussed by Cathryn Charnell-White in this volume) the growing dominance of London in Welsh literary culture, but the French Revolution clearly stimulated new ideas in both languages, increasing the traffic between them and bringing both into contact with other European languages.

This was not just a matter of an increase in the use of English at the expense of Welsh. The Welsh language shows extraordinary vitality in this period in its capacity to adapt its rich traditional modes of expression to deal with new concepts and genres. *Chwyldro*, corresponding to 'revolution' in its various senses, is just one of a host of words taking on new meanings at this time. Demand for reading matter in Welsh was evidently considerable, and although the three Welsh-language journals established in the mid-1790s were short-lived, there is reason to believe that their demise may have been due to repression by the authorities rather than lack of support.[19] The few numbers which were published contain a wealth of material, both translated and original, in which the Welsh language is seen to be engaging with the same issues as the English periodicals.[20]

Welsh-language publications were often suspected by the authorities of being vehicles for covert propagation of radical views, mostly, but not always, without justification. The Methodist movement in particular suffered a good deal of persecution on this account, and Methodist preachers were keen to emphasize that their opposition to the Established Church did not by any means imply disloyalty to the king. A revealing illustration of the atmosphere of the times is the following disclaimer which David Richard (Dafydd Ionawr) made in an English preface to a long Welsh-language poem on the Trinity, *Cywydd y Drindod*, published in 1793:

> Owing to the turbulence of the times, the Author thinks it necessary to premise, that his work has nothing to do with French Revolutions, nor British Politics.[21]

The very fact that he felt the need to say that, and to say it in English, perhaps suggests that his poem was not quite as apolitical as he liked to think.

The suspicions of the authorities were certainly not without substance in the case of some Welsh-language material, for the dramatic interlude discussed by Ffion Jones seems to have been able to go much further than anything on the English stage in enacting the executions of Louis XVI and Marie Antoinette. The very depiction of such events was controversial in itself, having the potential to undermine the authority of the monarchy. The anti-war stance of this interlude makes it a nice example of political ambiguity inherent in a fundamentally loyalist text.

Translation into Welsh was an opportunity to modify the political content of the source text, as shown by Marion Löffler in her discussion of the complex adaptation of the 'Marseillaise' into Welsh, partly via English and partly directly from the French, as 'Cân Rhyddid' (The Song of Liberty), in which the bloodthirsty chauvinism of the original is transformed into abstract Jacobin principles to an even greater degree than in the English version published in *Pig's Meat*. Conversely, translations into English of medieval Welsh poetry were a means of projecting contemporary ideals back to create a native radical tradition, depicting the heroic struggle of Welsh patriots against oppression.

Adaptation could be very free indeed, as in the case of the anti-monarchical pamphlet *Seren tan Gwmmwl* (1795) by John Jones (Jac Glan-y-gors). Although sometimes thought to be a Welsh version of Paine's *Rights of Man*, this corresponds only occasionally to the supposed source, and its debt to Paine is evident primarily in the democratic irreverence of its style.[22] Heather Williams's study of the reception of Rousseau in Wales reminds us that the transfer of ideas between cultures could occur not only in the form of texts but also as material manifestations such as the landscaped gardens of the Hafod estate.

'Political' responses, like people, are complex, after all, and even within a single poem or a letter, so called 'radical' and 'loyalist' elements may co-exist in unresolved tension. The closer one gets to the nuances of texts, and to the changing situations of lives lived in difficult times, the more obvious becomes the inadequacy of placing people on a political spectrum bisected by a clear political divide: as Stephen Roberts shows, the career of the 'anti-Jacobin' William Howels makes a neat enough contrast to that of his Glamorgan compatriot, the radical Iolo Morganwg – except in the matter of their consistently strident anti-Catholicism.

Above all, political responses shift with time, nowhere more markedly than in the 1790s, when convictions and ideologies were forever being caught, and occasionally overwhelmed, by the tide of events. A pivotal moment for Wales was the arrival of the French fleet at Fishguard (Abergwaun) in February 1797: for a few weeks, in a froth of invasion panic, all eyes turned to the Pembrokeshire coast, and Welsh loyalties came under sharp scrutiny in the British press. The ripples from those few anxious days were wide, affecting the Dissenting communities in particular, and hardening the popular anti-French, anti-Catholic stance. Hywel Davies's discussion of the aftermath of the event is an important reminder of the complexities and complicities (note the Welsh involvement in the brutal suppression of the Irish Rebellion in 1798) in relations between the Celtic peripheries and the British state. Those difficult relationships and troubled pasts push to the surface in other ways in Murray Pittock's exploration of the possibilities of 'national Gothic'. How writers after 1793 read the bloodier episodes of Welsh history against a contemporary backdrop of war is also considered by

Elizabeth Edwards, who shows that even landscape is not innocent of political meaning.

Historians have long understood the need to break down the bulky presence of *the* French Revolution – the great event, the beginning of European modernity – into highly charged, constantly moving atoms, and to trace the shifting relationships between them. If nothing else, this volume aims to hold and explore a series of such moments, and to suggest that, Dafydd Ionawr's strenuous disclaimer notwithstanding, writing from Wales in this period in fact has a great deal 'to do with French Revolutions, and with British Politics'.

Notes

[1] Simon Schama, *Citizens: A Chronicle of the French Revolution* (1989; paperback edn., London, 2004), p. 402.

[2] Timothy Morton, 'The Plantation of Wrath', in *idem* and Nigel Smith (eds.), *Radicalism in British Culture 1650–1830: From Revolution to Revolution* (Cambridge, 2009), pp. 64–85, at p. 65. See also David Erdman, *Commerce des Lumières: John Oswald and the British in Paris 1790–1793* (Columbia, 1986), on the vegetarianism of John Oswald.

[3] Williams's visit to Paris is explored by Mary-Ann Constantine, 'The Welsh in Revolutionary Paris', in this volume. For his life, see David Williams, *Incidents in my own Life which have been thought of some importance*, ed. Peter France (Brighton, 1980); J. Dybikowski, *On Burning Ground: An Examination of the Ideas, Projects and Life of David Williams* (Oxford, 1993); Whitney R. D. Jones, *David Williams: The Anvil and the Hammer* (Cardiff, 1986); Damian Walford Davies, *Presences that Disturb: Models of Romantic Identity in the Literature and Culture of the 1790s* (Cardiff, 2002); and the excellent entry in *ODNB*.

[4] See, e.g., Hugh Kearney, *The British Isles: A History of Four Nations* (Cambridge, 1989), and Murray G. H. Pittock, *Inventing and Resisting Britain: Cultural Identities in Britain and Ireland, 1685–1789* (New York, 1997).

[5] See, e.g., Leith Davis, Ian Duncan and Janet Sorensen (eds.), *Scotland and the Borders of Romanticism* (Cambridge, 2004); David Duff and Catherine Jones (eds.), *Scotland, Ireland and the Romantic Aesthetic* (Lewisburg, 2007); and for a recent overview, Murray Pittock, 'What is Scottish Romanticism?', in *idem* (ed.), *The Edinburgh Companion to Scottish Romanticism* (Edinburgh, 2011), pp. 1–9. See also *idem, Scottish and Irish Romanticism* (Oxford, 2008). Much of this work acknowledges as its stimulus Katie Trumpener's *Bardic Nationalism: The Romantic Novel and the British Empire* (Princeton, 1997), which, though thought-provoking, is problematic in its use of Welsh material.

[6] See Rémy Duthille, 'Le discours radical en Grande-Bretagne: entre patriotisme et universalisme, 1768–1789' (unpublished Paris Sorbonne / Edinburgh doctoral dissertation, 2009), pp. 311–15, for a discussion of the invisibility of Wales in the

writings of the Society for Constitutional Information (SCI). For the absence of a 'Welsh' category among British citizens abroad, see Constantine, 'The Welsh in Revolutionary Paris', in this volume.

[7] Pittock, *The Edinburgh Companion to Scottish Romanticism*, p. 5. See Cathryn Charnell-White, 'Networking the Nation: The Bardic and Correspondence Networks of Wales and London in the 1790s', in this volume for the societies of the London Welsh.

[8] See Gerard Carruthers and Alan Rawes, *English Romanticism and the Celtic World* (Cambridge, 2003); Davies, *Presences that Disturb*; *idem* and Lynda Pratt (eds.), *Wales and the Romantic Imagination* (Cardiff, 2007); Richard Gravil, *Wordsworth's Bardic Vocation 1787–1842* (London, 2003).

[9] Gwyn A. Williams, *Artisans and Sans-Culottes: Popular Movements in France and Britain during the French Revolution* (2nd edn., London, 1989), p. xi.

[10] Jennifer Mori, *Britain in the Age of the French Revolution, 1785–1820* (Harlow, 2000), p. 84. Clive Emsley's attractive book for students, *Britain and the French Revolution* (Harlow, 2000), does not mention Wales; Stuart Andrews's analysis of *The British Periodical Press and the French Revolution, 1789–99* (Houndmills, 2000) 'does not include the provincial press, whose reporting of national events usually relied on the reprinting of accounts from the London newspapers' (p. x): this is demonstrably *not* true of the Welsh periodicals. See Marion Löffler, *Welsh Responses to the French Revolution: Press and Public Discourse 1789–1802* (Cardiff, 2012). Wales is also missing from a volume of the *Annales historiques de la révolution française*,(342; October–December 2005) dedicated to 'Les îles britanniques et la révolution française' (the British Isles and the French Revolution). For Welsh absence from 'four nations' criticism, see Mary-Ann Constantine, 'Beauty spot, Blind spot: Romantic Wales', *Literature Compass*, 5, no. 3 (May 2008), 577–90.

[11] Publications to date include Ffion Mair Jones, *Welsh Ballads of the French Revolution 1793–1815*; Löffler, *Welsh Responses to the French Revolution*; Cathryn Charnell-White, *Welsh Poetry of the French Revolution 1789–1805*; Mary-Ann Constantine and Paul Frame (eds.), *Travels in Revolutionary France and A Journey Across America by George Cadogan Morgan and Richard Price Morgan*; Elizabeth Edwards, *English-Language Poetry from Wales 1789–1806*; John Barrell, *Edward Pugh of Ruthin 1763–1813: A Native Artist*. Volumes of letters and pamphlets and a volume on translation are currently in progress.

[12] David Davies, *The Influence of the French Revolution on Welsh Life and Literature* (Carmarthen, 1926); J. J. Evans, *Dylanwad y Chwyldro Ffrengig ar Lenyddiaeth Cymru* (Lerpwl, 1928).

[13] See Gwyn A. Williams, 'Romanticism in Wales', the essay which, somewhat startlingly, opens Roy Porter and Mikuláš Teich (eds.), *Romanticism in National Context* (Cambridge, 1988), pp. 9–36. Williams notes with some glee that the *Oxford Companion to Welsh Literature* (Oxford, 1986) struggles to find much evidence of 'Romantic sensibility' until well into the nineteenth century; he counters, as ever, with vividly described 'Romantic' lives (p. 9).

[14] See, especially, *CIM*; details of many further volumes exploring his life and work can be found at *http://www.iolomorganwg.wales.ac.uk*.

[15] See, e.g., John Davies, *Hanes Cymru: A History of Wales in Welsh* (London, 1990); Prys Morgan (ed.) *The Tempus History of Wales* (Stroud, 2001); *idem, The Eighteenth Century Renaissance* (Llandybïe, 1981); David J. V. Jones, *Before Rebecca: Popular Protest in Wales 1793–1835* (London, 1973); Peter D. G. Thomas, *Politics in Eighteenth-Century Wales* (Cardiff, 1998).

[16] Gwyn A. Williams, *The Search for Beulah Land: The Welsh and the Atlantic Revolution* (London, 1980); *idem, Madoc: The Making of a Myth* (London, 1979); *idem*, 'Druids and Democrats: Organic Intellectuals and the First Welsh Radicalism', in Raphael Samuel and Gareth Stedman Jones (eds.), *Culture, Ideology and Politics: Essays for Eric Hobsbawm* (London, 1982), pp. 246–76. For Morgan John Rhys, see Constantine, 'The Welsh in Revolutionary Paris', in this volume.

[17] An early attempt to do this should be acknowledged here: Trevor Herbert and Gareth Elwyn Jones (eds.), *The Remaking of Wales in the Eighteenth Century* (Cardiff, 1988) is a useful selection of key texts with interpretative essays aimed at encouraging students of history to interrogate their sources' use of language.

[18] See M. Wynn Thomas, *Morgan Llwyd* (Cardiff, 1984).

[19] See references noted in Dafydd Johnston, 'Radical Adaptation: Translations of Medieval Welsh Poetry in the 1790s', in this volume.

[20] See Löffler, *Welsh Responses to the French Revolution*.

[21] Dafydd Ionawr, *Cywydd y Drindod* (Gwrexam, 1793), [p. vii].

[22] Marion Löffler and Bethan Jenkins are currently working on a volume of Welsh radical pamphlets, which will include *Seren tan Gwmmwl*.

Wales as Nowhere: the tabula rasa of the 'Jacobin' imagination

CAROLINE FRANKLIN

Wales became a Utopia for the eighteenth-century literary imagination because it illustrated Thomas More's pun on eutopia (good place) and outopia (no place). Its desolate beauty attracted tourists in the 1770s and 1780s such as Dr Johnson, Arthur Young and William Gilpin.[1] Though geographically central within the British Isles, it was Nowhere from a metropolitan standpoint: as Geraint H. Jenkins notes, at this period 98% of the Welsh population were disenfranchised, 85% of the population of roughly half a million lived in villages of fewer than 1,000 inhabitants, and 90% of them spoke only Welsh.[2] Since 25 July 1689, when the Council of Wales was abolished, Wales had no civil institutions and it possessed no capital or metropolis. This made it a *tabula rasa* to urban writers when concocting fantasies of the good society.

Literature has always had its touchstones: mythological or religious heavens on earth, such as the land of Cockayne, Eden, Arcadia or the ideal commonwealth. From the time of Sir Thomas More and Sir Philip Sidney, pastoral idylls subverted courtly values. Then Enlightenment literary Utopias constructively criticized contemporary society by projecting ideal *man-made* societies for the first time. The typical literary form of these – a journey back or forward in time or space to a secret island or valley – conceded the political vision might be unreachable: 'The essentially contested nature of the concept of utopia . . . can be traced back to the paradox at the heart of the pun More coined.'[3] Economically backward Wales was a standing joke when judged in terms of Enlightenment stadial history, yet functioned as a wonderfully clean sheet upon which to construct a blueprint for a new golden age. Liberal and socialist concepts of progress towards perfectibility needed feasible pictures of an imaginary future situated in a recognizable present.[4] Their optimism in a civilizing process such as that outlined in Adam Smith's *Wealth of Nations* (1776) contested sceptical visions of decline from an ideal past, exemplified by Gibbon's *Decline and Fall of the Roman Empire* (1776–88). Here the Roman Empire was portrayed as initially bringing civilization to the barbaric Celtic culture it encountered before itself degenerating.[5] The aboriginal status of Celtic language and culture gave a patriotic glamour to Rousseauian nostalgia for the simple life. On the other hand, and ironically, Wales was in the vanguard of technological change in the 1780s. Her iron and coal were the raw materials needed for modern innovations in mechanical engineering, making possible an industrial revolution of the future.[6] Primitive Wales might be magically transformed. The Principality was a crucible to test one's progressive belief in the human ability to shape society.

Wales features prominently in fiction of the 1780s, for example: Robert Bage, *Mount Henneth* (1782); William Godwin, *Imogen: A Pastoral Romance from the Ancient British* (1784); Catherine Parry, *Eden Vale* (2 vols., 1784); Anna Maria Bennett, *Anna; or, Memoirs of a Welch Heiress* (4 vols., 1785); Richard Graves, *Eugenius, or, Anecdotes of the Golden Vale* (2 vols., 1785); Mrs H. Cartwright, *Retaliation, or, The History of Sir Edward Oswald and Lady Frances Seymour* (1787), *Powis Castle* (2 vols., 1788); Mr Nicholson, *Catherine, or, The Wood of Llewellyn* (2 vols., 1788); Charlotte Smith, *Emmeline, or, The Orphan of the Castle* (4 vols., 1788); Mary Wollstonecraft, *Original Stories* (1788); and Elizabeth Ryves, *The Hermit of Snowden, or, memoirs of Albert and Lavinia* (1789).[7] Of the so-called 'Jacobin' novelists, William Godwin, Robert Bage, Charlotte Smith and Mary Wollstonecraft all featured Wales in their earliest publications. The 'Jacobin' novel has come to be associated with the 1790s in recent studies,[8] but this chapter argues that it originated in novels of sensibility produced in the aftermath of the American War of Independence in 1776, which used Richardsonian paradigms to depict the exploitation of a virgin paradise.[9] Catherine Parry's *Eden Vale* (1784), for instance, tells of Welsh cousins fighting on opposite sides, and the grieving widow makes a passionate appeal to the king to cease making war: '"Surely our gracious Monarch is kept in ignorance of this scene of desolation and distress, or, attentive as he is to the religious and moral duties of life, he would not be unmindful of his subjects, who have an equal claim to his love, if melting beyond the torrid zone, or freezing amidst Canadian snows"' (I, p. 72).

The establishment of the new republic in America was greeted with rapture by Revd Richard Price, whose view of history was neither optimistic nor pessimistic but apocalyptic:

With heartfelt satisfaction I see the revolution in favour of universal liberty which has taken place in America – a revolution which opens a new prospect in human affairs and begins a new aera in the history of mankind – a revolution by which Britons themselves will be the greatest gainers, if wise enough to improve properly the check that has been given to the despotism of their ministers, and to catch the flame of virtuous liberty which has saved their American brethren.[10]

The Utopian visions of Richard Price and Joseph Priestley were a mutation of the seventeenth-century Millennialist tradition. They believed in a perfectability ordained by God yet necessarily brought about by heroic human will.[11] The shocking conflict between the mother country and the thirteen colonies in 1776 outweighed the British internal revolution of 1688 because it threw into question relationships within Protestantism. J. C. D. Clark argues that national identities inside Britain were not at this time imbricated with issues of race and language as they would be in the nineteenth century, but, rather, were rooted in a 'shared libertarian history within a polity defined and given coherence by the law, and a shared sense of Providential destiny'.[12] Language, however, was a major reason for the rejection of Anglicanism in Wales, delivered as it was through the medium of English. In 1780 Wales was brought into direct comparison with the colonies when Edmund Burke denounced the attempt of the Treasury to increase revenue from taxation from the impoverished Principality. Burke in 1774–5 had unsuccessfully argued for the abandonment of American taxation. Now the MP for Wales's mercantile 'capital', Bristol, wittily ridiculed the government who appointed the 'Preux Chevalier' John Probert at a salary of £300 p.a. 'to look for revenue' but who 'found rebellion'.[13] Burke went on to unsuccessfully propose a cost-cutting 'reform' instead: to unite 'all the five principalities to the crown and to its ordinary jurisdiction', and thus abolish the Welsh circuits entirely.

Wales and America were closely linked in terms of religious dissent, as Welsh Baptists and Quakers had emigrated in such numbers to Pennsylvania in the late seventeenth century that Penn had considered naming the settlement 'New Wales'.[14] The Welsh were instrumental in developing the American coal and steel industry there. America was also the new Eden of various radical sects such as the Moravians and Shakers, wishing to experiment with new co-operative and communistic ways of rural life which resisted centralized control. Disappointed revolutionaries fleeing the Terror or the reactionary backlash to the French Revolution would include Joseph Priestley himself. In the 1790s, Samuel Taylor Coleridge and Robert Southey planned a practice run in south Wales for their Pantisocracy in America, and Edward Williams (Iolo Morganwg) dreamed of an American expedition to find the descendants of Prince Madog who, according to the Welsh legend, had

discovered the New World before Columbus. The early socialist Robert
Owen founded his famous New Harmony project in Indiana in 1825. Such
social experiments were meant to be levers prompting change, but it would
only be in America that the religious socialism of the seventeenth century
evolved without a break into secular socialism, for the European Enlightenment engendered militant anti-clericalism.[15]

Godwin's sceptical yet Utopian romance *Imogen: A Pastoral Romance From
the Ancient British* (1784) imagines a society without possessions or wealth,
which by definition cannot see the point of war or conquest. It contrasts
strongly with the fatalistic universe of *Things as They Are, or, Caleb Williams*
(1794), written a decade later at the time of repressive clampdown in Britain
on supporters of the French Revolution.[16] Godwin's prophetic pastoral
imagined things as they might be, especially if the Old Country went back
to its pre-Norman, pre-Roman, democratic roots for revolutionary inspiration. Although he apparently had not yet visited the Principality in 1784,
the young writer combined Miltonic masque with Rousseauian pastoral in
an imaginary past doubtless inspired by Gray's primitivism, antiquarian
speculation about Stonehenge, and scholarly publications such as Evan
Evans's *Some Specimens of the Poetry of the Antient Welsh Bards, translated into
English* (1764), John Walters's *Translated Specimens of Welsh Poetry in English
Verse* (1782) and Edward Jones's *Musical and Poetical Relicks of the Welsh Bards*
(1784). Godwin would also have connected Wales with contemporary
nonconformist 'prophets' who combined scientific brilliance with religious
fervour for social change, such as Richard Price and his colleague and fellow-
mathematician, Abraham Rees, who had been head of Hoxton Academy
where Godwin had studied, and by 1786 was made fellow of the Royal
Society.[17]

Godwin's artful preface is modelled on that of Horace Walpole's Gothic
novel, *The Castle of Otranto* (1764), which masqueraded as a modern translation of an antiquarian book printed in Naples in 1529. The British 'editor',
William Marshall presents the stylized story of a villainous aristocrat whose
castle is destroyed by a gigantic apparition as a historical curiosity. It was
cobbled up by an 'artful priest' trying to 'enslave a hundred vulgar minds',
'confirm the populace in their ancient errors and superstition', and prop up
weakening clerical power.[18] Walpole implicitly asks contemporary readers
to see belief in aristocracy as itself a type of superstition. Godwin's ironic
preface to *Imogen* suggests that only a prehistoric society could be egalitarian
as this romance describes:

> The following performance, as the title imports, was originally composed in the
> Welch language . . . It appears under the name of Cadwallo, an ancient bard,

who probably lived at least one hundred years before the commencement of our
common æra. The manners of the primitive times seem to be perfectly understood
by the author, and are described with the air of a man who was in the utmost
degree familiar with them.[19]

Godwin cheekily wonders if Milton's masque, *Comus*, performed in 1634
in honour of John Egerton, earl of Bridgewater, lord president of Wales,
was based on this 'ancient' Welsh story, while conceding Milton improved
on the 'original'. This wittily pays tribute to Milton's literary stature, and
acknowledges him to be Godwin's model as a republican writer using the
masque genre to attack courtly values, while neatly registering Godwin's
dissociation from his precursor's Christianity.[20] For so very archaic is this
Welsh romance, 'it is impossible to discover in any part of it the slightest
trace of Christianity', and in 'a country so pious as that of Wales it would
have been next to impossible for the poet . . . to avoid all allusion to the
system of revelation' (p. 169, my emphasis). Godwin's editor later concedes
Imogen was probably written more recently than the Iron Age, perhaps by
one of his own forebears, Rice ap Thomas, from the reign of William III
(Godwin did have Welsh connections). Godwin must surely have been a
model for Iolo Morganwg in his use of pastiche and Celtic fakery to legitimize
democracy as both Ancient and British. So fond was Godwin of parody at
this time that, in his *Herald of Literature* (1784), he wrote a series of fictitious
works purportedly by Thomas Paine, R. B. Sheridan, Edmund Burke and
Frances Burney, then as Pamela Clemit notes, 'proceeded to review them
as if they were genuine'.[21]

   Godwin's Ossianic tale opens in an Edenic pastoral community living in
'happy equality' in the Vale of Clwyd: a remote 'inclosure' where 'the hoarse
din of war had never reached' (p. 173). The bards foster a natural religion
in which the very 'clods appeared to be informed with a conscious spirit'
(p. 185), and the magical story of Edwin and Imogen is told in a style
appropriate to their animist beliefs.[22] Yet nature encompasses thunderbolts
and savage wolves as well as lambs and doves of peace, and the pair cannot
be united until they confront power and violence in the fallen, hierarchical
world. The innocence of this pastoral Utopia functions dialectically with
experience of courtly values. So Imogen is abducted by Roderic 'Lord of a
hundred hills' (p. 9), in his goblin-powered car. Godwin follows Richardson
and Rousseau in using a woman's consent to sex as a political metaphor for
a society consenting to government in a narrative of sensibility. In the Welsh
Eden, Imogen stands firm against Roderic's temptations of flattery, sensuality
and wealth. Though the word 'rape' is used on the title page, a goblin warns
Roderic that the use of physical force will be fatal to him (p. 209).

Godwin puts Spenserian allegory to use in fostering political radicalism rather than inculcating obedience to authority. When Imogen is taken to Roderic's domain she sees the future: the Enlightenment which will succeed the Golden Age. For Roderic is son of the female magus Rodogune whose 'intellectual powers bestowed upon her by the Gods were great and eminent' (p. 196). Her son's applied science is the technical revolution which produced farming and the division of labour. He has iron ploughs to produce 'a rich scene of vegetable gold' (p. 214), and has amassed 'superfluous riches' (p. 217) and servants to call him lord. The political theory that social hierarchy arose from competition over property derives from Rousseau's *On the Origin of Inequality in Society* (1754).[23] Godwin seems to be wittily combining nostalgia for the more equal society that existed in Britain before the Norman Conquest with an allusion to the contemporary industrial exploitation of north Wales by entrepreneurs in touch with scientific and Dissenting circles in the Midlands, such as the Lunar Society. Perhaps the reason Godwin placed his Druids in the Vale of Clwyd rather than Anglesey was that the Bersham works near Wrexham were making a fortune for the brother-in-law of Joseph Priestley: ironmaster John Wilkinson (1728–1808). Wilkinson pioneered the use of steam engines in iron production and forged more accurate cannons and ordnance for the British armed forces.[24] Because north Wales still had a pastoral economy, based on cattle droving and textiles, the break with the past was sudden and revolutionary.

The gender politics of *Imogen* are crucial, for the culture of the shepherds of the valley is democratic, theocratic, patriarchal: male Druids and bards pass down communal wisdom through the ages. Roderic's neighbouring mountain kingdom is courtly, aristocratic and effeminate. Perhaps Godwin applied this Burkean gendering of the sublime and the beautiful after reading Lord Lyttelton's travel journal, where the mountains of Berwyn are described as Nature 'in the majesty of a tyrant' in contrast to the valley landscape inspiring 'meditations of love', which have 'great beauty but no majesty'.[25] He may also have ventriloquized Evan Evans's primitivist patriotic stance: 'I prefer the ancient British bards before the best English poets, and the ancient British verse as more manly and heroic than the wretched rhimes of the English.'[26]

In the masque's parodic reversal of roles, the lowly Imogen is placed on the throne in Roderic's mansion and crowned the goddess of simplicity as the praises of women are sung.[27] This allows her to see supernatural beings that previously were perceived solely by 'the consecrated priests' of the vale. A Marxist interpretation would suggest she is momentarily interpellated or tempted by the attraction of feudal chivalric ideology, which supposedly venerated women and protected the weak. Her own priests, this implies, indulge in comparable theatrical displays of power to mystify the populace. 'Those who believed themselves gifted with supernatural endowments must have felt themselves exempt and privileged from common rules, somewhat in the same way as the persons whom fiction has delighted to pourtray with immeasurable wealth', as Godwin would comment elsewhere.[28] We remember the chilling moment during the bardic recitals in the Vale of Clwyd when a story is told of the human sacrifice of a youth, Arthur, demanded to appease the wrath of the gods.

The Foucault of his time, Godwin theorized the attractions of ideologies of past ages. Even at the end of his life he still nicely balanced scepticism and sympathy in imagining why the Druidic priests of natural religion must also have been the most powerful poets:

> The supernatural appearances with which our ancestors conceived themselves perpetually surrounded must have had a strong tendency to cherish and keep alive the powers of the imagination and to penetrate those who witnessed or expected such things with an extraordinary sensitiveness.[29]

Even though Druidic priests are viewed with Enlightenment scepticism, Godwin's Calvinist background still makes him more inclined towards a theocracy than an aristocracy. He seeks to return the pastoral to the people in *Imogen*, and the same impulse would produce his masterpiece, the influential Utopian thesis of political anarchy: *Enquiry Concerning Political Justice* (1793). Clemit notes that Thomas Paine had posited American pastoral settlements as the opposite of British corruption in *Common Sense* (1776):

> Government, like dress, is the badge of lost innocence; the palaces of kings are built on the ruins of the bowers of paradise.[30]

In 'The Dream Interrupted' he allegorized the war as a tempest clearing the air in the New Eden:

> The pestilential atmosphere represents that ministerial corruption which surrounds and exercises its dominion over her, and which nothing but a storm can purify. The tempest is the present contest, and the event will be the same. She will rise with new glories from the conflict, and her fame be established in every corner of the globe . . .[31]

Godwin used Wales instead of America as shorthand for a natural, less hierarchical, society: not only in *Imogen*, but in *Things as They Are* (1794) and *Fleetwood* (1805).[32]

The spirited Imogen triumphantly surmounts all temptation by choosing the simple life over luxury. Next, she values 'Liberty, immortal, unvalued [i.e. priceless] liberty' (p. 238) over everything, including love itself. Even when Roderic assumes the shape of her intended, Edwin, she refuses to stay in his garden, rebuking the supposed Edwin for his refusal to escape and taking the lead herself: 'You shall see what an injured and oppressed woman can do' (p. 244). Imogen's inner chastity cannot be destroyed through violence, even when Roderic overcomes her and she falls unconscious: though Godwin fudges whether she had actually been violated. However he makes it abundantly clear that the sanctity of truth brings the whole ideological castle in the air tumbling down. For when Imogen refuses to admire aristocracy, Roderic sees himself as 'a monument of impotence and misery for all the world to gaze at' (p. 233). He becomes maddened by his own possessions, signalled by a play on words. The goblin Medoro demands:

> 'Art thou not possessed' – 'Talk not to me of possessions,' exclaimed Roderic
> . . . 'I give them to the winds'.

When the true Edwin appears and Roderic is unmasked as a fraud, he ceases to believe in his own authority: 'Oh Imogen, lovely, adorable Imogen, how vain has been my authority, how vain the space of my command! Let then my palaces tumble into ruin!' His phallic power has dwindled and he cries: 'Let that wand which once I boasted, shivered in a thousand fragments, be cast to all the winds of heaven!' (p. 255).

Although his career is often represented as a trajectory from rationalism to Romanticism, *Imogen* shows the young Godwin steeped in Rousseau and sensibility from the first: and in 1784 he was fascinated with cultural particularity just as he would be in 1831, when he asked:

> What is it that constitutes the manners of nations, by which the people of one country are so eminently distinguished from the people of another, so that you cannot cross the channel from Dover to Calais, twenty-one miles, without finding yourself in a new world? Nay, I need not go among the subjects of another government to find examples of this; if I pass into Ireland, Scotland or Wales, I see myself surrounded with a new people, all of whose characters are in a manner cast into one mould, and all different from the citizens of the principal state and from one another.[33]

Godwin's idealization of Welsh shepherds clearly rejected the *de haut en bas* approach towards contemporary Wales adopted by English travellers and novelists.[34] He also steered clear of the utilitarian paternalism of other liberals inventing Welsh Utopias, such as Robert Bage in the epistolary novel *Mount Henneth*, which had appeared two years earlier.[35] A paper manufacturer from Elford, near Tamworth, Bage was affiliated to the Birmingham Lunar Society. He was a close friend of Erasmus Darwin, and turned to literature after losing money when their ironworks at Wychnor failed. When Godwin toured the Midlands in 1797 and 1800 he would visit the provincial writer who first pioneered using popular fiction to air questions of social reform.

Bage adopted the Richardsonian theme of rape both as a political metaphor to denounce British oppression of its American colonies and simultaneously – in a much more unambiguous fashion than Godwin – he staged the feminist argument that a woman's honour cannot be lost when she is overpowered by force.[36] America is symbolized by Camitha Melton, who is captured by an English privateer and her body claimed as his rightful property which he could sell as 'a slave to the plantations' (I, p. 136) to defray the costs of her subsistence. The English captain attempts to prostitute her in Britain instead but Miss Melton 'acknowledged neither his power, nor his right' and cried out for her liberty. The doughty American stabs him with a pair of scissors when he attempts to rape her and escapes. The eventual reunion between Miss Melton and her missing father signals the restoration of the republic's self-determination as a future nation based on blood and birth.

Bage uses the notion of a cosmopolitan self-governing community in Wales as a Utopian alternative to the centralized state's warmongering for nationalistic self-interest. Not content with a single episode for political discussion, he juxtaposes three stories in different settings, each exemplifying a different type of imperialism: Wales, India and America. The rape and loss of America is contrasted with the tale of a wealthy nabob whose career in the East India Company coincided with its most notorious plundering of the subcontinent. Mr Foston confesses that in Calcutta 'We eat and drank, kept black slaves' and then when drunk he had desecrated a Hindu temple (I, p. 177). Foston is taught religious toleration by the priest's daughter, and when left destitute after an attack he learns sympathy for the native poor: 'I had seen patience, fortitude and resignation amongst the lowest of mankind' (I, p. 220).

As a lieutenant under Robert Clive, Mr Foston saves a Persian merchant and his daughter, Caralia, from some 'Mahrattoes', allies of the British in warfare over the possession of Calcutta, who had entered their house, brutally attacked the family and raped the women. When her rescuer proposes marriage, Caralia asks Foston if he does not view her as having been dishonoured as English novels do not 'permit a lady to live and marry, and be a woman after this stain' (I, p. 233). Foston's answer teaches the reader to distinguish between 'honour' of the spirit and the violation of the body by another. Their 'mixed marriage' is an image of harmony and reparation for the future of the subcontinent.

As a provincial intellectual who rarely travelled farther than 50 miles from Tamworth, Bage is conscious of the internal colonization within the British Isles and the impoverishment of the Celtic fringe. As a merchant, he extols the potential of colonial wealth to spark enterprise and to assuage colonial guilt through investment and philanthropy.[37] After Caralia's death, Foston brings his half-Persian daughter Julia home to Britain to make her a 'princess' (I, p. 69) and to create a Utopian commune in a dilapidated castle in poverty-stricken Cardiganshire, which stands as a reminder to the reader of English subjugation of the Welsh in the Middle Ages.[38] There he gathers together an assortment of characters who converse wittily on current affairs in the manner Peacock would adopt in his comic novels, two of which were also set in Wales. The English Mr Foston and the American Mr Melton are fathers to beautiful daughters Julia and Camitha whose nubility represents the future of their respective nations and their marriages at the conclusion suggest social harmony being restored.

Mr Foston proposes a type of Pantisocracy, and selected friends each take a wife and all marry on St David's day. Each contributes according to his/her talent or means. The wealthy 'projector' gives 'a moiety of his revenue' (II, p. 240); others teach, practise their professions, garden or drive the plough to cultivate the land:

> Our pursuit is happiness; let us first consider of our ways and means. In the first place we have four thousand acres of land to cultivate, and cause to be cultivated. We have houses to build; and the little village of Henneth to make into a town. We have two thousand fine oaks to fell and twice as many to plant. Now honest Hugh Griffiths assured me, yesterday, that he thought it impossible a man should be happy who has nothing to do. When he wore a tambour waistcoat, and indulged himself in the noble employment of lounging; my heart, says he, was as heavy as lead. But when he was ruined and had betaken himself to the awl and strap his heart was as light as a feather. This postulatum being granted, continues Mr Foston, that every man amongst us should be a man of business, of science and of pleasure (II, pp. 303–4).

Half of every day is devoted to business and half to scientific experiment and games of wit and wordplay, at which the Welsh are said to excel. Foston and Melton plan a linen manufactory and the 'erection of a dome to make glass bottles' and spectacles, which they will ship from Cardigan to Rhode Island, where they will build a dock. They will teach the litigious Welsh peasants both law and trade, and together create 'a thriving colony' there (II, p. 306).

If Robert Bage and William Godwin set Utopian fantasies in a Welsh *tabula rasa*, then the middle of the decade saw a questioning of history as progress in two novels inspired by the embryonic manifestations of the industrialization which was to come. Richard Graves's *Eugenius, or Anecdotes of the Golden Vale* (1785) and Anna Maria Bennett's *Anna, or, Memoirs of a Welch Heiress* (1785) had authors of Welsh ancestry or with Welsh connections, whose speculations on the future transformation of the Principality seemed 'to contain real facts in disguise', as the *Critical Review* remarked of the former.[39] Graves's novel of ideas has an epigraph from Ovid's *Metamorphoses*, alluding to Roman authors' preoccupation with decline, as when the reign of Jupiter succeeded that of Saturn's more glorious Golden Age. He frames the narrative with a discussion between two old friends on whether progress to a modern commercial society has effeminized men into 'fops and macaronis' and masculinized the women into 'viragoes, bold and abandoned'.[40] Footnotes, however, pay tribute to the female intellectuals Elizabeth Montagu, Hester Chapone, Anna Laetitia Aikin and Anna Seward, though Graves is somewhat unsettled by the literary success of Bristol milk-woman Ann Yearsley, who should be 'instructed to make cheesecakes and custards with her milk, as well as to make verses' (I, p. 181).

Graves's novel does give an eventual assent to progress, and his preface admits he had thought of calling his book 'the silver age'.[41] He is decidedly optimistic, even visionary: 'I think the Iron and Brazen Ages are gradually wearing off . . . I do not despair to see the Silver Age restored by which I would understand the bright polish of modern improvements joined to the innocence of simplicity of those primitive times, which form such amusing and delightful pictures in the pastoral writings of the ancient Greek and Roman poets' (I, p. 12).[42] His pacifist vision is that Europe 'may in time be formed into one grand commonwealth and even Rousseau's Utopian system, for a universal peace, to be guaranteed by the several states may be adopted, and at length prevail over the whole world' (I, p. 20).

Eugenius, or Anecdotes of the Golden Vale is a parable of the aesthetic enthusiasm for the primitivist picturesque reluctantly overthrown in favour of progress. The story is set in such a remote north Wales valley that it escaped the notice of Pennant (I, p. 27) and was inhabited only by peasants and a few freeholders until very recently.[43] Eugenius visits his college friend Williams whose family farm there. He and the reader are offered two ways of viewing the valley: in a utilitarian manner and aesthetically:

My friend Williams, looking round with an arch leer, "Well" says he, "what do you think of my native country?"
Though I was afraid this was the end of our journey, and felt my expectations

greatly disappointed, yet being unwilling to shock my friend's good nature, I observed that there was a noble view of the sea; and though the external appearance of the mountains was not very fertile or alluring, yet they *might* probably contain some rich veins of lead or copper in their bowels.

Williams felt the force of my sneer and smiling, "Well" said he, "you have made me as good a compliment as the case would admit of; but if I had promised to show you a fine woman, and should introduce you to a homely piece, you would not think it sufficient to be told that her *beauty* lay in her mind, or in her purse. – However when you see this valley in a different point of view you many probably like it better."

Then leaving again the direct road, which seemed to lead towards the seaport; we kept winding along the sides of the hills towards the cleft, where the road led us amidst a vast ridge of craggy rocks, which seemed to be the very boundaries of the creation; but instead of terminating in Milton's chaos – they opened on a sudden into a terrestrial paradise (II, pp. 30–2).

The young men compare their romantic love of the landscape with their priorities in viewing a woman. This analogy, however, leaves open to question whether more utilitarian motives might dictate the choice of a prospective bride. Eugenius, however, will always remain a romantic. He later demonstrates his Rousseauistic primitivism when he marries Williams's sister Flora, who was an apple-munching thirteen-year-old Eve when he first saw her.

Llan-dryffyd Dwr Llwiffen has already been renamed The Golden Vale by English incomers who cannot pronounce the name (I, p. 83). Lower middle-class professionals from Chester and Shrewsbury lord it over the poverty-stricken natives here, and flag this up by their ironic use of mock-colonial titles: 'Admiral Bombketch', 'Captain Spindle', the 'Archbishop' and 'Governor Howel', and institute a riotous dining club visiting each others' farm-houses, each tricked out in 'a whimsical style' (I, p. 43). In contrast, a more progressive English newcomer, Mr Hamilton, gives starving Welsh poachers employment as labourers, instead of prosecuting them, and is damned as a milksop by the boozy 'Captain' (I, p. 70). He also rescues the sixteen-year-old Jenny Cradoc, who has been groomed for the local squire's bed with the connivance of her family.

When Eugenius pays a second visit, some years later, he discovers that Mr Hamilton – though he too had first retired to the Golden Vale attracted by its beauty – has now gone into business there. He and an entrepreneur, Mr Jackson, have set up 'a manufactory of woollen stuffs' (I, p. 102): 'There were plenty of hands and their labour I knew would be cheap' (I, p. 144). Mr Jackson also acts as a factor for poor cottagers subsisting through knitting. The old winding path is now a wide road and Eugenius 'met several packhorses, and two or three busy people, going to or coming from the vale' (I, p. 97). He notices 'several new cottages and other buildings lately erected, which . . . gave [the prospect] the appearance of cheerfulness and industry' (ibid.). The unique 'beauty of the prospect' is now lessened by the straight lines of utilitarianism, but in exchange the poor are employed, the land more valuable and the population increases. 'Matters of taste should be only of secondary consideration and must frequently give way to convenience and utility' pronounces the projector, Mr Hamilton. The set of 'wretched, idle, unemployed and of course thievish inhabitants' have thankfully been easily 'civilised and converted to useful members of society' (I, pp. 143–4).

Eugenius chooses to live in the Golden Vale, solely for the sake of its spoiled but still beautiful view. However, his name, meaning 'well born', signals Graves's acknowledgement that it is a rich man's prerogative to enjoy an empty landscape and to choose Georgic retirement over urban life. When his Welsh sweetheart, Flora Williams, chooses the 'well born' narrator over the London merchant her mercenary aunt prefers, Eugenius looks forward to 'possessing her as my sole and most valuable property' (II, p. 168). The variegated 'union' roses scattered at their wedding suggest the marriage between the Englishman and Welshwoman is meant to symbolize a benevolent, personal and protective relationship between English capitalism and the beautiful land itself as well as with the money it yields.

We have seen how insistently the Principality was pictured as a feminine space, having no masculine public sphere or city life, and so it is not surprising that women writers in particular used Wales as a suitable setting for a female protagonist. Andrew Davies comments: 'Of the twenty Wales-related sentimental novels and novels of sensibility identified between 1780 and 1830, the majority have female central focalisers and almost all are socially displaced orphans.'[44] *Anna, or Memoirs of a Welch Heiress* was the debut of Anna Maria Bennett.[45] Published by William Lane, the leading fiction publisher of the decade, she became a phenomenally best-selling author, yet was well regarded by critics such as Coleridge and Mary Wollstonecraft. She prepared the way for Charlotte Smith and Charles Dickens in using the novel of sentiment to evoke social concern for liberal causes. *Anna* cleverly conflates a wish-fulfilment romance of upward social mobility with characters bearing recognizable names or even identities. For 'family names in the novel – Edwin, Herbert, Mansel, Turbville [*sic*] – are those of the gentry in eighteenth-century Glamorgan, while Anna's ancestral estate, Trevannion, brings to mind the great estate of Y Fan . . . inherited by the Countess of Plymouth, formerly Elizabeth Lewis in 1734', as Moira Dearnley notes.[46] Francesca Rhydderch observes that the emphasis on names in the novel signals 'anxiety focused on the relationship between changing inheritance patterns, that is,

weakened kinship and emergent Britishness', as it so happened that the
Welsh gentry abounded in heiresses at this time and dynastic names were at
risk.[47] Although the novelist shares a name with her protagonist and there may
well be autobiographical allusions, the main aims of the novel are to critique
the gentry's involvement in the industrialization of Wales and indict predatory male libertinism, rather than merely indulging in scandal-mongering.

The most vivid passage in the novel is the realistic portrait of Llandore
with its distinctive south-Walian lime-washed walls and a nearby ironworks
(I, p. 207): probably conflated with the novelist's birthplace, Merthyr Tydfil,
near the foundries at Cyfarthfa, Dowlais, and Hirwaun:

> The situation of the village of Llandore is beautifully picturesque and romantic;
> it stands in a fertile valley; through which runs the river Tave, whose frequent
> but harmless overflowings give a richness and verdure more captivating the eye;
> from the wild mountains which form to appearance an inaccessible chain on each
> side of the vale, irregularly interspersed with various old ruins, the sad memento
> of the faded glory and sunken dignity of the ancient inhabitants of Cambria. In
> the middle of a large green church-yard, stood the church, and round it, in two
> semi-circles, on the outside of the wall were whitewashed neat dwellings of the
> inhabitants, with here and there a break for a better house than common, such
> as the parsonage, the doctor's, lawyer's, exciseman's, and Presbyterian parson's
> (I, pp. 205–6).

At Llandore Castle, Anna meets Mrs Herbert who has inherited the ironworks
from her grandmother, just as the actual Charlotte Herbert's 'daughter-in-
law Alice owned part of the land on which the [Dowlais] ironworks was
built'.[48] Sarah Prescott notes that Mrs Herbert's brother-in-law, the traditional
landowner Sir William Edwin, is 'a literary reincarnation of Sir Watkin
Williams Wynn (third baronet)' and suggests that his family is endorsed by
the novel as 'ideal traditional landowners'.[49] They have certainly survived
financially, in comparison with the Herberts, chiefly owing to Lady Cecilia
Edwin's excellent managerial skills. Nevertheless she is mocked as a snob,
her son is a rake and her daughter a coquette, and the Edwins' residence at
Grosvenor Square is held up as the epitome of dissipated luxury in comparison with the rural simplicity of Wales. It is there that the poor relation,
Anna, is targeted by their guest the libertine nabob Patrick Gorget, lord
Sutton, recently 'graced with the favour of a virtuous prince' (II, p. 137).
This character, whose name cleverly yokes associations of greed and military
insignia, may allude to Robert Clive, who received an Irish barony in 1762
and who controlled political seats on the Welsh border. (His eldest son
married Lord Powis's daughter, Henrietta of Powis Castle.)

It is the Edwins' cousin Charles Herbert whom Anna chooses to marry and whose family she will redeem from bankruptcy and energize. Mrs Herbert's ironworks are mortgaged, owing to her dissipated husband's neglect. He spends his time womanizing at Bath while his young partner Mr Wilkinson, a lower-class technological genius, runs the business for a share of the profits. Mr Wilkinson, who is an industrialist yet also a man of feeling, falls in love with Anna, and behaves with generosity and dignity when she rejects him. The character invokes the pioneering ironmaster John Wilkinson mentioned earlier, who made a steam engine for Boulton and Watt, was a friend of Crawshay as well as Priestley, and became a folk-hero of the working people. The plot plays with the choice before the orphan heiress, who represents Wales, of marrying this industrial entrepreneur (another long-lost foundling like herself) or being captured and prostituted by the wealthy nabob colonialist, Gorget. Fears of Welsh despoliation or decline are eventually overtaken by fairy-tale dreams of future wealth, however. Both bourgeois newcomers Anna and Wilkinson eventually marry Herbert gentry in a wish-fulfilment union of entrepreneurial drive plus capital (Anna inherits £60,000) with the cachet of old blood. The younger generation are modernizers who reconcile the absurd Welsh patriotism of Sir William and Lady Edwin to loyalty to 'the British establishment and its Monarchy', as Jane Aaron remarks.[50] The vision for the future of Wales is that the rustic beauty spot of Llandore will be transformed into the iron capital of the world (as Merthyr Tydfil was), while retaining a paternal duty of care to the workers and Wales's distinct heritage (Anna learns Welsh in order to bring charity to the peasants).

Female 'Jacobin' writers towards the end of the decade took up Bennett's portrayal of an orphan in a desolate Welsh setting in order to indicate that *woman* is disinherited and exploited, rather than making the heroine a genius loci for Wales. Charlotte Smith's first novel *Emmeline, or, The Orphan of the Castle* (1788) opens in Pembroke castle, and she refers to her angelic harp-playing orphan heroine Emmeline as 'Welch', though she is also of Scottish descent for good measure. This imparts a Jacobite emphasis to the opening of the romance, where the female Celt represents all the disinherited subjects of the united kingdom. The ruinous 'castle of the state' image had just then featured in Book 5 of William Cowper's popular poem *The Task* (1785). Using it here alluded symbolically to the realm of Britain:

In a remote part of the county of Pembroke, is an old building, formerly of great strength, and inhabited for centuries by the ancient family of Mowbray; to the sole remaining branch of which it still belonged, tho' it was, at the time this history commences, inhabited only by servants; and the greater part of it was gone to decay. A few rooms only had been occasionally repaired to accommodate the proprietor, when he found it necessary to come thither to receive his rents, or to inspect the condition of the estate; which however happened so seldom, that during the twelve years *he* had been master of it, he had only once visited the castle for a few days . . .[51]

Placing the forgotten female orphan in Gothic ruins symbolizes woman as the last victim of the feudal laws of past ages. The choice of Pembroke in the poverty-stricken Principality made an emphatic contrast with the opulent mansions possessed by English patriarchs featured later in the novel. The bullying behaviour of Emmeline's aristocratic cousin, Delamere, who forces himself upon her, demonstrates the pointlessness of women relying on chivalry and protection by men. A young Walter Scott was shocked that Emmeline broke the engagement she had reluctantly agreed to, then later found herself a husband of her own choosing from the professional classes.

Smith based her plot on property law, for Emmeline was apparently illegitimate: 'a little, obscure creature, bred on the Welsh mountains, and who was born nobody knows how' (II, p. 37), but is later discovered to have been defrauded of her inheritance by her uncle for nineteen years. Foregrounding the heroine's quest for patriarchal recognition gives a feminist twist to the plot, as had Frances Burney's *Evelina* (1778). Defoe's and Richardson's earlier use of the bastard figure was a way of signalling that the apportioning of power through strict lines of genealogical descent had been abandoned in Britain. For them Monmouth's rebellion prefigured the Glorious Revolution itself.[52] But for later Jacobin novelists such as Charlotte Smith, 1688 was itself unfinished business, as further constitutional reform was needed.

The adventurous plot of the novel demonstrates Emmeline's fitness to inherit, for she attains the confidence to repudiate Delamere after gaining strength of character through exercising independent judgement in helping other indigent or ostracized female victims of society. We see the orphan surmounting her own experience of childhood neglect and then nursing her dying foster-mother, befriending poverty-stricken Mrs Stafford when she is fleeing debtors, and non-judgmentally assisting Lady Adelina during childbirth following an adulterous relationship with her brother-in-law. When she learns to assert herself, she looks into her late mother's life story and is rewarded by finding herself an heiress. Emmeline's progress to legitimacy and the property-owning classes is echoed by her journeys from west Wales to the quiet sea-bathing resort of Swansea, and then nearer still to the centre of metropolitan power in London.

Smith's first novel was the subject of the first signed review by novice reporter Mary Wollstonecraft in the first number of a new rational periodical, the *Analytical Review*. Though she acknowledged the power of the book, Wollstonecraft was suspicious of romance, and she feared such an idealized heroine would foster unrealistic expectations in girl readers.[53] Her own *Original Stories* for children of the same year castigated the false delicacy of conventional femininity, while the teacher-narrator Mrs Mason evokes 'true' sensibility in two aristocratic young girls, Mary and Caroline, by taking them to experience for themselves how poor people actually live.[54] 'Real life' incidents, graphically described, and didactic observations on the economic causes of poverty are juxtaposed with Mrs Mason's own religious stoicism and capacity for empathizing with other sufferers in this vale of tears. A harvest supper celebrates the girls' eventual maturity: they have turned from pupils to friends. For the first time, Mrs Mason speaks to them as equals, and her climactic confession, revealing that her personal experience of life as a woman has been unmitigatedly miserable, is dramatized by means of a dystopic Welsh setting. (Mary Wollstonecraft and her family had moved to Laugharne in 1777 and her father and sisters were still based in Wales.)

> She informed the children, that once travelling through Wales, her carriage was overturned near the ruins of an old castle. And as she had escaped unhurt, she determined to wander amongst them, whilst the driver took care of his horses, and her servant hastened to the neighbouring village for assistance. It was almost dark, and the lights began to twinkle in the scattered cottages. The scene pleased me, continued Mrs. Mason; I thought of the various customs which the lapse of time unfolds, and dwelt on the state of the Welsh, when this castle, now so desolate, was the hospitable abode of the chief of a noble family. These reflections entirely engrossed my mind, when the sound of a harp reached my ears. Never was any thing more opportune, the national music seemed to give reality to the pictures which my imagination had been drawing. I listened awhile, and then trying to trace the pleasing sound, discovered, after a short search, a little hut, rudely built. The walls of an old tower supported part of the thatch, which scarcely kept out the rain, and the two other sides were stones cemented, or rather plaistered together, by mud and clay (pp. 99–100).

Mrs Mason's pleasurable nostalgia for the past is ruptured by shocking contemporary reality when she comes upon the rude hut, where two families and their animals live separated by a partition of twigs and dried leaves. The cause of the harpist's fallen fortunes is his 'tyrant' landlord who enforces outdated feudal dues ('the fish they catch they must bring first to him', p. 103). This 'petty king' evicts anyone who refuses, and then abuses his position as Justice of the Peace to imprison the harpist's son-in-law 'on account of his killing a hare' (ibid.). Ironically, instead of denouncing aristocrats as one might expect, the Welshman begins to assert his own noble ancestry:

He then began one of the most dismal of his Welsh ditties, and in the midst of it cried out – He is an upstart, a mere mushroom! – His grandfather was cow-boy to mine! – So I told him once, and he never forgot it (ibid.).

As the sun goes down and the moon rises on the harvest scene which symbolically heralds her own evening of life, Mrs Mason takes stock of the past and confesses her failure to attain happiness: 'Heavy misfortunes have obscured the sun I gazed at when first I entered life' (p. 107). This seems a determinist static universe rather than a world where change and progress are likely.[55] Although Wollstonecraft eschews the Richardsonian theme of the threat of seduction or rape in order to concentrate on female education, women – like the Welsh – can look forward to no immediate improvement. They both epitomize tradition, and thus turn to the spiritual consolations of the next world rather than revolution in this. Prayer is Wollstonecraft's only remedy for society's ills in this early text.

Refusal to accept the violent subduing or economic exploitation of the colonies and Celtic nations of Britain triggered Utopian dreams in many 'Jacobin' fictions. Perhaps Wales featured so often because the preference for sublime and picturesque scenery over the merely beautiful took the tourist not into an Eden of natural abundance, but into mountainous regions where subsistence was shockingly difficult. The Enlightenment gave these writers faith in man's capacity to use reason and science to solve poverty, and their sociological vision was collective not individualist, organizational rather than escapist.[56] Dissenting culture encouraged perpetual striving for improvement, not only of the individual, but of society. Wales and other colonized spaces were gendered feminine in sentimental literature: usually to call for paternalist protection, but sometimes in order to depict women's marginality in society and desire to move into modernity. Few Utopians before Welshman Robert Owen imagined Utopian communities based on sexual egalitarianism as such.[57] Legend has it that in 1789, at the age of ten, he left Wales to make his fortune with forty shillings in his pocket. When this was accomplished he attempted to create a new world of socialism based on co-operation and communal living: dreams which would inspire his native land for over a hundred years.

The Utopian desires for pacifism and revolutionary social change could be seen to be mutually contradictory when taken to an absolute extreme, as Albert Camus commented when reviewing the use of force by totalitarian revolutionary regimes of left and right in the twentieth century. In 1946 he foresaw 'the end of ideologies, that is absolute Utopias which in reality destroy themselves through their enormous costs. Then it will be time to choose a new kind of Utopia – one that is more modest and less destructive.'[58]

Notes

[1]   Wales was described, for example, in Arthur Young, *A Six Weeks' Tour Through Southern Counties of England and Wales* (1768); Joseph Craddock, *Letters from Snowdon* (1770); Samuel Johnson, *A Diary of a Journey into North Wales* (1774); Thomas Pennant, *A Tour in Wales* (1778); Edward Lloyd, *A Month's Tour in North Wales, Dublin and its Environs* (1781); Henry Penruddocke Wyndham, *A Gentleman's Tour through Monmouthshire and Wales* (1781); William Gilpin, *Observations on the River Wye and Several Parts of South Wales* (1782).

[2]   See Geraint H. Jenkins, 'Wales in the Eighteenth Century', in H. T. Dickinson (ed.), *A Companion to Eighteenth-Century Britain* (Oxford, 2002), pp. 392–402.

[3]   See Barbara Goodwin and Keith Taylor, *The Politics of Utopia: A Study in Theory and Practice* (London, 1982), p. 15.

[4]   'The desire for a better way of being' was central to the Utopian imagination. See Ruth Levitas, *The Concept of Utopia* (Hemel Hempstead, 1990), p. 8.

[5]   Adam Rogers and Richard Hingley, 'Edward Gibbon and Francis Haverfield: The Traditions of Imperial Decline', in Mark Bradley (ed.), *Classics and Imperialism in the British Empire* (Oxford, 2010), pp. 189–209, at p. 196.

[6]   The term 'revolution' has been questioned by revisionist historians, but Brinley Thomas notes the dramatic transformation of Wales. This went together with a strong sense of cultural identity based upon the Welsh language, religious Dissent and scholarly leadership by the London Welsh at the end of the eighteenth century. See Brinley Thomas, *The Industrial Revolution and the Atlantic Economy: Selected Essays* (London, 1993), p. 216.

[7]   For fuller lists consult Moira Dearnley, *Distant Fields: Eighteenth-Century Fictions of Wales* (Cardiff, 2001), appendix pp. 237–40; Andrew Davies, '"The Reputed Nation of Inspiration": Representations of Wales in Fiction from the Romantic Period, 1780–1829' (unpublished Cardiff University PhD thesis, 2001). See also Sarah Prescott, *Eighteenth-Century Writing from Wales: Bards and Britons* (Cardiff, 2008), pp. 121–55.

[8]   Following the pioneering monograph by Gary Kelly, *The English Jacobin Novel, 1780–1805* (Oxford, 1976), attention focused mainly on the 1790s in studies such as Nicola J. Watson, *Revolution and the Form of the British Novel, 1790–1825* (Oxford, 1994); Angela Keane, *Women Writers and the English Nation in the 1790s: Romantic Belongings* (Cambridge, 2000); Nancy E. Johnson, *The English Jacobin Novel on Rights, Property and the Law: Critiquing the Contract* (Basingstoke, 2007); Miriam L. Wallace, *Revolutionary Subjects in the English 'Jacobin' Novel, 1790–1805* (Cranbury, 2009); A. A. Marley, *Conversion and Reform in the British Novel in the 1790s: A Revolution of Opinions* (Basingstoke, 2009).

[9]   See Caroline Franklin, 'The Novel of Sensibility in the 1780s', in Karen O'Brien and Peter Garside (eds.), *The Oxford History of the Novel, Volume 2* (forthcoming), for a survey of the fiction of the decade. The present chapter develops further brief observations on representations of Wales outlined there.

[10] Richard Price, *Observations on the Importance of the American Revolution and the Means of Making it a Benefit to the World* (Dublin, 1785).

[11] See Jack Fruchtman, 'The Apocalyptic Politics of Richard Price and Joseph Priestley', *Transactions of the American Philosophical Society*, 73, no. 4 (Philadelphia, 1983), 20.

[12] J. C. D. Clark, *English Society 1660–1832: Religion, Ideology and Politics During the Ancien Regime* (Cambridge, 2000), p. 40.

[13] 'Probert, thus armed, and accoutred,– and paid, proceeded on his adventure; – but he was no sooner arrived on the confines of Wales, than all Wales was in arms to meet him. That nation is brave, and full of spirit. Since the invasion of king Edward, and the massacre of the bards, there never was such a tumult, and alarm, and uproar, through the region of *Prestatyn. Snowden* shook to its base; *Cader Edris* was loosened from its foundations. The fury of litigious war blew her horn on the mountains. The rocks poured down their goatherds, and the deep caverns vomited out their miners. Every thing above ground, and every thing under ground, was in arms.' *Speech of Edmund Burke, Esquire, Member of Parliament for the City of Bristol On Presenting to the House of Commons: A Plan for the Better Security of the Independence of Parliament* (London, 1780), p. 24.

[14] See Ronald L. Lewis, *Welsh Americans: A History of Assimilation in the Coalfields* (Chapel Hill, 2008), p. 11.

[15] See Arthur Eugene Bestor, Jr., *Backwoods Utopias: The Sectarian and Owenite Phases of Communitarian Socialism in America: 1663–1829* (Philadelphia, 1950), p. 38.

[16] When it was rediscovered in 1963, critics were disappointed at the lack of psychological realism in *Imogen*. See for example, Martha Winburn England, 'Felix Culpa', appendix to *Imogen, A Pastoral Romance, from the Ancient British*, ed. Jack W. Marken (New York, 1963), p. 110. Burton R. Pollin in the same volume notes that *Imogen* was popular in America for at least twenty years, p. 113.

[17] See *ODNB*. Rees re-edited Chambers's *Cyclopaedia* in 1776. Godwin dedicated his first book of sermons to Richard Watson, bishop of Llandaff, perhaps on account of the latter's deeply controversial Restoration Day sermon, 'The Principles of the Revolution Vindicated', of 1776 which supported the American Revolution.

[18] Horace Walpole, *The Castle of Otranto* (3rd edn., London, 1766), pp. v–vi.

[19] Mark Philp (ed.), *Collected Novels and Memoirs of William Godwin* (8 vols., London, 1992), II, ed. Pamela Clemit, p. 169. Further quotation will be in parenthesis in the text.

[20] In 'Milton's *Comus* and the Politics of Masquing', Barbara K. Lewalski argues that *Arcades* and *Comus* were undertaken 'to reform the court genres and the values associated with them' though also rejecting 'excessive puritan joylessness'. See David M. Bevington and Peter Holbrook (eds.), *The Politics of the Stuart Masque* (Cambridge, 1998), pp. 296–320, at p. 297.

[21] Pamela Clemit, *The Godwinian Novel: The Rational Fictions of Godwin, Brockden Brown, Mary Shelley* (Oxford, 1993), p. 15.

[22] Moira Dearnley points out that Godwin is not uncritically proclaiming the attractions of a deistic natural religion in this novel, despite it being written during the decline of his religious orthodoxy. The Druidic faith is represented as a priest-led pagan polytheism and the happy valley itself is presented with a 'curious moral ambivalence'. See '"The venerable Name of Religion": Druidism in *Imogen* by William Godwin', in Dearnley, *Distant Fields*, pp. 114–29.

23   Clemit summarizes Godwin's intentions as 'to sketch the rise of government as a perversion of pastoral values' in *The Godwinian Novel*, p. 17.

24   John and his father Isaac had converted the Bersham furnace to coke smelting and for a time Denbighshire was an important part of the Industrial Revolution. In 1792 John bought Brymbo Hall Estate, Denbighshire. See *ODNB*.

25   'An Account of a Journey into Wales in two letters to Mr Bower', in *The Works of George, Lord Lyttelton* (London, 1774), pp. 736–51, p. 741. The account had been first written in 1756.

26   Evan Evans, *The Love of Our Country, a Poem with Historical Notes* (Carmarthen, 1772), p. viii.

27   This perhaps self-reflexively questions the genre of romance itself as a feminized domain. Compare Clara Reeve, *The Progress of Romance through Times, Countries and Manners, etc* (2 vols., Colchester, 1785), which approvingly associates romance writing with the 'heroes' of the court of Queen Elizabeth (I, p. 95). *Eden Vale* also shows a degenerate masquerade held by Sir James Evelyn where rural guests are attired as Floras and shepherdesses (I, p. 155).

28   William Godwin, *The Lives of the Necromancers* (London, 1834) p. 6. In 'Merlin', Stonehenge is described as a monument commemorating 300 British nobles massacred by the Saxons.

29   Godwin, *The Lives of the Necromancers*, p. 5.

30   Thomas Paine, *Common Sense. Addressed to the Inhabitants of America . . . by an Englishman* (1776), p. 1. Quoted by Clemit, *The Godwinian Novel*, p. 26.

31   Thomas Paine, 'The Dream Interrupted', *Pennsylvania Magazine* (June 1775), 173–4.

32   Note the Welsh name of the lower-class protagonist of *Things as They Are: Caleb Williams* (1794), and see the suggestion by Damian Walford Davies that Edward Williams (Iolo Morganwg) could be 'Caleb's second self and namesake': *Presences that Disturb: Models of Romantic Identity in the Literature and Culture of the 1790s* (Cardiff, 2002), p. 176. When Caleb Williams tries to flee the power of his master, Faulkland, it is an 'obscure market town in Wales' he deems most remote from his antagonist's reach. Likewise, Godwin's Wordsworthian 'new man of feeling', Fleetwood is from Merionethshire near Cader Idris, where much of the novel is set. See *Fleetwood, or, The New Man of Feeling* (3 vols., London, 1805). Kelly notes that Oliver Cromwell had used the alias of Williams, in *The English Jacobin Novel*, p. 205.

33   Godwin, 'Of Phrenology', in *Thoughts on Man, His Nature, Productions and Discoveries* (London, 1831), p. 185.

34   Evan Evans complained that 'ill usage' of Wales by 'despicable scribblers' such as the author of 'Letters from Snowdon' and Lord Lyttleton in his history of Henry II inspired this rebuttal, his first poem in English: *The Love of Our Country*, pp. v–vi.

35   Robert Bage, *Mount Henneth, A Novel in Two Volumes* (London, 1782), henceforth cited in parenthesis in the text. Lowndes paid £30 for *Mount Henneth*, which went into three editions. Walter Scott selected it for *Ballantyne's Novelists' Library* in 1824, probably unwilling to endorse the more radical later fiction such as *Man As He Is* (4 vols., 1792).

[36] Arianne Chernock notes that at least three members of the Lunar society, Thomas Beddoes, Erasmus Darwin and Robert Bage, endorsed rational education for women; and that Bage's *Hermsprong* (1796) was 'a Jacobin novel unabashed in its endorsement of women's rights'. See *Men and the Making of Modern British Feminism* (Stanford, 2009), pp. 24, 72.

[37] J. M. S. Tompkins notes Bage's regard for the merchant as the prime civilizer, and his use of the theme of international intermarriage 'to show reasonable men of all nations living in friendship together': *The Popular Novel in England, 1770–1800* (1932; repr., Lincoln, 1961), p. 204. Janet Sorenson comments that the dialogic form of the novel is 'reflective of the equally heterogeneous yet unified entity of the nation': 'Internal Colonialism and the British Novel', *Eighteenth-Century Fiction*, 15, no.1 (2002), 53–8, at 55.

[38] Betty Joseph comments: 'The feminizing power of sentimental discourse allows the woman to be placed as a figure within the paternal fiction of capital accumulation so the transfer of resources could be staged as a gift' in *Reading the East India Company 1720–1840: Colonial Currencies of Gender* (Chicago, 2004), p. 78.

[39] *Critical Review*, 60 (July 1785), 199–209, at 202.

[40] Richard Graves, *Eugenius, or Anecdotes of the Golden Vale, An Embellished Narrative of Real Facts* (2 vols., London, 1785), I, p. 5, henceforth cited in parenthesis in the text.

[41] Roman authors' universalizing narrative of decline, and writings investigating the possibilities for a renewed Age of Gold are discussed by Rhiannon Evans, *Utopia Antiqua: Readings of the Golden Age and Decline of Rome* (London, 2008).

[42] William Jackson in *The Four Ages, Together with Essays on Various Subjects* (London, 1798) also argues that the present age is iron but that gold is yet to come: 'Upon the restoration we advanced again, and have since been increasing in velocity towards perfection, like a comet as it approaches the sun' (p. 10).

[43] Dearnley notes that travel accounts such as Pennant's included graphic descriptions of industrial developments, like the Parys copper mines in Anglesey, and speculates that the novel may allude to the mill of the Cotton Twist company founded in 1783, though Pennant had not at that time published an account of it: Dearnley, *Distant Fields*, pp. 107–10. The Wye Valley and the nearby Forest of Dean, though visited by picturesque tourists, were also the site of ironworks and coal-mines in the eighteenth century.

[44] Davies, '"The Reputed Nation of Inspiration"', p. 64.

[45] Anna Maria Bennett, *Anna, or Memoirs of a Welch Heiress. Interspersed with Anecdotes of a Nabob* (4 vols., London, 1785), henceforth cited in parenthesis in the text.

[46] Dearnley, *Distant Fields*, p. 132.

[47] Francesca Rhydderch, 'Dual Nationality, Divided Identity: Ambivalent Narratives of Britishness in the Welsh Novels of Anna Maria Bennett', *Welsh Writing in English*, 3 (1997), 1–17, at 6.

[48] Dearnley, *Distant Fields*, p. 224.

[49] Prescott, *Eighteenth-Century Writing from Wales*, p. 135.

[50] See Jane Aaron, 'Seduction and Betrayal: Wales in Women's Fiction, 1785–1810', *Women's Writing*, 1, no. 1 (1994), 65–76, at 73.

[51]   Charlotte Smith, *Emmeline, or, The Orphan of the Castle* (4 vols., London, 1788), pp. 1–2. Henceforth cited in parenthesis in the text

[52]   Wolfram Schmidgen, *Eighteenth-Century Fiction and the Law of Property* (Cambridge, 2002), p. 102.

[53]   *Analytical Review*, 1 (July 1788), 327–33.

[54]   Mary Wollstonecraft, *Original Stories* (London, 1788); henceforth cited in parenthesis in the text.

[55]   As critics have noted, it probably inspired Blake's 'Nurse's song' in *Songs of Experience*.

[56]   See J. C. Davis on social engineering and organization, 'The History of Utopia: The Chronology of Nowhere', in Peter Alexander and Roger Gill (eds.), *Utopias* (London, 1984), pp. 1–18, at p. 10.

[57]   See Carol A. Kolmerten, *Women in Utopia: The Ideology of Gender in the American Owenite Communities* (Bloomington, 1990), p. 9.

[58]   Albert Camus, 'To save lives, 20 November 1946', in *Between Hell and Reason: Essays from the Resistance Newspaper 1944–7*, trans. Alexandre de Gramont (Hanover NH, 1991), p. 125.

Rousseau and Wales

HEATHER WILLIAMS

Jean-Jacques Rousseau is one of the names most readily associated with the French Revolution and its causes. And yet his ideas also held appeal for those who feared revolution. Privileged reference point for the likes of Robespierre and Wollstonecraft, few reputations are as paradoxical as his, few reception histories as complex and as international. Clearly Rousseau had different meanings for different people, or perhaps for different peoples. Though there have been studies of his significance for a number of non-Francophone cultures, including England,[1] Ireland,[2] Scotland,[3] and Sweden,[4] investigation of his various meanings in Wales or for the Welsh people has never been attempted.[5]

As far as the French Revolution and reactions to it are concerned, Rousseau is unique in that he seems to have appealed in equal measure to radicals and to conservatives. Though Rousseau was undoubtedly used by Revolutionaries, and therefore condemned by Burke and his followers, he was nevertheless loved by counter-Revolutionary émigrés (though not for his *Contrat social*),[6] and conservative types in Britain, especially women.[7] While Robespierre would praise him in revolutionary speeches, Marie Antoinette had been to visit his grave. In a Welsh context, the Francophile Ladies of Llangollen loved Rousseau and nature while hating the Revolution, and the Hafod household created a Rousseau-inspired landscape in upland Ceredigion, but was terrified of the threat from France.[8]

The level of paradox associated with Rousseau's thought and legacy earned him a key place in Roger Chartier's argument that books may not after all be responsible for the ideological erosion that leads to revolutionary rupture.[9] Work by Chartier, and more recently Swenson, has shown how Rousseau was used when revolutionaries constructed a continuity that was primarily

a process of justification and a search for paternity.[10] In other words it was
the Revolution that first made Rousseau into one if its major causes, by
praising and invoking him, especially in the debate leading to the transfer
of his remains to the Panthéon. This chapter will examine how this Rousseau
paradox plays out in a Welsh context, focusing on the contrasting examples
of Welsh radical writer and cultural nationalist Iolo Morganwg, and the
landowner and landscaping pioneer Thomas Johnes of Hafod.

However, I shall begin with perhaps the biggest irony of Romanticism
in Wales. Though Rousseau's teachings can be held partly responsible for
changing the attitudes of English travellers towards Wales in the latter parts
of the eighteenth century,[11] his own interest in the place and his plan to
make his home in Wales have been largely forgotten.[12] How ironic that Iolo
Morganwg – recently described as a 'one-man Welsh Romanticism'[13] – had
no knowledge of the great *philosophe*'s pronouncements on the Welsh and
their landscape, and how ironic that the London Welshman Thomas Phillips,
whose copies of Rousseau's works are today in the Founder's Library at
Lampeter, did not know of Rousseau's plans to settle in his own ancestral
Radnorshire.

A browbeaten Rousseau was brought to London in January 1766 by David
Hume and J.-J. de Luze, but the *philosophe*'s first instinct was to escape to
the country, in search of peace and solitude. He first mentions Wales in a
letter of 18 January 1766:

> j'apprends que M. Hume a trouvé un seigneur du pays de Galles qui dans un
> vieux monastére où loge un de ses fermiers lui fait offre d'un logement précisement
> tel que je le désire. Cette nouvelle, Madame, me comble de joye. Si dans cette
> contrée éloignée et sauvage je puis passer en paix les derniers jours de ma vie
> oublié des hommes, cet intervalle de repos me fera bientot oublier toutes mes
> miséres et je serai redevable à M. Hume de tout le bonheur auquel je puisse
> encore aspirer.[14]

> (I understand that Mr Hume has found a lord from Wales who can offer him
> accommodation of precisely the kind that I desire, in an old monastery where
> one of his farmers lodges. This news, Madam, fills me with joy. If in this remote
> and wild country I may pass the last days of my life forgotten by men, this interval
> of rest will soon make me forget all my miseries and I shall be indebted to Mr
> Hume for all the happiness that I can yet hope for.)

The 'seigneur' in question was Chase Price (1731–77), Tory MP for Radnorshire from 1768 until his death, whom Rousseau met two days later to
discuss his plans, and the house was Monaughty, a corruption of the Welsh

mynachdy (monastery), near Bleddfa, Radnorshire.[15] Chase Price assures him he is making the right choice, for his country abounds 'in nothing but solitude and independency',[16] and what is more, the cost of living is low. Rousseau accepts the invitation,[17] his heart set on spending the remainder of his days in Wales ('Puissai-je y mourir en paix', Oh! To die there in peace).[18] Unfortunately, the exasperated Hume does not share Rousseau's enthusiasm for Wales:

> yet he is absolutely determined to retire and board himself in a Farmer's House among the Mountains of Wales for the sake of Solitude. He has refus'd a Pension from the King of Prussia and Presents from hundreds . . .[19]

and mounts a concerted campaign against the plan.

But Wales holds a special appeal for Rousseau, largely on account of its similarity with his native Switzerland: 'Le pays de Galles ressemble entiérement à la Suisse, excepté les habitans'[20] (Wales is exactly like Switzerland, except for the inhabitants). He is undaunted even by the Welsh language, as he is confident that Welsh hearts will conquer any linguistic divide:

> j'ai résolu d'aller à tout risque me jetter tout au fond de la Province de Galles où l'on n'entend pas même l'Anglois, mais dont les habitans bons et hospitaliers tireront de leurs coeurs l'intelligence qui ne sera pas dans leurs oreilles.[21]

> (I have decided that whatever the risk, I shall throw myself into the depths of the province of Wales, where not even English is to be heard, but where the good and hospitable inhabitants will draw from their hearts the intelligence that their ears lack.)

However, the plan falls through, and Rousseau goes instead to Staffordshire, where a place was ready for him ('un logement tout prêt'), but with one eye on a possible future visit to Wales.[22]

Rousseau may never have made it to Wales, but his ideas certainly did. Within Welsh bibliography, provenance studies are in their infancy, because libraries have not compiled provenance indexes for their holdings, and private libraries in Wales have not been the subject of the kind of statistical investigation that has looked at the presence of *philosophes*' writings in English ones.[23] Nevertheless there is a significant number of eighteenth-century editions of Rousseau's works, both in French and in English translation, in libraries in Wales today. Such books found at the National Library, and at university libraries at Aberystwyth, Bangor, Swansea and Lampeter, are presumably traceable to other, mostly private, libraries, such as those at

Hafod, or at Plas Newydd, Llangollen. It is worth remembering at this juncture that there were times when just owning Rousseau's books would have been daring. On the Continent, these books had been burned, and just across the Welsh border in Shrewsbury in 1798 a library voted to expel books including Rousseau and others.[24] It was brave, then, of Iolo Morganwg to have Rousseau's works in his shop in the 1790s.[25]

It seems likely that just as many people in Wales learnt about Rousseau in a less direct way, perhaps through relatively short extracts translated into English in periodicals or digests. Though there are no passages from Rousseau translated in any of the Welsh-language periodicals of the 1790s, nor in those border English-language periodicals that served a Welsh readership, publications such as *Pig's Meat* and *The Manual of Liberty*, which contained passages of Rousseau in English, were read and used in Wales.[26] For instance, the radical editor and writer Tomos Glyn Cothi translated a paragraph of Rousseau's *Emile* from the English of *The Manual of Liberty* into Welsh in his private notebook.[27] Thus Rousseau's main route into Wales may have been indirect; a Rousseau mediated by an Anglophone, London-based culture. However, this mediation is complicated by the fact that Wales had its own community of cultural hybrids in London to speed up the exchange of ideas. The connections of 'full Welsh Europeans'[28] such as David Williams and Richard Price with France and French culture are well known,[29] and need not be repeated here, save for brief mention of Williams's direct connection with Rousseau.

The story contained in a supplement to the *Town and Country Magazine* in 1778 that David Williams met Rousseau is apocryphal,[30] but he certainly sent a copy of his *Liturgy*, with accompanying letter, to Rousseau in Paris, through the agency of Thomas Bentley. According to the latter's diary, Rousseau described the *Liturgy* as a 'truly noble and respectable undertaking; I approve of it entirely and greatly respect the man'. The account of the meeting in Williams's autobiography adds that Rousseau claimed to be: 'one of his most devoted disciples', and that he urged Bentley to 'tell Williams it is a consolation to my heart that he has realized one of my highest wishes, and that I am one of his most devoted disciples'.[31] The prominent role played by David Williams in British culture (not to mention French) should not obscure the fact that he remained in contact with his native Welsh culture via London's colourful community of Welsh expats,[32] but he was arguably more London than Welsh.

Unlike Williams and Price, the Welsh naval surgeon and writer David Samwell was actively and heavily involved in the Welsh cultural revival.[33] Through his work he travelled to the South Seas, where he famously witnessed the murder of Captain Cook, and was later posted to Versailles to care for British prisoners of war in 1798. As he was surely the Welshman who came into the closest contact with real 'savages', noble or otherwise, we might expect the writings of Rousseau, with their attention to primitive people, living in a state of nature, to strike a chord with him. When summing up on his exotic experiences in a letter to Matthew Gregson, his overall attitude is indeed in tune with Rousseau's: he claims that 'the natives of all the South Sea Islands Matt are a good natured humane and well disposed people, in my opinion much superior to ourselves in those respects'.[34] It would not be surprising if he did have some knowledge of Rousseau's ideas, but as there is no scholarly apparatus in his *Journal* relating his musings to any reading or studying, we can only guess that a passage such as the following description of people who seem to live in paradise might be a variety of British Rousseauist discourse. Samwell speaks of people who live 'where Summer for ever smiles where Nature appears in her gayest attire', and far from 'artificial society', but who then shock us by seeming to display 'brutal Violence & savage Barbarity!' Far from then condemning these people, Samwell takes the opportunity to blame their chiefs, and the power structure in which they live, for this behaviour.[35] However, the closest we can get to proving that he knew or read Rousseau is a tantalizing report by Frank Holden in a letter to William Roscoe that in many of his meetings with Samwell in the early 1780s they discussed 'the comparative happiness of a savage and civilized [state] and we both seem to be of our friend Rousseau's sentiment'.[36]

The remainder of this chapter will explore the presence of Rousseau in Wales through a re-evaluation of Iolo Morganwg and Thomas Johnes of Hafod. Two figures seemingly in opposition yet drawn together by their zeal for the preservation and recovery of Welsh manuscripts. Thomas Johnes of Hafod Uchdryd in upland Ceredigion was a man of broad cultural horizons, who received his formal education in Edinburgh, and made his grand tour in 1768–71, visiting Switzerland, as well as France, Spain and Italy, and spending some months in Paris. He inherited the Hafod estate in 1780 and became Whig Member of Parliament for the borough of Cardigan, and also its lord lieutenant. His translations from French (most famously Froissart) leave us in no doubt about his ease with the French language and his Franco-philia, as do casual references to Voltaire's *Candide* in his letters.[37] He was also a collector and bibliophile, and is most famous for the landscape that he created. It is in this very practical, if indirect, way that we see some of Rousseau's ideas come right into the heart of Wales.

Thomas Johnes made the Hafod estate into an eighteenth-century paradise landscape, planting trees, creating flower gardens and picturesque walks.[38] An important influence on his ideas about landscape was *The English Garden*, a long poem in four books, by William Mason, a friend of William Gilpin,

Figure 1. 'Hafod House (1810)', engraving by Joseph C. Stadler,
after a painting by John 'Warwick' Smith.

the author of the *Observations of the River Wye* (1782). So keen was Johnes
that Hafod should be included in any subsequent editions of this work
(indeed it was included in 1789), that he took some sketches by Thomas
Jones to show him, and claimed that Mason's *English Garden* had been his
guide when landscaping. Their meeting is described by Gilpin in a letter to
Mason in April 1787:

> The walks, & lawns were laid out by Mr. Mason whose English garden he took
> in his hand; & wanted no other direction. So if you want to see an exact translation
> of Yr. book into good Welsh, you myst go to Mr. Johnes's seat in Cardiganshire.[39]

Rousseau was Mason's 'favourite philosopher',[40] and in the garden that
Mason created for Lord Harcourt at Nuneham Courtney he placed a bust
of Rousseau and inscribed some pantheistic words from *La Nouvelle Héloïse*
above a gate.[41] Rousseau is directly invoked in notes by the author's friend
William Burgh, that were included in the second edition of *The English
Garden* (1783). Burgh refers us to 'Rousseau's charming descriptions of the
Garden of Julie, *Nouvelle Eloise*, 4 partie, lett. 11th.'[42]

Rousseau's sentimental novel, *Julie, ou La Nouvelle Héloïse* (1761) was
phenomenally popular, came out in seventy-two editions before the end of
the century, and 'changed lives and fashions' across Europe.[43] It was translated
rapidly into English as *Eloisa, or a Series of Original Letters* by William Kenrick,[44]

and made a huge impact on English literature, leading to countless novels featuring Julies, Julias, and Juliettes, and still others that reworked its plot in some way.[45] Julie's garden, like Sophie's in *Emile*, is a haven of beauty and fertility in which the hand of the gardener is invisible. It was the antithesis of the tradition of formal gardening exemplified in Versailles. Johnes also wished the gardener's hand to be invisible. He wrote to George Cumberland, author of *An Attempt to Describe Hafod* (1796,) that 'by beautifying it I have neither shorn or [*sic*] tormented it'.[46] Caroline Kerkham has suggested that Johnes's landscape was modelled jointly on the estates of Mason's poetic hero and that of Rousseau's Julie at Clarens, further describing 'Thomas Johnes's empathy with Rousseau's perception of nature [as] remarkable'.[47]

The affinity between the Hafod household and Rousseau goes beyond the aesthetic. In *La Nouvelle Héloïse* Clarens is also the model of a fertile, productive and harmonious rural community, overseen by Julie and her husband Wolmar. One year later in *Emile* (1762), the main characters' very different educations also prepare them for a life as benevolent landlords. Thomas Johnes was keen to innovate in order to improve agricultural productivity at a time when debates in Parliament warned of food shortages resulting from the war effort. Johnes brought experts from Scotland, attempted to import Swiss peasant families (but the scheme failed for lack of government backing),[48] and published a handbook *A Cardiganshire landlord's advice to his tenants*, and ensured its translation into Welsh by William Owen Pughe. But his motivation clearly went beyond the economic, as he saw the value of educating his tenants, and was familiar with the work of Griffith Jones, Llanddowror.[49] This putative Clarens at Cwmystwyth also employed a doctor for tenants, and ran a school where Mrs Johnes ensured girls could learn reading and needlework, and for which she procured bibles and Hannah More as reading material: 'yr oedd llyfrwerthwr yn Llundain rywdro'n sôn am yrru dau focsaid o Feiblau, a mil o lyfrynnau bach o waith Hannah More, at Mrs Johnes'.[50]

While devoted to Hafod, Thomas Johnes and his wife Jane and daughter Mariamne were also very much in contact with London-based culture. Mariamne corresponded with Edward Smith of the Linnean Society, such was her passion for botany.[51] She also made a deep impression on William Shepherd, the Unitarian minister from Liverpool and friend of the family, who says that she read 'the best authors in the English, French, and Italian languages . . . with diligence, and remembered with accuracy'.[52] Given her interest in nature and the huge popularity of Rousseau's novels, it is hard to believe that she had not read one of them. She is perhaps more likely to have read Rousseau than her father, though we can prove neither. Rousseau and much of the eighteenth-century French canon, including Voltaire, were part of the Pesaro library purchased by Johnes, but this collection did not arrive at Hafod until after the fire of 1807, and despite the existence of various catalogues, it is difficult to pinpoint what could have been read when.[53] Besides, in the case of Mariamne, Shepherd mentions that her books were in 'her apartments', rather than in her father's library.

One of the scholars fortunate enough to receive permission from Johnes to work at the famous library was Iolo Morganwg, whose political radicalism ultimately seems to have got in the way of their scholarly arrangement.[54] Though he lacked the money to travel as far as the Continent, Iolo did spend the heady years that followed the outbreak of the French Revolution in London,[55] and despite lacking formal education his energetic reading ensured that his cultural horizons were broad. The name Jean-Jacques Rousseau has frequently been juxtaposed to Iolo's. Indeed critical attempts at rapprochement between the two thinkers are something of a leitmotiv in Iolo scholarship, often accompanied by a retelling of the anecdote about Iolo's experimentation with eating grass.[56] References to Rousseau begin early, with J. J. Evans's *Dylanwad y Chwyldro Ffrengig ar Lenyddiaeth Cymru* (1928),[57] and his influence is stressed in numerous more recent pieces. For Prys Morgan the fact that he has 'imbibed rather too much of Rousseau's nature-worship' leads to him posing as a 'noble savage' in English drawing rooms,[58] and he is 'like a Celtic Jean-Jacques Rousseau'.[59] Ceri Lewis has also written a piece laden with references to Rousseau, whom he holds responsible for Iolo's wish to return to nature, whose *Du Contrat social* was an important influence on Iolo, and whose ideas on primitive man represent a parallel to his thinking on ancient Druids.[60]

These, and other, very general references to Rousseau have been used, more often than not, to prove something about Iolo; that is they have been part of a critic's agenda. Sometimes the aim is simply to prove that this Glamorgan man was no parochial figure, and in these cases Voltaire's name is dropped in for good measure, as in the following:

> On no account should it be thought that Iolo was unfamiliar with the wider world. His letters bristle with political information and literary quotations, and he was thoroughly conversant with the geography of America, the course of the war with France, and the writings of Rousseau, Voltaire, Hume, Franklin and many others.[61]

At other times Rousseau's name is invoked in order to stress Iolo's scholarliness, and at others 'Rousseau', or the title of one of his texts – such as *Du Contrat social* – functions as a shorthand for 'radicalism'. Never have such juxtapositions been backed up by a search for hard evidence. What follows is a contribution to this task.

Firstly, would Iolo have known Rousseau in the original French? His abilities in languages including French have been stressed by Iolo scholars. This has sometimes been a way of proving his scholarliness, as in Geraint Jenkins's description: 'He learned to read French and Latin, dabbled with Sanskrit and Greek, and turned himself into a self-styled authority on language and literature, history etc.'[62] But we might ask why there is a history of claiming that he read French 'with considerable ease',[63] without mentioning that the evidence suggests that he used translations of major French works. We might also ask, with Gwyn Alf Williams, whether such stress on his cosmopolitan reading actually diminishes him, as it obscures his real originality as organic intellectual. Williams makes the opposing claim that: 'he was . . . free of English [sic] and, to some extent, French and Latin'.[64] Iolo's knowledge of French was probably that of a lexicographer,[65] and it seems that English is the language which gave him access to ideas from France. Secondly, what evidence is there that he knew Rousseau's works? He certainly knew the titles, as he stocked some in his shop. Geraint Jenkins tells how, on his return from London to Cowbridge in 1795:

> he deliberately stocked his bookshop with incendiary literature brought in from London and Bristol, and turned it into a Jacobin den, where works by Milton, Godwin, Priestley, Cowper, Voltaire, Rousseau and Paine were stacked openly on the shelves.[66]

There is little doubt that Iolo was interested in books. He possessed hundreds, and was an avid reader in both Welsh and English; he also sold books, and planned to set up a circulating library at Cowbridge.[67] The book-lists that he drew up, relating to the shop, the planned library, and simply of 'books in my possession', enable us to begin to trace his reading, or at least his familiarity with titles. For instance a list headed 'Books at present in my possession proper for a circulating Library. Sepr 1ˢᵗ 1795' gives us Rousseau's *Social Compact*.[68] Another list entitled 'Reading society' gives 'Rousseau', but does not identify the book.[69] We know that these rubbed shoulders on the shelves with volumes of Voltaire, and other French works in English translation, such as Marmontel's *Tales*, Bernardin de Saint Pierre's *Indian Cottage*, and Lesage's *Gill Blas*. But, of course, no amount of book-lists can account for books that Iolo may have borrowed from elsewhere, for instance a tantalizing note in a 'Daily Journal for 1780' to 'Eloisa by Rousseau', under the heading 'Jewel's Library', leaves us wondering whether he borrowed it, read it in a library, or never got around to doing either.[70]

However, some of Iolo's unpublished work shows that Rousseau was more than a name for him. In an essay on Welsh literature Iolo makes a comment on Rousseau's *Discours sur les sciences et les arts*, the piece that won

the Academy of Dijon prize in 1750, in which he first sketched out his
vision of human history as a fall from harmonious nature into corrupt society.
In this early piece, which first brought him to fame on publication in 1751,
Rousseau argued that intellectual progress, as manifested in 'the sciences
and the arts' was both a cause and a symptom of moral decline. In his essay
Iolo argues that Welsh literature escapes the problems that other literatures
may have and 'that afforded Rousseau too many powerful arguments on
the side that he took of the prize question proposed by the Academy of
Dijon'.[71] Iolo is thus using a reference to Rousseau to bolster his argument
that Welsh literature is morally superior to English and has the potential to
make the Welsh 'wiser and better'.[72] Another reference to Rousseau's work,
this time his novel *Emile ou de l'éducation*, also shows Iolo disagreeing with
Rousseau. In a paragraph headed: 'Preface to the New Robinson Crusoe',
Iolo grudgingly accepts that Rousseau's novel is of some value:

> The errors of great men are remarked and the discussion of them frequently leads
> to the Truth from which they have deviated.
>
> Thus Rousseau's Emilius will, in spite of the false opinions advanced in it,
> always be a valuable book, both on account of the important Truths which it
> contains, and those which it has caused to be discovered; and it would be unjust
> not to attribute to it at least a considerable enlargement in our ideas concerning
> education.[73]

He cites the title in English (though the full English title was *Emilius and
Sophia*). The connection with Robinson Crusoe is no accident. This is one
of the very few books that Emile is allowed to read in the novel, and the
fact that Iolo seems to know this suggests a knowledge of the content of the
book, not just its title. An English translation by William Kenrick appeared
in 1762–3 and was more widely read than a rival translation produced by
Thomas Nugent in 1763. In any case these ideas on education were widely
diffused, either via extracts or reviews in periodicals and digests, such as *Pig's
Meat* (which Iolo knew),[74] and *The Manual of Liberty* (1795), used by Tomos
Glyn Cothi, as mentioned above. Ideas also passed via other writers, such
as David Williams, whom Iolo knew,[75] or Thomas Day, whose *The History
of Sandford and Merton* (1783–9) has been called 'the English Emile';[76] Iolo
owned a copy of this, along with *Telemachus*, which functions as a leitmotiv
in *Emile*. Rousseau is mentioned by Iolo in a polemical piece entitled 'Notes
for A push at the pillars of Priestcraft', in which he claims that:

> The best indeed the only true friends of mankind from <u>Jesus Christ and his
> Appostles</u> down to <u>George Fox</u>, I would say down to Tom Paine, but that Sir
> Archy Macblunder would furiously gnash his teeth at me, have almost without

exception appeared amongst the lower classes or very rarely above the middle Newton, Franklin, Ganganelli, Rousseau.[77]

In the same piece Iolo writes of waiting for revolution: waiting 'in peace for the interposition of divine providence to accomplish a revolution in the political world',[78] which suggests that he is interested in the radical Rousseau, or the Rousseau who was perceived at the time to be a precursor of the Revolution. Although there is a strong suggestion that he read *Eloisa*, and even stronger evidence that he read *Emilius*, it is the political Rousseau that he writes about in this passage. Iolo's Rousseau, then, is the Rousseau created for and by the Revolution, rather than Rousseau the lover of nature, as has sometimes been assumed.

Beyond the establishment of actual engagements with Rousseau in Iolo's texts, comparative work on the two figures can look for echoes, such as the following in a short essay by Iolo on 'Religion, Legislation, and National Manners':

> By looking into history we shall see that the primary or fundamental principles of almost every Code in the originated [*sic*] with people that were in a state of nature or savages. Moses, Athens, Sparta, Rome, England. So however excellent in themselves they can not be adduced as proofs of progressive civilization. For I hope to be able to prove that we have rather corrupted than improved these laws. We have certainly found out the means of evading their force.[79]

True comparative work would not be about simply looking for references to, or points of real, verifiable contact with the more famous thinker. It would not be about reducing Iolo's, or anyone else's, text to a series of sources, or pinning it down to specific influences that would 'explain' him. Rather, it would entail using the figure of Rousseau as a parallel, taking a pan-European view, looking at similarities between them that Iolo himself probably did not realize, such as their passion for walking, or feeling uncomfortable with the patronage of polite society. Pursuing these less tangible connections can lead us to truly speculative comparative work, which might suggest why Iolo, on the one hand, ended up advocating self-government for Wales, and Rousseau, on the other, urged the Poles to turn their energies to a patriotic focus on their own language and customs and to go as far as to invent these latter if they could not be preserved or recovered (in *Considérations sur le gouvernement de Pologne* (1771), posthumously published).[80] Similarly, Iolo's vision of Druids, with the emphasis on open-air worship, could be examined as 'a version of Rousseau'.[81]

Tracing the influence of one very famous thinker on a much less famous one, with a view to bolstering the latter's claims to a place in the world

canon will always work to the detriment of the latter. This, though, is the
legacy of a model of analysis familiar from Enlightenment studies that traces
a movement from centre to periphery or from Francophone to vernacular.
True, such hierarchical thinking has been superseded by work that acknowledges that 'men and women of the peripheries talked back'.[82] This new
approach is exemplified in a recent volume of essays that sets out to 'persuade
dix-huitiémistes that the study of the peripheries of the Enlightenment yields
insights about the movement as a whole'.[83] But such 'peripheral' or 'foreign'
figures as Iolo or Tomos Glyn Cothi surely did not think in terms of reflecting
something back to an ostensible centre. What is needed is a truly comparative,
international, multi-lingual consideration of how people in different places,
but in parallel with each other, did not so much talk back to a centre, as just
talked. This must go beyond the rather blinkered notion of literary studies
that the era of the nation state has left us, because these people did not act
or talk in isolation, but in complex patterns of direct or indirect connections,
transcending geographical and linguistic boundaries.

Notes

1   See James H. Warner, 'The Reaction in 18th-Century England to Rousseau's
    Two *Discours*', *Proceedings of the Modern Languages Association*, 48 (1933), 471–87;
    H. Roddier, *Jean-Jacques Rousseau en Angleterre au 18e siècle* (Paris, 1950); Jacques
    Voisine, *Jean-Jacques Rousseau en Angleterre à l'époque romantique* (Paris, 1956). For
    more recent surveys, see Gregory Dart, *Rousseau, Robespierre and English Romanticism*
    (Cambridge, 1999); Edward Duffy, *Rousseau in England: The Context for Shelley's
    Critique of the Enlightenment* (Berkeley, 1979). Also Rousseau-inflected conservative
    writing is traced in Kevin Gilmartin, *Writing Against Revolution: Literary Conservatism
    in Britain: 1790–1832* (Cambridge, 2006). On the more specific question of
    translations of Rousseau's works into English, see Peter France, 'Voltaire and
    Rousseau', in Stuart Gillespie and David Hopkins (eds.), *The Oxford History of
    Literary Translation in English, Volume 3 1660–1790* (Oxford, 2005), pp. 381–91.
2   Michael O'Dea, 'Rousseau in Eighteenth-Century Irish Journals: "A Wanton and
    Romantic Imagination"', in Graham Gargett and Geraldine Sheridan (eds.), *Ireland
    and the French Enlightenment* (Basingstoke, 1999), pp. 90–106; Maire Kennedy,
    French Books in Eighteenth-Century Ireland (Oxford, 2001).
3   Peter France, 'Primitivism and Enlightenment: Rousseau and the Scots', *The
    Yearbook of English Studies*, 15 (1985), 64–79; R. A. Leigh, 'Rousseau and the
    Scottish Enlightenment', *Contributions to Political Economy*, 5, no. 1 (1986), 1–21.
4   Marie-Christine Skuncke, 'Jean-Jacques Rousseau in Swedish Eyes around
    1760', in Richard Butterwick, Simon Davies and Gabriel Sanchez Espinosa (eds.),
    Peripheries of the Enlightenment (Oxford, 2008), pp. 87–103.

[5] This chapter began as a paper given at the Edward Lhuyd Conference, University of Wales Centre for Advanced Welsh and Celtic Studies, Aberystwyth, 2009. In preparing the topic for publication I have incurred numerous debts to the expertise of colleagues, and would like to warmly thank the following: Katherine Astbury, Cathryn Charnell-White, Mary-Ann Constantine, Michael Cronin, Mark Darlow, Martin Fitzpatrick, Angelica Goodden, Robin Howells, Bethan Jenkins, Dafydd Johnston, Ffion Mair Jones, Caroline Kerkham, Marion Löffler, Geraint Philips, Darach Sanfey, Gwyn Walters.

[6] Roger Chartier, *Les Origines culturelles de la Révolution française* (Paris, 1990), p. 106.

[7] Rousseau's reception by women in Britain is a complex field of its own. His 'ambiguous radical legacy' for women writers is discussed in Annette Wheeler Cafarelli, 'Rousseau and British Romanticism: Women and the Legacy of Male Radicalism', in Gregory Maertz (ed.), *Cultural Interactions in the Romantic Age: Critical Essays in Comparative Literature* (New York, 1998), pp. 125–55. See also Mary Seidman Trouille, *Sexual Politics in the Enlightenment: Women Writers Read Rousseau* (Albany, 1997).

[8] See NLW, Dolaucothi Correspondence, V7/77, Jane Johnes, Hafod, to her 'dear Brother', Dolaucothi, n.d. ['Thursday morning'], cited in Marion Löffler, *Welsh Responses to the French Revolution: Press and Public Discourse 1789–1802* (Cardiff, 2012), p. 17.

[9] Chartier, *Les Origines culturelles de la Révolution française*, p. 103. Chartier looks at books owned by émigrés and condemned persons that were confiscated by the Revolutionary authorities after 1792, and claims that their reading matter did not differ fundamentally from that of the most deeply committed Revolutionaries (pp. 105–6). For further discussion of this point, see Haydn Trevor Mason, *The Darnton Debate: Books and Revolution in the Eighteenth Century* (Oxford, 1998), where, unsurprisingly, Rousseau receives much attention.

[10] See Chartier, *Les Origines culturelles de la Révolution française*, and James B. Swenson, *On Jean-Jacques Rousseau: Considered as One of the First Authors of the Revolution* (Stanford, 2000).

[11] For a survey of these attitudes, see Prys Morgan, 'Wild Wales: Civilizing the Welsh from the Sixteenth to the Nineteenth Centuries', in Peter Burke, Brian Harrison and Paul Slack (eds.), *Civil Histories: Essays Presented to Sir Keith Thomas* (Oxford, 2001), pp. 265–84.

[12] Very brief mention is made in David Edmonds and John Eidinow, *Rousseau's Dog* (London, 2007), p. 129. Maurice Cranston skates over it in *The Solitary Self: Jean-Jacques Rousseau in Exile and Adversity* (London, 1997), the third volume of his biography (p. 163). It is almost totally elided in John Viscount Morley, *Rousseau and his Era* (2 vols., London, 1923), II, p. 125. However, it is described in Roddier, *Jean-Jacques Rousseau en Angleterre*, p. 276, and in J. Churton Collins, *Voltaire, Montesquieu and Rousseau in England* (London, 1908), pp. 206–10. Also recently in the psycho-geographical portrait of Radnorshire by Peter J. Conradi, *At the Bright Hem of God: Radnorshire Pastoral* (Bridgend, 2009).

[13] Damian Walford Davies and Lynda Pratt (eds.), *Wales and the Romantic Imagination* (Cardiff, 2007), p. 2.

[14] Rousseau to Marie-Charlotte de Campet de Saujon, comtesse de Boufflers-Rouverel, 18 January 1766, in R. A. Leigh (ed.), *Correspondance complète de Jean-Jacques Rousseau* (52 vols., Oxford, 1965–98), XXVIII, pp. 199–200. All the following extracts from Rousseau's correspondence are from this edition.

[15] Named after an earlier grange of Abaty Cwmhir, *pace* the notes in Rousseau's correspondence: Leigh (ed.), *Correspondance complète*, XXVIII, p. 217, note a. The house is described as: 'A residence of the year 1636 which has retained many of its original features' in *The Royal Commission on the Ancient and Historical Monuments and Constructions in Wales and Monmouthshire, Inventory, Volume III, Radnor* (London, 1913), entry 51. See also Richard Suggett, *Houses and History in the March of Wales: Radnorshire 1400–1800* (Aberystwyth, 2005), figs. 161–3, and description on pp. 153–4. An image of Monaughty is also contained in Gavin De Beer, *Jean-Jacques Rousseau and his World* (London, 1972), p. 78. It is likely that the Chase Price correspondence and commonplace books, Hatfield House, Hertfordshire, contain reflections on Rousseau.

[16] Leigh (ed.), *Correspondance complète*, XXVIII, p. 211, Chase Price to Jean-Jaques Rousseau, 20 January 1766.

[17] Ibid., p. 218, Rousseau and David Hume to Chase Price, 22 January 1766.

[18] Ibid., p. 237, Rousseau to François-Henri d'Ivernois, 29 January 1766.

[19] Ibid., p. 267, David Hume to John Home de Ninewells, 2 February 1766.

[20] Ibid., p. 275, Rousseau to Marie-Charlotte-Hippolyte de Campet de Saujon, comtesse de Boufflers-Rouverel, 6 February 1766.

[21] Ibid., pp. 218–19, Rousseau to Marie-Madeleine de Brémond d'Ars, 22 January 1766.

[22] Ibid., XXIX, p. 31, Rousseau to Chase Price, 15 March 1766.

[23] R. S. Crane, 'Diffusion of Voltaire's Writings in England, 1750–1800', *Modern Philology*, 20 (1923), 264. Crane's data is used by Warner, 'The Reaction in 18th-Century England to Rousseau's Two *Discours*'. The situation in Ireland is discussed in Kennedy, *French Books in Eighteenth-Century Ireland*, pp. 129–30.

[24] See Heather Jackson, *Marginalia, Readers Writing in Books* (New Haven, 2001), cited in William St Clair, *The Reading Nation in the Romantic Period* (Cambridge, 2004), p. 259.

[25] Geraint H. Jenkins, 'The Urban Experiences of Iolo Morganwg', *WHR*, 22, no. 3 (2005), 483.

[26] On these periodicals and their readerships, see Löffler, *Welsh Responses to the French Revolution*.

[27] NLW 6238A, 'Y Gell Gymysg'. I am grateful to Marion Löffler for bringing this passage to my attention.

[28] R. J. W. Evans, *Wales in European Context: Some Historical Reflections* (Aberystwyth, 2001), p. 10.

[29] See Mary-Ann Constantine, 'The Welsh in Revolutionary Paris', in this volume. See also David Williams, 'The Missions of David Williams and James Tilly Matthews to England (1793)', *English Historical Review*, LIII, no. 212 (1938), 651–68. Also

Roddier, *Jean-Jacques Rousseau en Angleterre*; and Whitney R. D. Jones, *David Williams: The Anvil and the Hammer* (Cardiff, 1986). On Richard Price, see Paul Frame and Geoffrey W. Powell, "'Our first concern as lovers of our country must be to enlighten it'": Richard Price's Response to the French Revolution', in this volume, and David Oswald Thomas, *The Honest Mind: The Thought and Work of Richard Price* (Oxford, 1977).

[30] Jones, *David Williams*, p. 89.

[31] David Williams, *Incidents in my own life which have been thought of some importance, edited with an account of his published writing by Peter France* (Brighton, 1980), p. 21.

[32] For discussion of his connections, see Damian Walford Davies, *Presences that Disturb: Models of Romantic Identity in the Literature and Culture of the 1790s* (Cardiff, 2002), esp. p. 21 ff.

[33] See Cathryn Charnell-White, 'Networking the Nation: The Bardic and Correspondence Networks of Wales and London in the 1790s', in this volume.

[34] David Samwell, *The Death of Captain Cook and Other Writings*, ed. Nicholas Thomas, Martin Fitzpatrick and Jennifer Newell (Cardiff, 2007), p. 108.

[35] See Samwell's journal in James Cook, *The Journals of Captain James Cook on his Voyages*, ed. J. C. Beaglehole (4 vols., Cambridge, 1955), III, part 2, pp. 989–1300, at pp. 1021–2.

[36] Correspondence LRO, Roscoe Papers, 920 ROS 2065, Frank Holden to William Roscoe, 1 May 1781, cited in Martin Fitzpatrick, 'The "cultivated understanding" and "chaotic genius" of David Samwell', in Geraint H. Jenkins (ed.), *A Rattleskull Genius: The Many Faces of Iolo Morganwg* (Cardiff, 2005), pp. 383–402, at 394.

[37] See Richard J. Moore-Colyer (ed.), *A Land of Pure Delight: Selections from the Letters of Thomas Johnes of Hafod, Cardiganshire (1748–1816)* (Llandysul, 1992), p. 209.

[38] For a general account of this episode in the history of landscape gardening, see Mark Laird, *The Flowering of the Landscape Garden: English Pleasure Grounds, 1720–1800* (Philadelphia, 1999). For accounts of Johnes's landscaping at Hafod, see Stephen Briggs and Caroline Kerkham, 'A Review of the Archaeological Potential of the Hafod Landscape, Cardiganshire', *CBA Research Report*, 78 (1991), 160–74, and Caroline Kerkham, 'Hafod: Paradise Lost', *Journal of Garden History*, 11, no. 4 (1991), 207–16.

[39] Bodleian Eng. Misc. d. 571, f. 8ᵛ. I am extremely grateful to Bethan Jenkins for providing this transcript. This is cited and discussed in Kerkham, 'Hafod: Paradise Lost', 212, and Mavis Batey, 'The English Garden in Welsh', *Journal of Garden History*, 22, no. 2 (1994), 157–61.

[40] Mavis Batey, 'William Mason, English Gardener', *Journal of Garden History*, 1, no. 2 (1973), 12.

[41] Jean-Jacques Rousseau, *Julie, ou, la Nouvelle Héloïse*, ed. Henri Coulet (Paris, 1993), part 4, letter 11, note.

[42] Burgh's note to Book 4, line 358 in William Mason, *The English Garden: A Poem in Four Books, new edition, corrected, to which are added a commentary and notes, by W. Burgh* (Dublin, 1786), p. 252.

[43] Maurice Cranston, *The Romantic Movement* (1994; repr. Oxford, 1995), p. 11.

[44] France, 'Voltaire and Rousseau', pp. 381–91, at p. 387.

45   For accounts of the specific influence of this novel on English novels, see Gary Kelly, *Women, Writing, and Revolution* (Oxford, 1993), p. 33, Nicola J. Watson, *Revolution and the Form of the British Novel* (Oxford, 1994), pp. 4, note 9, 23. Also Cafarelli, 'Rousseau and British Romanticism'.

46   Cumberland MSS, Thomas Johnes to George Cumberland, 28 July 1794, cited in Kerkham, 'Hafod: Paradise Lost', 209.

47   Ibid., 213.

48   Dafydd Jenkins, *Thomas Johnes o'r Hafod, 1748–1816* (Caerdydd, 1948), p. 50.

49   Two volumes by him are listed in Ifan Kyrle Fletcher, *A Catalogue of Rare Books from Famous Libraries* (London, 1940).

50   Jenkins, *Thomas Johnes o'r Hafod*, p. 37.

51   A letter by Mariamne Johnes is reproduced in Margot Walker, *Sir James Edward Smith, 1759–1828: First President of the Linnean Society of London* (London, 1988), p. 23.

52   A portrait of Mariamne is contained in Thomas Johnes's obituary, written by Shepherd, cited in Caroline Kerkham, 'The Rev. Dr William Shepherd and the death of Mariamne Johnes', *Friends of Hafod Newsletter*, 14 (1996–7), 26–33.

53   See *Bibliotheca Alchorniana* (held at NLW); Fletcher, *A Catalogue of Rare Books from Famous Libraries*; Herbert Lloyd-Jones, 'The Hafod Library in 1807', *NLWJ*, XVII, no. 2 (1971), 207–8, Eiluned Rees, 'An Introductory Survey of 18th Century Welsh Libraries', *Journal of the Welsh Bibliographical Society*, 10, no. 4 (1971), 197–258, at 229.

54   *CIM*, II, p. 189, William Owen Pughe to Iolo Morganwg, 14 June 1799, 'some body must have insinuated something to him respecting your kingophobia and other demon matters'.

55   For an account of this period of his life, see Davies, *Presences that Disturb*, pp. 135–92, and Jenkins (ed.), *A Rattleskull Genius*.

56   As in Prys Morgan, *Iolo Morganwg* (Cardiff, 1975), p. 75, or in John James Evans, *Dylanwad y Chwyldro Ffrengig ar Lenyddiaeth Cymru* (Lerpwl, 1928), pp. 88–9.

57   Evans, *Dylanwad y Chwyldro Ffrengig*, p. 88, 'Dywed bywgraffwyr Iolo, hefyd, ei fod y pryd hwn yn credu syniadau Rousseau, mai melltith yw gwareiddiad ac mai'r ddelfryd yw'r cyflwr naturiol yn y goedwig.'

58   Morgan, *Iolo Morganwg*, pp. 75, 14.

59   *Idem*, 'Romanticism and Rationalism in the Life of Iolo Morganwg', in T. M. Charles-Edwards and R. J. W. Evans (eds.), *Wales and the Wider World: Welsh History in an International Context* (Donington, 2010), p. 155.

60   Ceri W. Lewis, 'Iolo Morganwg', in Branwen Jarvis (ed.), *A Guide to Welsh Literature c.1700–1800* (Cardiff, 2000), pp. 135, 129, 157.

61   'Introduction', *CIM*, p. 4.

62   Jenkins (ed.), *A Rattleskull Genius*, p. 12.

63   Lewis, 'Iolo Morganwg', p. 131. This echoes G. J. Williams, *Iolo Morganwg, y Gyfrol Gyntaf* (Caerdydd, 1956), p. 106.

64   Gwyn A. Williams, 'People's Remembrancers to a Welsh Republic', *Radical Wales*, 12 (1986), 18.

65 Indeed we know that he coined words for Welsh that demonstrate a lexicographer's knowledge of French and Latin. On his lexicographical teachers and the question of language skills, see Richard M. Crowe, 'Thomas Richards a John Walters: Athrawon Geiriadurol Iolo Morganwg', in Hywel Teifi Edwards (ed.), *Llyfni ac Afan, Garw ac Ogwr* (Llandysul, 1998), pp. 227–51.

66 Jenkins, 'The Urban Experiences of Iolo Morganwg', 483.

67 Ibid., 483.

68 NLW 21407C. I am grateful to Ffion Mair Jones for guidance on Iolo's book-lists.

69 Ibid.

70 NLW 21326A. Mentioned in Geraint H. Jenkins, *Bard Of Liberty: The Political Radicalism of Iolo Morganwg* (Cardiff, 2012), p. 41 n. 64.

71 NLW 13121B. The essay is reproduced in Cathryn Charnell-White, *Bardic Circles: National, Regional and Personal Identity in the Bardic Vision of Iolo Morganwg* (Cardiff, 2007), pp. 272–6, this quotation is on p. 275. Iolo includes the item 'Rousseau on civilization' in at least two of his book-lists: NLW 13136A, p. 27, and NLW 21407. It seems likely that this refers to an English translation of Rousseau's *Discours*. On these translations, see Warner, 'The Reaction in 18th-Century England to Rousseau's Two *Discours*'.

72 Charnell-White, *Bardic Circles*, p. 272.

73 NLW 13141A, p. 114.

74 It features in Iolo's 'London Booklist', NLW 13136A, p. 148. *Pig's Meat*, II (1794), 135, contains an extract entitled 'On the Common People (From Rousseau's Emilius)'. I am grateful to Marion Löffler for bringing this to my attention.

75 Roddier says of David Williams: 'avec une réelle intelligence critique il tamise en quelques sorte l'enseignement de Rousseau à l'usage du grand public', Roddier, *Jean-Jacques Rousseau en Angleterre*, p. 151. The public he has in mind is British, not just Welsh.

76 Ibid., p. 153: '*l'Emile* anglais'.

77 NLW 13123B, pp. 157–64, at p. 161.

78 Ibid., p. 162.

79 Ibid., p. 74.

80 This text is discussed briefly in Richard Butterwick, Simon Davies and Gabriel Sánchez Espinosa (eds.), *Peripheries of the Enlightenment* (Oxford, 2008), pp. 9–10.

81 Gwyn Alf Williams hints promisingly at this, but does not analyse: 'Theirs [London-Welsh radicals] was a version of Rousseau's natural religion', Gwyn A. Williams, 'Druids and Democrats: Organic Intellectuals and the First Welsh Radicalism', in Raphael Samuel and Gareth Stedman Jones (eds.), *Culture, Ideology and Politics: Essays for Eric Hobsbawm* (London, 1982), p. 52. A similar hint is made in E. Gwynn Matthews, 'Denbighshire's Democratic Druids', *Denbigh and its Past*, 8 (1994), 21–4.

82 For a discussion of such work see Butterwick, 'Introduction', in Butterwick, Davies and Sánchez Espinosa (eds.), *Peripheries of the Enlightenment*. This quotation is on p. 7.

83 Ibid., p. 16.

Figure 2. 'Richard Price, D.D. F.R.S.', engraving by Thomas Holloway, 1793, after a painting by Benjamin West.

'Our first concern as lovers of our country must be to enlighten it': Richard Price's response to the French Revolution

PAUL FRAME AND GEOFFREY W. POWELL

Born at Llangeinor in south Wales in 1723 and dying at Hackney, London in 1791, the Dissenting minister and political radical Richard Price lived through the period we choose to call the Enlightenment. If we were asked to suggest a text which could be read to understand this period, we are, perhaps, most likely to recommend Immanuel Kant's 1784 essay *Answering the Question: What is Enlightenment?*, a highly influential piece which opens with the quintessential observation: 'Enlightenment is man's emergence from his self-incurred immaturity'.[1] However, there is another equally moving and equally pivotal text to recommend, composed a mere five years later, in 1789, in which Richard Price responded to the news that the French king was 'by his own desire . . . conducted amidst acclamations never before heard in France to Paris, there to shew himself to his people as the restorer of their liberty'.[2]

The advent of revolution in France can be seen as the fulfilment of Price's own prescience. 'There seems . . . to be an important revolution approaching', he had written in January 1784 to Thomas McGrugar, secretary to the Committee of Citizens of Edinburgh who, like others in Britain at the time, were seeking political and social reform:

> The ideas of men are changing fast. Their minds are growing more enlightened; and a general conviction is like to take place, that "all legitimate government . . . is the dominion of men over *themselves*; and not in the dominion of communities over communities, or of any men over other men." When this happens, all slavish governments must fall, and a general reformation will take place in human affairs.[3]

Though these hopes were to be dashed in the Britain of 1785, when parliamentary reforms proposed by Pitt the Younger failed to pass, they were
rekindled by later events in France about which, in October 1788, Price
wanted to know more. 'What is now passing in France is an object of my
anxious attention', he informed Thomas Jefferson, then United States representative in Paris:

> I am by no means properly informed about the nature and circumstances of the
> struggle; but as far as it is a struggle for a free constitution of government and the
> recovery of their rights by the people I heartily wish it success whatever may be
> the consequences to this country, for I have learnt to consider myself more as a
> citizen of the world than of any particular country, and to such a person every
> advance that the cause of public liberty makes must be agreeable.[4]

Delighted by what he read in Jefferson's subsequent detailed letters, Price
wrote, just two weeks before the fall of the Bastille, to the Comte de Mirabeau
in Paris concerning both current events and future possibilities:

> A revolution so important brought about in a period of time so short by the spirit
> and unanimity of a great Kingdom without violence or bloodshed, has scarcely
> a parallel in the Annals of the world. May the contagion of an example so striking
> extend itself to surrounding nations; and may its influence spread till it has over-
> thrown every where the obstacles to human improvement and made the world
> free, virtuous and happy.[5]

By 1789 Mirabeau, who had translated into French the 1776 pamphlet
Observations on the Nature of Civil Liberty in which Price supported the earlier
American revolutionaries, stood at the very heart of French matters as a
member of the new National Assembly. Price's letter to him now was by
way of introducing his nephew, George Cadogan Morgan. Like his uncle,
Morgan was 'anxiously attentive to the glorious struggle in France for the
blessings of Liberty' and wanted to travel there. Finding himself in Paris on
the fateful day of 14 July Morgan had, by the 21st, written two letters to
his uncle detailing the extraordinary and exhilarating events he witnessed
there. As Price noted in his private journal on 2 August:

> My *nephew* George . . . has been *witness* at *Paris* to the glorious *scene*. He has seen
> all the events that have attended the revolution in the great kingdom that now
> astonishes *Europe*, that has *scarcely* a *parallel* in the history of the world, and that
> is likely to be the commencement of a general reformation of the governments
> of *Europe*. Heaven grant that it may be settled without much more *bloodshed*.[6]

As Morgan continued his travels through France, Price spent most of August and the early part of September enjoying swimming, riding and walking at Southerndown on the coast of south Wales. He kept an eye on French events via the *Gazetteer*, which arrived each morning from London, and on 9 September wrote from Southerndown to his friend the marquis of Lansdowne: 'What an instruction to the world are the [French] Patriots . . . now giving by their declaration of rights, abolition of tithes etc etc.'[7] By mid-September he was back in Hackney, where Tom Paine visited him and found him 'all Joy and happiness at the Progress of Freedom in France'.[8] Even the traumatic events of 3 and 4 October – the so-called October Days when Louis XVI and his family were forced by a violent mob to remove themselves from Versailles to Paris and into effective incarceration – did little or nothing to diminish Price's enthusiasm for the Revolution. Up to this point, his enthusiasm had been a largely private matter, but on 4 November 1789 that changed. He was asked to preach a sermon to fellow-members of the *Society for Commemorating the Revolution in Great Britain*, a group dedicated to celebrating annually the Glorious Revolution of 1688 that ended the reign of Catholic James II and brought Protestant William and Mary to the throne. His sermon was entitled *A Discourse on the Love of Our Country*.

Price discussed in this sermon some of the principal concerns of his life and work: natural rights, religious tolerance, civil liberties, and political reform, as well as the relationship between nations and communities. He also celebrated what he believed to be the principles of the 1688 Glorious Revolution: the right to liberty of conscience in religious matters, the right to resist power when abused, and the 'right to chuse our own governors, to cashier them for misconduct, and to frame a government for ourselves'.[9] Only later in his peroration did he directly address and celebrate events in France. He did so by first linking them to the Revolution of 1688 and the American Revolution of 1776:

> After sharing in the benefits of one Revolution, I have been spared to be a witness to two other Revolutions, both glorious. And now, methinks, I see the ardor for liberty catching and spreading, a general amendment beginning in human affairs, the dominion of priests giving way to the dominion of reason and conscience.[10]

Then, in two memorable closing paragraphs, he offered up encouragement to his fellow-reformers and a warning to those who continued to oppose their aims:

> Be encouraged, all ye friends of freedom and writers in its defence! The times are auspicious. Your labours have not been in vain. Behold kingdoms, admonished

by you, starting from sleep, breaking their fetters, and claiming justice from their oppressors! Behold, the light you have struck out, after setting America free, reflected to France and there kindled into a blaze that lays despotism in ashes and warms and illuminates Europe!

Tremble all ye oppressors of the world! Take warning all ye supporters of slavish governments and slavish hierarchies! Call no more (absurdly and wickedly) reformation, innovation. You cannot now hold the world in darkness. Struggle no longer against increasing light and liberality. Restore to mankind their rights and consent to the correction of abuses, before they and you are destroyed together.[11]

Ageing and ailing as he now was, Price had wondered whether he possessed enough strength to give this sermon but, in the event, all went well. He even managed to attend the feast that followed and to move a Congratulatory Address to the French National Assembly, a copy of which was duly forwarded to the Assembly and read there on 25 November to considerable applause. The rest of November he spent preparing his sermon for publication, which took place on 5 December. Within a week a second edition appeared and on 17 January 1790, perhaps still flushed with this success, his journal records a very rare instance of self-praise:

The revolution in *Fr*[an]*ce* will for ever distinguish the last year and will form an *epoch* of the greatest importance in the history of human kind. It is an event wonderful and *unparalleled*. I am refreshed and animated whenever I turn my thoughts to it and I *exult* in the hope that possibly I may have contributed a little towards producing and confirming it. I am afraid, however, that this Revolution is not yet perfectly out of danger.[12]

At about the time Price wrote this entry, the parliamentarian Edmund Burke perused the published version of the *Discourse* and was appalled by what he read. Convinced that Price, and others like him, were seditionists seeking to overthrow the British constitution and monarchy by spreading revolutionary ideas and ideals, Burke determined to write an immediate reply. By November 1790 his work had been published under the title *Reflections on the Revolution in France*.

Aside from a vituperative and largely disingenuous personal attack (which Price chose largely to ignore) Burke attempted to counter his rationalist thinking by appealing to the superiority of prescriptive rights. By this, he meant the rights of an established hierarchy, of privilege based on property and with hereditary and aristocratic position as qualifications for political leadership. Though he acknowledged that change and reform were sometimes necessary, they should, he felt, always proceed incrementally. The rationalist and natural-rights-based thinking advocated by Price and the French Revolutionaries must, he felt, inevitably lead to the impetuous radical change of long-established institutions and modes of living. In fact, in Price's case, nothing could have been further from the truth. Not only had he spent his entire adult life seeking progressive reform through the only institution available to him – an unreformed parliament – but he had always adopted a pragmatic and cautionary approach to the major changes he wished to see. Revolutionary upheavals, of the kind he welcomed in France, were sometimes necessary, but always as a last resort.

Burke also predicted in his *Reflections* what the consequences of the Revolution in France might be: increasing violence and bloodshed, the likelihood of war and even the rise of a military despot. In these, of course, he was to be proved correct, but this does not negate the value of Price's approach. To read Price's Old Jewry address as dangerously inflammatory, as Edmund Burke did, is to miss the point of what Price was trying to say.

Burke can be excused for misunderstanding what he read, for the *Discourse* is a more profound and subtle work than it might at first appear. Moreover, someone of Burke's perspicacity would have realized just how potentially threatening the address really was, for this *was* an incitement – not to resort to violence to overthrow a particular power – but to cultivate a way of life which, through its respect for legitimate authority, had no place for power at all. Here was a Dissenting minister and philosopher unequivocally applying the teaching of Jesus to the world.

Price's address 'on the love of our country' allowed him to explore what the teaching of Jesus meant for living, not just in the place in which one happened to find oneself, but anywhere in the world. Like many others, he was convinced that this teaching was rational and therefore could be accepted by all, irrespective of local belief. His attention was thus not focused primarily on 1688, 1776 or 1789, but on the human presence in the world as such. He argued not for a rushing to the barricades but a coolly rational exploration of the teaching of the Gospels through reliance on independent and critical thought (by thinking of all things 'as they are')[13] rather than on imposed belief or, in Burke's terms, on 'the old ecclesiastical modes'.[14] His address was an opportunity for him to show how 'the chief blessings of human nature are . . . truth, virtue and liberty'[15] and that these are attainable, not through the exercise of power to exploit and conquer, but universal benevolence and all that it entails.

In a country which was amassing wealth precisely through the exercise of power to conquer and exploit this must have been a troubling message, and, indeed, it remains so. Perhaps because of this, Price's sermon seldom receives the recognition it deserves, though it stands among the best products of the Enlightenment and has lost none of its persuasiveness over time. The subject itself, the love of our country, might have been expected to encourage a narrow nationalism and even xenophobia, but, provocatively, Price set out to show how the new ideas about knowledge and reason could build truth, virtue and liberty even from this foundation.

His first step was to examine what constituted a country or people. He set about undermining the egocentric belief that it is the securing of territory for ourselves which makes us into a nation and enables us to distinguish ourselves from others and to assert our superiority over them. Like other Welsh-born writers of this period (the educationalist David Williams, for example) Price is often referred to as an English thinker, and although Price himself makes very little of his Welshness in his own writings, it is perhaps possible to speculate that it was his experience of being a London Welshman which taught him that people are not merely the occupants of a piece of territory but members of a community which transcends the particular space it occupies.

Even this communal view of identity, however, was not primarily what he was affirming. After all, it could still have been the basis for a narrowly conceived self-centredness. That he was after something more radical becomes clear as we follow his argument. When we recognize and cherish our communal identity we do not, in so doing, claim that all our institutions and processes are outstandingly good and superior to those of others. (At least, we only do so if we are deluded.) If we view things as they are, we find good and bad in all communities, including our own. The world is made up of groups of people with differing beliefs and practices, some of which are good and some bad. While we might expect co-operation for mutual improvement to result from this perception, in fact something very different happens. 'What has the love of their country hitherto been among mankind? What has it been but a love of domination, a desire of conquest, and a thirst for grandeur and glory, by extending territory and enslaving surrounding countries?'[16] This has come about through a spirit of rivalry and ambition, which not only wreaks havoc internationally but within communities too since the rights and liberties of individuals suffer from private self-seeking at the expense of the common good.

The logic of social living is simple enough. It leads us to universal benevolence and to seeing ourselves as citizens of the world. This is why 'offensive wars are always unlawful and to seek the aggrandizement of our country by them, that is, by attacking other countries in order to extend dominion, or to gratify avarice, is wicked and detestable'.[17] But what of the spirit of rivalry and ambition? Price had to recognize its existence, and he did so by describing how a society built on ambition actually functions; and how those committed to universal benevolence have to maintain their vigilance to resist its incursions.

The notion that humans are inherently self-interested, competitive creatures has a long history. Hobbes went so far as to say that unless a strong power could enforce order, life in a society full of such creatures would be solitary, poor, nasty, brutish and short. Especially through Locke's response to this, there developed the idea that a controlling power must be chosen as a representative for those who were to be controlled. Government must be by consent if abuses of power were to be avoided. Price himself adopted this view, though with a consistency which Locke might have found disturbing. Unless a person set in authority was chosen as a servant, and, crucially, treated as no different from his fellows, other than in the special trust put in him and in the authority granted him, rivalry and ambition would govern his conduct. He would exercise power rather than authority. Those in power, thought Price, 'are always endeavouring to extend their power'.[18] In effect, governments based on the power principle are 'contrivances for enabling the *few* to oppress the *many*'.[19] They always tend towards despotism, both within their own territory and outside.

In his Old Jewry sermon Price painted a vivid picture of how a society which runs on encouraging individual self-interest might try to function. It was, of course, an easy picture to create since all he had to do was open his eyes and view the society in which he lived. The most obvious manifestation of it was the huge gap between rich and poor. There was, evidently, no free and just exchange between those who provided services for each other. Out of these exploitative relationships grew luxury, vice and debt. High status mattered, and if servility and sycophancy did not secure advantage, there was always bribery. If the oppressed citizens tried to rebel against their lot they could always be put down by force. Force was also used in extending territory and wealth beyond the State's boundaries. The struggle for more power had become a wonderful engine for the accumulation of wealth in the hands of those who held power. Britain, like other countries with which it was locked in commercial or military conflict, had grown rich on exploitation and plunder. This way of life was, he argued, deeply untenable: 'Restore to mankind their rights', he declared, 'and consent to the correction of abuses, before they and you are destroyed together.'[20]

What he proposed, instead, was constant vigilance against the abuse of power, a form of self-defence, which is of quite a different order from the violence of dispossessing and exploiting others. This vigilance is all: 'Whenever it is withdrawn and a people cease to reason about their rights and to be awake to encroachments, they are in danger of being enslaved and their servants will soon become their masters.'[21] He does not suggest, therefore, that we can have a new world order in which the abuses of power can be eliminated and forgotten, but, with the growth of understanding, we can, at least, become more effective in creating greater space for authoritative and benevolent living.

If we were able to keep rivalry and ambition under control, a community of co-operating individuals would result, but how could this be achieved? Price, along with other Enlightenment figures, believed the advancement and dissemination of knowledge was the solution. If we can understand the machinations of the self-seeking and catalogue the consequent follies of indulgence on the one hand and oppression on the other, a reasoned order could be established, in which individuals would join together to create an authoritative structure for themselves to secure liberty for all. Such a society would live in peace with its neighbours. He would doubtless have been surprised if he could have foreseen the scale of barbarism into which his world would later fall, especially in the twentieth century.

In his *Review of the Principal Questions in Morals*, Price said 'the more we enquire, the more indisputable, I imagine, it will appear to us, that we express necessary truth, when we say of some actions, they are right; and of others, they are wrong'.[22] That 'indisputable' is itself, of course, disputable. Concern for self and competitiveness seem equally self-evident to those who hold opposing views (and we live in a part of the globe where they have long been taken as the sure foundation of the State). For Adam Smith, rivalry, far from being the root of evil, was the spur to 'excellency'. As he observed, in his *Wealth of Nations*, 'great objects . . . are evidently not necessary in order to occasion the greatest exertions'.[23] In effect, his flourishing society would be one fuelled by the very competition and ambition that Price saw as destructive of universal benevolence.

David Hume was perhaps the most accomplished exponent of this moral point of view. Unlike Price, he believed morality 'is more properly felt than judged of'.[24] It is not an object of reason, and the rules of morality are not conclusions of our reason. Virtue is an affair of taste and moral good is an agreeable emotion or feeling which certain actions produce in us. When it comes to morality, he thought reason was no guide, and that only 'an appeal to general opinion'[25] could provide a standard of conduct. In the first volume of his *Treatise of Human Nature*, in which he dismantled much of what had hitherto passed as received opinion in philosophy, he conceded that, when it came to conduct, he found himself 'absolutely and necessarily determined to live and talk, and act like other people in the common affairs of life'.[26] As we discover in the second volume of his *Treatise*, his philosophical method was much more accommodating when it came to morality. Basing moral standards on what people actually did was an appealing idea for the bene-ficiaries of a flourishing economy.

This was the crux of the matter when it came to moral theory. Those, like Hume, who claimed that morality was a matter of natural feelings, would locate the 'moral' in what people actually experienced; others, like Price, found the moral law to be secured by objective reason, outside or above common experience. The contrast was, in effect, between the conserver of the established order and the radical who sought to change things for the better. Accepting life as it was may have been a comfortable state of affairs for the oligarchs and those who were well placed in the political and economic order, but it was not so comfortable for those subject to the injustice and exploitation on which that order depended. As a Dissenter, Price had more reason than most to want to change the established order, but it was his commitment to an alternative moral vision, rather than personal experience, which made his rationalism necessary.

Price's rationalist scheme of universal benevolence involves an economic order in which individual participants are not self-centred competitors but benevolent co-operators. His liberty is not freedom of choice to do anything for self-gratification, because it is governed by a determination to have the same expectations for others that we have for ourselves, and, since we are to be citizens of the world, the 'others' are, literally, everyone.

At a point in time when the bankruptcy of the old ideology of the free market is all too evident, a careful reconsideration of Price's approach is long overdue. His intuitionism arguably provides a more realistic basis for progressive reform than Kant's. This is particularly evident if we compare Kant's treatment of the Gospels' injunction to 'love thy neighbour' with that of Price. When, in his *Fundamental Principles of the Metaphysic of Morals*, Kant tried to make sense of this command to love our neighbour,[27] he used the fact that it is a *command* to rule out the possibility that we are to love others through actual affection or feeling. (In the same spirit, von Hayek said, more recently, in his *Constitution of Liberty*, that 'general altruism'[28] was a meaningless idea because, in effect, nobody can care for others in general.) Why else, he thought, would it be a command? On this basis, what he expected of society is obedience, out of duty, to what is rationally imposed. We are to see the behaviour of, say, the Good Samaritan as involving an act of will rather than intuition, or feeling.

In contrast to Kant, Price realized that universal benevolence could not depend, alone, on an intellectual acceptance of the principle to love our neighbour. There had to be a similar universality of feeling too. There had to be 'both a *perception of the understanding*, and a *feeling of the heart*',[29] and, unlike Kant, he included both in his eternal and immutable morality. He also observed acutely that 'it may be difficult to determine the precise limits between these two sources of our mental feelings; and to say, how far the effects of the one are blended with those of the other'.[30] His peaceful world order would not be established, as Kant's *Perpetual Peace* argued, through pure practical reason alone but through a brotherhood of all who, if clear-sighted and knowledgeable, would feel a universal benevolence. This would make the selfish exploitation of others, whether close or distant, impossible.

For a few years following Price's sermon, 'brotherhood and co-operation' were certainly in the air. In a London speech celebrating the first anniversary of the Revolution, on 14 July 1790, Price lauded the French Assembly's resolution of 22 May that year renouncing forever, as he put it, 'all views of conquest, and all *offensive* wars'.[31] In celebrating this fact he did not begin his speech with the sort of airy and metaphysical speculation Burke ascribed to him. He began, instead, by stressing the importance of peace to the continued security of a Britain sinking 'under a load of debts' consequent upon the series of wars it had recently fought. The prospect of peace, there-fore, formed an 'instance of wisdom and attention to human rights which has no example'. For too long, he argued:

> The passions of Kings and their Ministers . . . involved nations in the calamities of war. But now, (thanks to the National Assembly of France) the axe is laid to the root of this cause of human misery; and the intrigues of Courts are likely to lose their power of embroiling the world.

All of which promised the 'new and better order in human affairs', which he went on to outline thus:

> In this kingdom we have been used to speak of the people of France as our *natural enemies*; and however absurd, as well as ungenerous and wicked, such language was, it admitted of some excuse while they consisted only of a monarch and his slaves.

But the French had now 'broke their yoke . . . asserted their rights, and made themselves as free as ourselves'.[32] Britain, he argued, had been an example to France through the Glorious Revolution of 1688, which had finally established full constitutional monarchy in contrast to the absolute monarchy that persisted in France up to the Revolution. In the wake of that revolution, however, he claimed, 'THEY are now become an example to US'. Having abandoned absolute monarchy, France was now engaged in sweeping political and social reforms of the kind he wished to see in Britain. He had information too, from 'a very respectable authority', that the National Assembly had formed 'a design' to propose an alliance with Britain that would act as a crowning glory to the actions in France:

> Thus united, the two kingdoms will be omnipotent, they will soon draw into their confederation HOLLAND, and other countries on this side the Globe, and the United States of AMERICA on the other; and, when alarms of war come, they will be able to say to contending nations, PEACE, and there will be PEACE.[33]

This hope for an early form of NATO was an entirely rational suggestion at the time, though one destined to fail.

Price died on 19 April 1791. By May, Edmund Burke was already arguing for a war against Revolutionary France. But in France itself, there were still some who voiced sentiments akin to those of Price. On slavery for example, which Price abhorred and had urged the Americans to abolish as quickly as humanly possible, Robespierre voiced his opposition: 'The moment you pronounce, in one of your decrees, the word *slave*, you will be pronouncing your own dishonour and the overthrow of your constitution', he declared of a proposal to insert into the new French constitution a clause allowing slavery to continue in her colonies. 'Perish your colonies, if you are keeping them at that price. Yes, if you had either to lose your colonies, or to lose your happiness, your glory, your liberty, I would repeat: perish your colonies.'[34]

On the question of property generally, Price had declared in 1767 that he could not 'think it necessary that the world should continue for ever divided, as it is now, into a multitude of independent states whose jarring interests are always producing war and devastation. A scheme of government may be imagined that shall, by annihilating property and reducing mankind to their natural equality, remove most of the causes of contention and wickedness.'[35] He understood this could be seen as mere Utopian reverie but, as with so many of his arguments, it represented a long-term aspiration derived from a more immediate reality – the disparity between rich and poor – and the knowledge 'that there is an equality in society which is essential to liberty, and which every state that would continue virtuous and happy ought as far as possible to maintain'.[36] While introducing his *Draft Declaration of the Rights of Man and of the Citizen* into the National Convention in April 1793, written in opposition to a Girondist constitution written by Condorcet (a correspondent of Price), Robespierre argued: 'In defining liberty, the first of mankind's assets, the most sacred of the rights it receives from nature, you said, rightly, that its limits were the rights of others; why did you not apply that principle to property, which is a social institution?' He then proposed four clauses that echo much of Price's position:

> Property is the right every citizen has to enjoy and dispose of the portion of goods guaranteed to him by law. The right to property is limited, like all others, by the obligation to respect the rights of other people. It cannot prejudice either the security, or the liberty, or the life, or the property of our fellows. Any possession or any trade that violates that principle is illicit and immoral.[37]

By the time Robespierre spoke these words relations between Britain and France had moved even further away from 'brotherhood and co-operation'. Not only had Revolutionary France declared war on Britain in February but, in France itself, the moderate Girondists were soon coming under attack from the more extreme Jacobins led, of course, by Robespierre. The bloody events that followed need no reiteration here; Price's intellectual legacy was one of many casualties.

Though it can be argued that by calling for war against France as early as May 1791 Burke helped push the French Revolutionaries into adopting a more extreme course than they might otherwise have taken, his argument that 'the oppression of the minority will extend to far greater numbers, and will be carried on with much greater fury, than can almost ever be apprehended from the dominion of a single sceptre'[38] had the ring of prescience in the shadow of Robespierre, the Committee of Public Safety and mistress guillotine. In short, Burke came to be seen as the man who bested the 'unfortunate Dr. Price', a verdict bolstered too by the fact that nineteenth-century Britain went on to adopt precisely the sort of expansionist and imperialist policies, backed by an empirical and utilitarian outlook, that Price opposed in all his work. After his death, indeed, the Revolution appeared to undermine so many principles of his life. These included not only his belief in a creator, his hatred of dogmatism and his constant desire to question everything (including his Christian beliefs), but the very ideals of truth, freedom and virtue: truth lost through the development of entrenched factionalism and stereotyping, freedom lost as justice became arbitrary and relied on denunciation rather than the rule of law, and virtue lost when Robespierre allied it to terror.

Would this have turned Price from the ideas he outlined in the *Discourse*? It seems unlikely. He understood that revolution, as a last resort, might be necessary, but his rationalist vision of natural rights and civil liberties was always tempered by an understanding that revolutionary activity was inherently dangerous. He knew things could go wrong because he understood the frailty of human nature when under the influence of the passions. It was a crucial element of the moral philosophy he had outlined in 1758. 'Actions', he claimed, 'may have all the form of virtue without any of its realities'; he understood too the nature of mob violence – 'the odium of a cruel action, when shared among the many, is not regarded'. Such concerns, however, did not mean reforms should not be attempted. As he had told Thomas McGrugar in 1784:

> The danger of producing confusion, and of setting government afloat, is often urged as a reason against attempts to reform. But this is an argument that proves too much. Ought it to influence in France, Spain, Turkey, &c. were the people there duly sensible of their rights, and of the evil of arbitrary governments? If so, all the vile tyrannies of the world must be suffered to continue as they are.[39]

The situations between countries also differed and might have unforeseen consequences in revolutionary times. Though he wanted to see good come from the Revolution in France he worried over their lack of a middle ground to act as a buffer between the ruling élite and the largely uneducated and grossly abused Third Estate. As he told Thomas Jefferson in 1789, 'A better representation than ours it may easily obtain; but the want of such a body of free-holders and respectable yeomanry as there is in this country and in yours seems in this respect a great disadvantage to it.'[40]

None of the dire consequences of the Revolution were a direct result of the ideas Price outlined in his *Discourse*. They were the consequence of decisions made by those with power, and the fact that all too often their power went unchallenged by those over whom they wielded it. While power still existed, it needed to be constantly watched, and, for that, an enlightened population cognizant of its rights and liberties and with a willingness to defend them was crucial. We began this short study by acknowledging that Kant's essay on enlightenment is better known for defining the character of that phenomenon than Price's sermon; it is time, perhaps, to give Price his due. After all, in his essay, Kant was, it seems, so busy paying due homage to King Frederick of Prussia (a liberal in intellectual matters but also a militarist) that he did not see just how pusillanimous his version of enlightenment was. He summarized the practical significance of it in the sentence: 'Argue as much as you like and about whatever you like, but obey'.[41] What is crucial here is what has to be obeyed. If what is to command obedience is authoritative, then performing roles obediently would be thoroughly reasonable, but to combine free rational thought with obedience to what has to be uncritically accepted has nothing other than expediency to commend it. Kant does recognize that the rational touchstone for a law must be in a people's wish to impose it on itself, but obedience to the State in the performance of one's role, come what may, ensures that there will always be containment of radical enlightenment by the power of the State. While Price also recognized the need for obedience to the State, for him this has to presuppose that citizens see its requirements as being genuinely authoritative. When they are not, it is their duty to 'resist abuses as soon as they begin'.[42] Performance of any role in the service of the State has to be a matter of rational commitment, not uncritical compliance.

Both recognize the need for obedience, therefore, but Price's understanding of it is rather different from Kant's. While Kant gives the example of the clergyman who, as a scholar, can freely expose the failings of his church but, as a priest, must perform his role in maintaining the institution as though he had not, Price can allow no such division between thought and practice. His approach may at first seem more incendiary, as Burke claimed it was, but, in its consistency and integrity, we believe that it provides a better model for enlightenment than Kant's essay, and should be far better known.

> Our first concern as lovers of our country must be to enlighten it. Why are the nations of the world so patient under despotism? Why do they crouch to tyrants, or submit to be treated as if they were a herd of cattle? Enlighten them and you will elevate them. Shew them they are *men* and they will act like *men*. Give them just ideas of civil government and let them know that it is an expedient for gaining protection against injury and defending their rights, and it will be impossible for them to submit to governments which, like most of those now in the world, are usurpations on the rights of men and little better than contrivances for enabling the *few* to oppress the *many*.[43]

Notes

[1]   Immanuel Kant, 'An Answer to the Question: "What is Enlightenment?"', in Hans Reiss (ed.), *Kant: Political Writings* (2nd edn., Cambridge, 1991), p. 54.

[2]   Richard Price, 'A Discourse on the Love of Our Country (Preface to the Fourth Edition)', in D. O. Thomas (ed.), *Price, Political Writings* (Cambridge, 1991), p. 177.

[3]   Rémy Duthille, 'Thirteen Uncollected Letters of Richard Price: Letter 3', *Enlightenment and Dissent*, 27 (2011), 105, Richard Price to Thomas McGrugar, 27 January 1784. Price's internal quote is said to be from Montesquieu (see ibid.,105, n. 47).

[4]   W. Bernard Peach and D. O. Thomas (eds.), *The Correspondence of Richard Price* (3 vols., Durham, 1983–94), III, p. 182, Richard Price to Thomas Jefferson, 26 October 1788.

[5]   Peach and Thomas (eds.), *The Correspondence of Richard Price*, III, pp. 229–30, Richard Price to Count Mirabeau, 2 July 1789. The quoted text is from a postscript to the letter of 2 July, which is dated 4 July 1789. Price, however, must have mistaken the date as by 4 July Morgan was already in France.

6   Beryl Thomas and D. O. Thomas, 'Richard Price's Journal for the Period 25 March 1787 to 6 February 1791', *NLWJ*, XXI, no. 1 (1980), 390–1. For Morgan's letters from France, see Mary-Ann Constantine and Paul Frame (eds.), *Travels in Revolutionary France and A Journey Across America by George Cadogan Morgan and Richard Price Morgan* (Cardiff, 2012).

7   Peach and Thomas (eds.), *The Correspondence of Richard Price*, III, p. 256, Richard Price to the marquis of Lansdowne, 9 September 1789.

8   J. Graham, *The Nation, The Law and The King, Reform Politics in England, 1789–1799* (2 vols., Lanham, 2000), I, p. 131 and note 33, Thomas Paine to Thomas Walker of Rotherham, 19 September 1789.

9   Price, 'A Discourse on the Love of Our Country', pp. 189–90.

10   Ibid., p. 195.

11   Ibid., pp. 195–96.

12   Thomas and Thomas, 'Richard Price's Journal', 392–3.

13   Price, 'A Discourse on the Love of Our Country', p. 178.

14   Edmund Burke, *Reflections on the Revolution in France*, ed. William B. Todd (New York, 1959), p. 121.

15   Price, 'A Discourse on the Love of Our Country', p. 181.

16   Ibid., p. 179.

17   Ibid., p. 188.

18   Ibid., p. 187.

19   Ibid., p. 181.

20   Ibid., p. 196.

21   Ibid., p. 187.

22   Richard Price, *A Review of the Principal Questions in Morals by Richard Price*, ed. D. D. Raphael (Oxford, 1974), p. 47.

23   Adam Smith, *An Inquiry Into the Nature and Causes of the Wealth of Nations* (2 vols., London, 1910), II, p. 246.

24   David Hume, *A Treatise of Human Nature* (2 vols., London, 1956), II, p. 178.

25   *Idem*, 'Of the Original Contract', in *idem*, *Essays, Moral, Political and Literary* (London, 1903).

26   *Idem, A Treatise of Human Nature*, I, p. 254.

27   Immanuel Kant, 'Fundamental Principles of the Metaphysic of Morals', in Thomas Kingsmill Abbott (ed. and trans.), *Kant's Critique of Pratical Reason and Other Works on the Theory of Ethics* (London, 1967), p. 15.

28   F. A. Hayek, *The Constitution of Liberty* (London, 1960), p. 78.

29   Price, *A Review of the Principal Questions*, p. 62.

30   Ibid.

31   Thomas and Thomas, 'Richard Price's Journal', 399.

32   Ibid.

33   Ibid.

34   Maximilien Robespierre, 'On the Condition of Free Men of Colour, 13 May 1791', in Slavoj Žižek (with Jean Ducange and John Howe), *Virtue and Terror, Maximilien Robespierre* (London, 2007), pp. 20–1.

[35] Richard Price, *Four Dissertations* (3rd edn., London, 1772), p. 138n.

[36] *Idem, Observations on the Importance of the American Revolution and the means of making it a benefit to the world* (2nd edn., London, 1785), p. 71.

[37] Maximilien Robespierre, 'Draft Declaration of the Rights of Man and of the Citizen, 24 April 1793', in Žižek et al., *Virtue and Terror*, p. 67.

[38] Edmund Burke, *Reflections on the Revolution in France* (2nd edn., London, 1790), p. 186.

[39] Duthille, 'Thirteen Uncollected Letters', 105–6, Richard Price to Thomas Macgrugar, 27 January 1784.

[40] Peach and Thomas (eds.), *The Correspondence of Richard Price*, III, p. 218, Richard Price to Thomas Jefferson, 4 May 1789.

[41] Kant, 'An Answer to the Question: "What is Enlightenment?"', p. 59.

[42] Price, 'A Discourse on the Love of Our Country', p. 187.

[43] Ibid., p. 181.

The Welsh in Revolutionary Paris

MARY-ANN CONSTANTINE

Adresse présentée à la Convention Nationale, par les Anglois, Irlandois, & Écossais, résidans à Paris, & aux environs, le 23 Septembre 1793, l'an deuxième de la République.

Nous nous présentons devant la Convention Nationale, au nom de ceux de nos frères les Anglois, les Irlandois & les Écossois, résidans à Paris & dans les environs, qui chérissent comme nous les principes de la liberté, & qui souffrent de la rigeur des décrets que votre justice & votre sagesse nous persuadent n'avoir été rendus, que pour frapper d'un coup mortel les énnemis de la République. À la vue des malheurs dont nous allons êtres les victimes innocents, nous venons, avec confiance, réclamer votre protection, les droits de la justice, & ceux de l'hospitalité.

Il n'est pas étonnant qu'une révolution, qui doit anéantir les limites factices qui séparent les nations, & qui a permis fraternité à tout le genre humain, ait engagé les habitans des contrées voisines à voyager ou à résider en France. Les malheureux, les persécutés ont couru y chercher un asyle; les amis de la liberté universelle y sont venus par goût. Nous sommes les représentans des uns et des autres, & ce sont les interêts de tous dont nous prenons la défense auprès de la Convention Nationale.[1]

(An Address presented to the National Convention, by the English, Irish, & Scottish residents of Paris and its environs, 23 September 1793, second year of the Republic.

We come before the National Convention in the name of our English, Irish and Scottish brothers resident in Paris and the environs, who, like ourselves, hold the principles of liberty dear, and who are suffering under the severity of the decrees that your justice and wisdom have, we know, only passed in order to strike a mortal blow at the enemies of the Republic. Foreseeing that we will be the innocent victims of troubles ahead, we come, with confidence, to demand your protection, and the rights of justice and hospitality.

It is not surprising that a revolution which, aiming to destroy the factitious boundaries separating nations, has granted fraternity to all human beings, should have attracted the inhabitants of neighbouring countries to travel or to reside in France. The wretched and the persecuted have fled here seeking asylum; the friends of universal liberty have come of their own inclination. We are the representatives of both, and we are here before the National Convention to defend the interests of all.)

In August 1793 the French government, officially at war with Britain since January, issued a decree stating that foreigners not domiciled in France before 14 July 1789 were liable to be arrested; this was followed in September with a further decree which allowed for the sequestration of their property. Petitions such as this, presented by anxious 'résidans', show how acutely vulnerable foreign nationals became as the Terror gathered strength and turned increasingly on supposed enemies within. Many of those who had come to France to work or study, as well as those who came in the cause of 'universal liberty', found themselves caught up and then overtaken by the rapidly evolving politics of the early 1790s.[2]

As the above Address shows, three of the four nations of the British Isles (the ideal eradication of 'factitious' national boundaries notwithstanding) are clearly inscribed in the official language of Revolutionary France. To be English, Scottish, or Irish means something to the authorities in Paris, and with good reason. Scots and Irish had been evident as distinct cultural groupings in the city from medieval and early modern times, thanks in part to the presence of their internationally renowned Catholic colleges within the University of Paris, which formed around existing scholarly communities from both countries: the Collège des Écossais, formally established in 1333, and the two Irish colleges (the Collège des Lombards was constructed 1676–7, and the Collège des Irlandais between 1769 and 1776).[3] In 1762–3, indeed, during a period of university restructuring, the 'distinctness' of the Irish was put forward as a reason against amalgamation; that distinctness recurs in the rhetoric used by the colleges themselves when fighting for their survival during the nationalization of ecclesiastical property in 1790.[4]

The Welsh, as ever, are much harder to spot. The absence of separate educational institutions (Catholic Welsh scholars would have studied at the Collège des Anglais) obviously worked against public recognition; there were no Welsh radical groups such as the United Irishmen (and the more shadowy United Scotsmen) working with the French authorities to undermine the British state, and there were no official societies like the Cymmrodorion or the Gwyneddigion of the London Welsh to act as cultural nuclei and encourage the Welsh to define themselves as a separate group. Numbers

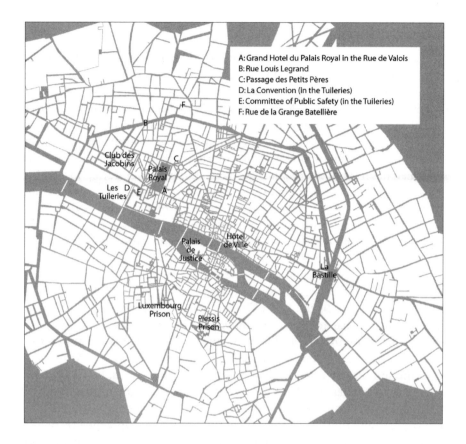

A: Grand Hotel du Palais Royal in the Rue de Valois
B: Rue Louis Legrand
C: Passage des Petits Pères
D: La Convention (in the Tuileries)
E: Committee of Public Safety (in the Tuileries)
F: Rue de la Grange Batellière

Figure 3. Map: Revolutionary Paris.

can never have been great, and so most traceable attributes of Welshness must have melted into the larger British and Irish expatriate community, making it hard to track their historical presence in the city. Nevertheless a few notable individuals did, for a variety of reasons, find themselves in Paris between 1789 and 1798. Their stories offer a series of vivid snap-shots of the course of the Revolution itself, and reveal some of the historical and social factors that caused Welsh men and women to engage directly with events in France. Their presence in Paris invokes larger questions, too, of how identities – personal, political and national – are formed and adapted during a period of breathtakingly rapid change.[5]

1789: 'witness to the glorious scene'

One of the key players in the Revolution debate was the Dissenting
minister Richard Price, from Llangeinor near Bridgend in Glamorgan. His
Discourse on the Love of Our Country of 1789, discussed elsewhere in this
volume, provoked Burke's *Reflections on the Revolution in France* and effectively
began the pamphlet wars which would soon involve Price's friends and
protégés, among them Thomas Paine and Mary Wollstonecraft. Price, by
then famous for his support for the American cause, became a close and
informed observer of the political developments in France during the 1780s.
Among the contacts sending him news and pamphlets was Thomas Jefferson,
then America's representative in Paris; he also corresponded with figures
who would play key roles in the Revolution itself, such as the Comte de
Mirabeau and the Duc de la Rochefoucauld.[6] But in the summer of 1789
Price had a new informant, his own nephew, George Cadogan Morgan.

Morgan, born in Bridgend in 1754, attended Cowbridge Grammar School
and, briefly, Jesus College, before studying mathematics and science at the
Hoxton Academy. In the late 1770s he preached in Norwich and Great
Yarmouth and married into an influential Dissenting family of shipping
merchants before moving to Hackney, where he worked as an assistant to
Richard Price, and lectured in science at the New College.

In the summer of 1789, in the company of three friends, he set off on a
tour that, following a beaten tourist route, would take them straight down
through France, from Calais via Paris to Marseilles, along the coast to Nice,
up to Turin and then on to Geneva and the Alps. Morgan kept a record of
his impressions in a series of letters, written as a journal, to his wife, and in
two lengthy letters to Price. The letters to his wife have survived and have
recently been edited and published;[7] the two crucial letters to Richard Price,
written from Paris at the height of the uprising, are now lost. Nor, it seems,
are there any surviving copies of the *London Gazetteer* in which they were
published in August and September that year: only a couple of extracts
survive, quoted by other people in the ensuing debate. But the letters home,
and the letters and journals of two of his travelling companions, Edward
Rigby and Samuel Boddington, allow us to follow him closely during those
extraordinary days around 14 July 1789.

They reached Paris on the evening of the 7th. By the time they left, not
without some difficulty, on the 19th, they had attended a meeting of the
National Assembly at Versailles, been at the theatre the night Necker was
dismissed and witnessed the subsequent explosion of angry crowds onto the
streets; they had seen the formal dismantling of the Bastille and watched the
king enter the city 'without his guards' and, somewhat awkwardly, accept

the cockade of the new order. By a stroke of fortune, they were based at the expensive but convenient Grand Hotel du Palais Royal: 'However, we have not grudged the money as our situation at the awful moment of revolt enabled us to see what others who lodged in a different part of the town heard from us with astonishment.' The most dramatic letter, written from the hotel at four o'clock in the morning of 13 July, vividly captures the 'boiling and unsettled state of commotion' in the narrow streets below:

> Our company partook of the hurry and terrors of the crowd – and once more we lodged ourselves safely in our citadel. It was now night and we could only hear the steps and shouts of those who pass'd to and fro. The sky was red with the several fires. We could hear the reports of the guns from a variety of quarters and we witness'd the cries of mothers and wives who stuck to their husbands and their sons pressing them not to unite with the general rage. About 10 o'clock the uniformity of the noise was interrupted by the violence of a party who assail'd the doors of a gunsmith living in a room just under ours. The crash of the stones and stakes which the populace drove against the doors set our whole hotel into an uproar.[8]

Fortunately, finding no guns in the shop below, the crowd 'retired in great tranquility' and left the agitated guests in peace.

Morgan is an excellent reporter: vivid, persuasive, and, given the chaos he is describing, surprisingly calm-headed. He has a particularly endearing knack, too, of putting his own personal inconvenience in a greater, historical, perspective. At various stages on their journey the group find themselves in threatening situations: on one of many attempts to leave the city they are turned back – 'amidst taunts, hissings, abuse and insults to our own lodging where they searched every rag of our baggage and treated us in every respect as if we had been spies';[9] outside Joigny they are 'fairly stop'd by the inquisitive multitude', and just beyond Dijon their traces are cut, leaving 'our carriage immoveable & altogether at the mercy of the crowd'.[10] Each time, their own enthusiasm for the progress of 'Liberty' carries them through these difficult moments. The admiration, at this point, is often reciprocal: to be British in France in 1789 is, after all, to embody an ideal of liberty already attained through the Glorious Revolution of 1688. Edward Rigby noted in a scrawled journal entry for the night of 13 July: 'as we were always known to be English every one who spoke to us considered us their Friends & said they were going to be as free as we are in England'.[11]

Morgan, acutely aware that he has been privileged to see these events at first hand, wrote on finally leaving Paris: 'the King's entrance without his guards into Paris, the demolition of the Bastile, and the restoration of Peace and Liberty to the noble Parisians amply repaid our loss of time and the fatigue of our spirits'.[12] Not all witnesses to what Richard Price called the 'glorious scene' were quite as moved. A fellow-Welshman, Frederick Jones, following almost exactly the same route two months later was less impressed (tourist 'relics' notwithstanding) by the Revolution's greatest signifier:

> On the morning after our arrival in Paris we could not avoid going to see the ruins of that bugbear of France, the Bastile . . . We walked upon them, and I have also brought away a bit of wood and another of stone as relics . . . However, upon the whole . . . it certainly makes no further impressions, as a fabric, upon a person who actually sees it, than what might be conceived at the sight of any other prison.[13]

Because of the loss of the letters to Richard Price, George Cadogan Morgan's contribution to the British perception of events in France in the summer of 1789 has been obscured from the historical record; as argued elsewhere in this volume, it has implications for assessing Price's own universalist position, often tendentiously viewed through a post-Burkean lens. In the years that followed his visit, Morgan kept a close eye on events in the capital, and, if anything, became more enthusiastic for the principles of liberty and equality promised in the thrilling first year of the Revolution. He also became a more explicitly convinced republican, and in August 1792, at a moment when the future of the French monarchy hung in the balance, he published, anonymously, and possibly only for circulation in France, *An Address to the Jacobine and Other Patriotic Societies of the French Urging the Establishment of a Republican Form of Government*. Written at a pivotal moment, with the king effectively a prisoner, and Austria and Prussia threatening 'exemplary and memorable revenge on the nation [of France] if the royal family are harmed', it suggests in no uncertain terms that the French should seize this opportunity to rid themselves of kings and courts, 'the most destroying pestilence that ever desolated the universe':

> With all these evidences of his voracious appetites before your eyes, will you yet keep the Monster? The Eggs of the devouring brood are in your hands – will you expect to hatch from them anything that is not poisonous and fatal?[14]

Read with hindsight the piece seems brutal, even bloodthirsty, but Morgan does not argue for the execution of the king ('An Example of Severity would answer to no purpose'). His solution, a kind of monarchical theme park, is more elegant, and much wittier: 'In some distant, but safe enclosure, he should sport and fatten amongst his stags. – He should indulge all his natural propensities and display to your infant Republic the full brutality of his Species.'[15] The text, fascinatingly, sits on a faultline. As has recently been emphasized, British responses to events in Paris crystallized around the violence of the August Days, with many initial enthusiasts retreating from their commitment to revolution in the wake of the attack on the Tuileries and the imprisonment of the king.[16] Morgan's decision to publish the *Address* in the weeks after these events underlines his continued support for the revolutionary government in France.

1792: 'the energy of those principles that shake Europe to the centre'

1792 was a year of very different possible futures for Europe. Some months earlier, one of George Cadogan Morgan's compatriots also believed that the French stood at a cross-roads. Morgan John Rhys (1760–1804), a Baptist minister from Llanbradach near Caerphilly, had (after two failed attempts to emigrate to America) spent the years 1787–91 preaching in Pontypool and in north Wales.[17] He had also become involved with the London Bible Mission, which aimed to promote the Protestant message abroad.

In August 1791 Rhys was advised to spend some time in Devon for reasons of health, and boarded a ship bound for Exeter. After several days waiting in harbour for the right tide, the wind changed – providentially, as Rhys interpreted it – and he decided to head instead for Calais. His mission then became, as Hywel Davies has put it, 'a Protestant crusade to preach the Gospel *and* to disseminate civil and religious liberty amongst the French papists'.[18] Part of his remit was to set up a French Bible Society, and ensure a supply of books. Two lengthy and reflective autobiographical letters written to his fellow-Baptist John Rippon in November 1791 and February 1792 reveal a great deal about the course of Rhys's life as he saw it, and (though frustratingly short on hard facts) offer some hints as to his experiences across the Channel.[19] He spoke no French, but, nothing daunted, began to preach in Calais, Dunkirk and Boulogne to an assortment of expatriates who were, it seems, badly in need of guidance: 'the English there I found were numerous but they had gone to sleep on beds of ivory & wallowed in the mire of immorality'.[20] By this time organized religion in France was in a state of vacuum: Church property had been nationalized since November 1789, and so Rhys was able to rent a former Catholic church to preach his gospel. This can only have confirmed his sense – shared by many Dissenters, Joseph Priestley prominent among them – that the Revolution itself revealed an unfolding of the divine plan: 'From what the Lord has already done in France

we have every reason to believe we will carry on his work.'[21] Still, things
did not all go smoothly: 'Now I firmly believe', he wrote to Rippon, 'what
you said once, that a preacher in France has need of ten times as much grace
as one in England. Here if he has a notion of being useful he must keep
company with all sorts and make himself everything to see if he can win
some. – He has all the temptations to fight with that the Devil on this earth
can produce.'[22]

Rhys had some thoughts of going to Brittany, but ended up in Paris.
By February 1792 he was lodging with a 'monsieur Gamble' at the corner
of the Boulevard and the Rue Louis le Grand – soon to be renamed, less
monarchically, the Rue des Piques (Street of Pikes). His host was James
Gamble, a printer and engraver who shared a premises with the paper manu-
facturers Arthur and Robert,[23] and who would, some months later, sign an
Address presented to the Assembly on 14 August warmly congratulating the
French on the overthrow of the monarchy four days earlier.[24] Gamble may
have been part-owner of Whites Hotel, Passage des Petits Pères, and would
also sign the notorious Address drawn up there by members of the British
and Irish community during a dinner in November 1792.[25] This Address
congratulates the French government on their commitment to the ideals of
liberty and universal rights, and looks forward to the formation of 'a close
union between the French republic and the English, Scotch and Irish nations,
a union which cannot fail to ensure entire Europe the enjoyment of the
rights of man'.[26] Among the other signatories were the notable radical figures
John Oswald, Lord Edward Fitzgerald, John Hurford Stone and John Frost;
a large number of those present were Irish. It seems likely that Thomas Paine
(who had arrived in Paris in mid-September) and Helen Maria Williams
were also present, but did not sign.[27] Rhys's connection with James Gamble
raises the possibility that he too was at least peripherally involved with this
network of radical expatriates, but the second letter to Rippon, full of
alarming hints at catastrophes and failures, financial and moral, frustratingly
tells us almost nothing about the circles he moved in during his stay in Paris.
We do not know how many of the subsequent signatories to the Whites
Hotel Address could be counted among the 'English [who are] are numerous
enough here to establish two churches – a few goes to the Ambassadors
Chappel and the greatest part nowhere'.[28] We do not know if Rhys attended
the debates in the Assembly, or the Jacobin club, which at this time dealt
frequently with the possibilities and practicalities of a closer relationship with
the radical societies of Britain.[29] Nor, most crucially of all, do we know how
long he stayed in Paris during the critical year of 1792.

The renaming of the street on which he lodged captures as well as anything
the extraordinary flux and contingency of life in Paris at this period. Towards

the end of his letter, written in a snow-bound city sporadically erupting into food riots, he set out four of the possible futures facing the French nation in February 1792:

> You'll naturally enquire something about the signs of the times – It is best perhaps to be silent – everything is quiet at present but disturbances are expected. In regard to Politicks which is the general topick of conversation the nation is divided into four classes – some for preserving the present constitution as it is – others for having 2 chambers as in England – others for the old monarchical government and the 4th for reform of the constitution & making it consistent with itself as they say by taking away all vetos & even Kings out of the way – if the first will not stand it is very probable the last will make a bold attempt, if they happen to meet with an Oliver to lead them.[30]

History in the making is so very tangible here it seems almost to torment a man who believes fervently that events are unrolling in line with the will of God: 'But what', he declares piously, 'need we trouble ourselves about these things, it is the Lord omnipotent that reigneth & his will shall stand'. To which, as if he cannot help himself, he immediately adds: 'but when each work is going forward we cannot be altogether idle spectators. The danger is gazing too much so as to forget the one thing needful.'[31]

Though the period in France seems to have ended in some disappointment, Rhys retained his zeal. On returning to Wales he set about editing, writing for and publishing a ground-breaking radical Welsh-language periodical, *Cylch-grawn Cynmraeg*, the first instalment of which appeared in February 1793. Through it, he voiced his own thoughts on class privilege and oppressive taxes, war, the slave trade, the missionary movement, disestablishment, education and parliamentary reform. But he also provided a forum for debate on these matters in the Welsh language, and thus laid the true beginnings of what, in the following century, would become a crucial aspect of the Welsh public sphere.[32] Financial difficulties and the increasing tension of the political climate meant the journal ran to only five issues: by October 1794 Rhys had emigrated (or, according to some accounts, fled) to America, where he travelled widely, preaching, particularly in the South, against slavery and in favour of religious liberty. In 1797 he contributed a series of *Letters on Slavery* to the periodical *American Universal Magazine*, set up by another strongly abolitionist, milenarian and recently-arrived British radical, Richard 'Citizen' Lee.[33] In 1798 Rhys bought a large swathe of land in the Alleghany mountains and christened it Cambria: hundreds of Welsh emigrants were encouraged to join him in founding and developing the town of Beulah. He married, had five children, and died aged only 44 in 1804:

'Morgan John Rhys', wrote Gwyn A. Williams, 'burns in the mind like a sudden flame, all warmth and brilliance and brevity.'[34]

Rhys's letters, and fascinating journal, from the period of his travels in the South refer occasionally to his time in France, and as Gwyn A. Williams notes, 'the release of political inhibitions is tangible.'[35] The Paris of early 1792 and its galvanizing effect on his subsequent actions is recalled most memorably in Charleston, a place to which he had booked his passage a full decade earlier, but had twice been prevented from reaching:

> Had Providence then permitted me to cross the ocean, I should not have borne my testimony against many bad laws and iniquitous practises in my native country, nor perhaps have drank so deep of the cup of manumission. Having stood on the ruins of the Bastile in Paris, and still feeling the energy of those principles which shake Europe to the centre, I am now constrained to preach Liberty to captives, and proclaim the acceptable year of the Lord.[36]

1793–6: 'the Principles of a Nation'

The latter end of 1792 saw the arrival in Paris of two men whose involvement in French politics could, perhaps, have produced a different sequence of events to those we now know as history.[37] The historian and educationalist David Williams (1738–1816), was initially taught (like Morgan John Rhys) by another David Williams (1709–84), an Independent minister who kept a school at Cwm, near Watford, just south of Caerphilly. Following a promise made to his dying father, he subsequently attended the Dissenting academy at Carmarthen and served congregations in Frome and Highgate, London. He did not last many years as a formal preacher of Dissent, however, but became a deist, and, with a group of friends who included Benjamin Franklin, drew up a *Liturgy on the Universal Principles of Religion and Morality* (1776), welcomed by Voltaire (some of whose works he translated) and Rousseau.[38] By the 1780s Williams was running a school in Chelsea, and increasingly occupied with the theory and practice of education for both children and adults. Between 1785 and 1787 he delivered a well-attended series of lectures on political philosophy from Great Russell Square, and it is quite likely that James Tilly Matthews came into his orbit then: 'he is my tutor', said Matthews later of Williams, 'and as all mankind know his staunch republican principles, it cannot be wondered that I should possess the same principles'.[39] Almost the only other certain fact about the early life of James Tilly Matthews is that he was a wholesale tea merchant, trading from Leadenhall Street where the East India Company had its offices, and living in a smartish town house in Camberwell Grove. The location of his Welsh forebears (discussed below) is not known.

David Williams became involved with some of the key players in the French Revolution at this period when he met the journalist Jacques-Pierre Brissot, who was trying at the time to set up an international journal in London.[40] When the venture failed, and Brissot returned to Paris, he continued to correspond with Williams, drawing heavily on his educational theories for his own work, with the result that Williams became far better known as a writer in France than at home.[41] By 1789 Brissot was among the leaders of the New France; he was a member of the National Assembly and among the founders of the Jacobin Club. In August 1792 Williams was included, with Thomas Paine and Joseph Priestley, amongst the number of honorary French citizens, and in November 1792 he was formally invited over to help a committee drafting a new constitution for the Republic. His letter to Roland accepting citizenship emphasizes the full gravity and potential of the political moment:

> All the Friends of that regulated humane and comprehensive justice, which is the ultimate object of political knowledge, have their eyes intensely fixed on the National Convention of France. The conspiracy of European Tyrants is defeated; the obstructions of hereditary royalty & Aristocracy are removed; & France is distinguished by the first opportunity, afforded to Philosophy, of applying the principles of reason & virtue to the construction of a political Constitution.[42]

When Williams travelled to Paris, James Tilly Matthews went too.

The timing of this visit turned out to be fateful; Brissot and another minister, Le Brun, were by now running foreign affairs in a manner that has been judged 'amateurish in the extreme'.[43] The new French republic's war against Austria and Prussia had resulted – against Brissot's own more moderate intentions – in the overthrow of the king, whose subsequent trial (which Williams attended) completely overshadowed the business of constitutional reform. Although he did manage to produce a written commentary on the constitution of 1791, his time in Paris was evidently frustrating: 'I had not been in Paris a week', he wrote in his memoirs, 'before I perceived I could be of no use. The Convention was dividing into factions, while the Commune of Paris was seizing its power and the whole country crumbling into anarchy.'[44] As Manon Roland, awaiting execution in 1793, would recall, the 'sage penseur, véritable ami des hommes' was highly disturbed at the manner in which Assembly proceedings were conducted: 'Comment peuvent discuter, me disait-il, des hommes qui ne savent point écouter?' (How, he asked, can men discuss if they will not listen?).[45]

Throughout December, as relations with Britain deteriorated rapidly, Brissot seems to have been simultaneously urging the Convention towards an inevitable war while consulting Williams on the possibilities of maintaining peace. By 24 January news of the king's execution reached London and all French ambassadors were expelled. On 1 February, the Convention in turn declared war on Britain. Yet that very same evening, at a dinner, Williams was asked to take a letter to Lord Grenville expressing France's extreme regret, and urging that the ports of Dover and Calais be kept open; as the historian David Williams remarks, this is an extraordinary document in the history of foreign diplomacy, openly expressing a desire to avoid hostilities on the very day that war was declared. Its postscript, in Le Brun's own hand, expresses the hope that 'le philanthrope, David Williams' will be able to persuade his countrymen to adopt 'des sentiments plus pacifiques et plus convenables a l'interêt des deux pays' (an inclination to peace more in the interests of both countries).[46] According to Williams himself, he was also asked to put another, unwritten, proposal before the British government: if they would support the Girondists (Brissot's party) in their internal power struggle against the Jacobins, and help them gain control of the Convention, France would make peace and might then follow a moderate 'British' model of parliamentary reform.[47]

Williams, who knew that his influence in Britain was nowhere as potent as his friends in France imagined, returned home, delivered his letter, and was frustrated but not surprised *not* to be granted an audience with Grenville; he never got an opportunity to pass on the Girondists' proposal. Two months into the war, however, the foreign minister Le Brun made another (and, to historians of both sides, baffling) overture of peace; and this time, the 'ambassador' was James Tilly Matthews.

Matthews had spent his time in Paris using Williams's name to get involved with French political society; when nothing came of the first peace initiative he headed back to France again, announced himself to Le Brun as Williams's representative (which he was not), and explained – apparently acting on his own – that Britain would be prepared to negotiate if certain demands were met. A thirteen-page document outlined these demands; the French government took this seriously enough to draft a reply, offer their own terms for peace, and send Matthews back with a sealed letter for Grenville. The British government, puzzled by the unorthodox channel of communication, and having already declared war, decided to ignore it. Matthews proceeded to make himself as much of a nuisance as possible, even publishing accounts of the content of the letters in the opposition press.[48]

Over the next few months Matthews continued to wage his rogue pacifist mission of diplomacy back and forth across the Channel, completely confusing both sides as to the true intentions of the other. Meanwhile, in France, the Girondist party fell, Brissot and his friends went to the guillotine, and, in August 1793, as the Committee of Public Safety under Robespierre began to legislate more harshly against foreign residents, Matthews was placed under arrest as a British spy. For some months he was restricted to his hotel lodgings in the Rue de la Grange Batellière and various interviews were conducted to try and ascertain his true motives; finally, when he could no longer afford to pay the rent, he was confined in Plessis prison, a converted college near the Sorbonne (see Fig. 3).[49] Throughout his detention he bombarded the French government with reams of pages of memoranda in minute, neat handwriting, complaining bitterly about his treatment, protesting his pacifist intentions, expanding on the great service he had done to France, his committed republican principles, and bemoaning his increasing ill health: 'Among the numerous occurrences which occupy your attention', he writes, with superb understatement, in November 1793, 'I fear you have quite forgot me.'[50]

These letters, preserved in the Archives des Affaires Étrangères, are interestingly reminiscent of certain other writers of the period; a similarity which may, perhaps, suggest something about Matthews's background and education. They recall in particular the voice of the radical Welsh stonemason Edward Williams (Iolo Morganwg) at its most paranoid: the same blend of righteous indignation and frustration, the same tendency to pile clause upon clause, to back-track half-way through a thought, and to bolster every statement with laborious justifications. The many drafts of the preface to Williams's collection of *Poems, Lyric and Pastoral* (1794), written under great physical and mental stress during his period in London, 1792–3, reveal a writer visibly struggling with language to create a plausible narrative of himself (and for himself) in the face of perceived hostility and betrayal.[51] Like Williams, Matthews claims the language of moral rectitude:

Citizens,
I think I may use an abridged style as I have only to utter the language of Truth. If it was possible that I could for a moment deviate from the . . . line of Conduct which has now for three years actuated my mind, I would long ago have turned imposter. I would in a thousand ways have flattered the committee, promised wonders; for as many ways are open to deceive the most rigid observer, but most assuredly, any other than the steps I have followed wd have been deception indeed. Even now Citizens it perhaps wd not be the most difficult of all things to play the Hypocrite. You will recollect that though I am under the surveillance of a gendarme, I can say what I please now & laugh at you when I have passed the Frontiers, but no Citizens, it is not in my Soul. As I speak little but think much, I am perhaps, more alive to harsh insinuations than many others; every

word of this nature is a wound, because it is returning evil for Good, but perhaps
you cannot satisfy yourselves of this truth, & certainly you have every reason to
be suspicious.[52]

What on earth, one wonders, was the Committee of Public Safety (itself no
stranger to paranoia) to make of that? Mike Jay has warned against reading
Matthews's madness – which would ruthlessly define him in later years –
backwards into the letters from this period, and it is true that the syntax,
though stressed, is not quite broken. But it is not quite true to claim, as Jay
does, that at this point the French authorities still took him entirely seriously.
Not long after Matthews's arrest in 1793, the Committee's official translator
(a United Irishman called Nicholas Madgett, a key figure among the signatories to the Whites Hotel Address) felt impelled to add his own comment
to his translation of Matthews's letter:[53]

> Conforme a l'original qui me paroit écrit par un homme qui a perdu la raison.
> J'ai traduit il y a quelques mois une lettre du meme auteur qui sans être aussi
> extravagante que celle ci, donnait de fortes indications de démence. Madgett.[54]

> (Conforms to the original which appears to have been written by a man who
> has lost his senses. Several months ago I translated a letter by the same writer
> which, although not as extreme as this one, showed clear signs of madness.
> Madgett.)

The letters continued, increasingly tortuous and disturbed. As others have
noted, one passage in particular is especially valuable for throwing some
light on Matthews's origins and his sense of identity. In it, he defends his
integrity in terms of his nationality:

> With respect to any suspicions against me as to the reality of my Patriotism that
> is equally unjust. First, if the Example of ones Ancestors is of any weight, or if
> the Principles of a Nation are any Proof; mine claim the preference to all others.
> I am Welch; tho English by being a Subject of Great Britain; from the time of
> Caesar to this Moment, we have preserved our Liberty and Laws, and History
> cannot furnish an Hundred instances in this period of a man having forsaken the
> Cause for w. you are now fighting. I say if obstinacy of Principle is of any weight,
> the Welch have the Preference over all mankind.[55]

Clearly the idea of a Welsh past mattered a great deal to Matthews. The
narrative of that past is presented as one of resistance to external military
power, and of the preservation of cultural integrity – 'our Liberty and Laws'.

The Welsh nation itself is 'principled', even obstinately so, and its values (including, of course, opposition to England) are the values of the new France: 'the Cause for which you are now fighting'. Inevitably, he does not stop there:

> But I may add something more; my Mothers family are French, of the name of Tilly, who were obliged to leave France at the Revocation of the Edict of Nantes. I bear this name, having been Christened James Tilly (and as Arms are [borne] with us I have always borne the Arms also which are French) – I do not use the name Tilly when writing generally, because in Wales 3 names is considered so much an Ostentation, & I respect my Fathers Whims; but in all Deeds, & w[h]ere property is in Question, I am obliged to use it. The Constitutional Assembly proclaimed the reestablishment in their rights of Citizens to all descendants of these refugees; being dissatisfied with the Government in England, I determined to embrace it, and it is this which made me interest myself first in the [affairs] of France.

Again, the tumble of clauses and ideas makes this difficult to interpret in places, but Matthews's paternal Welshness, coupled with his mother's French blood, becomes, in a sense, his pledge of total republican authenticity. Political convictions are no longer sufficient. This declaration of not-being-English twice-over is, one suspects, grimly significant: a measure of how far the Revolution itself has moved along the trajectory mapped by Michael Rapport from cosmopolitanism to an 'exclusive nationalism'.[56]

Many of the prisoners in Plessis were executed, but it seems that even French bureaucracy was no match for the relentless drip-drip of Matthews memoranda, and in February 1796 he was released on grounds of insanity and given a passport. He begged his way home. Although for the purposes of this chapter that is effectively the end of his story, it is only now that the events for which he is most famous begin. Matthews came to believe that the 'Air Loom Gang', a group of criminals with extraordinary powers, led by 'Bill the King' and the 'Glove Woman' were controlling his mind (and the minds of others, notably leading government ministers) from an underground base in Moorfields. The Air Loom was a kind of 'influencing machine', which channelled thought waves and, by inflicting terrible pain, caused its victims to lie. Armed with this explanation for the otherwise inexplicable conduct of government ministers who seemed hell-bent on war when peace was offered them, Matthews continued to plague the government, dramatically accusing Lord Liverpool of 'Treason' from the gallery of the House of Commons. The result, brutally, was his committal to Bethlem Lunatic Asylum. Despite the continual protestations of his

Figure 4. David Samwell, 1798. A 'physionotrace' portrait
taken in Paris by Gilles-Louis Chrétien.

extremely loyal family that in every respect but the belief in the Air Loom
Gang he was sane and harmless, Matthews, the would-be champion of
Liberty, would spend the rest of his life incarcerated. A book-length study
of his delusion, *Illustrations of Madness*, published by his doctor, John Haslam,
in 1810, is considered to be the first fully documented case of paranoid
schizophrenia.[57] That Matthews was mentally ill seems indisputable, and it
is not surprising that his version of events in Paris was easily dismissed, and
then forgotten: as Mike Jay has argued, Haslam used his authority to over-
write, and overrule his patient's still coherent, still fluent account of his
patently 'unbelievable' role in high-level international diplomacy.

1798: return to Versailles

In May 1798 the Welsh naval surgeon David Samwell (Dafydd Ddu Feddyg) was settling into his new apartment in Versailles, where he was tending the British prisoners of war.[58] In a cheerful letter to his friend the Liverpool businessman Matthew Gregson[59] he reveals that he has lost no time in getting to know the expatriate community in Paris:

> Where any poetical folks are to be found and I have the least acquaintance with them, they are sure to be first objects of my attention. The first House I entered at Paris was that of Helen Maria Williams – she shewed me every friendly attention, made me guest for 2 days & took every means to satisfy my curiosity of seeing the Town as much as it could be in so short a time – you may guess how interesting almost every spot of it was to me. I have a great deal to say, but must hold my tongue, lest my letter should be stopped on this or your side of the water –

One result of that time in 'Town' was a striking picture of Samwell made by the artist Gilles Chrétien, using a technique, perfected around 1786, known as the 'physionotrace', which permitted close-to-life portraits of sitters in profile (Fig. 4).[60] Helen Maria Williams, who had returned to Paris with John Hurford Stone after a period of exile in Switzerland, was living in comfortable lodgings and had resumed her artistic *salons*. Samwell, in airy but empty rooms, writes that he is at a loss for furniture (which his Liverpool friend could so easily have supplied!) and awaits the return social call with mock trepidation: 'I expect Miss Williams every day to pay me a visit and I am busy in framing poetical apologies for the trim she will find my apartments in!'

The conditions of the seven or eight hundred prisoners held at the camp, he notes, are not too bad (indeed, 'as I do not relish French cooking', he rather envies them their plain mess food); Versailles itself pleases him too:

> The palace and Gardens I shall not attempt to describe but only say that they are always open to the public of course to a Welshman, who like me chuses (by the by it is Hobson's choice) to wear the French national cockade instead of his own, the Leek – perhaps you will say for once that I am a prudent man in so doing, no such thing. Every body in France is obliged to put it in his hat, or be obliged by the sentries &c. in short not a single person is to be seen without it. Carrying that mark about me, I pass in the crowd without any one knowing or car[ry]ing what country I am of, and find myself, as I expected, as much at ease & freedom here as in England.

In the summer of 1789 George Cadogan Morgan had also swiftly adopted the 'French national cockade' as a passport to 'ease and freedom'. Back then, though, it seemed a gesture of solidarity with the people of France, who themselves saw 'their' revolution as cutting across national divides – 'seeming to rejoice more', in the words of Edward Fitzgerald, 'on account of its effect on Europe in general than for their own individual glory. *Ah! Nous sommes tous frères.*'[61] Restrictions on foreigners did ease after the Terror, but a culture of surveillance and suspicion persisted: wearing the cockade is 'Hobson's choice', and its purpose is to disguise foreignness, to allow even the Welshest of Welshmen (which Samwell undoubtedly was) to pass for a citizen, not of the world, but of France. And Versailles, where Morgan had watched the newly fledged Assembly debate the first draft of the Declaration of the Rights of Man, is now a camp for the British prisoners of a war that will not end anytime soon.

The foreboding of the Address cited at the beginning of this essay seems amply fulfilled: 'a revolution aiming to destroy the factitious boundaries between nations', a revolution which promised to grant 'fraternity to all human beings' has narrowed into the most constrictive parameters of nationality, and Richard Price's open-hearted 'love of our country' has turned to a bitter *amour de patrie* curdled by fear and suspicion. But Samwell's letter offers something else besides. He is annoyed, he admits, to be missing 'the grand meeting of Welsh Bards', held that year (mainly at Samwell's instigation) at Caerwys in Flintshire: 'I long to have an account of it, which I expect soon from the Welsh Shakespeare[62] in his native language.' Cultural revivals, and particularly the cultural revivals of what Gwyn A. Williams calls the 'non-historic' peoples ('small, of no account, the debris of a past', lacking 'even the vestiges of a state and . . . doomed to disappear'), also surged forward on the criss-crossing waves of responses to the events in France.[63] Some of these too, in the century that followed, would harden into nationalisms of the more belligerent kind, but the Welsh bards of the 1790s were not, by and large, the type to oblige the wearing of the Leek by force.

Notes

[1] Archives des Affaires Étrangères (La Courneuve, Paris), 588, item 1.

[2] Michael Rapport, *Nationality and Citizenship in Revolutionary France: The Treatment of Foreigners 1789–1799* (Oxford, 2000). See also Jennifer Huer, 'Enemies of the Nation? Nobles, Foreigners and National Citizenship in the French Revolution', in Len Scales and Oliver Zimmer (eds.), *Power and the Nation in European History* (Cambridge, 2005), pp. 275–94.

3   See Michael Rapport, 'A Community Apart? The Closure of the Scots College in Paris During the French Revolution 1789–1794', *The Innes Review*, 53 (2002), 81–4; Liam Chambers, 'Revolutionary and Refractory? The Irish Colleges in Paris and the French Revolution', *Journal of Irish Scottish Studies*, 2, no. 1 (2009), 29–50.

4   Liam Chambers notes that the principal deliberately distanced the Irish college from its Scots and English counterparts to ensure its survival, stressing 'a shared pro-revolutionary Franco-Irish anti-Britishness'. 'Revolutionary and Refractory?', 37.

5   The contingency of political identity during the revolutionary decade is nicely evoked by Mark Philp, 'The Fragmentary Ideology of Reform', in *idem* (ed.), *The French Revolution and British Popular Politics* (Cambridge, 1991), pp. 50–77.

6   See Paul Frame and Geoffrey W. Powell, '"Our first concern as lovers of our country must be to enlighten it": Richard Price's Response to the French Revolution', in this volume; for a recent re-evaluation of Price's French contacts, see Rémy Duthille, 'Thirteen Uncollected Letters of Richard Price', *Enlightenment and Dissent*, 27 (2011), 83–142.

7   Mary-Ann Constantine and Paul Frame (eds.), *Travels in Revolutionary France & A Journey Across America by George Cadogan Morgan and Richard Price Morgan* (Cardiff, 2012).

8   Ibid., p. 49.

9   Ibid., p. 52.

10 Ibid., pp. 55, 58.

11 Oxford, Bodleian Library, Special Collections, Dep. e. 43, 'Rigby Journal', p. 28^{v}.

12 Constantine and Frame (eds.), *Travels*, p. 53.

13 Jones (brother of the better-known artist, Thomas Jones of Pencerrig) spent a few days in Paris in September 1789 and wrote a letter home which goes into pungent detail about the collection of night soil outside his hotel window in Versailles. He seems to have followed the beaten tourist route, admiring chateaux and palaces, and making only minimal reference to the 'unsettled state of national affairs'. Frederick Jones, *Copies of letters merely intended for, and by the desire of, intimate friends* (n.p., 1795), p. 11 (from facsimile copy held at NLW). I'm grateful to Mr Charles Parry for bringing this rare text to my attention. For souvenir-hunters and the 'afterlife' of the Bastille, see Simon Schama, *Citizens: A Chronicle of the French Revolution* (1989; paperback edn., London, 2004), pp. 344–58.

14 Constantine and Frame (eds.), *Travels*, p. 100.

15 Ibid., p. 116.

16 Attitudes to the August Days are explored by Rachel Rogers, 'Vectors of Revolution: The British Radical Community in Early Republican Paris 1792–1794' (unpublished University of Toulouse PhD thesis), pp. 349–59.

17 For Rhys, see Gwyn A. Williams, *The Search for Beulah Land: The Welsh and the Atlantic Revolution* (London, 1980).

18 Hywel M. Davies, '"Transatlantic Brethren": A study of English, Welsh and American Baptists with particular reference to Morgan John Rhys (1760–1804) and his friends' (unpublished University of Wales PhD thesis, 1984), pp. 366–7.

[19]   BM Add. 25388, pp. 399–404. I am grateful to Hywel Davies for passing on copies of this manuscript.

[20]   Ibid., p. 402.

[21]   Ibid., p. 403.

[22]   Ibid., p. 404.

[23]   See Rogers, 'Vectors of Revolution', and J. G. Alger, 'The British Colony in Paris 1792–93', *English Historical Review*, XIII, no. 52 (1898), 672–94. For details on Gamble, see 682–3.

[24]   David Erdman, *Commerce des Lumières John Oswald and the British in Paris 1790–1793* (Columbia, 1986), pp. 163–4. The Address was drawn up by James Watt, son of the inventor.

[25]   For a lively account of expatriate activity (and the extraordinary amount of cross-Channel intellectual traffic), see ibid. Rogers, 'Vectors of Revolution', adds considerable further insight.

[26]   Alger, 'The British Colony in Paris', 673.

[27]   Williams is thought to have been the 'English lady' who composed 'an English song to the tune of the Marseillaise' noted in the list of toasts. Erdman, *Commerce des Lumières*, p. 230.

[28]   BM Add 25388, p. 404.

[29]   See Erdman, *Commerce des Lumières*.

[30]   Ibid.

[31]   Hywel Davies reads this comment as an expression of Rhys's moderate Calvinism: 'God employed rational human agents to realize His Will. Involvement in "politics" was thus, as far as Rhys was concerned, an obligation to God on the part of the conscientious Christian.' Davies, '"Transatlantic Brethren"', pp. 370–1.

[32]   See Marion Löffler, *Welsh Responses to the French Revolution: Press and Public Discourse 1789–1802* (Cardiff, 2012); extracts from the journal are given on pp. 179–224.

[33]   Jon Mee has recently suggested that both Lee and Rhys were disappointed by the ambivalence of Philadelphian radicals towards abolitionism. I'm grateful to Jon Mee for a copy of his unpublished paper '"Written on the Atlantic Ocean": 'Citizen' Lee and the Dispersal of Radical London'.

[34]   Williams, *In Search of Beulah Land*, p. 53.

[35]   Ibid., p. 76.

[36]   See John T. Griffith, *Rev. Morgan John Rhys: The Welsh Baptist Hero of Civil and Religious Liberty of the Eighteenth Century* (2nd edn., Carmarthen, 1910), p. 162. This edition (unlike the 1899 one) includes extracts from the journal as well as the more formal letters, but much is missing. A complete version based on the original manuscripts is currently in progress as part of the 'Wales and the French Revolution' series.

[37]   For biographical information on David Williams, see above, p. 8 n. 3. The narrative which follows is much indebted to the excellent article by (yet another) David Williams, 'The Missions of David Williams and James Tilly Matthews to England (1793)', *English Historical Review*, LIII, no. 212 (1938), 651–68, with additional material from the Archives des Affaires Étrangères.

[38] David Williams, *Incidents in my own Life which have been thought of some importance'*, ed. Peter France (Brighton, 1980), p. 4. For Williams and Rousseau, see Heather Williams, 'Rousseau and Wales', in this volume.

[39] Cited by Williams, 'The Missions', 661–2. For Matthews see Roy Porter, 'Introduction', in John Haslam, *Illustrations of Madness* (London, 1988), and the highly readable biography by Mike Jay, *The Air Loom Gang: The Strange and True Story of James Tilly Matthews and his Visionary Madness* (New York, 2004).

[40] See J. P. Brissot, *Mémoires (1754–1793)*, ed. C. Perroud (2 vols., Paris, 1910), I, pp. 367–8, and Eloise Ellery, *Brissot de Warville: A Study in the History of the French Revolution* (Boston, 1915). Responding to an earlier article by Robert Darnton, Frederick A. De Luna puts up a robust defence of Brissot's reputation in 'The Dean Street Style of Revolution: J-P. Brissot, jeune philosophe', *French Historical Studies*, 17, no. 1 (1991), 159–90.

[41] Williams confidently assesses his own influence thus: '*Letters on Political Liberty* – This work was translated into French & much made use of by some of the Authors of the French Revolution – . . . The Principles of Constitution and Liberty were further developped – in *Lectures on Political Principles* & in *Lessons to a Young Prince*. They were partly reduced to practice in the French Constitution – but they do not appear to be yet fully understood.' NLW 10336E, p. 44.

[42] Cardiff, David Williams Collection, Letters, MS 5.36: item 12. For an analysis of Williams's *Observations sur la dernière constitution de la France* (1793) in the context of other British writings on the French constitution at this time, see Rogers, 'Vectors of Revolution', pp. 278–93.

[43] Williams, 'The Missions', 655.

[44] Williams, *Incidents in my own Life*, p. 27.

[45] See S-A Berville and J-F Barrière (eds.), *Mémoires de Madame Roland* (2 vols., Paris, 1820), II, pp. 10–11. Roland thought Williams would have been a much wiser choice than Thomas Paine for the Convention. Brissot, in his memoirs, was equally flattering, judging him 'de tous les hommes de lettres anglais celui qui me paraît avoir une philosophie plus universelle, plus dégagée de tous préjugés nationaux' (of all English men of letters the one who seems to me to have the most universal philosophy, the most free from national prejudice), ibid., p. 367.

[46] Williams, 'The Missions', 659–60.

[47] Williams, *Incidents in my own Life*, p. 31.

[48] 'Letters from M. Le Brun', *The Times*, 22 May 1793. Accessed from *The Times* Digital Archive at *http://mlr.com/DigitalCollections/products/Times*.

[49] A (suspiciously literary) account of conditions can be found in C. A. Daubin, *Les Prisons de Paris sous la Révolution d'après les relations contemporains* (Paris, 1887).

[50] Archives des Affaires Étrangères, 588, item 35, p. 63 (18 Brumaire An II = 8 November 1793).

[51] For the autobiographical drafts, see Mary-Ann Constantine, *The Truth Against the World: Iolo Morganwg and Romantic Forgery* (Cardiff, 2007), pp. 50–3. It is almost tempting to posit a typical 'persecution style' for the 1790s: one might further compare, for example, the attitude and language of Sampson Perry, the radical editor of the proscribed journal *Argus* (and another member of the Whites Hotel

group), who, like Matthews, spent many unpleasant months in French prisons during the Terror, and who repeatedly defined himself as the victim of persecution on both sides of the Channel. His case was discussed by Rachel Rogers, "'I declare myself beginning the world again": The Tenacious Defiance of Sampson Perry, "late editor of the Argus", in 1790s Paris and London', unpublished paper, British Association for Romantic Studies conference, Glasgow, 2011. I am grateful to the author for a copy of her paper.

52   Archives des Affaires Étrangères, 588, item 158, pp. 370–5 (30 Floréal An III = 19 May 1795).

53   See Alger, 'The British Colony in Paris', 684. Nicholas Madgett (born in Kinsale in 1740) was educated in Paris and subsequently worked for the French Foreign Office; he was much involved in negotiations prior to the expeditions to Ireland. Somewhat confusingly, Madgett's cousin, also called Nicholas Madgett (born in Tralee in 1758), worked as a spy for the British government. See Richard Hayes, *Biographical Dictionary of Irishmen in France* (Dublin, 1949), pp. 194–6, and *idem*, *Ireland and Irishmen in the French Revolution* (London, 1932), pp. 105–6; the careers of both men are discussed further in Liam Swords, *The Green Cockade: The Irish in the French Revolution 1789–1815* (Glendale, 1989).

54   Archives des Affaires Étrangères, 588, item 46, p. 84 (18th Brumaire An II = 8 November 1793).

55   Ibid., item 158, pp. 370–5 (30 Floréal An III = 19 May 1795). Extract at pp. 371–2. The letter is hard to read in places but the sense is made clearer by the accompanying French translation.

56   Rapport, *Nationality and Citizenship*, p. 206; against this broad trajectory Rapport is careful to show that the xenophobic rhetoric of government from 1793 was not always matched in practice, and that some foreigners did manage to live and work in French society ('useful' artisans in particular were exempted from many of the draconian decrees). Being on the wrong side in the factional power struggles of 1792–3 was (for example in the case of Thomas Paine or Helen Maria Williams) as much a contributory factor in their imprisonment as nationality.

57   Roy Porter's introduction to the 1988 edition of this work includes two more extraordinary letters written by Matthews after his return to England in 1796, and a brilliant exposition of the nature and circumstances of Matthews's paranoia and of Haslam's attitude to his patient. Porter, 'Introduction', in Haslam, *Illustrations of Madness*.

58   London Record Office, 920, Samwell Correspondence, Gregson Papers, GRE 2/17, letter no. 54. I am very grateful to Martin Fitzpatrick for a copy of this letter. Samwell, who sailed with Captain Cook on his last voyage, and wrote an eye-witness account of his death, was a lively member of several London-Welsh societies. See William Ll. Davies, 'David Samwell (1751–1798): Surgeon of the "Discovery", London-Welshman and Poet', *THSC* (1926–7), 68–133; Martin Fitzpatrick, 'The 'Cultivated Understanding' and Chaotic Genius of David Samwell', in Geraint H. Jenkins (ed.), *A Rattleskull Genius: The Many Faces of Iolo Morganwg* (Cardiff, 2005). It was in Versailles on 8 April 1798 that Samwell inscribed in his copy of the Welsh Book of Common Prayer the last words of Louis XVI: ibid., pp. 389–90.

59   Matthew Gregson (1749–1824), a prominent public figure in Liverpool, was involved in the Liverpool Library, the Royal Institution, and the Botanic Gardens; he became a Fellow of the Society of Antiquaries.

60   The Samwell portrait is held at NLW; for the technique and its popularity in Paris during the revolutionary decade, see Anthony Halliday, *Facing the Public: Portraiture in the Aftermath of the French Revolution* (Manchester, 1999), pp. 43–7.

61   Cited in Hayes, *Ireland and Irishmen*, p. 104.

62   Thomas Edwards (Twm o'r Nant; 1739–1810) was one of Samwell's favoured poets.

63   Gwyn A. Williams, 'Romanticism in Wales', in Roy Porter and Mikuláš Teich (eds.), *Romanticism in National Context* (Cambridge, 1988), pp. 9–36, at pp. 16–17. See also Cathryn Charnell-White, 'Networking the Nation: The Bardic and Correspondence Networks of Wales and London in the 1790s', in this volume.

Figure 5. 'Marche des Marseillois', published in London in 1792.

The 'Marseillaise' in Wales

Marion Löffler

The 1942 film *Casablanca*, which itself has attained near-mythical status, features a scene that confirms the symbolic power of song at its 'full expressive potential: the moment of performance'.[1] When a group of German officers in Rick's Café Américain intones 'Die Wacht am Rhein' (The Watch on the Rhine), Czech resistance leader Victor Laszlo strikes up a song whose original title was 'Chant de Guerre pour l'Armée du Rhin' (War Song for the Rhine Army). The owner of the café, Rick Stein, authorizes his band to join in and the audience rises to drown out the German officers, singing what they and we know as the 'Marseillaise'. 'Die Wacht am Rhein' had been composed in direct response to 'La Marseillaise' a hundred years earlier; both had sought to arouse patriotic feelings on opposite banks of the contested river Rhine and been used as national hymns, their titles and lyrics resonant of their original, military purpose.[2] Written by Swabian Max Schneckenburger in 1840 and put to music by the Swiss organist J. Mendel, the German song had implored all who spoke German to unite in guarding father Rhine against the common French enemy.[3] Like so many symbols of attempted German unity, it had later become associated with militarism and Nazism, a symbol of German expansionism whose performance might evoke a strong negative reaction. In *Casablanca*, this reaction took the form of performing 'La Marseillaise', whose purpose and early history had been similarly patriotic. It had been written and composed by Joseph Rouget de Lisle in response to a request by the mayor of Strasbourg, Philippe de Dietrich, as the French Republic declared war against the king of Bohemia and Hungary. The resulting 'Chant de Guerre pour l'Armée du Rhin' was first performed publicly by the mayor himself on 26 April 1792. From Alsace, the song quickly made its way to the south of France, where the *fédérés* each received a copy on leaving Marseilles and entered Paris singing it. Soon it was intoned by patriotic crowds in theatres all over the Republic, it accompanied their revolutionary activities and fired the military campaigns of the various republican armies.[4] It was the battle-song of a nation at war.

Outside France, however, the bloody patriotism of 'La Marseillaise' was superseded by its revolutionary angle, as it became symbolic of the French Republic and therefore of liberty itself as well as the values of a new world. Through adoption by liberal and revolutionary movements (together with the tricolour and the central motto of 'Liberty, Equality, Fraternity') it came to be one of the enduring symbols of the events which rang in the age of modern politics.[5] Adopting the 'Marseillaise', however, was not a simple act of performance or of literal translation. In this period of complex cultural exchange it involved its reshaping to fit both the cultural landscape and the topical circumstances within which the radicals of various European countries operated; the score became a vessel to fill with very different emotions and political messages. This chapter sketches the initial transformation of the 'Marseillaise' beyond the borders of France, focusing on its remodelling as 'Cân Rhyddid' (Song of Liberty) and on its expedition into west Wales, where it became part of the manuscript and traditional culture of a country which was only just on the cusp of modernization; an example of the domestication and dissemination of revolutionary ideas in a deeply rural society.[6]

From France with love: across borders and oceans

'La Marseillaise' advanced swiftly beyond the borders of France. Less than eight months after it had been written, the German Jacobin Johann Friedrich Franz Lehne published a 'Lied freier Landsleute nach der Melodie des Marsches der Marseiller' (Song of free Compatriots on the Tune of the March of the Marseillans), which was performed as part of the public pageant of planting a 'Freiheitsbaum' (Tree of Liberty) for the Republic of Mainz on 13 January 1793.[7] The German lyrics resounded with liberty and threats to those who curtailed it, but accentuating the peaceful symbolism of the Tree of Liberty, focused on an organic imagery of sowing, crops and free yeomen; a far cry from the blood-filled trenches and wasted landscape of the French source text:

> Seht diesen Baum, all' ihr Despoten!
> Wir pflanzten unsern Rechten ihn;
> Und in des Vaterlandes Boden
> Soll er noch unsern Enkeln blüh'n.

Wir wollen ihn mit Mut beschützen,
Bis die Gerechtigkeit gesiegt;
In seinem Schatten dann vergnügt
Am Abend unseres Lebens sitzen.

Wohlan! Die Wahl ist leicht!
Nur Freiheit oder Tod!
Weh' dem! Fluch dem!
Der je es wagt und unsrer Freiheit droht![8]

(Behold this tree, all ye despots!
We planted it for our rights;
and in the fatherland's soil
it shall flower for our grandsons still.
We shall guard it with courage,
until justice has carried the day;
in its shade we shall then sit
enjoying the evening of our life.

Now then! The choice is easy!
Only liberty or death!
Woe betide him! A curse upon him!
Whoever dares to threaten our liberty!)

By 1793, the 'Marseillaise' had certainly crossed the Channel, too. In late October 1792 the journalist Pierre Lebrun, then French Minister of Foreign Affairs, had sent copies to the London Revolution Society, whose members sung it 'with enthusiasm' at their annual dinner on 5 November.[9] It was swiftly followed by its first dated edition in England, a broadside which combined the six-stanza French lyrics and the musical notation with an etching of 'A Party of the Sans Culottes Army marching to the Frontiers' by the anti-royalist artist Richard Newton, published by William Holland on 10 November 1792.[10] Along with other political caricatures, it was most probably shown at his 'Holland's Exhibition Rooms', 50 Oxford Street, and perhaps even appeared pasted up on a wall, like the satirical mock handbills of the time.[11] Thus, radical Welsh 'Jenkin' and ironic Irish 'Patrick' in 'The Porters' Gossip' may have stood discussing *Rights of Man* in front of it. Jenkin's Welsh accent, whose 'calediad' (hardening) betrayed his south-Walian origins, may well be what men like Edward Williams (Iolo Morganwg) and Morgan John Rhys sounded like to English ears:[12]

Cot pless hur, what pustle and rout;
Come tell hur, coot frient, if you can,
What all that creat pook is apout,
Which hur thinks they call Paine's Rights of Man!

They tell hur such wonderful things,
A Welchman's as goot as a LORT;
There's no more occasion for kings
Than hur crantmoter hat for a swort.[13]

The score of 'La Marseillaise' was heard in the meetings and at the dinners of radical organizations such as the LCS, along with the older 'Ça Ira' and the 'Carmagnole', though accused and witnesses alike at the Treason Trials of 1794 pointedly denied that any of them were *sung* by those present.[14] Yet we know that it had been sung in November 1792 and English lyrics on the tune had been available from 1793, when an English adaptation of four of the six original stanzas had appeared in Robert Thom[p]son's *A Tribute to Liberty*, in *An Asylum for Fugitive Pieces*, and in the first volume of *Pig's Meat*.[15] Thom[p]son, an active member of the LCS, had left for France late in December 1792, 'threatened with prosecution for his political poems'.[16] By 1793 he had returned, running a bookshop at 'No. 4, Bell Yard, Temple-Bar', where he also printed *A Tribute to Liberty*.[17] His version soon crossed the Irish Sea to appear on song sheets in Dublin in the 'early 1790s'.[18] In 1795 the 'Marseilles March', 'Ça Ira' and the 'Carmagnole' featured in John Lawrence's radical subversion of the traditional almanac, the *Patriot's Calendar, for the Year 1795*.[19] In the same year all three also appeared in the first of the *Paddy's Resource* song-books published by the United Irishmen,[20] and *A Tribute to Liberty* was reprinted in New York as *A Tribute to the Swinish Multitude . . . collected by the celebrated R. Thomson*.[21] They all featured the same English adaptation of four stanzas of the 'Marseillaise', mostly entitled the 'Marseilles March' and occasionally endowed with a subtitle to explain that it had been 'sung by the Marseillois going to battle, by General Kellerman's army'.[22]

In the Anglo-Atlantic world, this 'Marseilles March' became part of the battle over the 'contested space of cultural practice' which was public singing, as the power of song in general and of this song in particular was recognized by radicals and loyalists alike.[23] The LCS advised its branches that 'for every meeting of its affiliated divisions held to discuss specific proposals and policies, they were to hold another at which political texts were read aloud and discussed, with everyone present obliged to contribute'.[24] The government spies embedded in its divisions certainly took note of these 'songs of a very treasonable tendency'.[25] At the trials of the Scottish Jacobins William Skirving and Maurice Margarot in January 1794, the prosecution stressed that 'the use of French words [and] the singing of French songs . . . showed that the members of the British Convention were prepared to take all the measures of the French revolutionaries'.[26] Later in the year, the report issued by the 'Secret Committee of the House of Commons' also included 'songs, seditious toasts, and a studied selection of the tunes which have been most in use in France since the revolution' in the repertoire of radical propaganda.[27] In Ireland, the satirical conversations between 'Squire Firebrand' and his spy 'Billy Bluff' published in the *Northern Star* in 1796 counted the reading of newspapers among seditious United Irishmen activities, but judged that it was 'songs that is most to be dreaded of all things . . . singing patriotic lies, national impudence, and united treason'.[28] The anonymous Dublin publisher of the *Political Harmonist: or Songs and Political Effusions Sacred to the Cause of Liberty* highlighted the particular power of three songs:

> The Americans obtained their liberty by the heart-chearing [*sic*] sound of *yankee doodle*, and the French by the more exhilarating ones of *ça ira* and the Marseillois Hymn; such charming and inspiring Harmony is sufficient in itself to inspire men with a love of Liberty, particularly when under such musical influence they have achieved the salvation of their country.[29]

There are no known Welsh versions of 'Ça Ira' and 'Yankee Doodle' (though Iolo Morganwg wrote his own English version of the 'Carmagnole' and a seditious English and Welsh 'Rights of Man' to the tune 'God Save the King'),[30] but en route to Ireland and hence to America, both the original French and the English adaptation of the 'Marseillaise' were received into Wales, England's internal colony whose cultural otherness was well rehearsed.[31] Irish Gaelic was rarely referred to as an obstacle in communicating with local people by late eighteenth-century travellers in Ireland, but they 'often enough . . . mention[ed] the Welsh language as a difficulty' which they encountered on their way there.[32] In Wales translation into the indigenous Celtic language was necessary for empowering this song.[33]

The potential Welsh translator must be sought within the ranks of its small organic intelligentsia, most of whom had plenty of opportunity to come into contact with the text of the French original or the English translation. Radical Welsh authors and poets enmeshed in the London-Welsh circles of the Gwyneddigion and Cymreigyddion societies, men like Edward Williams (Iolo Morganwg), John Jones (Jac Glan-y-gors) and Thomas Roberts (Llwyn-rhudol), would have heard it in meetings and lectures they attended.[34] The list of authors and books in the possession of Hugh Maurice (Huw Morus),

jotted down in his copy of *Y Geirgrawn*, contained not only entries such as
'Fr Constitution–1' and 'T Paine–1', but also 'Thomson–1', which may
have referred to one of Robert Thom[p]son's publications.[35] Others such
as Morgan John Rhys, Thomas Evans (Tomos Glyn Cothi), David Davies
(Holywell) and William Richards (Lynn) may have read the English version
in publications like *Pig's Meat* or the *Patriot's Calendar* somewhere between
Norwich and west Wales.[36] One of them, successfully hiding behind the
occasional pseudonym 'Gwilym' (William), created the only Celtic version
of the 'Marseillaise' then current in the British Isles.[37]

Political Welsh radicalism in the 1790s was not an organized mass movement, but a fragile web of like-minded men who dared oppose the hegemony
of landowner, state and Church in their under-urbanized world. They did
not publish song-books fit for rebellion (rioting in Wales was still mainly
spontaneous and economically induced),[38] but they succeeded in bringing
out three radical periodicals in their own language between 1793 and 1796.[39]
Gwilym used the fourth number of *Y Geirgrawn* to bring his creation to the
attention of the Welsh public.

The first striking difference between this print version of the 'Marseillaise'
and those which had appeared in England was the introductory prose text.
Like the preface to the *Political Harmonist* above, it ascribed great power to
the song, but it updated this by referring to very recent French victories. In
addition, Gwilym highlighted the very act of translation by inviting critical
feedback:

DDINESYDD,
OS yw'r Gân ganlynol wrth eich bodd, y mae i chwi gyflawn ryddid i'w rhoddi
yn y *Geirgrawn*. Am y cyfieithiad, nid oes gennyf ddim i'w ddywedyd, ond *barned
y deallus*. Y mae lluoedd *anorchfygol* y Wladwriaeth Ffrangaeg yn ddyledus iddi,
mewn mesur mawr, am eu buddugoliaethau ardderchoccaf. Yn ddiweddar, fe'i
dadseiniwyd gan uchel fynyddoedd yr *Eidal*; a hi a gyrrhaeddodd Frudain, megis
ar adenydd y gwynt. O bydd neb yn ei beio, gwneled ei gwell. Y mae iddo
gyflawn roesaw o ran GWILYM.[40]

(CITIZEN,
IF the following Song is to your taste, you are at perfect liberty to put it in the
Geirgrawn. About the translation, I have nothing to say but *let the knowledgeable
judge*. The *invincible* forces of the French Republic are indebted to it, to a great
extent, for their greatest victories. Lately, it has been echoed by the high mountains
of *Italy*; and it reached Britain as if on the wings of the wind. If anyone should
find fault with it, let him do it better. He is full welcome as far as GWILYM is
concerned.)

A second difference was the transformation of the song title, which followed the Mainz adaptation in becoming 'Cân Rhyddid' – a 'Song of Liberty'. The explanatory paratext closed with a third innovation by citing the opening line of the original,[41] '*Allonz enfans de la patriæ, &c.*' Thereby the reader's attention was focused back on the French original, perhaps to establish the provenance of what followed, for 'Cân Rhyddid' was a complex adaptation.

'*To mete and vend the light and air*': the twice-adapted '*Marseillaise*'

The anonymous English translator,[42] while not creating an entirely new song like J. F. F. Lehne, had prepared much ground for Gwilym by writing four English stanzas that matched the British domestic situation and the political principles of its radicals. Only the first line of stanza one referenced France with 'Ye sons of France, awake to glory', and only this stanza may be said to resemble the original relatively closely. The following three stanzas moved the action to Britain itself by using the first person plural in phrases like 'Our fields and cities blaze'. The translator picked suitable lines and couplets from stanzas two, three and six of the original French and mixed them with new material to create a song which was still warlike, yet less bloodily patriotic than the original. Stanza three, for instance, opened with the image of the despots and hired traitors of the original stanza two, but continued with a reference to the British window tax which had just been attacked in the second part of *Rights of Man*,[43] before rejecting both oppression and slavery, while elevating 'man' in general:

> With luxury and pride surrounded,
> The vile insatiate despots dare,
> Their thirst of power and gold unbounded,
> To mete and vend the light and air;
> Like beasts of burden would they load us,
> Like gods, would bid their slaves adore;
> But man is man, and who is more?
> Then shall they longer lash and goad us?

Stanza four similarly utilized material from stanza six of the original, but replaced the 'amour sacré de la patrie' (sacred love of the fatherland) which gave liberty its home with 'Liberty!' alone. The chorus still called on all to march 'to victory or death', but it did not demand that 'sang impur' (impure blood) should fill the trenches. No material from the fourth stanza of the original, which directly threatened tyrants, was used in this English version.

Also missing was any reference to the additional seventh stanza, the 'couplet des enfants' (children's stanza).[44] The domestication of the text had been achieved by replacing most references to France and the French with such to liberty and peace, though the threatening atmosphere of war and destruction was maintained.[45]

This manifestly well-known and successful English adaptation became one source of Gwilym's 'Cân Rhyddid'. The first three of his five stanzas adapted the corresponding English stanzas for a Welsh audience, translating relatively closely, though adding emphasis to some of the key changes introduced by the English translator through italicization and multiple exclamation marks. This was the case with the reference to the window tax, '*Mesurant, gwerthant oleu'r dydd!!!*' (*They measure, sell the light of day!!!*), and in the key line on the importance of man himself.[46] In addition, Gwilym moved the language and imagery of these stanzas even further away from bloody patriotism to abstract concern for mankind. Where J. F. F. Lehne had bound 'Freiheit' (liberty) to peaceful German soil and 'Landmann' (yeoman, compatriot), and the English translator had moved the battle for liberty to Britain, Gwilym focused on oppression and liberty as abstract opposites whose collision transcended race, nationality, gender and class. The French 'enfants de la patrie' (children of the fatherland) and the English 'sons of France' became 'meibion Rhyddid' (the sons of Liberty). The sword was not raised in defence of 'nous' (us) or the 'français' (French), nor of English 'children, wives and grandsires', but it was 'plant gorthrymder' (the children of oppression) who were crying out for help. In the chorus, the very principles of 'R[h]yddid, hêdd a chariad' (Liberty, peace and love) were at stake and Welsh citizens were not called to fill trenches with impure blood or go to 'victory or death', but to 'farw, neu fyw'n rhydd' (die or to live free).

Gwilym did not translate the fourth of the published English stanzas. Instead, stanzas four and five of the published 1796 version of 'Cân Rhyddid' resemble the French source text. In the absence of a published English version of the same character, we must assume them to be direct translations from French. Stanza four threatened the oppressors directly, almost exactly as in the French original:

> O crynwch, crynwch, euog dreiswyr;
> Ac mwyach byth na lawenhewch;
> A chwitheu hefyd gas fradychwyr
> O ffrwyth eich llafur y bwyttewch:
> Ac er i'ch hên fyddinoedd dawnus,
> Guro ein hifaingc wyr i dre;
> O'u llwch daw eraill yn eu lle,
> I yrru'n oll eich lluoedd dawnus.

(Tremble, tyrans et vous perfides
L'opprobre de tous les partis,
Tremblez! Vos projets parricides
Vont enfin recevoir leurs prix
Tout est soldat pour vous combattre,
S'ils tombent, nos jeunes héros,
La terre en produit de nouveaux,
Contre vous tout prêts à se battre!)

The Welsh song concluded with an equally close translation of the 'children's stanza', which had not been on the illustrated song sheet of the French 'Marseillaise' or part of the well-known English version of 1793. Both stanzas four and seven of the original may have come to Gwilym's attention in 1795, when they were circulating in the *Patriot's Calendar*, complete with the score and alongside a total of four entirely new French stanzas.[47] Stanza seven was clearly marked 'Les Enfans' in the *Patriot's Calendar* and Gwilym, too, closed his contribution with a footnote stating that 'Y pennill hwn a genir gan y plant bychain' (This stanza is sung by the small children). 'Cân Rhyddid', published in *Y Geirgrawn* in north-east Wales in May 1796, had thus absorbed and domesticated ideas and vocabulary of the French Revolution in two ways. Stanzas one to three had been filtered through the English context and thereby undergone a two-stage process of far-reaching adaptation. The final two stanzas, however, like the prize medals engraved for the Gwyneddigion eisteddfodau of 1789 by Augustin Dupré, General Engraver of French Money to the National Assembly of France, represented a direct link between the ideas of the French Revolution and radicalism in Wales.[48]

'Addition to the Song of Liberty': the song journeys on

Of published radical poems in Wales, few were copied into multiple manuscripts and performed publicly. 'Cân Rhyddid' was not only copied by more than one author, its text was amended and extended, it was translated back into English, it was performed publicly and became part of a case for sedition. Though it had appeared in *Y Geirgrawn* in north-east Wales, most of the later activity occurred in south-west Wales, an area where 'surface deference and quietism in matters political' masked a society characterized by economic tension and the alienation of an extended pocket of Dissent from all establishments.[49] Religious radicalism had flourished along Teifi and Tywi since the early eighteenth century, the Dissenting academy at the regional centre Carmarthen had followed the currents of Enlightenment for almost as long, and it employed Arians and Arminians as teachers.[50] Welsh Unitarianism, a rare 'enduring experiment in rural Enlightenment', sprang from here and took deep root.[51]

It does not surprise that we encounter 'Cân Rhyddid' in this area, in a commonplace book belonging to one John Davies of Llanfihangel Ystrad, a small hamlet south of Lampeter. John Davies was not a 'usual suspect' of Welsh radicalism, but a simple cobbler and bookbinder whose only trace in Welsh history is the diary for the last years of his life, 1796 to 1799, which perfectly illustrates the distribution of texts from various sources in a rural society.[52] Into it Davies copied directly from publications, transcribed printed material second-hand from other manuscripts, and jotted down what he heard from friends and neighbours. The sources for some material were serials like, for instance, the *Hereford Journal* and the *Gentleman's Magazine*.[53] Others, such as the subversive lines 'found in St. Petry [*sic*] Church yard in Colchester on Tuesday the 19 of Dec. 1797. being the Day appointed for a general thanksgiving' were most probably copied second-hand, perhaps from Tomos Glyn Cothi's commonplace book 'Y Gell Gymysg' (The Miscellaneous Repository), where they appeared more correctly transcribed and ascribed to the 'Camb Intell. For Jan 20 1798'.[54] Pieces like the friendly 'epitaph' for Joseph Priestley composed by the Arian minister and school-master David Davis of nearby Castellhywel, which would not appear in print for another thirty years, may have been jotted down on hearing them.[55] On 28 April 1797, John Davies copied 'Cân Rhyddid' into this volume exactly as it had been published in *Y Geirgrawn* a year earlier, complete with the footnote to the 'children's stanza'.[56] In two places, however, words have been replaced as if in a draft version by a much younger hand. Ten pages on, the same hand added a 'Chwanegiad at Gân Rhyddid' (Addition to the Song of Liberty) which consisted of a strong new stanza and chorus:

> Ein gwragedd meibion merched siriol
> Sy'n gwaeddi amddiffynwch ni.
> A gwaed ein brodyr dewrion gwrol,
> Sy'n llefain dial ychel cri
> Ar ein anrheithwyr drwg[llwyr]erlidgawr.
> Syn gwasgar llid a rhyfel llawn
> Gan ddiffodd pob rhyw ddynol ddawn
> Er peri gofid trwm a galar.

> Trwy'r tan Trwy'r tan ar mwg
> I'r maes awn oll yn un
> Ar frys ar frys eu lluoedd drwg
> Can dderbyn synwyr pryn.[57]

(Our wives, sons, merry daughters
are crying out defend us.
And the blood of our brave heroic brothers
calls vengeance with a loud cry
on our bad^{wholly} persecuting despoilers.
Who are driving forward rage and full-on war
extinguishing all human virtue
to cause heavy grief and sorrow.

Through the fire, through the fire and the smoke
to the field let's all go as one;
rush, rush, their evil forces
will receive redeemed sense.)

While the lyrics manifested the same resolve to withstand any aggressor as pervaded the French original and the battle terminology is similar, both stanza and chorus were original Welsh compositions inspired by the published translation. In Llanfihangel Ystrad, 'Cân Rhyddid' acquired six stanzas, two choruses and, perhaps, a second author.

About the same time, the published version of 'Cân Rhyddid' had been noted even further south. Iolo Morganwg had by then returned from London to run a shop in Cowbridge which sold 'sugar uncontaminated with human gore' and stocked copies of the *Cambridge Intelligencer*, the *Watchman* and *Rights of Man*.[58] Iolo was not content with just perusing his copy of *Y Geirgrawn* or noting down its poetry. His way of making the text his own was to translate it into English. 'No. 29' in a volume of drafts and revisions of poems like 'John Bull's Litany' and 'Ode on Converting a Sword into a Pruning Hook' was a song just headed 'Translated from the Welsh Magazine Y Geirgrawn, for May 1796'.[59] Here, Iolo furnished a literal translation into English of the entire contribution, including the introduction and the footnote, exactly as it had been published in *Y Geirgrawn*. His motivation is unclear, but he may have intended to make this text accessible to English radical circles. Like other texts in this manuscript volume, the translation had been edited, albeit to a lesser extent than other pieces which had undergone a whole series of revisions.[60] Perhaps this was one of his 'castles in the air', a project forgotten once his attention was drawn to different matters. It may, on the other hand, have been the 'literal translation of your hymn' asked for by John Prior Estlin in 1801 in relation to the trial of Tomos Glyn Cothi.[61]

Laura Mason has judged that the 'moment of performance' marks the instant at which a song achieves its full potential, as the text leaves print and manuscript to enter oral culture, supported by a tune.[62] Radicals, loyalists and state authorities all recognized its power as we have seen above, and for 'Cân Rhyddid' this decisive 'moment' is recorded for spring 1801, when it was sung at a traditional *cwrw bach* (bid-ale) in the village of Brechfa, Carmarthenshire, in aid of one of its inhabitants. The record survived because the song was part of the court case against Tomos Glyn Cothi, the weaver who had preached Welsh Unitarianism since 1786, translated and published subversive hymns and pamphlets into Welsh, and edited a radical Welsh journal in 1795.[63] An opportunity to silence him arose in the wake of this apparently charitable social gathering, which went horribly wrong. Arguments ensued and Tomos was accused of singing an English version of the 'Carmagnole' ascribed to Iolo Morganwg.[64] Iolo Morganwg took it upon himself to organize the defence for his fellow-Unitarian and friend by collecting affidavits to be presented during the trial. Most of these agreed that the company:

> was engaged in convivial conversation, several songs were sung, amongst others a lyrical version in Welsh of Gray's Elegy in a Country Churchyard, a Welsh hymn was also sung; and amongst other things, a Welsh song to the tune of the Marseillois hymn which had been printed in a Welsh magazine, the 4th No. for May 1796; . . . but after high words had occurred, a song was sung . . . of a satirical nature . . . George Thomas took great offence at this, and supposed that this song had been written by the Revd. Thomas Ev[ans].[65]

As we have seen, the 'Carmagnole' and the 'Marseillaise' had often been printed and performed together, so it does not surprise that they were mentioned together in this trial for sedition, too.[66] It is more likely that the gathering would have sung the Welsh song of liberty which was clearly circulating among the Unitarians of the area than a song with English lyrics they may have found difficult to pronounce, but the indictment for 'sedition' centred around the English version of the 'Carmagnole', because it was easier to gain a conviction with a seditious song in the language Judge George Hardinge understood. On the basis of this charge, Tomos Glyn Cothi was sentenced to two years in prison, to stand in the stocks twice and to keep the peace for seven years after.[67] Hardinge's report stressed, however, that 'the Prisoner was in the habit of composing, singing and teaching others to sing songs in the Welch language of a very seditious tendency',[68] which brought the Welsh element of the conviction back into the picture. In addition, rumours circulating well into the nineteenth century insisted that Tomos had actually performed a stanza of Iolo Morganwg's 'Breiniau Dyn' (Rights of Man), the lyrics of which were in his 'Cell Gymysg'.[69] Among

the dozen or so witnesses in support of Tomos Glyn Cothi whom Iolo
Morganwg secured were several Unitarians from the parish of Llanfihangel
Ystrad, in their midst the well-known and revered farmer-benefactor David
Jenkin Rees.[70] They, too, used songs as evidence, albeit to underscore Tomos
Glyn Cothi's loyalty in the wake of the attempted invasion of Britain via
Fishguard in 1797:

> . . . soon after the French were taken Prisoner in Pembrokeshire these Deponents
> severally heard the said Thomas Evans testify his joy thereat and he wrote a Welsh
> song in celebration of ancient British valour and in abhorrence of the French
> designs against our Government of which he delivered copies to the Deponents.
> D. J. Rees, Jacob Evans, John Evans.[71]

There exists, indeed, a poem with which Tomos Glyn Cothi responded to
the Fishguard debacle, and it seems to have been well known in south-west
Wales.[72] But Iolo Morganwg used a different verse to further assist his friend
and advertise his plight. On what looks like the title page of a publication,
he wrote out a 'Pennill a wnaeth Thomos Glyn Cothi er annog y Cymry i
fynd yn wrol yn erbyn y Ffrancod a diriasant yn Aber Gwaun yn y flwyddyn
1797' (A stanza made by Tomos Glyn Cothi to urge the Welsh to go heroically against the French who landed in Fishguard in the year 1797). At the
bottom of the same page, an English note advised 'This to be introduced in
the Preface or introduction to the Trial of Tho'. Evans'.[73] Iolo was planning
a pamphlet similar to those published on behalf of the defendants in the
famous Treason Trials of 1794. Tomos Glyn Cothi knew of this, but Theophilus Lindsay warned against it as it was likely to 'increase prejudices' against
Tomos and might land Iolo in the same 'confinement'.[74] The pamphlet was
never written and only the title page survives. The stanza which features
prominently on it is not from the anti-French poem cited by the supporters
of Tomos Glyn Cothi in their affidavits, but it is the addition to 'Cân
Rhyddid' from the manuscript of John Davies, here attributed to Tomos
Glyn Cothi for the first time.[75] Iolo was a great poetic forger who loved to
hide behind various alter egos, but he never ascribed his work to another
living poet, let alone a close friend. We may safely assume, therefore, that
the additional stanza was composed by Tomos Glyn Cothi.

Iolo Morganwg died in 1826 and Tomos Glyn Cothi moved to be minister
at the Unitarian Hen Dŷ Cwrdd in Aberdare in 1811, where he died in
1833. When the Welsh Unitarians first published a periodical, *Yr Ymofynydd*
(The Inquirer), in 1848, it featured a contribution entitled 'Cân Rhyddid,
gan y diweddar Barch T. E., Glyn Cothi. A gyfansoddwyd tua diwedd y
cannrif [*sic*] diweddaf. Ar y don Marseillaise' (The Song of Liberty, by the

late Revd T. E., Glyn Cothi, composed towards the end of the last century on the tune of the Marseillaise).[76] The second stanza of this published version is the addition to 'Cân Rhyddid' noted in John Davies's diary in 1797 and ascribed to Tomos Glyn Cothi by Iolo Morganwg in 1801. The first stanza is a relatively close, though slightly more optimistic, rendering of stanza four of the English 1793 version, which had not been translated for the 1796 *Y Geirgrawn* version. Tomos Glyn Cothi thus appears to have translated one stanza from the 1793 English adaptation in the style employed by Gwilym for his 1796 *Y Geirgrawn* version and composed one stanza and two choruses in emulation of them. Significantly, this mixture of adaptation and original creation was characteristic of his work as translator and author.[77] The new chorus, published for the first time in 1848, gave the song a decidedly internationalist timbre:

> Hawl dyn – trwy'r byd,
> Llwyr deg ennillo'r dydd;
> Heb fraw – drwy unol fryd,
> O'n rhwymau awn yn rhydd.[78]

> (The right of man – through the world,
> may it fairly and squarely win the day;
> fearlessly – with united will,
> we shall walk free from our bonds.)

All seven stanzas of 'Cân Rhyddid' were reprinted in Welsh periodicals and popular volumes until the end of the nineteenth century, separately and together, but mostly linked with the name and court case of Tomos Glyn Cothi.[79] Final proof for all seven stanzas eludes us while the identity of 'Gwilym', resident at 'Tŷ'r Crochennydd' (The Potter's House),[80] remains hidden. We can safely credit Tomos Glyn Cothi with composing at least two additional stanzas of 'Cân Rhyddid', but we cannot, as has been done in the past, ascribe the authorship of the printed version to either Tomos Glyn Cothi or Iolo Morganwg.[81] Tomos and Iolo, who in the latter's words had been 'for many years on very intimate and friendly terms',[82] were both deeply impressed with the ideas and vocabulary of the French Revolution; they corresponded with the same well-known English Unitarians and they spent convivial hours together copying each other's manuscripts and composing poetry with and to each other.[83] The song may well have been a co-operative effort.

Postscript

The 'Marseillaise' continued to be powerfully attractive in Britain, as in other countries, its famous tune perfect for publicizing widely differing political messages.[84] In Britain, loyalist parodies and patriotic rewrites soon turned against the 'ferocious Gaul invading' and called on Britons to defend 'our land'.[85] Percey Bysshe Shelley attempted his own translation in 1811, often cited on the internet as the first English version of the 'Marseillaise'.[86] In Wales, the Carmarthen Chartist and Rebecca Riot leader Hugh Williams included three English-language versions of the 'Marseillaise' as representative of 'France' in his internationalist volume *National Songs and Poetical Pieces, dedicated to the Queen and her Countrywomen*.[87] The 1793 version was reproduced here with the usual title, albeit footnoted that it may be altered to 'Ye sons of Britain, wake to glory'.[88] The seven stanzas of the 'Marseillaise Hymn. Translated by Dr. Bowring', and the two stanzas of 'Death or Liberty. Adapted to the National French Air of the "Marseillois Hymn" by J. S. Buckingham, Esq., M.P.' were both new attempts at close renderings.[89] They do not appear to have left much trace in the Welsh working-class movement. Welsh miners and socialists preferred to sing the four stanzas first published in 1793 at meetings and festive banquets in honour of men like Keir Hardie.[90]

New Welsh adaptations also appeared well into the twentieth century. *Y Cerddor Cymreig* (The Welsh Musician) published a thoroughly nationalized version in 1871, whose lyrics, written by the popular Welsh poet Richard Davies (Mynyddog), called on 'feibion dewrion gwlad y bryniau' (the brave sons of the land of hills) to follow the dragon banner of their last Prince Llewelyn to fight for the rights of Wales.[91] Similar nationalist, though British, sentiments led to the most recent translation of the 'Marseillaise' into Welsh during the First World War. To support the war effort it was felt that Cardiff's school children should perform the national anthems of Britain's allies in their St David's Day celebration. William Thomas supplied a suitably close translation.[92] By then, however, the 'Marseillaise' was once more counted among the 'Caneuon a Chaniadau Rhyfel' (War Songs and Canticles).[93] None of the later adaptations came close to the version first printed in *Y Geirgrawn* in 1796 and its early additions in articulating the epoch-making spirit of the French Revolution conjoined with Welsh humanism.

Notes

[1]   Laura Mason, *Singing the French Revolution: Popular Culture and Politics 1787–1799* (Ithaca, 1996), p. 3.

2   Michel Vovelle, 'II. La Marseillaise: War or Peace', in Pierre Nora (ed.), *Realms of Memory: The Construction of the French Past. Volume III: Symbols*, English-language edn. ed. Lawrence D. Kritzman, trans. Arthur Goldhammer (New York, 1998), p. 51.

3   Hans Jürgen Hansen (Hrsg.), *Heil Dir im Siegerkranz. Die Hymnen der Deutschen* (Oldenburg, 1978), pp. 28–31.

4   For detailed accounts of the early French history of the song, see Vovelle, 'II. La Marseillaise: War or Peace', pp. 30–40; Mason, *Singing the French Revolution*, pp. 94–100.

5   Significantly, *Realms of Memory: The Construction of the French Past. Volume III: Symbols* opens with chapters on the tricolour, the 'Marseillaise' and the main motto. See Raoul Girardet, 'I. The Three Colors: Neither White nor Red', in Nora, *Realms of Memory*, pp. 3–26; Mona Ozouf, 'III. Liberty, Equality, Fraternity', ibid., pp. 77–114.

6   On the lack of urbanization, see Harold Carter, *The Towns of Wales* (Cardiff, 1965); Philip Jenkins, 'Wales', in Peter Clark (ed.), *The Cambridge Urban History of Britain. Volume II: 1540–1840* (Cambridge, 2000), pp. 133–49.

7   Helmut Klapheck und Franz Dumont (Hrsg.), *Als die Revolution an den Rhein kam: Die Mainzer Republik 1792/93. Jakobiner – Franzosen – Cisrhenanen* (Mainz, 1994), p. 43. For the history of Mainz during the Revolutionary years, see T. C. W. Blanning, *Reform and Revolution in Mainz 1743–1803* (Cambridge, 1974), pp. 267–302.

8   Hans-Werner Engels (Hrsg.), *Gedichte und Lieder Deutscher Jakobiner* (Stuttgart, 1971), pp. 49–51.

9   Albert Goodwin, *The Friends of Liberty: The English Democratic Movement in the Age of the French Revolution* (London, 1979), p. 247. I owe this reference to Mary-Ann Constantine.

10 A. Hyatt King, 'The First Illustrated and Dated Edition of the Marseillaise', *The British Museum Quarterly*, 20, no. 1 (1955), 1–2. The broadsheet is reproduced there, and also opposite p. 28 in Nora, *Realms of Memory*, and on the cover of Malcolm Boyd (ed.), *Music and the French Revolution* (Cambridge, 1992).

11 For the relationship between Holland and Newton, see John Barrell, 'Radicalism, Visual Culture, and Spectacle in the 1790s', *Field Day Review*, 4 (2008), 43–6; idem, *'Exhibition Extraordinary!!' Radical Broadsides of the Mid 1790s* (Nottingham, 2001), pp. vii–x.

12 The 'hardening' of voiced consonants to denote the Welshness of characters in English dialogue – a literary device since Shakespeare – is based on the phonetic feature of 'calediad' associated mostly, but not exclusively, with the dialect of the Tawe valley in south-west Wales. See Siân Elizabeth Thomas, 'A Study of Calediad in the Upper Swansea Valley', in Martin John Ball (ed.), *The Use of Welsh: A Contribution to Sociolinguistics*, Multilingual Matters, 36 (Clevedon, 1988), pp. 85–96.

13 J. Walker, 'The Porter's Gossip', in Robert Thompson (ed.), *A Tribute to Liberty. Or, A New Collection of Patriotic Songs* (London, 1793), pp. 64–5.

14 John Barrell and Jon Mee (eds.), *Trials for Treason and Sedition 1792–1794* (8 vols., London, 2006–7), III, pp. 119, 401; For history and symbolism of 'Ça Ira' and 'La Carmagnole', see Mason, *Singing the French Revolution*, pp. 42–57, 94, 173; *eadem*, '"Ça Ira" and the Birth of Revolutionary Song', *History Workshop Journal*, 28, no. 1 (1989), 22–38; Vovelle, 'La Marseillaise: War or Peace', pp. 30–1, 33.

15 'The Marseilles March', in Thompson, *A Tribute to Liberty*, pp. 59–60; 'The Marseilles March', *Pig's Meat*, I (1793), 67–8; 'The Marseilles March', in *An Asylum for Fugitive Pieces. Volume IV* (London, 1793), pp. 25–6.

16 Mary Thale (ed.), *Selections from the Papers of the London Corresponding Society 1792–1799* (Cambridge, 1983), pp. 29, 36, 41, 42.

17 Thompson, *A Tribute to Liberty* [copy in Bodleian Library, Harding Collection C 3541], title page.

18 Georges-Denis Zimmermann, *Songs of Irish Rebellion: Political Street Ballads and Rebel Songs 1780–1900* (Dublin, 1967), p. 39.

19 [John Lawrence], *Patriot's Calendar, For the Year 1795 Containing the Usual English Almanack, the French Calendar, with the Corresponding Days of our Stile; the French Declaration of Rights, and Republican Constitution, the American Constitution, Magna Charta . . .* (London, [1794]), p. 77, appendix, pp. 3–19.

20 *Paddy's Resource: Being a Select Collection of Original and Modern Patriotic Songs, Toasts and Sentiments, Compiled for the Use of the People of Ireland* ([Belfast], 1795), pp. 32–4, 59–61. Their later song-books, *Paddy's Resource: Being a Select Collection of Original and Modern Patriotic Songs, Toasts and Sentiments, Compiled for the Use of the People of Ireland* ([Belfast], 1796) and *Paddy's Resource: Or The Harp of Erin, Attuned to Freedom. Being a Collection of Patriotic Songs Selected for Paddy's Amusement* ([Dublin], 1798 and 1803), did not feature any songs of French origin. For a detailed analysis of all, see Mary Helen Thuente, *The Harp Re-strung: The United Irishmen and the Rise of Irish Literary Nationalism* (Syracuse, 1994), pp. 125, 133–69.

21 *A Tribute to the Swinish Multitude: Being a Choice Collection of Patriotic Songs Collected by the Celebrated R. Thomson* (New York, 1795), pp. 61–2; 'Ça Ira' was reprinted on pp. 81–2. According to an anecdote contributed by 'P. J.' to *The American Universal Magazine*, 20 March 1797, 284, 'R. Thompson, author of the well known volume of patriotic songs', was believed to be 'an officer in the French army' by then. I owe this reference to Jon Mee, University of Warwick.

22 Thompson, *A Tribute to Liberty*, p. 55; *An Asylum for Fugitive Pieces*, p. 25; *A Tribute to the Swinish Multitude*, p. 61.

23 Michael T. Davis, '"An Evening of Pleasure Rather Than Business": Songs, Subversion and Radical Sub-Culture in the 1790s', *Journal for the Study of British Cultures*, 12, no. 2 (2005), 115.

24 Barrell, 'Radicalism, Visual Culture, and Spectacle in the 1790s', 46.

25 Thale, *Selections from the Papers of the London Corresponding Society 1792–1799*, pp. xxv, 67, 122, 127.

26 Ibid., p. 105.

27 Barrell, 'Radicalism, Visual Culture, and Spectacle in the 1790s', 47.

28 Thuente, *The Harp Re-strung*, pp. 12–13.

29 'A Cosmopolite' (ed.), *Political Harmonist: or Songs and Political Effusions Sacred to the Cause of Liberty* (4th edn., Dublin, 1797), p. v; cited in Thuente, *The Harp Re-strung*, p. 151.

30 Mary-Ann Constantine and Elizabeth Edwards, '"Bard of Liberty": Iolo Morganwg, Wales and Radical Song', in John Kirk, Andrew Noble and Michael Brown (eds.), *Poetry and Song in the Age of Revolution. Volume 1: United Islands? The Languages of Resistance* (London, 2012), pp. 63–76. For the text of this 'Carmagnole', see 'Y Parch. Thomas Evans, Aberdar', *Yr Ymofynydd*, cyfres newydd, XIII, rhif 4 (1888), 82. It is discussed in John James Evans, *Dylanwad y Chwyldro Ffrengig ar Lenyddiaeth Cymru* (Lerpwl, 1928), p. 144. For 1790s versions of 'God Save the King', see Davis, '"An Evening of Pleasure Rather Than Business"', 118–20, 127. For a Chartist version in Wales, see 'God Save our Native Land!', in Hugh Williams (ed.), *National Songs and Poetical Pieces, dedicated to the Queen and her Countrywomen* (London, 1839), pp. 6–70.

31 Peter Lord, *Words with Pictures: Welsh Images and Images of Wales in the Popular Press, 1640–1860* (Aberystwyth, 1995), pp. 53–74.

32 C. J. Woods, *Travellers' Accounts as Source-Material for Irish Historians* (Dublin, 2009), p. 34.

33 For the linguistic situation in Wales at the time, see Geraint H. Jenkins, 'The Cultural Uses of the Welsh Language 1660–1800', in *idem* (ed.), *The Welsh Language Before the Industrial Revolution* (Cardiff, 1997), pp. 368–406.

34 For Iolo Morganwg in London, see Constantine and Edwards, 'Bard of Liberty'. For Glan-y-gors, Thomas Roberts, and the Gwyneddigion, see Middleton Pennant Jones, 'John Jones of Glan-y-Gors', *THSC* (1911), 61–3, 66–72; R. T. Jenkins and Helen M. Ramage, *A History of the Honourable Society of Cymmrodorion and of the Gwyneddigion and Cymreigyddion Societies (1751–1951)* (London, 1951), pp. 108–9, 110–12, 122–3.

35 Inscription in the miscellaneous printed volume NLW YX2 GEI. For the gifted scribe and artist Hugh Maurice (Huw Morus), nephew of the Cymreigyddion patron Owen Jones (Owain Myfyr), see E. D. Jones, 'Hugh Maurice (?1775–1825), a Forgotten Scribe', *NLWJ*, I, no. 4 (1940), 230–2. For Owen Jones, 'Owain Myfyr', see Geraint Phillips, 'Forgery and Patronage: Iolo Morganwg and Owain Myfyr', in Geraint H. Jenkins (ed.), *A Rattleskull Genius: The Many Faces of Iolo Morganwg* (Cardiff, 2005), pp. 403–23.

36 Marion Löffler, *Welsh Responses to the French Revolution: Press and Public Discourse 1789–1802* (Cardiff, 2012), pp. 4–5.

37 The pseudonym 'Gwilym', resident at 'Tŷ'r Crochennydd' (The Potter's House), was only used three times: in *Y Geirgrawn*, I (February 1796), 15–16, ibid., IV (May 1796), 123, and in connection with the 'Marseillaise' translation. See also below 106 and note 80.

38 For the lack of politically inspired popular radical action in Wales, see David J. V. Jones, *Before Rebecca: Popular Protests in Wales 1793–1835* (London, 1973), pp. 60–6.

39 Löffler, *Welsh Responses to the French Revolution*, pp. 26–34.

40 *Y Geirgrawn* (May 1796), 127–8.

41 For the notion of the paratext, see Paul Magnuson, *Reading Public Romanticism* (Princeton, 1998), pp. 5–6.

42 Although the translation appeared in Thom[p]son's collections alongside his own works, we cannot be sure that he was the translator. The indexes in several of his publications mention that 'those marked thus (★) are by other authors', and the 'Marseilles March' was 'marked thus (★)'. See Thompson, *A Tribute to Liberty*, p. 97.

43 For the attack, see Mark Philp (ed.), *Thomas Paine: Rights of Man, Common Sense, and Other Political Writings* (Oxford, 1995), pp. 303, 311.

44 According to Vovelle, 'II. La Marseillaise: War or Peace', p. 37, the seventh verse was added by an unknown author in late 1792, because 'the young had begun to play an increasingly important part in civic celebrations'.

45 For different translation strategies, such as 'domestication' and 'foreignization', see Friedrich Schleiermacher, 'On the Different Methods of Translating (1813)', in Douglas Robinson (ed.), *Western Translation Theory from Herodotus to Nietzsche* (Manchester, 1997), pp. 233–4.

46 These are therefore not, as assumed by E. Gwynn Matthews, 'original and striking concepts'. See E. Gwynn Matthews, 'Holywell and the Marseillaise', *Flintshire Historical Society Journal*, 38 (2010), 117–31.

47 'Marche des Marseillois', in [Lawrence], *Patriot's Calendar, For the Year 1795*, appendix, pp. 9–18. This included the score of the song. Scores and French lyrics of 'Ça Ira' and the 'Carmagnole' were also published here.

48 Iorwerth C. Peate, 'Welsh Society and Eisteddfod Medals and Relics', *THSC* (1937), 293, plate 1.

49 Gwyn Alf Williams, 'Druids and Democrats: Organic Intellectuals and the First Welsh Nation', in *idem, The Welsh in their History* (London, 1982), p. 46.

50 Ibid., pp. 42–3; H. P. Roberts, 'The History of the Presbyterian Academy Brynllewarch-Carmarthen II', *Transactions of the Unitarian Historical Society*, V, part I (1931), 24–42.

51 Martin Fitzpatrick, 'Enlightenment', in Iain McCalman (ed.), *An Oxford Companion to the Romantic Age: British Culture, 1776–1832* (Oxford, 1999), pp. 302–3.

52 Kenneth R. Johnston, 'Whose History? My Place or Yours? Republican Assumptions and Romantic Traditions', in Damian Walford Davies (ed.), *Romanticism, History, Historicism: Essays on an Orthodoxy* (London, 2009), pp. 79–102.

53 NLW 12350A, 'Diary &c. of John Davies, Ystrad, 1796–99', ff. 95–102.

54 Ibid., ff. 108–9; NLW 6238A, 'Y Gell Gymysg', ff. 150–2. The latter fills over four hundred pages with transcripts and translations from English sources, such as the *Cambridge Intelligencer*, the *Chester Chronicle* and the *Protestant Dissenting Magazine*, as well as with original radical material by Tomos Glyn Cothi himself and by friends like David Davis, Castellhywel, and Iolo Morganwg.

55 NLW 12350A, 'Diary &c. of John Davies, Ystrad, 1796–99', f. 90. For the text of 'An Epitaph, Intended for Dr. Priestley, referring to his belief of Materialism', see *Telyn Dewi; Sef Gwaith Prydyddawl y Parch. David Davis o Gastell-Hywel, Ceredigion* (Llundain, 1824), p. 148.

56 NLW 12350A, 'Diary &c. of John Davies, Ystrad, 1796–99', ff. 88–9.

57   Ibid., f. 103.
58   Andrew Davies, '"Uncontaminated with human Gore"? Iolo Morganwg, Slavery and the Jamaican Inheritance', in Jenkins, *A Rattleskull Genius*, p. 292; *CIM*, III, pp. 801, 811.
59   NLW 21401E, f. 29.
60   For Iolo's obsessive revising, see Elizabeth Edwards, *English-Language Poetry from Wales 1789–1806* (Cardiff, 2013), pp. 25, 35. For the various drafts of his 'John Bull's Litany', see Constantine and Edwards, 'Bard of Liberty'.
61   *CIM*, II, p. 382, John Prior Estlin to Iolo Morganwg, 23 September 1801. This explanation of the translation, however, is difficult due to the earlier dating of the pieces with which it occurs in this manuscript.
62   Mason, *Singing the French Revolution*, pp. 2–3.
63   Löffler, *Welsh Responses to the French Revolution*, p. 30.
64   The whole tale has been narrated skilfully by Geraint H. Jenkins, '"A Very Horrid Affair": Sedition and Unitarianism in the Age of Revolutions', in R. R. Davies and *idem* (eds.), *From Medieval to Modern Wales: Historical Essays in Honour of Kenneth O. Morgan and Ralph A. Griffiths* (Cardiff, 2004), pp. 175–96.
65   NLW 2137D. The content of this file has been outlined in G. J. Williams, 'Carchariad Tomos Glyn Cothi', *LlC*, III (1954–5), 121–2.
66   Writers on the French Revolution often cite them together, too. See Mason, *Singing the French Revolution*, pp. 1–2; David Charlton, 'Introduction: Exploring the Revolution', in Boyd, *Music and the French Revolution*, pp. 4–5.
67   NLW, Great Sessions, 4/753/1–3; NLW 21373D; Geraint Dyfnallt Owen, *Thomas Evans (Tomos Glyn Cothi): Trem ar ei Fywyd* (Abertawe, 1963), p. 36.
68   PRO HO 47/27, Judge's Report, 20 March 1802.
69   *Nodion am y Parch. Thos. Evans (Glyn Cothi), Aberdar, 1764–1833* (Dowlais, 1893), p. 3; NLW 6238A, 'Y Gell Gymysg', ff. 215–28.
70   For David Jenkin Rees, see Löffler, *Welsh Responses to the French Revolution*, pp. 1, 53.
71   NLW 21373D, 'Carchariad Tomos Glyn Cothi', 'Copy No. XIV'.
72   NLW 6238A, 'Y Gell Gymysg', f. 287. Published versions are found in *Gardd Aberdar, Yn Cynwys y Cyfansoddiadau Buddugol yn Eisteddfod y Carw Coch, Aberdar, Awst 29, 1853* (Caerfyrddin, 1854), p. 105; Owen, *Thomas Evans (Tomos Glyn Cothi)*, p. 31. The poem itself is ambiguous. It commenced with anti-French stanzas, but ended in a threat to 'holl wrthwynebwyr gwaedlyd pob gwynfyd hyfryd hedd, / Holl dreiswyr y tylodion, rai gwaelion oer eu gwedd' (all bloody opponents to every pleasant paradise of peace, / all the rapists of the poor, the wretched and miserable of appearance).
73   NLW 13144A, f. 175.
74   *CIM*, II, p. 384, Thomas Evans (Tomos Glyn Cothi) to Iolo Morganwg, 30 September 1801.
75   NLW 13144A, f. 175; NLW 12350A, f. 103.
76   'Cân Rhyddid, gan y diweddar Barch T. E., Glyn Cothi. A Gyfansoddwyd tua Diwedd y Cannrif [*sic*] Diweddaf. Ar y Don Marseillaise', *Yr Ymofynydd*, I, rhif 16 (1848), 380.
77   Löffler, *Welsh Responses to the French Revolution*, p. 47.

[78] 'Cân Rhyddid, gan y diweddar Barch T. E., Glyn Cothi', 380.

[79] Cynddelw, 'Traethawd ar Fywyd, Athrylith, Helyntion Barddol, a Theithi Dewi Wyn', in *Blodau Arfon, sef Gwaith yr Anfarwol Fardd Dewi Wyn (Mr. Dafydd Owen,) o Eifion* (2nd edn., Caernarfon, 1869), atodiad, pp. 5–6; 'Y Parch. Thomas Evans, Aberdar', 81–3; T. C. U., 'Y Parch. Tomos Glyn Cothi (1769[*sic*]–1833)', *Yr Ymofynydd*, cyfres newydd, XIV, rhif 29 (1890), 113; 'Can Rhyddid', in *Nodion am y Parch. Thos. Evans (Glyn Cothi)*, pp. 4–5. I owe the first reference to Cathryn Charnell-White.

[80] This meant, judging by the contemporary definition of 'y crochenydd' (the potter), that the translator was a minister of God, like Tomos Glyn Cothi. See *Geiriadur Ysgrythyrol; yn Cynnwys Arwyddocad Geiriau Anghyfiaith, ynghyd ac Enwau ac Hanesion yr Amrywiol Genedloedd, Teyrnasoedd, a Dinasoedd . . . Y Llyfr Cyntaf* (Bala, 1805) s.v. 'Cro'.

[81] Geraint H. Jenkins claimed authorship for Iolo Morganwg on the basis of a remark in a letter by J. S. Estlin, see note 61, and E. G. Millward did the same for Tomos Glyn Cothi on the basis of his singing 'Cân Rhyddid' at the 'bid-ale' which led to the accusation of sedition against him. See E. G. Millward (gol.), *Blodeugerdd Barddas o Gerddi Rhydd y Ddeunawfed Ganrif* (Llandybïe, 1991), pp. 265–6, 332.

[82] D. Lleufer Thomas, 'Iolo Morganwg a Thomas [*sic*] Glyn Cothi', *Yr Ymofynydd*, cyfres newydd, XX, rhif 101 (1896), 129.

[83] NLW 6238A, 'Y Gell Gymysg', ff. 215–26, 279, 342–6; 'Traethawd o Hanes Bywyd y Diweddar Barch. Thomas Evans (Tomos Glyn Cothi,) Aberdar', in *Gardd Aberdar*, p. 105.

[84] For further international versions of the 'Marseillaise', see Vovelle, 'II. La Marseillaise: War or Peace', pp. 66–72.

[85] 'Song. Adapted to the original Music of the Marseillois Hymn', *Chester Chronicle*, 7 October 1803; Old Nick, 'The Britons March, Or, the Marche des Marseillois Parodied', in *The Antigallican* (London, 1804), pp. 201–2. I owe both references to Elizabeth Edwards.

[86] '58. To Edward Fergus Graham [Undated apparently drafted after 19 June 1811]', in Roger Ingpen (ed.), *The Letters of Percy Bysshe Shelley Containing Material never before Collected* (new edn., 2 vols., London, 1915), I, pp. 100–1.

[87] Williams (ed.), *National Songs and Poetical Pieces*, pp. 36–40. The volume also contained songs for countries like Switzerland and Scotland, and 'To Poland. From the Mountains of Wales', pp. 43–4.

[88] Ibid., pp. 38–9.

[89] Ibid., pp. 36–7, 39–40.

[90] 'The Marseillaise', in The Aberdare Socialist Society, *A Complimentary Banquet to Keir Hardie, M.P., 1 March 1901* (Aberdare, 1901).

[91] 'Hymn Marseillaise: Geiriau gan Mynyddog. Cynghaneddwyd gan Isalaw', *Y Cerddor Cymreig*, II, rhif 130 (1871), 333–6.

[92] W. C. Elvet Thomas, *Tyfu'n Gymro* (Llandysul, 1972), pp. 112–13. I owe this reference to Meic Birtwistle, Trefenter.

[93] Robert Bryan, 'Caneuon a Chaniadau Rhyfel', *Y Cerddor*, XXVI, no. 312 (1914), 129.

The 'Rural Voltaire' and the 'French madcaps'

GERAINT H. JENKINS

Among the many commercially astute natives of Cardiganshire who went up to London in the late eighteenth century was Evan Williams. One of five sons born to a blacksmith and a Methodist exhorter, Williams had sat at the feet of Edward Richard, the celebrated classical scholar and poet, at Ystradmeurig and gained a reputation as a shrewd and enterprising young man. In 1787, in partnership with his brother Thomas (who later became a banker), he set up a bookselling business at the Strand in London.[1] In all his dealings this arch-loyalist and churchman struck a hard bargain. Iolo Morganwg, who used to keep hefty tomes at hand to hurl at a bookseller's head, memorably described him as 'Skin-Devil-Williams, bookseller (or rather book-swindler) of the Strand'.[2] Williams gave politically radical works a wide berth and specialized in selling antiquarian books, bibles, maps, sermons and descriptions of tours, some of which were elegantly bound and were far beyond the means of the common reader. To Iolo's anguish, he liked to describe himself as 'bookseller to the Prince Regent, and to the Duke and Duchess of York'.[3] Not surprisingly, therefore, when Williams rather rashly invited the Glamorgan republican to edit a new Welsh journal to be called the *Cambrian Register* he was turned down.[4] Undeterred, Williams persuaded the already overworked William Owen Pughe to take up the editorial reins and to promise that its content would give no encouragement to Dissenters or Jacobins.

This ambitious undertaking roused considerable interest. Intrigued by its promise to contain 'every curious occurrences, both ancient and modern', Thomas Jones, an ebullient exciseman from Denbighshire who was living in Bristol by 1795, reckoned that 'if it keeps pace with the proposals' it might serve a useful purpose.[5] Aimed at zealous Cambro-Britons with disposable income, the periodical was designed to celebrate the ancient memorials of the Welsh and to 'enrich the fund of historical and antiquarian knowledge'.[6] In spite of the fanfare, however, the *Cambrian Register* was poorly received. William Owen Pughe was so overwhelmed with work that finding subscribers and drumming up articles proved to be a thoroughly depressing experience. Only three issues – in 1795 (published in 1796), 1796 (published in 1799) and 1818 – appeared and, as the editor confessed, its eventual demise was chiefly attributable to 'want of support'.[7] Even Evan Williams's nose for business and devious cunning could not save it.

In the first number a terse note recorded the death of William Jones, Llangadfan, a man 'noted for his skill in the treatment of the scrophula. He was a man of considerable reading and knowledge; a good Welsh poet, and philologist.'[8] In the difficult circumstances of wartime Britain, few would have expected the editor to add that the said William Jones was also a natural contrarian, a Jacobin free-thinker and a sworn enemy of every John Bull, English-speaking bishop and Calvinistic Methodist, as well as being a warm-hearted Welsh patriot. Always a model of discretion, Pughe did not broach such indelicate matters. Yet he made partial amends by publishing in the second issue 'A Sketch of the Life of William Jones',[9] an obituary penned by Walter Davies who, in London-Welsh circles, was better known by his bardic nom de plume Gwallter Mechain, which he derived from Llanfechain, his birthplace in Montgomeryshire.

The son of a craftsman, Davies served an apprenticeship as a cooper until he was twelve. His mother, who believed that he had the makings of a bishop, taught him to read and plied him with books. He mastered Latin, Greek and arithmetic at a local endowed free school, and gained a firm grasp of the rules of Welsh prosody at the feet of the tenant-farmer William Jones at Llangadfan. He set his heart on going to university and, with the financial assistance of the Gwyneddigion Society, enrolled as a student at St Alban Hall, Oxford, in 1791 and graduated from All Souls four years later, before gaining an MA from Trinity College, Cambridge, in 1803.[10] Davies revelled in these distinguished centres of learning and acquired a reputation as a 'hard-reading man' and something of a pedant.[11] He loved hobnobbing with the upper classes and fawning on those luminaries who helped to advance his ecclesiastical career. Convinced that his untutored countrymen could never achieve what privileged graduates aspired to and that the 'strong-winged genius' of Isaac Newton would never have soared had he been a Montgomeryshire man, he became a rather unpleasant snob.[12] Ordained in 1795, he climbed the ecclesiastical ladder, ministering at Meifod and Llan-wyddelan before becoming rector of Manafon in July 1807 where, over a period of thirty years, he basked in his reputation as the 'Sage of Manafon'.[13]

In cultural matters, too, Davies shamelessly curried favour with influential patrons. Happy to be bracketed with 'free-born' Englishmen, he championed the established order and supported the right of the State to institute punitive measures to protect the security of the realm. Fearful of the possible effects of Welsh-language versions of the *Rights of Man* or the libertarian subjects chosen by the Gwyneddigion Society for leading competitions in the revived eisteddfodau held from 1789 onwards, he supported the formation of loyalist associations in the county and, in a discursive essay on 'Rhyddid' (Liberty) at the St Asaph eisteddfod in 1790, he urged the Welsh to count their blessings, complain less, and thank their lucky stars that they inhabited a land in which the poor were granted the same protection as the rich.[14] He was none too scrupulous in winning public attention. Deep down he knew that he was an indifferent poet – to this day he is known as a one-stanza poet[15] – and he outraged his rivals when he gained an unfair advantage by persuading his London-Welsh allies, Owain Myfyr and William Owen Pughe, to forewarn him of the subjects chosen for supposedly impromptu declamations at eisteddfodau.[16] In the politically fraught year of 1798 he published a Welsh translation of John Bowdler's loyalist tract *Reform or Ruin: Take Your Choice*.[17] Walter Davies lived to be eighty-eight and over that long period his inflated view of himself was matched by his gritty attachment to crown, church and country.

In the light of Davies's political prejudices and his animus against supporters of the French Revolution, he was hardly the best qualified writer to pay tribute to his former mentor. William Owen Pughe must surely have guessed that he would cast the radical firebrand in an unfavourable light, especially since Davies was still smarting under the slights and injuries he had suffered at William Jones's hands. The obituary, riddled with omissions, evasions and half-truths, has been accurately described by Gwyn A. Williams as 'clever, witty and repulsive'.[18] It merits close attention because it tells us as much about the obituarist as his subject. While Davies expressed grudging admiration for the way in which William Jones had overcome the social obstacles of his upbringing and lack of formal education to become 'a scholar, a poet, and philosopher', his portrayal was mean-spirited and sometimes malevolent. Like most 'rustics', as Davies dubbed tenant-farmers and labourers, his parochialism had made him indolent and shiftless, while his mean appearance, uncouth demeanour and broken English betrayed his reluctance to engage with the outside world, soften his manners and be less critical of his superiors. His tendency to rake up the past, make invidious national distinctions and adopt 'the insinuating stile and specious reasonings of Voltaire' reflected his 'eccentric' and 'reprehensible' behaviour. According to Davies, his mentor had read some of the writings of Voltaire in early life and had admired them greatly. Indeed, he bore more than a passing physical resemblance to the French philosopher, so much so that he became known as the '*Rural Voltaire*'.[19] He shared Voltaire's hatred of religious intolerance and political oppression, became known as a mimic and satirist, and generally made a nuisance of himself. Harshly, Davies concluded that the career of this misanthrope showed very clearly 'how men are led into error by false and partial conceptions of things; by an obstinate attachment to one side of the question, without having prudence or candour, either to give ear to, or examine the apologies and arguments of the opposite party'.[20]

Even though the crusty old Jacobin had clearly teased and browbeaten his modestly gifted pupil on many occasions, that Davies should have written such an unpleasant account of his life and work was deeply regrettable. He clearly had misgivings about it. The sketch had been hastily written in three or four days, some fifteen months after William Jones's death, and, as Davies readily recognized, it had not struck a fair balance between Jones's virtues and shortcomings. On submitting it, he asked William Owen Pughe and Owain Myfyr to 'give it the smoothing plane, if not a total new arrangement'.[21] If the fair-minded Pughe did recast the obituary, then the original version must have been even harsher. But Pughe was always reluctant to interfere, even in matters as sensitive as this, and he would have known that the balance of the sympathies of his readers lay with Walter Davies.

Obituaries often colour the thinking of future generations and William Jones's posthumous reputation clearly suffered at the hands of his pupil. During the Victorian period writers were so anxious to portray the Welsh as a law-abiding, morally upright people[22] that a flinty, pleasure-loving rural Voltaire like William Jones was airbrushed out of the annals. Local antiquaries averted their eyes whenever they encountered his satirical and bawdy poems, and puritanical Nonconformists tut-tutted sternly whenever the infidel's name was mentioned. The result was that Gwilym Cadfan (to give him his pen name as a poet) was repackaged as a poet and an antiquary. That is how he is described in the *Dictionary of Welsh Biography* and articles in scholarly journals usually depict him as a rather eccentric, if many-sided, literary figure.[23] Only comparatively recently has this benign mask been removed to reveal a decidedly unrespectable plebeian radical and libertarian.[24] During the age of revolutions, and especially after the fall of the Bastille, he emerged as one of the most vigorous defenders of republican principles, *sans-culottism* and religious toleration in Wales. 'Of a Deist', wrote Thomas Jones the exciseman of him, 'he is the firmest friend I ever met with – a'r mwya' tin-boeth a'r welais i erioed (and the hottest-arsed I ever saw).'[25]

Within the context of the French Revolution in Wales, the uniqueness of William Jones lies in the fact that, as far as we know, he was the only

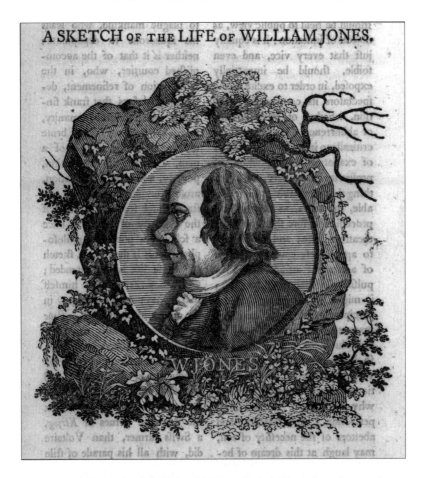

Figure 6. 'A Sketch of the Life of William Jones'. Unattributed engraving
from *Cambrian Register*, II (1799).

Welsh tenant-farmer to speak up loudly for the rights of man, to attack
inequality and privilege in church and state, and to express his independent-
mindedness in spiritual and moral spheres. The tiny band of radicalized
plebeian Welshmen in the 1790s were generally artisans and craftsmen. Iolo
Morganwg was a stonemason, for instance, and Tomos Glyn Cothi a weaver.
Both men prided themselves on their independence and their freedom,
insofar as the government allowed them, to express liberal and egalitarian
sentiments. William Jones's circumstances were rather different and the
manner in which this tenant on the Wynnstay estate emerged as an advocate
of heterodox ideas and French Revolutionary ideals is an intriguing story
in itself.

For the most part, William Jones's early life is shrouded in mystery. Baptized in Llangadfan parish church on 18 June 1726, he was the youngest of three sons born to William John David (1666–1758) and his second wife Catherine (1686–1760). When his elder stepbrother, William Siôn Dafydd of Bwlch Llety Griffith, died in December 1750, he was persuaded by his father to take up the tenancy of Dolhywel, a 57-acre farm owned by the Wynns of Wynnstay and located in the parish of Llangadfan, close to Cwm Nant-yr-eira.[26] By this stage he had acquired the reading habit even though, having been 'born, bred & confined in this obscure corner',[27] he was forced to spend most of his time eking out a bare living husbanding sheep and cattle on barren upland wastes and boggy marshland:

> Here is but a small quantity of level ground, being but narrow slips along the sides of the rivers. The soil on the rising ground is but thin, lying chiefly on a stiff clay, or a brittle slate; and most commonly so poor as not to be capable of producing any manner of corn and without paring, burning or being well manured. About one third part of the country is an uncultivated waste, which is likely to continue in that state, a great part thereof being moorish or boggy.[28]

His wife Ann, whom he married in 1756, bore him a son (William) and two daughters (Elizabeth and Ann) before falling victim to a debilitating illness which confined her to her bed until her death in 1774. For Jones and many other small farmers, earning a living on such inhospitable terrain, often in wet, stormy and cold weather, was an exhausting challenge and one which he resented keenly, not least because it kept him from his beloved books and 'the pleasure of conversing with men of knowledge'.[29]

Yet we should not exaggerate the social isolation of upland communities in which the daily language was Welsh. In William Jones's heyday it was much easier to venture by coach, carriage and horseback into rural Montgomery-shire than it had been in Tudor and Stuart times. Living in Llangadfan did not mean that he was necessarily isolated from the world of print or from the ferment which accompanied the American and French revolutions. His papers reveal detailed knowledge of the locality and his essay on the social features of the parishes of Llanerfyl, Llangadfan and Garthbeibio shows that he was a perceptive and well-informed observer. But he yearned for more reading matter and wider horizons. One critically important link with the wider world was Cann Office, a staging post at Llangadfan on the main road from London to Holyhead and from Shrewsbury to Aberystwyth. Local patriots used to believe that its origins lay buried in the medieval past, but Cann Office was the name given by 1662 to the Tynydomen inn which had become a staging post that sported the sign 'The Three Cans'.[30] William

Jones's father had served as a guard on the stage coaches which rattled noisily through the parish and at Cann Office he eagerly awaited a supply of letters, books, pamphlets, newspapers and ballads sent to him by his friends in Shrewsbury and London. He also often met Walter Davies and William Owen Pughe there. He read voraciously, steeping himself in astronomy and physics, geography, topography, history, music and philosophy. The Celtic scholarship of Edward Lhuyd, the poems of Milton and the civilization of the Incas were all grist to his mill.[31] He immersed himself in etymology, lexicography and orthography, wrote a Welsh grammar,[32] and, with admirable common sense, showed how the Celtic languages had a common origin but were then 'separately cultivated, or moulded, according to the state of knowledge and genius of the nations speaking them'.[33]

But in order to slake his thirst for literature he needed additional sources of income. During his boyhood he had contracted scrofula, a hideous disease popularly known as 'the King's Evil' since it was thought that the king's touch was the only reliable cure. Sores, blisters and tumours disfigured his body and after so-called reputable physicians had been found wanting he resorted to self-medication and healed himself by placing the powder of half-burnt rags on the tumours.[34] Having read as many medical treatises as he could and familiarized himself with herbal lore, he became a part-time country healer and ventured as far afield as Oswestry, Shrewsbury and London to attend the sick, especially objects of charity. Sickness and pain were endemic in Georgian Wales and there was no shortage of work for itinerant nostrum-mongers whose pills and potions helped to soothe or cure ailments. William Jones broadcast his particular expertise in a handbill printed by Stafford Prys, a master-printer at Shrewsbury:

> To the Publick, William Jones of *Llangadfan, Montgomeryshire,* having (in the Course of twenty Years diligent Research into the Nature and Practice of Physick) discovered a safe and effectual method of cure for the King's Evil, whether hereditary or adventitious, now offers his Service to all who shall think proper to apply for his advice and Assistance. Whereas 'tis generally thought that the Evil is never radically cured; Any Person entertaining such an Opinion may be convinced to the contrary by being referred to many in *Montgomeryshire, Merioneth-shire* and *London,* who were perfectly cured of that distemper; none having ever relapsed who observed his Rules and Directions. He cures likewise *Fistulous* and *running Ulcers,* the *Fistula Lachrymalis* and other Disorders of the *Eyes,* glandulous *Tumors,* Oedematous and *Dropsical Swellings,* white *Swellings* of the *Joints, Rheumatick,* fixt and wandering Pains, and many other Diseases Incident to human *Bodies.*[35]

Like many untrained healers, he knew how to promote himself and his wares, patching together 'some intellectual credibility from whatever shreds and tatters he could'.[36] Whenever sceptics mocked his methods and questioned his competence, he used to pull up his shirt and point to the scars which allegedly bore witness to his success in conquering scrofula.[37] He, for his part, told tales of the ham-fisted and maladroit failures of trained physicians. For a fee of half a guinea each, three surgeons (or 'men carpenters' as Jones dubbed them) had advised the son of William Rowland of Peniarth that there was no alternative but to amputate his injured foot. The distraught family immediately called for the Llangadfan healer and, having cured the son, he was rewarded with the measly sum of five shillings. 'I shall soon become rich', he wrote drily, 'Thus am I frequently used for want of being legally qualified. Blessed be the Aristocracies!! and the Constitution, magna Diana Ephesorum.'[38] He did not consider himself to be a quack. Indeed, he loathed the stigma attached to the word and bristled whenever he encountered the dubious nostrums – 'suitable Hogwash for the swinish multitude'[39] – peddled by charlatans. He stubbornly refused to comply with the Medicine Duties Act of 1785 which obliged him to apply for a licence to operate as a quack, thereby, as he sarcastically commented, enabling him to 'kill as many as I please cum privilegio Regis', and continued to serve the local community by purging, blood-letting, excising tumours, extracting teeth and plying paupers with copious amounts of buttermilk.[40] Nothing ever came of his plan to publish a book of household remedies,[41] but he always relished the opportunity to take time out from his tedious routine on the farm to visit the sick, enjoy convivial company and cultivate romantic, even lewd, liaisons in a variety of watering-holes on the borders and as far afield as London. William Jones was assuredly not the stay-at-home depicted in Walter Davies's obituary. Outgoing, outward-looking and convivial, his idea of happiness was strong drink, lively company and a pretty girl on his knee. A Voltairean could not live by draining, hedging, carting and herding alone.

During his travels he sampled the tavern-based culture of different towns and cities. A widower at forty-eight, his papers are full of accounts, real and imagined, of amorous adventures, bawdy poems and lewd tittle-tattle. 'I am sometimes fond of fun',[42] he cried as he ventured into the shadowy under-world of alehouses, cellars and brothels where 'unrespectable' plebeians gathered to flirt and ogle, sing raucous songs, crack obscene jokes and generally let off steam.[43] It was a world familiar to many of the men who frequented the Cymmrodorion and, more especially the Gwyneddigion, societies. On his visits to London and to eisteddfodau in north-east Wales he would have heard David Samwell's tales about the promiscuous habits of the Tahitians;[44] Iolo Morganwg, whom he met at Oxford and corresponded with, might well have acquainted him with his bawdy 'Cân Morfudd i'r

Gyllell Gig' (Morfudd's Song to the Meat Knife).[45] Many of Jones's own pieces are exuberantly libidinous, full of suggestive references to pen-knives and staffs.[46] One of his most audacious poems, 'The enraptur'd lover to the Tune of Jack ye Latin', a work redolent of Lewis Morris's song to 'The Fishing Lass of Hakin', is published fully here for the first time:

> In Pool there lives a pretty Lass
> I promise that my Jenny
> In mien & beauty doth surpass
> The brightest Dames of Guinea
> She is so swift in ev'ry drift
> There's not a Devil can catch her
> Nor 'ere an Elf but Nick himself
> In lying can over match her.
>
> Her snotty nose & drooping eyes
> And charming monkey features
> Have taken my fancy by surprise
> Most loving of all creatures!
> When in the dark I'll want no mark
> As I shall never miss her
> Her bum will crack at every smack
> When I'll attempt to kiss her.
>
> My love I'll swear is monstrous fair
> In Town there's not her fellow
> With the Devill she may compare
> In tawny black & yellow
> Her froglike voice makes me rejoyce
> Whene'er I hear her squeaking
> How sweet she screams when in her dreams
> She wants to stop her leaking.
>
> A Fireship full rigg'd & man'd
> In glorious warlike order
> May put my courage at a stand
> When I'll attempt to board her
> But when she reels upon her heels
> Most sweetly drench'd in Liquor
> And like a Sled is dragg'd to bed
> I'll have a chance to nick her.

Her empty scull is like a Bell
That's in a miller's hopper
Her lolling tongue I know full well
Will suit it for a clapper
She try'd her fate at Billing's gate
And off she came victorious
And top'd the shrews in all the stews
Her actions all are glorious.

To you my merry lads of Pool
I recommend my Doxy
I am not a jealous fool
That will not woo by proxy
If you'll adorn me with a Horn
As nature may invite you
I vow I will not take it ill
Your serv^t. sirs good bye t' you.[47]

Even when he was a greybeard of sixty-five, he sang of his desires for a young girl in a manner which would have been more familiar to Moll Flanders than Lady Huntingdon.[48] In poems like these, reflecting 'a tradition of plebeian unrespectability and irreverence',[49] Jones cocked a snook at the culture of politeness.

In other, more important, fields, William Jones also set his face against prevailing ideals and modes of conduct. Uniquely in the deeply deferential county of Montgomeryshire, he risked his own livelihood as a tenant-farmer by showing his contempt for the behaviour of the landed gentry and their villainous agents and stewards. Over the course of the eighteenth century the socio-economic gulf between the affluent landed gentry and the lower orders widened markedly. Of the 132 estates with resident owners in the county in the 1690s, only twenty-three had survived by 1810.[50] Estates had become larger units and the smaller proprietors had slipped down the social scale as a result of biological failures (male heirs had become a rare commodity), crippling mortgages, improvidence and heavy drinking.[51] The most powerful estate owners in the county were the Powis and Wynnstay families and under their watch the mood changed appreciably in the rural countryside from the 1770s onwards. At his bleak upland farm in Llangadfan William Jones kept a close eye on how the Wynns of Wynnstay, his absentee masters, asserted their dominion over their patrimonies. When Sir Watkin Williams Wynn, third baronet of Wynnstay, had married Anne Vaughan, the future heiress of Llwydiarth, Llangedwyn and Glanllyn, in 1719, the Wynnstay estate had replaced Llwydiarth as the most influential force in the Llangadfan area.[52]

Indeed, the Wynnstay influence radiated over seven counties in north Wales and the borders, and it was commonly said that the peasantry only committed themselves to any course of action if it pleased God and the Wynns of Wynnstay. Under the third baronet, the Tory and Jacobite sympathizer known as the 'Great Sir Watkin',[53] the family began to employ hard-headed, ruthless agents to advance their territorial and political interests. Since the fourth baronet was a dilettante, more interested in the fine arts, Druidism and music than in auditing his accounts (he had run up debts of £160,000 by 1789), he allowed his estate agents to flout age-old conventions.[54] Three-life leases were replaced by annual tenancies at rack rent. Between 1770 and 1800 rents in general were raised by up to 50 per cent on Montgomeryshire estates and this led to an erosion of trust and confidence between landlord and tenant.[55] Critics maintained that 'Great Self'[56] was the primary consideration of landed Titans and William Jones roundly condemned their 'insatiable avarice'.[57] The ten pounds which he paid in rent to the Wynns of Wynnstay in 1786 had trebled by 1795,[58] and he laid much of the blame on unscrupulous and unfeeling agents.

Chief among them was Francis Chambre of Oswestry whose disagreeable nature ensured that Sir Watkin's name became a synonym for 'Tyrant' and 'Oppressor'. Chambre was determined to screw every single penny of rent from tenants, no matter what their personal circumstances might be. Although he conceded that adverse seasons in 1780–2 had occasioned 'a time of scarcity that memory can scarcely equal',[59] his clunking fist slammed down on tenants who defaulted or expressed their disaffection. Over the summer of 1783 tenants in Oswestry were served with notices to quit in order 'to make some few Individuals know themselves a little better than they do at present and to convince them the property they enjoy is yours [i.e. Sir Watkin Williams Wynn IV] & not theirs, & that they shou'd pay you what another thankfully wou'd, and not lay claim to your indulgence'.[60] Infuriated, William Jones wrote in December 1786 directly to the fourth baronet to remind him that his 'renowned father' had happily received letters and petitions in Welsh from penurious tenants, had replied in Welsh in his own hand, and had done all within his power to redress their grievances. But the callous and unforgivable deeds of Wynnstay agents in recent years had tarnished the reputation of the family among 'your poor Tenants in the mountainous parts of this country':

May the Distresses of a number of laborious families subsisting on coarse fare, cultivating an ungrateful soil, & driven to the grievous alternative of quitting the country or sooner or later be reduced to beggary, be taken into your own immediate consideration. Cruelly rack'd, harrass'd, insulted & oppressed by an

insidious circumvention bordering very near on fraud & extortion, not daring
to complain least it compleat their ruin by drawing upon them the resentment
of haughty and insolent superiors who might, on a slight pretence, let loose upon
them their rapacious Bailiffs Bums etc Bullies to make a havoc of their property
& plunge them in a few Days into the utmost Distress & Poverty.[61]

It is inconceivable that Chambre would have allowed such a pungent letter
to be read by Sir Watkin and, following the latter's death in the year of the
French Revolution, the abusive practices continued. Many commentators
noted what they saw as a decline in gentry circles of natural affection and
noblesse oblige. Agents were allowed to act with impunity, with the result
that growing numbers of innocent people were 'bending their heads to the
heavy Yoke of rack rents, poor rates and many other ponderous impositions,
and charity long ago has been kicked out of doors, and scarcely considered
any more as a virtue'.[62]

Those who believed in justice, rights and human dignity also had little
cause to feel heartened by the state of politics in Montgomeryshire. Conservative diehards praised the political somnolence of the county. The ruling
clique held the political reins and very few adult males were entitled to vote.
Contested elections were so infrequent that many of the enfranchised lived
and died without ever having the opportunity to go to the polls. On the
surface, peace and harmony reigned, and the bitterly fought county election
in 1774 was something of a landmark simply because of its novelty.[63] The
Powis Castle interest prevailed – at great financial cost – on that occasion,
though the Wynnstay interest soon recovered its monopoly and held a
stranglehold on the seat from 1799 until 1880.[64] Sir Watkin's agents had
unnerved voters during the 1774 election by employing hard-line coercion.
Freeholders were reminded of the burdensome duties involved in seeking
assessment for the land tax or were threatened with the withdrawal of ancient
rights to graze sheep or cut peat on common lands located on the Wynnstay
estate. Challenging the Titans of Wynnstay could have ruinous consequences,
as William Jones would discover.

The monopoly exercised by the landed élite also had important cultural
consequences. In their pursuit of land, wealth and their own personal
pleasures, the Wynns were generally heedless of the status and fortunes of
the Welsh language and the indigenous literary culture. Convinced that 'our
own Anglified gentry' thought of Welsh as a coarse patois fit only for peasants,
Jones sarcastically referred to those who, 'suckled by English nurses whose
milk transubstantiated them', were more than happy to be called 'mere
Englishmen'.[65] Native literary heritage was undervalued and, in a bid to
rescue some of the manuscript treasures left to moulder in gentry homes,

he offered his services to leading figures among the London Welsh as a collector and transcriber of words, songs and antiquities. He was well placed to undertake this work. Fluent in Welsh and English, he had a sufficient grasp of Latin to enable him to translate into Welsh parts of Ovid's *Metamorphoses* and odes by Horace. He was steeped in the Welsh poetic tradition and could compose *cywyddau* and *carolau plygain*.[66] A skilful violinist, he was a connoisseur of Welsh dances.[67] He was known to Welsh-language luminaries like Rhys Jones Blaenau, Twm o'r Nant, Edward Jones 'Bardd y Brenin' (the King's Bard), Owain Myfyr, William Owen Pughe and Iolo Morganwg, all of whom considered him a prickly but immensely able man. His poverty and sufferings were also well-known to relatively affluent expatriates who, though conscious of his apparent inability to toe the line, felt that he deserved support. One generous ally was Pughe, who received from Jones a regular supply of words and phrases in common use on the Welsh borders as well as names of subscribers for his proposed dictionary.[68]

William Jones's main client, however, was Edward Jones, of Llandderfel, Merioneth, who went up to London *c*.1774 to follow a career as a harpist and harp tutor.[69] As he entertained prosperous Londoners in concerts and soirées, he learned how to bow and scrape, ingratiating himself with the likes of Fanny Burney and, more significantly, the Prince of Wales, to whom he became the King's Bard when he ascended to the throne in 1820. His musical talents were somewhat uninspiring – Iolo Morganwg memorably dubbed him 'Humstrum Jones'[70] – and he was also known as a literary scavenger and a plagiarizer. Yet he did some sterling work in preserving traditional Welsh music. Adept at persuading others to work on his behalf, he recruited William Jones and indeed paid him handsomely for visiting private libraries and transcribing a large corpus of musical and literary material which was incorporated into *The Musical and Poetical Relicks of the Welsh Bards* (1784) and in a revised edition published in 1794. For Jones's part, this search for manuscripts spurred an intense interest in their preservation. He devoted as much time as he could spare to visiting private libraries to seek out old manuscripts for his patrons in London. He was turned away at Wynnstay and cursed loudly when he discovered that priceless material had been removed to Jesus College, Oxford, to be held as 'perpetual prisoners'[71] there. Many landowners believed that Welsh manuscripts were worthless. At Cyfronnydd a maidservant was ordered to burn such trash in an oven, while at an auction held at Rhiwsaeson manuscripts which contained the poems of Dafydd ap Gwilym were sold for a measly groat. At Melin-y-grug an eleventh-century Latin concordance was tossed into a river. William Jones was enraged by such wanton neglect: 'In this lamentable manner we are bereaved of the pleasure of the works of our ancestors.'[72] No longer could he pin his faith on the landed gentry, for evidently few of them cared a fig for the Welsh language and its associated culture.

He was also beginning to despair of the capacity of the Established Church to protect and nurture Welsh-language worship. Nigel Yates has argued that the image of the Hanoverian church in Wales as an agent of Anglicization was nothing more than 'a fiction'.[73] This verdict would have greatly surprised Welshmen like Evan Evans, Richard Morris and Iolo Morganwg, all of whom were convinced that the Established Church was desperately seeking to shed its Welshness. Why else would a group of hard-working clerics like Walter Davies, John Jenkins, W. J. Rees and others have come together at the turn of the eighteenth century to promote a cultural agenda designed to Cymricize an ailing institution?[74] Time and again the point was made that prelates in Wales were a pale shadow of their Welsh-born predecessors who had conscientiously ministered to the needs of Welsh speakers in Tudor and early Stuart times. During William Jones's lifetime he was denied the opportunity of conversing in Welsh with any of the bishops of St Asaph. Following the translation of John Wynne to the diocese of Bath and Wells in 1727, the see became home to ten bishops between 1727 and 1802, none of whom was Welsh. All of them were well-educated, distinguished and perhaps well-meaning men, but they were remote from their flocks, prone to install their own nominees in lucrative posts and at best indifferent to the well-being of the native tongue. Some of them were openly contemptuous of the Welsh language. Robert Hay Drummond, an unlikeable Scot, devoted a good deal of time to persuading monoglot Welsh people that it was in their true interests to learn English. Embracing English at the expense of their own language would 'enlarge their views and notions', and enable them 'to unite with the rest of their fellow-subjects in language, as well as government'.[75] His successor Richard Newcome also ascribed superior status to the English tongue and it was during his watch (1761–9) that Evan Evans felt the need to thunder and rage against those 'oppressive strangers', 'ravenous wolves' and 'useless rogues' who were bringing his beloved church into disrepute.[76]

During these years, too, churchmen throughout Wales and among the London Welsh were scandalized by what became known as 'the Bowles affair'.[77] In 1766 John Egerton, bishop of Bangor, inexplicably appointed Thomas Bowles, an English septuagenarian who spoke no Welsh, to minister to the needs of the parishes of Trefdraeth and Llangwyfan in Anglesey, where virtually everyone spoke and understood only Welsh. Evan Evans referred to the egregious Bowles as 'y Sais brych' (the mottled Englishman)[78] and the appointment provided further evidence that the status of Welsh as the language of religion in Wales was under threat, even in its major heartland.

When the new rector alienated his flock by ministering in polished English and also wilfully deceiving his churchwardens, a suit was brought against him in the Court of Arches. Here his advocates let the cat out of the bag by insisting that 'Wales is a conquered country, it is proper to introduce the English language, and it is the duty of the bishops to promote the English, in order to introduce the language.'[79] William Jones was so incensed by this blatant example of linguistic imperialism that he denounced prelates for foisting on the Welsh 'their voracious offspring, like so many wasps, to suck the sweet fruits of the labours of others' ('eu gwehilion gwangcus fel cynnifer o gaccwn geifr i sugno melusdra ffrwythau llafur eraill').[80] In his own diocese, the tradition of having resident pastors with close connections with the Welsh-speaking majority was increasingly flouted. Newcomers called Baker, Newcome and Tamberlain were 'planted' in vacant livings in Montgomery-shire and were encouraged to promote the English language.[81] As Eryn M. White has clearly shown, the effects of creeping Anglicization may be seen in the provision of church services in Montgomeryshire by c.1810: 47 per cent of services were in Welsh, 30 per cent were in English and 23 per cent were bilingual.[82]

Yet the mother church remained an extremely powerful institution. The number of regular worshippers might have been declining, but it was still reckoned to offer the only legitimate and reliable means of personal salvation. Even in 1791 the parish of Llangadfan had no Dissenters or Roman Catholics.[83] To the overwhelming majority, the Established Church was still the guardian of the true faith and however much William Jones might have loathed absentee bishops and their favourites he was even more hostile to the contagious enthusiasm associated with Calvinistic Methodism. Although Howel Harris, the most dynamic of the early enthusiasts, had been given a cool reception in the county, his converts had managed to establish around twenty societies by 1750. Little further ground was made, however, and when Harris resumed his evangelical tours in the 1760s he discovered that country folk were still antagonistic to his harshly worded sermons and overbearing manner. 'Who ever heard of our Saviour sitting in a chaise!'[84] they cried. Although William Jones genuinely loathed the 'strange fire' emitted by Methodist preachers, his hostility towards them was based on their self-righteous attitudes, their morbid obsession with sin, and their prejudice against 'head knowledge' and rational thought. He joined forces with Harri Parry, a diminutive poet from Craig-y-gath, Llanfihangel-yng-Ngwynfa, in exposing in verse the hypocrisy and cant practised by these Pharisees.[85] Both were aware of Howel Harris's scandalous liaison with the self-styled prophetess Madam Sydney Griffith, and joined other writers in depicting the young enthusiasts as philanderers who preyed on credulous

young women and lured them into darkened houses to indulge in forni-
cation.[86] A bawdy satirist like Jones was instinctively critical of the extent
to which such alleged hypocrites breached their own ethical code:

> Da gan sant os caiff fantais
> Dynu y boen o dan bais
> Poen fydd ar dduwiol pan fô
> Ei ganol yn egino
> A byd syn ydyw bôd sant
> Yn methu trechu trachwant.[87]
>
> (A saint will gladly take advantage
> by seeking relief under a petticoat
> the pious feels the pain
> when his erection sprouts
> and a strange world it is that a saint
> cannot conquer lust.)

Jones also resented the fact that Methodist exhorters maintained that traditional Welsh dances were the work of the Devil. Sanctimonious evangelists
were perfectly happy to witness their own followers leaping in praise of the
Lord, but drew the line at watching earthy dances performed by the vulgar
sorts. 'The Charms of Music' are many,[88] claimed Jones, and he prepared
detailed descriptions of feisty Welsh dances which his father had taught him
during his youth. To the accompaniment of tunes like 'The Roaring Horn-
pipe', 'Aly Grogan' and 'The Galloping Nag', these dances made heavy
physical demands on participants and served to enliven communal festivities.[89]
The young Ann Griffiths of Dolwar Fach was, during Jones's lifetime, as
yet untouched by the evangelical cause and preferred to dance the night
away in nosweithiau llawen. Had Jones lived to read her impassioned hymns
he might have admired them, but he would certainly have deplored her
conversion from a dance-loving girl into a Methodist hymnist. With some
feeling, he wrote: 'the Enthusiasm of the Methodists together with the tyranny of the Landowners have spread an universal gloom over the country'.[90]
When Walter Davies was unwise enough to sympathize with the new
enthusiasts Jones mocked him in a clever macaronic poem entitled 'The
Pedant's Soliloquy or the Owl's Dream':

> In School bûm nes cael bôd
> In Skill Hector 'Scolheigtod
> Alpha, Beta, jota, well!
> Gamma in Hebrew Gimel
> Mine Hebrew mae yn o brin
> Mine Greeg mae'n o gregin

Lag lag lag gag gag o gêg
I Ddiawl dyna Wyddeleg
Diawl etto ond yw Latin
Fel plû yn tyfu om tîn
Omnibus stercus bestow
Item dyna ladin etto
Gibberish or English wrangling
Begad Sirs dat be good sing.
In mine addle brain mae'n odli
Noun mood mine Awen me
Bara gwyn heb eiriau gwâd
A menyn yw nymuniad
Myn tân wel dyna ganu
A lâdd o brydyddion lu!
Cael caws ar ei draws ryw dro?
Item dyna ganu etto
Clul clol, sâl siol, bwl breles
Clolyn a lolyn di lês.[91]

William Jones had a special gift for satire, and the exciseman Thomas Jones believed that he seldom missed an opportunity to mock his enemies: 'O! fel y tru ei weflau a'i lygaid – os gwel o achos i Satyr ymddangos – dyna fo yn y munud yn ei ddewis Elfen' (Oh! How his lips and eyes turn – if he sees the need for a satire to appear – he is at once in his element).[92] But by the coming of the French Revolution his writings had acquired a more strident political edge. Over the years the works of Voltaire had influenced his tone and style and had emboldened him to champion civil liberties. So had the American Revolution. Gwyn A. Williams maintained that he had already become 'a spiritual American',[93] but his interest in the New World was largely triggered by the Madog legend and the possibility that Welsh-speaking Indians still existed there. Far more significant in his political development, however, was the thrilling news which arrived from France in the summer of 1789. To him, the French Revolution seemed to open the way to comprehensive change in society. His correspondence with the likes of Walter Davies and William Owen Pughe in the early 1790s reveals that he felt that he no longer had anything to gain by holding his tongue. If he was not in a position to contribute to the popular print culture of the day, he reckoned that he could play a significant part by composing odes on freedom and oppression, singing on the rights of man and seeking to politicize fellow-poets and correspondents.[94] In a Wales beset with loyalists and time-servers, he spoke out fearlessly of his admiration for the French for 'defending the natural privilege of mankind' ('amddiffyn braint naturiol dynolryw').[95] A few months before the fall of the Bastille he celebrated in verse the king's recovery from his first bout of madness, but he also used the occasion to remind the sovereign of his duty to 'his mean subjects . . . to relieve the innocents . . . and support the weak'.[96] His tone became more trenchant in the wake of the success of the French insurgents. All over Europe, he cried, distressed people yearned to be freed from the shackles of despotism. The images of liberty – liberty trees, caps, Tom Paine's *Rights of Man* – caught his imagination and he looked forward to the day when a Welsh Paine 'screeched in Wales' ('ysgrechian ynghymru').[97]

Absentee landowners and their agents had become, in Voltairean language, 'the despicable tools of Despotism' and society had become divided between oppressors and slaves, shearers and feeders.[98] In the eyes of their masters, the swinish multitude were 'brutes' who spoke a tiresome jargon and were destined either to remain in a state of slavish dependence or be 'shoved by Devils into the sea to be drown'd or slaughtered'.[99] In a passage included in an undated letter to William Owen Pughe, he was scathing about the manner in which landowners and agents were making life unbearable for tenant farmers like himself:

> . . . these primary planets [landed gentry] or blazing stars move eastward (as usually contrary to the heavens) towards the capital in quest of places, preferments, plays, or ladies of pleasure, and leave us under the malignant influence of their satellites, the supercilious and insolent agents and bailiffs; these rapacious cormorants, not satisfied with open racking, frequently join the fox tail to the bear's claw to make use of base circumstances to fleece us more effectually; and if tenants cannot make prompt paiment on fix't days, a train of Bums bailiffs and other understrappers will be let loose upon them . . .[100]

Those who dared raise a cry of protest were swiftly silenced by these merciless taskmasters and 'told in a true Aegyptian phrase "that we are idle"'.[101] While affluent landlords had all the comforts they required, the lower orders were suffering great hardships as a result of inflated grain prices, steep rent increases, exorbitant tithe demands and various other indignities.[102] William Jones, now at the end of his tether, informed everyone prepared to listen that he would no longer serve tyrants by draining bogs, planting crops and refurbishing his property.[103]

He had also become thoroughly disenchanted with the insensitivities of the Anglican establishment. Having served as a churchwarden and an overseer of the poor in the past, he no longer worshipped at St Cadfan's church. He vigorously advocated rational inquiry – Thomas Jones the exciseman dubbed him a deist[104] – and the presence of a so-called 'rural Voltaire' in the fastnesses

of Montgomeryshire increasingly disturbed orthodox Christians. Matthew
Worthington, the absentee rector of Llangadfan, pursued him relentlessly
and informed his parishioners that the 'rank Republican' who dwelt among
them was determined to level society and reduce him personally to the status
of 'a poor scrub of a Curate'. He longed for an opportunity to empty his
shotgun in his direction.[105] Jones responded by attacking the 'Soulslaving'
trade of 'the Tithing Tribe' whose dissimulation, rapaciousness and tyranny
were a scandal to the Christian religion. Small wonder, he claimed, that the
'French madcaps' had renounced it.[106] As Welsh-speaking clerics were passed
over in favour of monoglot English 'blockheads' from Oxford and Cambridge,
the once widely admired and cherished *fam eglwys* (mother church) had
become a thoroughly discredited institution.[107] Just as odious in his eyes was
the 'abominable methodistical jargon'[108] peddled by Calvinistic Methodists
– 'the most pestiferous & enthusiastic of all sects'[109] – who demonized him
at every opportunity. Writing to Walter Davies, he was both vulnerable and
defiant:

To be short, there exists not a more piteable Biped than your humble Servant
– not a little, not a bit of comfort left, for this world nor the next; you too well
know that I have offended the Elect in these parts sometime ago & am excluded
for ever from the Lists of saints which are so regularly kept here, that the Book
of Life is to be, as it were, a transcript of the methodistical Registers. As for my
temporal affairs, Bad enough![110]

Those who believed in fostering a sense of Britishness also found him
obstinate. Jones was fully aware that the French had proclaimed the doctrine
of the sovereignty of the nation in 1789 and, as his brushes with authority
became more frequent, he furiously denounced those Saxon and Norman
usurpers who had robbed the Welsh of their land and liberties. He deplored
the 'belchings' of English historians who were 'reviler[s] of our nation',
expressed his commitment to liberty by singing 'Ça Ira' and 'La Marseillaise'
in his drinking dens, and reacted against loyalist anthems like 'God Save the
King' and 'Rule Britannia' by composing a Welsh national anthem – 'Toriad
y Dydd' (Daybreak) – which, with its rousing refrain 'Fe unwn lawen ganiad
ar doriad têg y dydd' (And join in joyful song at the fair break of dawn),
was meant to celebrate the survival of the Welsh people and to articulate
popular resistance.[111] Though none of this potentially inflammatory material
was published the loyalist cause remained steadfastly hostile to him. He had
become a pariah in his own locality.
    In a bid to whip up what his enemies liked to call 'Welsh Feaver',[112] he
attended eisteddfodau, sponsored by the Gwyneddigion Society, which

had been revived by 1789 with a view to promoting libertarian principles.[113] Knowing full well that the 'old brothers' ('hên frodyr')[114] from south Wales were more likely to become Jacobins than their hidebound northern counterparts, he argued that they should be encouraged to return to the fold to invigorate (and radicalize) the eisteddfodic muse. To his sorrow, however, poets from north Wales continued to run the show and, awash with alcohol, they sang poems in loyalist vein, involved themselves in fist-fights, and demonized the likes of Tom Paine. Whereas taverns and ale-houses in London were invariably the foci for sedition, those of north Wales frequented by the bards at eisteddfodau were militant in their loyalism. In their midst William Jones's reputation as a Voltairean heretic led to much bitter wrangling.

Fear of conspiracies, treason and armed rebellion was rife during the 1790s, generated by the publicity which surrounded the local loyalist associations founded from 1792 onwards and by the outbreak of war with France in February 1793. Local magistrates were urged to keep a vigilant eye open for agitators and a raft of measures passed by Parliament at the instigation of William Pitt was designed to harass, prosecute and incarcerate the most prominent and defiant radicals. William Jones became keenly aware of prying eyes in his neighbourhood. The rector Matthew Worthington deliberately stirred up feelings against him, and postmasters at Llanfair Caereinion intercepted and confiscated his mail.[115] Jones retaliated by devising a form of stenography which local blockheads could not hope to decipher.[116] John Jones, a liberal gentleman who lived at Stonehouse, Llangadfan, bravely took up his cause, but the old curmudgeon refused to hold his tongue:

> . . . he has harboured for some time a Republican disposition, which I frequently as a friend desired him to drop every particle into total oblivion; but my advice made no effect, his correspondence gave rise to suspicion, his letters were opened, some never came to his hands, one letter from a member of parliament came opened. I was desired at a publick meeting of the Gentlemen & Justices of this County at Llanfair [Caereinion] to warn M[r]. W[m]. Jones to be cautious what he wrote or said in publick company . . .[117]

One suspects that William Jones irresistibly invited confrontations with the authorities.

During the early 1790s he became convinced that Pitt's government was an immoral regime and that there was every justification for seeking asylum elsewhere. He knew that for many farmers and craftsmen America was the most attractive land of opportunity for persecuted or deprived peoples.[118] The material and spiritual benefits were incontrovertible and the fertile and extensive lands of Kentucky – a 'new discovered Canaan', according to the Baptist minister Samuel Jones[119] – beckoned. There was also the Madog legend to fire the imagination.[120] William Jones shared the view of the Welsh chattering classes in London that a tribe of white-skinned, Welsh-speaking Indians, known as the Padoucans or the Madogwys, existed somewhere in the upper reaches of Missouri. These were reputedly the descendants of Madog, the mythical son of the medieval prince Owain Gwynedd who had supposedly discovered America in 1170. Obsessed with the ill-starred campaign to discover the Madogwys, Jones distributed an English address entitled 'To all indigenous Cambrobritons' at the Llanrwst eisteddfod in 1791, calling on the oppressed Welsh to emigrate and establish a Welsh colony in the land of the free where, like the Padoucans, they could become 'a free and distinct people', true to the values and precepts of their ancestors.[121] He bombarded influential persons with requests for assistance. Sir William Pulteney MP, widely believed to be the richest American stockholder of the day, rebuked him for seeking to rob this happy island of its loyal and obedient work-force, and when he turned to Thomas Pinckney, the American ambassador in London, for support in establishing a joint-stock company to bolster the plans of emigrants he received another dusty response.[122] But still he persevered and eight months before his death he was reported to be 'piping hot for a journey to Kentucky',[123] in order to pursue a career as a physician. Nothing came of his plans, however, for he died in his seventieth year and was buried on the last day of November 1795.[124]

As we have seen, although Walter Davies was a man of the cloth he was not overblessed with scruples. In a tiny footnote included in his obituary to William Jones he claimed that shortly before his death his mentor had expressed his wish 'of having the sacrament administered unto him, which he received with all the symptoms of sincere penitence'.[125] Given what we know of his life and writings, it is inconceivable that Jones, any more than Voltaire, would have genuinely recanted on his deathbed and taken communion. The Welsh Voltaire would surely have preferred to sup with the Devil. He was laid to rest, according to his own wishes, in unconsecrated ground on the northern side of the graveyard at St Cadfan's church. The epitaph on his grave, composed by his grandson Evan Breeze (Ieuan Cadfan), commemorated his gifts as a poet, an antiquary and a country healer,[126] but made no mention of his commitment to freedom, tolerance and justice. In 1995, on the occasion of the bicentenary of William Jones's death, the parishioners of Llangadfan raised funds for a memorial to be set in the west wall of the parish church. The inscription included the words 'Ysgolhaig, Athronydd, Bardd, Cofnodydd Dawnsiau Llangadfan' (Scholar, Philosopher, Poet, Recorder of the Llangadfan Dances).[127] But, as we have seen, there is much more to William Jones than that. If anyone needs to be saved from the condescension and squeamishness of posterity, it is the unrespectable Welsh political radical known as the 'rural Voltaire'.

Notes

[1] *DWB*; Eiluned Rees, 'The Welsh Book Trade from 1718 to 1820', in Philip Henry Jones and Eiluned Rees (eds.), *A Nation and its Books: A History of the Book in Wales* (Aberystwyth, 1998), pp. 127–8.

[2] *CIM*, II, p. 154, Iolo Morganwg to Owen Jones (Owain Myfyr), 15 November 1798.

[3] *Cambrian Register*, II (1799), [v–vi].

[4] *CIM*, I, p. 806, William Owen Pughe to Iolo Morganwg, 21 March 1796.

[5] NLW 1806E, f. 774, Thomas Jones to Walter Davies, 20 October 1795; NLW 13221E, f. 256, Thomas Jones to William Owen Pughe, 20 October 1795.

[6] *Cambrian Register*, I (1796), viii.

[7] Glenda Carr, *William Owen Pughe* (Caerdydd, 1983), p. 58; Huw Walters, *Llyfryddiaeth Cylchgronau Cymreig 1735–1850 / A Bibliography of Welsh Periodicals 1735–1850* (Aberystwyth, 1993), pp. 10–11.

[8] *Cambrian Register*, I (1796), 460.

[9] Ibid., II (1799), 237–51. The essay was accompanied by an engraved likeness of Jones.

[10] For Davies, see *DWB*, *ODNB*, and for his works, see D. Silvan Evans (ed.), *Gwaith y Parch. Walter Davies, A.C. (Gwallter Mechain)* (3 vols., Caerfyrddin, 1868).

[11] According to C. Grant Robinson, the likes of Davies at All Souls College found themselves in 'the blessed euthenasia of eighteenth-century Oxford', *All Souls College* (London, 1899), p. 176; Charles Crawley, *Trinity Hall: The History of a Cambridge College 1350–1975* (Cambridge, 1976), p. 142; Elisabeth Leedham-Green, *A Concise History of the University of Cambridge* (Cambridge, 1996), p. 120. According to the latter, a good number of scallywags left with a degree but few other attainments beyond 'advanced skills in drinking and driving a coach and pair'. Ibid.

[12] Evans (ed.), *Gwaith y Parch. Walter Davies*, III, p. 24.

[13] Mari Ellis, 'Rhai o Hen Bersoniaid Llengar Maldwyn', in Gwynn ap Gwilym and Richard H. Lewis (eds.), *Bro'r Eisteddfod: Cyflwyniad i Maldwyn a'i Chyffiniau* (Abertawe, 1981), p. 89. For his relationship with Iolo Morganwg, see Geraint H. Jenkins, 'An Uneasy Relationship: Gwallter Mechain and Iolo Morganwg', *MC*, 97 (2009), 73–99.

[14] Evans (ed.), *Gwaith y Parch. Walter Davies*, II, pp. 1–109; Hywel M. Davies, 'Loyalism in Wales, 1792–1793', *WHR*, 20, no. 4 (2001), 687–716.

[15] This is the *englyn* 'Y nos dywyll yn distewi' (Silence brought by the dark night) in his poem 'Cwymp Llywelyn' (The Fall of Llywelyn) in 1821. Gwyn Jones, *The Oxford Book of Welsh Verse in English* (Oxford, 1977), p. 203.

[16]   Graham Thomas, 'Gwallter Mechain ac Eisteddfod Corwen, 1789', *NLWJ*, XX, no. 4 (1978), 408; Geraint Phillips, *Dyn heb ei Gyffelyb yn y Byd: Owain Myfyr a'i Gysylltiadau Llenyddol* (Caerdydd, 2010), chapter 5.

[17]   Walter Davies, *Diwygiad neu Ddinystr: wedi ei dynnu allan o lyfr Saesneg a elwir Reform or Ruin* (Croesoswallt, 1798).

[18]   Gwyn A. Williams, *The Search for Beulah Land* (London, 1980), p. 72.

[19]   *Cambrian Register*, II, 245. Voltaire was noted for his 'beak-like nose and the eccentricity of his dress'. Roger Pearson, *Voltaire Mighty: A Life in Pursuit of Freedom* (paperback edn., London, 2006), p. 336. For the influence of his deistic thought, see Norman L. Torrey, *Voltaire and the English Deists* (New Haven, 1930).

[20]   *Cambrian Register*, II, 250–1. These comments are reflected in Richard Williams, *Montgomeryshire Worthies* (2nd edn., Newtown, 1894), pp. 164–5, and Elias Owen (ed.), *The Works of the Rev. Griffith Edwards (Gutyn Padarn)* (London, 1895), pp. 24–8.

[21]   BL Add 15031, f. 43, Walter Davies to Owen Jones (Owain Myfyr), 30 April 1797.

[22]   For this theme, see Hywel Teifi Edwards, *Gŵyl Gwalia: Yr Eisteddfod Genedlaethol yn Oes Aur Victoria 1858–1868* (Llandysul, 1980), chapter 5.

[23]   Tecwyn Ellis, 'William Jones, Llangadfan', *LlC*, I, no. 3 (1951), 174–84; Enid Roberts, 'William Jones, Dolhywel', *MC*, 70 (1982), 40–6.

[24]   Gwyn A. Williams, *Madoc: The Making of a Myth* (London, 1980), pp. 89–95; Geraint H. Jenkins, *Y Chwyldro Ffrengig a Voltaire Cymru* (Caerdydd, 1989); *idem*, '"A Rank Republican [and] a Leveller': William Jones, Llangadfan', *WHR*, 17, no. 3 (1995), 365–86.

[25]   NLW 13221E, f. 257, Thomas Jones to William Owen Pughe, 20 October 1795.

[26]   E. H. C. Davies, 'Property and Landownership in Llangadfan', *MC*, 79 (1991), 80–1.

[27]   NLW 168C, f. 145, William Jones to Edward Jones, 12 November 1791.

[28]   NLW 1641B, vol. 2, f. 55. This description occurs in Jones's essay 'A Brief Description of the Parishes of Llanerfyl, Llangadfan and Garthbeibio', dated 29 April 1792 and published posthumously in the *Cambrian Register*, II, 366–85.

[29]   NLW 168C, f. 145, William Jones to Edward Jones, 12 November 1791.

[30]   Enid P. Roberts, 'Cann Office', *NLWJ*, XVIII, no. 4 (1974), 418–26.

[31]   References to these are made in Jones's correspondence with Walter Davies in NLW 1806E and with William Owen Pughe in NLW 13221E and NLW 13222C. See also Jenkins, '"A Rank Republican [and] a Leveller"', 366–7.

[32]   NLW 22B, pp. 65–84.

[33]   Caryl Davies, *Adfeilion Babel: Agweddau ar Syniadaeth Ieithyddol y Ddeunawfed Ganrif* (Caerdydd, 2000), pp. 270–2.

[34]   NLW 1806E, f. 788, William Jones to Walter Davies, 22 October 1794; J. Glyn Penrhyn Jones, 'A History of Medicine in Wales in the Eighteenth Century' (unpublished University of Liverpool MA thesis, 1957), pp. 142–4.

[35]   Powys Archives, M/EP/24/Z/MT/2, Llangadfan Parochial Records, no. 1, f. 127^v; NLW 1949E, unpaginated. Stafford Prys (1732–84) was a Montgomeryshire man. See *DWB*.

[36]   Roy Porter, *Quacks: Fakers and Charlatans in English Medicine* (Stroud, 2000), p. 66.

[37]   *Cambrian Register*, II, 244.

[38]   NLW 1806E, f. 796/C.

[39]   NLW 1806E, f. 788, William Jones to Walter Davies, 22 October 1794.

[40]   Ibid. See payments made to him for dispensing drugs and cures, in Powys Archives, M/EP/24/O/RT/I, Llangadfan Parochial Records, no. 4, for the years 1764–88.

[41]   Jones, 'A History of Medicine in Wales', p. 143.

[42]   Powys Archives, M/EP/24/Z/MT/2, Llangadfan Parochial Records, no. 1, f. 45^r.

[43]   For some of the literature on this subject, see Gillian Russell and Clara Tuite (eds.), *Romantic Sociability: Social Networks and Literary Culture in Britain, 1770–1840* (Cambridge, 2002); Jon Mee, 'Rough and Respectable Radicalisms', *History Workshop Journal*, 56 (2003), 238–44; Michael T. Davis, '"An Evening of Pleasure rather than Business": Songs, Subversion and Radical Sub-Culture in the 1790s', *Journal for the Study of British Cultures*, 12, no. 2 (2005), 115–26; Michael T. Davis and Paul A. Pickering (eds.), *Unrespectable Radicals? Popular Politics in the Age of Reform* (Aldershot, 2008).

[44]   Martin Fitzpatrick, 'The "Cultivated Understanding" and Chaotic Genius of David Samwell', in Geraint H. Jenkins (ed.), *A Rattleskull Genius: The Many Faces of Iolo Morganwg* (Cardiff, 2005), pp. 383–402; Russell Davies, *Hope and Heartbreak: A Social History of Wales and the Welsh, 1776–1871* (Cardiff, 2005), pp. 281–2.

[45]   NLW 21390E, nos. 22, 23; *CIM*, I, pp. 134–9, Iolo Morganwg to Owen Jones (Owain Myfyr), 6 March 1779.

[46]   See Powys Archives, M/EP/24/Z/MT/2, Llangadfan Parochial Records, no. 1, ff. 35–6, 61$^{r–v}$, 62^r.

[47]   Ibid., ff. 49^v–50^r. For Lewis Morris's poem, see Raymond Garlick and Roland Mathias (eds.), *Anglo-Welsh Poetry 1480–1990* (Bridgend, 1982), pp. 90–2, and for other examples of his bawdiness, see Geraint H. Jenkins, 'Lewis Morris: "The Fat Man of Cardiganshire"', *Ceredigion*, XIV, no. 2 (2002), 1–23.

[48]   Powys Archives, M/EP/24/Z/MT/2, Llangadfan Parochial Records, no. 1, f. 53^v, and NLW 171E, ff. 9–10. He coyly described his 'trifling love adventures' in NLW 1806E, f. 787, William Jones to Walter Davies, 14 April 1794.

[49]   Iain McCalman, *Radical Underworld: Prophets, Revolutionaries, and Pornographers in London, 1795–1840* (Cambridge, 1988), p. 237. See also Peter Wagner, *Eros Revived: Erotica of the Enlightenment in England and America* (London, 1987), and G. S. Rousseau and Roy Porter (eds.), *Sexual Underworlds of the Enlightenment* (Manchester, 1987).

[50]   Melvin Humphreys, *The Crisis of Community: Montgomeryshire 1680–1815* (Cardiff, 1996), p. 99.

[51]   See ibid., chapter 5; Philip Jenkins, *The Making of a Ruling Class: The Glamorgan Gentry 1640–1790* (Cambridge, 1983); David W. Howell, *Patriarchs and Parasites: The Gentry of South-West Wales in the Eighteenth Century* (Cardiff, 1986).

[52]   Askew Roberts, *Wynnstay and the Wynns* (Oswestry, 1876), p. 13; Davies, 'Property and Landownership in Llangadfan', 75.

53   He was also often referred to as 'Prince of Wales', Geraint H. Jenkins, *The Foundations of Modern Wales: Wales 1642–1780* (Oxford, 1987), p. 157.

54   T. W. Pritchard, 'Sir Watkin Williams Wynn, Fourth Baronet (1749–1789)', *TDHS*, 28 (1979), 18–67.

55   David W. Howell, *The Rural Poor in Eighteenth-Century Wales* (Cardiff, 2000), p. 51.

56   Evan Evans, *Casgliad o Bregethau* (2 vols., Mwythig, 1776), I, sig. B3ʳ.

57   NLW 13221E, f. 387, William Jones to William Owen Pughe, undated.

58   NLW, Longueville Deeds and Documents, nos. 858, 925.

59   Howell, *The Rural Poor in Eighteenth-Century Wales*, p. 51.

60   NLW, Wynnstay 125, vol. 14, ff. 403–5.

61   Powys Archives, M/EP/24/Z/MT/2, Llangadfan Parochial Records, no. 1, ff. 98ᵛ–99ʳ.

62   NLW 821C, f. 122ᵛ. So wrote William Williams, Llandygái.

63   Peter D. G. Thomas, 'The Montgomeryshire Election of 1774', *MC*, 59, Parts 1–2 (1965–6), 116–29.

64   Bryn Ellis, 'Parliamentary Representation of Montgomeryshire', ibid., 63, Part 2 (1974), 74–96.

65   NLW 13221E, f. 282, William Jones to William Owen Pughe, 15 November 1793; NLW 168C, f. 147, William Jones to Edward Jones, 23 June 1789. He believed that the landed behemoths reckoned that the Welsh 'can scarcely be distinguished from Brutes but by the number of our supporters! & that our Language was but an incoherent Jargon'. NLW 13221E, ff. 377–8, William Jones to William Owen Pughe, 19 May [1794].

66   *Cambrian Register*, II, 239; Enid P. Roberts, *Braslun o Hanes Llên Powys* (Dinbych, 1965), pp. 66–7.

67   Lois Blake and W. S. Gwynn Williams (eds.), *The Llangadfan Dances* (3nd edn., Llangollen, 1954); Eddie Jones, 'William Jones, Dôl Hywel, Llangadfan 1726–1795', *Dawns* (2006), 42–8.

68   See, for instance, NLW 13221E, ff. 373–6, William Jones to William Owen Pughe, 24 October 1789, and f. 282, William Jones to William Owen Pughe, 15 November 1793.

69   Tecwyn Ellis, *Edward Jones, Bardd y Brenin 1752–1824* (Caerdydd, 1957).

70   *CIM*, I, p. 626, Iolo Morganwg to Edward Jones [?1794]; ibid., p. 632, David Pugh to Iolo Morganwg [?1794].

71   NLW 168C, f. 145, William Jones to Edward Jones, 12 November 1791.

72   Ibid.

73   Nigel Yates, 'Part III: 1780–1850', in Glanmor Williams, William Jacob, Nigel Yates and Frances Knight, *The Welsh Church from Reformation to Disestablishment 1603–1920* (Cardiff, 2007), p. 223.

74   Bedwyr Lewis Jones, *Yr Hen Bersoniaid Llengar* (Penarth, [1963]), *passim*.

75   Robert Hay Drummond, *A Sermon preached in the Parish-Church of Christ-Church, London* (London, 1753), p. 22; C. L. S. Linnell (ed.), *The Diaries of Thomas Wilson DD 1731–37 and 1750* (London, 1964), p. 235.

76   NLW 2009B, *passim*; Geraint H. Jenkins, 'Yr Eglwys "Wiwlwys Olau" a'i Beirniaid', *Ceredigion*, X, no. 2 (1985), 131–46; Gerald Morgan, 'Ieuan Fardd (1731–1788):

"Traethawd yr Esgyb Eingl"', ibid., XI, no. 2 (1990), 135–45. William Jones described Evans as 'that unfortunate true Briton' who had 'emitted some sparks of light, in the Time of Aegyptian darkness'. NLW 168C, f. 147ᵛ, William Jones to Edward Jones, 23 June 1789.

[77] Geraint H. Jenkins, '"Horrid Unintelligible Jargon": The Case of Dr Thomas Bowles', *WHR*, 15, no. 4 (1991), 494–523.

[78] Hugh Owen (ed.), *Additional Letters of the Morrises of Anglesey (1735–1786)* (2 vols., London, 1947–9), II, p. 666.

[79] *The Depositions, Arguments and Judgment in the Cause of the Church-Wardens of Trefdraeth, in the County of Anglesea, against Dr Bowles* (London, 1773), p. 59.

[80] Owen (ed.), *Additional Letters of the Morrises of Anglesey*, II, p. 745.

[81] NLW, Records of the Church in Wales, SA/MB/19.

[82] Eryn M. White, 'The Established Church, Dissent and the Welsh Language', in Geraint H. Jenkins (ed.), *The Welsh Language before the Industrial Revolution* (Cardiff, 1997), pp. 253–4, 278.

[83] NLW, Records of the Church in Wales, SA/QA/7, 9.

[84] Gomer M. Roberts, 'Howel Harris and Montgomeryshire', *MC*, 63, Part 1 (1973), 104.

[85] NLW 1817E, ff. 73ʳ–74ᵛ; Roberts, *Braslun o Hanes Llên Powys*, p. 71; E. G. Millward, 'Rhai Agweddau ar Lenyddiaeth Wrth-Fethodistaidd y Ddeunawfed Ganrif', *Cylchgrawn Cymdeithas Hanes Eglwys Methodistiaid Calfinaidd Cymru*, LX, no. 1 (1975), 3–4; Geraint H. Jenkins, '"Peth Erchyll Iawn" oedd Methodistiaeth', *LlC*, XVII, nos. 3–4 (1993), 195–204.

[86] See, for instance, the insinuations of Lewis Morris (NLW 67A, ff. 57–68) and Rhys Jones (A. Cynfael Lake (ed.), *Blodeugerdd Barddas o Ganu Caeth y Ddeunawfed Ganrif* (Cyhoeddiadau Barddas, 1993), pp. 79–80), and Iolo Morganwg's rousing 'Jumper's Hymn', with its suggestive refrain 'And a jumping we will go' (NLW 6238A, pp. 394–6).

[87] Powys Archives, M/EP/24/Z/M7/2, Llangadfan Parochial Records, no. 1, f. 38ᵛ. See also ff. 39ᵛ–40ʳ and NLW 1817E, f. 73.

[88] NLW 171E, f. 40. For the resurgence of Welsh music and dance, see Prys Morgan, *The Eighteenth Century Renaissance* (Llandybïe, 1981), pp. 124–32, and Phyllis Kinney, *Welsh Traditional Music* (Cardiff, 2011).

[89] NLW 171E, ff. 17–18, 35–40; Blake and Williams, *The Llangadfan Dances, passim.*

[90] NLW 168C, f. 147ᵛ, William Jones to Edward Jones, 23 June 1789.

[91] Powys Archives, M/EP/24/Z/M7/2, Llangadfan Parochial Records, no. 1, f. 40ᵛ.

[92] NLW 13221E, f. 257, Thomas Jones to William Owen Pughe, 20 October 1795.

[93] Williams, *The Search for Beulah Land*, p. 40.

[94] See his ode to liberty in Welsh, in Powys Archives, M/EP/24/Z/M7/2, Llangadfan Parochial Records, no. 1, ff. 53ᵛ–54ᵛ, and in NLW 1806E, f. 795. In an English poem, 'On the Times', he claimed that despots from Lisbon to St Petersburg were uniting 'to cramp mankind with Fetters'. Powys Archives, Llangadfan Parochial Records, no. 1, f. 58ʳ.

[95] NLW 13221E, f. 415, William Jones to William Owen Pughe, Easter Monday 1791.

[96] Powys Archives, M/EP/24/Z/M7/2, Llangadfan Parochial Records, no. 1, ff. 41^r, 46^v.

[97] NLW 13221E, f. 311, William Jones to William Owen Pughe, 15 July 1792.

[98] For the strongest Voltairean overtones, see NLW 13222C, ff. 287–8, William Jones to William Owen Pughe, 21 January 1792; NLW 13221E, ff. 267–70, William Jones to William Owen Pughe, 2 December 1792; NLW 13222C, ff. 431–4, William Jones to William Owen Pughe, 2 April 1793; NLW 1806E, f. 787, William Jones to Walter Davies, 14 April 1794; NLW 13221E, ff. 303–6, William Jones to William Owen Pughe, 7 May / 1 June 1794.

[99] NLW 1806E, f. 782, William Jones to Walter Davies, undated.

[100] NLW 13221E, f. 387, William Jones to William Owen Pughe, undated.

[101] Ibid.

[102] David J. V. Jones, *Before Rebecca: Popular Protests in Wales 1793–1835* (London, 1973), pp. 18–19, 22, 57, 59, 61, 64.

[103] NLW 13221E, f. 343, William Jones to William Owen Pughe, 7 August 1791.

[104] NLW 13221E, f. 257, Thomas Jones to William Owen Pughe, 20 October 1795.

[105] NLW 1806E, f. 786, William Jones to Walter Davies, 18 October 1793. Worthington was also master of the free school at Deuddwr and minister at Newchapel in Montgomeryshire. *Gentleman's Magazine*, I (1796), 441.

[106] NLW 1806E, f. 787, William Jones to Walter Davies, 14 April 1794. For other echoes, see Justin Champion, 'May the Last King be strangled in the bowels of the Last Priest: Irreligion and the English Enlightenment, 1649–1789', in Timothy Morton and Nigel Smith (eds.), *Radicalism in British Literary Culture, 1650–1830: From Revolution to Revolution* (Cambridge, 2002), chapter 1.

[107] When an Englishman was appointed to serve the Welsh at Meifod, Jones caustically commented that 'the parishioners must learn English, or go to Hell with the sans culottes'. NLW 1806E, f. 782, William Jones to Walter Davies, undated.

[108] NLW 1806E, f. 782, William Jones to Walter Davies, undated. Jones was referring here to the works of the Revd Peter Williams, best known for his annotated Welsh Bible in 1770 and his expulsion from the Calvinistic Methodist movement in 1791.

[109] NLW 13222C, f. 320, William Jones to William Owen Pughe, 12 September 1790.

[110] NLW 1806E, f. 786, William Jones to Walter Davies, 18 October 1793.

[111] NLW 13221E, f. 339, William Jones to William Owen Pughe, 6 August 1791; Laura Mason, *Singing the French Revolution: Popular Culture and Politics, 1787–1799* (Ithaca, 1996); Powys Archives, M/EP/24/Z/M7/2, Llangadfan Parochial Records, no. 1, f. 59^{r-v}; NLW 13221E, f. 369, William Jones to William Owen Pughe, [1 April 1792].

[112] NLW 13221E, f. 368, William Jones to William Owen Pughe, [1 April 1792].

[113] J. Lloyd Thomas, 'Eisteddfod Talaith a Chadair Powys (The Powis Provincial Chair Eisteddfod)', *MC*, 59, Parts 1–2 (1965–6), 60–81; Hywel Teifi Edwards, *Yr Eisteddfod* (Llandysul, 1976), pp. 22–34; Phillips, *Dyn heb ei Gyffelyb yn y Byd*, chapter 5.

114 NLW 1806E, f. 777, William Jones to Walter Davies, 28 June 1789.

115 NLW 13221E, f. 302, William Jones to William Owen Pughe, undated.

116 Ibid., f. 343, William Jones to William Owen Pughe, 7 August 1791.

117 NLW 323E, f. 44, John Jones to Edward Jones, 24 November 1795.

118 Hywel M. Davies, "'Very Different Springs of Uneasiness": Emigration from Wales to the United States of America during the 1790s', *WHR*, 15, no. 3 (1991), 368–98.

119 *Idem, Transatlantic Brethren: Rev. Samuel Jones (1735–1814) and his Friends* (London, 1995), p. 164.

120 Williams, *Madoc: The Making of a Myth*. For Jones's interest in this legend, see his letters to William Owen Pughe in NLW 13221E, ff. 301–2, 303–6, 311–12, 339–42, 415–17.

121 NLW 13221E, f. 340, William Jones to William Owen Pughe, 6 August 1791.

122 Ibid., ff. 267–8, William Jones to William Owen Pughe, 2 December 1792; NLW 13221E, ff. 301–2, William Jones to William Owen Pughe, undated.

123 NLW 1806E, f. 773, Thomas Jones to Walter Davies, 4 April 1795.

124 *Montgomeryshire Records: Parish of Llangadfan* (Montgomeryshire Genealogical Society, 2005), p. 105.

125 *Cambrian Register*, II, 250.

126 NLW 1806E, f. 791; *Y Gwyliedydd* (March 1837), 89.

127 NLW, William Jones (Llangadfan) Committee Papers A 1996/38, 1–9.

Networking the nation: the bardic and correspondence networks of Wales and London in the 1790s

CATHRYN A. CHARNELL-WHITE

With its worthy patrons, patriotic competition subjects, and silver medals for the assembled bards, the revived Eisteddfod of the 1790s embodied the imagined Welsh nation;[1] a nation whose cultural memory was safeguarded by its bards' unique knowledge of Welsh history, mythology and genealogy.[2] This deliberate evocation of Wales's bardic tradition not only accorded with the self-image of the Welsh, but also with the dominant view of eighteenth-century antiquaries and Romantics who fixed their gaze on Wales and the Welsh.[3] The timing of the revival of the Eisteddfod in the year of the French Revolution was purely serendipitous. Jonathan Hughes (1721–1805), an elderly Welsh bard, had only the interest of the ancient art of Welsh strict-metre poetry in mind when he organized the small eisteddfod at Llangollen in January 1789. Yet events in Paris in July of 1789 excited the political enthusiasm and patriotism of eisteddfodic bards, organizers and patrons in Wales and London, albeit to different degrees. In turn, the cultural legacy of the French Revolution and Revolutionary Wars in Wales is apparent in the poetic output of the eisteddfodau of the 1790s and their increasingly (British) loyalist tenor.[4] This chapter explores the contours of bardic and associational culture in Wales's regional bardic circles and in the societies of the Welsh diaspora in London. The final section surveys the Eisteddfod both as a locus of network activity between London and Wales in the 1790s and as a triumph of those combined communication networks.

Poetic circles and networks in Wales

Medieval Wales's professional poetic guild represented the pinnacle of élite Welsh culture, but following the loss of Welsh independence in 1282 and

Wales's absorption into the English administration at the Tudor Acts of Union (1536, 1543), increasing Anglicization of traditional patrons – the noble and ecclesiastical classes – forced the bardic profession into a spiral of decline. By the middle of the seventeenth century, strict-metre poetry survived as the preserve of amateur country poets who, nonetheless, considered themselves active participants of a venerable, living tradition. The fortunes of strict-metre poetry changed with the intervention of the Morris brothers of Anglesey and their coterie. Through London's Welsh societies these middle-class Welsh patriots stimulated a revival of Welsh (and Welsh-language) culture and antiquities,[5] and in the process, validated bardic identity as a worthwhile form of Welsh cultural nationalism.[6]

The literary circle or coterie as a means of stimulus, transmission and criticism for writers is largely a feature of Renaissance literary culture,[7] and during this period the Welsh term *cylch barddol* (bardic circle) seems to have been adopted in this sense. Partly as a result of Wales's notoriously poor infrastructure (which was largely orientated east towards London and west towards Holyhead and Dublin), eighteenth-century bardic circles tended to be intimate, irregular phenomena reliant on geographical proximity: they consisted of individuals who belonged to the same locality and who were, broadly speaking, neighbours who gathered at a member's home or at a tavern. This, however, did not preclude correspondence between circle members, nor between members of a circle and individuals whose main (or indeed only) experience of circle life was conducted through correspondence. Circles tended to have a pedagogic dynamic: pupils clustered around a central tutor in a relationship that was, in spite of its implied hierarchy, often confirmed by friendship. Consequently certain poetic genres – *ymddiddan* (dialogue), *ymryson* (contention), *canu gofyn a diolch* (poems of request and thanks) and occasional poetry – reveal the cut and thrust of circle life as well as the mutual support it provided for its members. Bardic circles did not exist exclusively for the practice of the strict metres,[8] yet free-metre poetry was often sneered at as the preserve of Welsh balladeers, who had their own country-wide network of publishers, ballad singers and sellers existing in tandem with the Welsh book trade.[9] As a locus of poetic training, practice and encouragement, bardic circles had a strong oral character, yet many poets and poetic circles received their knowledge of strict-metre verse from a treatise by the poet, publisher and compiler of almanacs, Siôn Rhydderch (John Roderick; 1673–1735). Based on the medieval bardic 'Statute of Gruffudd ap Cynan', Rhydderch's *Grammadeg Cymraeg* (Welsh Grammar; 1728) was the most influential text in the eighteenth-century revival of both Welsh strict-metre poetry and the Eisteddfod.[10] With growing levels of literacy in eighteenth-century Wales, reading was also a vital source of learning for poets. Frustrated by the disparate nature of poetic circles in south Wales, and having little opportunity to discuss poetry with like-minded people, David Davis of Castellhywel (1745–1827) gleaned much from the printed works of English poets.[11]

The public performance of poetry remained an important aspect of bardic culture in the eighteenth century, but this was increasingly enriched by written and print culture, transforming it to such a degree that the structure of geographically disparate bardic circles became increasingly reticulated; interlinked into a more nuanced and open-ended network.[12] A network structure is also a more versatile organizing concept than the 'circle', allowing for the manifold forms of association that emerged in eighteenth-century Britain.[13] The local, national and London interconnections of Wales's bardic communities bear out their resourceful and intricately networked nature.

The bardic career and social advancement of the weaver turned schoolmaster David Thomas (Dafydd Ddu Eryri; 1759–1822) was almost entirely shaped by the widespread and well-connected bardic circles of north Wales. A fellow-pupil at John Morgan's school at Llanberis lent him a copy of Rhydderch's treatise on Welsh metrics, and another teacher, the clergyman David Ellis, nurtured his interest in Welsh poetry and manuscript culture.[14] The Gwyneddigion Society regarded Ellis's textual criticism of medieval poetry highly and he became a corresponding member in the late 1780s.[15] His pupil, however, formed his own direct link with London through the poet Robert Hughes of Penmynydd, Anglesey (Ceint Bach, Robin Ddu yr Ail o Fôn; 1744–85). During a twenty-year career in London as a legal clerk, Hughes had been a key figure amongst the Gwyneddigion, until ill health brought him back to Wales where, in 1783, he worked as a schoolteacher in Caernarfon.[16] Hughes discussed the Gwyneddigion with Thomas. The latter became a corresponding member in 1785, and exchanged letters primarily with Owen Jones (Owain Myfyr; 1741–1814) and William Owen Pughe (1759–1835), and through them with other corresponding members, namely the excise collector Thomas Jones (Rhaiadr) of Corwen and Bristol, Edward Williams (Iolo Morganwg; 1747–1826) of Glamorgan, and Walter Davies of Montgomeryshire (Gwallter Mechain; 1761–1849). Thomas was fortunate enough to be patronized by a local gentleman, Paul Panton, who had himself been a corresponding member of the Cymmrodorion Society since the 1760s,[17] and who had also previously been a benefactor of Evan Evans. While Thomas did not have direct contact with Evans, who died in 1788, he at least had access to Evans's manuscripts at Panton's extensive library at Plas Gwyn, Anglesey. Written at Panton's behest, Thomas's anti-Paineite song of 1793, 'Cân Twm Paine' (The Song of Tom Paine), was written in imitation of an unidentified English original and bears the hallmarks of the vulgar conservatism of the contemporary backlash against the Revolution in Britain.[18]

Emboldened by his own direct connections with members of the Gwynedd-igion, Thomas established Cymdeithas Lenyddol Beirdd Arfon (The Literary Society of the Poets of Arvonia), known colloquially as 'Cymdeithas yr Eryron' (The Society of Snowdonia Men). 'Eryron' may also be translated as 'eagles' and so Thomas's bardic apprentices were also known as his 'chicks' ('cywion'). John Roberts (Siôn Lleyn; 1749–1817) and Griffith Williams (Gutyn Peris; 1769–1838) were foremost among his protégés and together they formed a regional network that spanned Arfon, Llŷn and Eifionydd.[19] They met at his home, at taverns, or at the homes of other members during Thomas's peripatetic tours of Llŷn and Eifionydd.[20] On these occasions they exchanged and transcribed poems and manuscripts. Thomas also maintained a written correspondence with his pupils, most notably with Roberts.[21] Thomas was ideally positioned to mediate between them in Caernarfonshire and the Gwyneddigion Society in London, and his influence and knowledge were, in turn, mediated by his protégés to yet another layer or lower stratum of poets: Dafydd ap Dafydd (who briefly resided in London), John Hughes, Gruffydd Isaac, and Evan Owen.[22] Thomas became equally well connected to poets and poetic circles in the neighbouring counties of north Wales: the main poets of north-east Wales, Jonathan Hughes and Thomas Edwards (Twm o'r Nant; 1739–1810);[23] and through them with John Thomas of Pentrefoelas.

Naturally, the extent to which David Thomas became networked to individuals and groups in Wales and London changed throughout his lifetime. His bardic stature was enhanced by the eisteddfodau of the 1790s: indeed, he became the first Welsh bard to be defined by eisteddfodic success, and his status as adjudicator later made him an attractive point of contact for seasoned and up-and-coming bards alike. Thomas also published English-language poetry in the *North Wales Gazette* that was as neoclassical in taste as his Welsh poetry. This brought him into contact with Richard Llwyd (Bard of Snowdon; 1752–1835),[24] an Anglophone Welsh poet equally well aligned with Welsh and London-Welsh networks. He not only contributed to the periodical press of the 1790s, but even established his own Welsh-language magazine (which ran to only one issue) in 1800.[25] His rootedness in the overlapping bardic and correspondence networks provided a binding sense of identity in his own immediate circle; his protégés gained notoriety in Welsh polite society by falling out irrevocably after his death.

In contrast to north Wales, bardic circles were relatively scarce in south Wales at the beginning of the eighteenth century.[26] But in the uplands of Glamorganshire, a group of bards instigated a local cultural revival that fed into the broader revivalist programme emanating from the London-Welsh societies.[27] They called themselves 'gramadegyddion' (grammarians), in a nod to the printed poetic treatises by Renaissance humanists and contemporary revivalists such as Siôn Dafydd Rhys, Wiliam Midleton, and Siôn Rhydderch. By the 1760s their meetings centred on Lewis Hopkin of Llandyfodwg, and also involved two cultured clerics and lexicographers in the Vale of Glamorgan: John Walters of Llandough and Thomas Richards of Coychurch.[28]

The circle's poetic activity shows the influence of high and low print culture on bardic culture and communications, as well as how Wales's emerging public sphere actively stimulated the convergence of bardic circles on one another. Guided by the eisteddfodic rubric set out in Rhydderch's treatise, they held occasional eisteddfodau at Llantrisant which in 1771 formed the kernel of a short-lived society aiming to uphold the Welsh language and to give practical support to Welsh writers, the Gwrth-Hengistiaid (The Anti-Hengistians).[29] In the late 1760s they inspired the young self-educated stonemason, Edward Williams, introducing him to the domestic and London-based networks that would shape, not only his own literary career but also the contours of Welsh national identity. Thus Williams was encouraged to send a poem to the editors of Wales's first, short-lived Welsh-language periodical of 1770, *Trysorfa Gwybodaeth; Neu Eurgrawn Cymraeg* (Treasury of Knowledge; Or Welsh Magazine).[30] He also contributed to Welsh-language almanacs.[31] In addition to practical information, pocketbook almanacs printed light reading material and poetry by contributors from every part of Wales. David Thomas and Walter Davies also published poetic juvenilia in them. Crucially, the almanacs allowed poets to expand their horizons beyond their immediate localities, and gave poets like Edward Williams and his fellow-grammarians a sense of belonging to a national network, albeit a virtual one.[32]

This sense of interconnection was enhanced by the more concrete links with the London Welsh enjoyed by John Walters, Thomas Richards, and the poet and weaver John Bradford of Betws.[33] Around 1774 Williams introduced Walters to Owen Jones, a relative newcomer to the London-Welsh social scene whose commitment and financial support was to play a vital role in the Society's cultural achievements from 1789 to 1807.[34] Like David Thomas in north Wales, Williams's exposure to the vibrant associational culture of the London Welsh motivated him to establish a literary society of his own. Although Brodoliaeth Beirdd Morgannwg (The Fraternity of Glamorgan Poets; est. 1780) was not limited to poets, it followed the model of the societies for Welshmen in the metropolis, and welcomed every man 'proficient in the [Welsh] language'.[35] It was nonetheless predisposed towards poetry and aimed to hold an annual 'association' (in effect, an eisteddfod) at Llantrisant to endorse the neoclassical literary standards promoted by the London Welsh and to experiment with Welsh metrics.[36] The exact make-up of its membership is unclear, but Williams counted fellow-grammarians John Bradford, William Davies and Edward Evan amongst its members, as well as Evan Evans. Williams had spent much time in Evans's company around this period and benefitted from his insight into the intricacies of the Welsh poetic tradition, the debate surrounding Macpherson's Ossian poems, and personal anecdotes about Lewis Morris.[37] Williams clearly envisaged the relationship between the Gwyneddigion and the Glamorgan fraternity as one of equals and he invited various London Welshmen to join as corresponding members. Without financial support and a strong local membership, the fraternity lost momentum: its only lasting legacy was the treatise of metrical innovations that, by the late 1780s, had become the corner-stone of Williams's ambitious alternative vision of Wales's genuine poetic tradition, Bardism.

But Bardism was more than an alternative reading of Wales's poetic tradition. It was a highly subjective system constructed by Williams to counter popular stereotypes of the Welsh, proving that Wales was in fact a civilized nation whose native culture deserved the attention of the whole world: '. . . a noble spirit of liberality, genuine morality, and liberty runs through it [=Bardism], and it does very considerable honour to the nation that gave it existence'.[38] The significance of the three bardic orders and their coloured robes sums up Bardism's contemporary resonance nicely: the white, blue and green robes of the Druids, Bards and Ovates respectively signified peace, truth and learning.[39] Furthermore, that their robes were unicoloured symbolized truth; the byword of Jacobins and Rational Dissenters and also the sentiment of Williams's most iconic bardic motto, 'Y Gwir yn erbyn y Byd' (the Truth against the World).[40] Bardism's basic primitivist frame was established during the 1780s, but it was fine-tuned in the years that followed the French Revolution, during Williams's residence in London in the heady years between 1791 and 1795 while he steered his *Poems, Lyric and Pastoral* (1794) through the press.[41]

Many of the Glamorgan grammarians were Rational Dissenters, and Williams was already receptive to the politics of reform when he arrived in London.[42] Many of Bardism's supposedly ancient Welsh features – liberty, equality, religious toleration, freedom of speech, and opposition to war – attest his engagement with the political culture of the 1790s through the intersecting metropolitan political and London-Welsh networks.[43] This dynamic engagement is most clearly seen in his anthem of bardic Jacobinism and radical fellowship, 'Breiniau Dyn' (Rights of Man), loosely based on a

militant reworking of 'God Save the King'.[44] He found like-minded friends
in the London-Welsh societies: John Jones (Jac Glan-y-gors; 1766–1821),
Owen Jones, William Owen Pughe, Thomas Roberts of Llwynrhudol, and
David Samwell (Dafydd Ddu Feddyg; 1751–98). Pughe, suspected 'of very
seditious tendency' by native Welshmen,[45] was on intimate terms with
members of the SCI and LCS and may have introduced Williams to figures
such as John Thelwall, Horne Tooke, Robert Southey, Gilbert Wakefield
and perhaps even Thomas Paine himself, with whom Williams identified
strongly both in his letters and poetry.[46] When the defendants of the notorious
Treason Trials of 1794 were released, Williams composed an English song,
Trial by Jury (1795), for the celebration at the Crown and Anchor tavern, 5
February 1795.[47] Samwell too was on the cusp of Unitarian circles and
introduced Williams to Anna Seward, the Aikins, Theophilus Lindsey,
George Dyer and, perhaps, Joseph Priestley.[48] Williams also came into contact
with the radically sympathetic printer Joseph Johnson and his circle. Another
link was the philosopher David Williams (discussed elsewhere in this volume)
who apparently introduced Edward Williams to Talleyrand at his home.[49]

The careers of both David Thomas and Edward Williams demonstrate
that by the end of the eighteenth century bardic circles had converged,
forming a more expansive network that dovetailed with the native Welsh
book trade and literary culture (both high and low), the cultural revivalist
movement, and the London-Welsh societies. In effect, geographically isolated
poets were not bereft of support. William Jones of Llangadfan (Gwilym Cadfan;
1726–95) often complained of his seclusion in rural Montgomeryshire, yet
(as shown elsewhere in this volume) he was remarkably well connected.[50]
The Arian minister David Davis of Castellhywel found support in the re-
ligiously and politically radical Unitarian circle (the 'Black Spot') in Cardiganshire, to which Edward Williams also belonged.[51] Involvement at a distance
with the associational culture of the metropolis stimulated both Thomas and
Williams to instigate their own literary societies, although neither posed a
serious threat to the cultural dominance of the London-based Gwyneddigion.

London-Welsh associational culture and its networks

Just as the London-Welsh societies gained prestige from their high-profile
patrons,[52] connections with London conferred status on Welsh bards and
their circles. The London Welsh were not unaware of their privileged
position. As William Owen Pughe declared, London was 'in our rustic
conversations the primary point in the geography of the world'.[53] The city's
cultural pull was a corollary of its economic and political influence that had,

by the beginning of the century, proved a 'powerful agency of cohesion and centralization' for the British state.[54] As Pughe's comment suggests, the countless Welsh men and women amid the tides of economic migrants to London sharpened awareness of national and British concerns. Though the Welshness of many migrants to London was obliterated by metropolitan life, an important portion of the Welsh diaspora maintained a self-conscious identity – referred to by Murray Pittock in a Scottish and Irish context as 'Fratriotism'[55] – by creating their own associational life, culture, and ritual in London.[56]

The history of Welsh societies in London has been fully charted.[57] More than the earlier Honourable and Loyal Society of Antient Britons (est. 1715), whose raisons d'être were patriotic and charitable,[58] the Honourable Society of Cymmrodorion (1751–87) had specific cultural aims for the cultivation of the Welsh language and its literature and for encouraging research into the nation's antiquities:

> To this End, a considerable Number of Persons, Natives of the Principality of *Wales*, now residing in and about *London*, inspired with the love of their Common Country, and consulting the honour of the *British* Name, propose to establish a general Monthly Society, distinguished by the Name and Title of *Cymmrodorion* (or Aborigines).[59]

Alive to the power of the printing press, they were committed to the publication of Welsh antiquities. Although their actual achievements were modest, the society asserted London's cultural dominance and their own reputation as modern-day patrons of Welsh literature. By the 1790s, however, Cymdeithas y Gwyneddigion (the Society of the Men of Gwynedd) was the driving force of London-Welsh social life and a significant influence on cultural life in Wales. It was established in 1770 by members of the Cymmrodorion – principally Owen Jones – who considered that society too élitist, and its members too acquiescent to its wealthy influential patrons.[60] However, the Gwyneddigion was a new society rather than a rival one and both societies enjoyed considerable cross-membership until the Cymmrodorion disbanded in 1787. In turn, the Gwyneddigion spawned several short-lived offshoots that revitalized Welsh associational life in the city, namely the Ofyddion (Ovates; 1794), the Cymreigyddion (Welsh Scholars; 1795), and the Caradogion (The Caractacans; 1790). Little is known of the latter, a debating society founded by David Samwell, because its papers were confiscated by government agents in the repressive political climate of the decade's middle years.[61]

Full membership of the Gwyneddigion was open to Welshmen resident in London. Its leading figures have received much scholarly attention: John

Jones (Jac Glan-y-gors),[62] Owen Jones,[63] William Owen Pughe,[64] David Samwell,[65] and (less well known) the diligent Edward Charles (Siamas Wynedd; 1757–1828).[66] Society membership was inevitably relatively fluid: Robert Hughes spent two decades in the capital, while Robert Davies (Bardd Nantglyn; 1769–1835) was a temporary resident from 1800 until 1804. As we have seen, corresponding membership was important for both sides.[67] William Jones of Llangadfan undertook research for both Edward Jones and William Owen Pughe; Edward Williams was paid to transcribe and collate material for the three-volume compendium of medieval Welsh poetry and prose, *The Myvyrian Archaiology of Wales* (1801–7).[68]

The Gwyneddigion were generally more politically radical than their predecessors: the skinner Owen Jones supported John Wilkes in the 1770s and, along with David Samwell, he responded favourably to news of the French Revolution. Geraint Phillips has shown how much the Gwyneddigion owed to both Pughe's scholarly application and Jones's vision, zeal and generous financial backing.[69] The society's Welsh patriotism was expressed through its sociability, with Welsh functioning as the language of conviviality through poetry, harp-playing, singing and debating. This was not at all incompatible with Britishness, as illustrated by Thomas Jones's bilingual ode to the 'Gwyneddigion's Feast', 15 July 1799, with its concluding Cambro-British toasts:

> In cheerful bumpers drink, "success
>   "To the Heroes of our Isle."
> "May length of days and happiness,
>   "on our mighty Monarch smile."
> "To our Ancient BRITISH tongue,
>   "Unsullied honors to the end of time,
> "And may this SOCIAL BAND continue long
>   "To raise the pow'rs of BRITISH song
>   "Lofty and sublime!"[70]

As Jones's poetic toast suggests, the Gwyneddigion were no less fond of alcohol than the Cymmrodorion. Edward Charles's 'Brychlyfr' (Miscellany) gives us a privileged insight into their rowdy meetings, and shows how a sense of communal identity was articulated in texts that are replete with private or running jokes.[71] Edward Williams's ribald 'Cân Morfydd i'r Gyllell Gig' (Morfydd's Song to the Meat Knife),[72] and David Samwell's mock heroic poem, 'Padouca Hunt' (1791),[73] are excellent examples of clubbable entertainment since both provide roll-calls of society members and an indication of the group's dynamics. Samwell's poem in particular reflects the

Figure 7. John Jones (Jac Glan-y-gors), from
frontispiece to 1923 edition of *Seren Tan Gwmmwl*.

spectrum of opinion accommodated by associational culture, something also played out in the friendship and correspondence of two Gwyneddigion who hailed from the same area in north Wales: the loyal Church-and-king man, Edward Charles,[74] and the republican John Jones (Jac Glan-y-gors). Jones, the landlord of a tavern where the society often met, was often the butt of Charles's literary squibs, some of which were intended for his proposed anthology 'Bruttwn Gwynedd' (The Briton of Gwynedd). This volume was advertised on the final page of Jones's radical, Paineite pamphlet, *Seren Tan Gwmmwl* (A Star Under a Cloud; 1795), a volume attacked by Charles in print in 1796.[75] The mutual support that associational life offered was some-times expressed in more material ways and Charles's abject poverty in his later years was ameliorated by donations from the societies to which he had contributed so much during his lifetime.

The correspondence networks of the London Welsh were largely an extension of their associational culture. But while London's cultural pull and the focus of London-Welsh societies on cultural revival was an important facet of Welsh relations with London, this structure was not rigidly prescribed and it allowed for levels of direct and indirect (as well as official and unofficial) contact, provided the protocols of the republic of letters were observed.[76] For example, in his links with London, John Roberts (Siôn Lleyn) occasionally circumvented David Thomas as mediator by corresponding directly with two natives of the Llŷn Peninsula living in London: David Davies (Dafydd ap Dafydd) of Pwllheli and Thomas Roberts of Llwynrhudol.[77] Some Welsh correspondents also had family connections with London: Jonathan Hughes's son, Rhys, lived in the city,[78] as did the daughters of John Roberts.[79]

The most prolific correspondents amongst the Gwyneddigion in the 1790s were Owen Jones, William Owen Pughe and David Samwell. Owen Jones's reputation amongst the Gwyneddigion was not matched in London's polite society,[80] but the personal archives of Pughe and Samwell reveal that they were particularly well connected in London and beyond. Pughe had been in London for six years, unaware of the existence of the London-Welsh societies, before he was introduced to the Gwyneddigion by Robert Hughes in 1783. It proved a cultural awakening for him: his talents were nurtured by Owen Jones, and Pughe owes much of his renown as a lexicographer and scholar to the opportunities provided by his involvement with the Gwyneddigion's publications. He was also linked into wider antiquarian and lexicographical networks that included Robert Southey, William Godwin, Walter Scott and, possibly, William Blake. More controversially, and to the ultimate detriment of his reputation, he was also linked with the 'prophetess' Joanna Southcott.[81] Samwell's reputation rested on his surgical career in the navy and his eye-witness account of the death of Captain James Cook,

A Narrative of the Death of Captain Cook (1786).[82] He counted John Aikin, Anna Laetitia Barbauld (née Aikin), Anna Seward and Helen Maria Williams amongst his friends. The broader connectivity enjoyed by Pughe and Samwell was not necessarily a corollary of their status within London's Welsh societies, although the Gwyneddigion (and the Cymmrodorion before them) would have been an obvious first port of call for anyone in learned circles wishing to learn more about Wales and the Welsh.

The Eisteddfod: networking the imagined nation

As a meeting for professional poets and aristocratic patrons to confirm poetic rights and the rules of strict-metre poetry, and to license appropriately trained poets, an eisteddfod was a means of upholding the professional guild and its traditions in the face of social change.[83] Self-preservation against Anglicization and diminishing patronage provided the impetus for the eisteddfodau held at Caerwys in 1523 and 1567. Similarly, the revival of the Eisteddfod in early eighteenth-century Wales was the response of antiquaries and poets to a culture in crisis.[84] In the early eighteenth century, almanacs promoted numerous small, informal eisteddfodau which were held in taverns throughout Wales and known as 'eisteddfodau'r almanaciau' (almanac eisteddfodau). At this time, the Eisteddfod was essentially a nexus for lone poets and for Wales's regional poetic circles. This changed as the alliance of Welsh and London-Welsh networks in the 1790s effected its transformation into a recognizable movement. A narrative of this change can be gleaned from their correspondence.[85]

Eisteddfodau were discussed and organized in private correspondence between poets in Wales and London, and poetic compositions were also submitted by post for consideration by adjudicators. The postal nature of competition resulted in occasional subterfuge and partisanship, as competitors from Wales tried to curry favour, and their London-Welsh supporters provided them with inside knowledge and tried to influence decisions.[86] The initial stimulus came from the aged bard Jonathan Hughes of Llangollen who had been taught in poetic circles in Denbighshire and was held in high esteem by David Thomas. Multi-authored poems by Hughes and his associates, published in almanacs and anthologies,[87] attest the healthy nature of these networks. Such was his reputation that in 1803 Richard Llwyd, through the Duke of Somerset, secured Hughes a payment of £15 from the Royal Literary Fund,[88] an institution founded in 1790 by the Welshman David Williams. With the support of local clergy and gentry Hughes arranged an eisteddfod at Llangollen at the feast of Epiphany, January 1789. It was poorly attended: David Thomas was hampered by cold weather,[89] but Hughes recognized that the thin attendance was due to the penury of amateur poets.[90] He wrote to the Gwyneddigion requesting a small financial gift for the winning poet in the next eisteddfod, at Corwen, 12–13 May 1789.[91] Despite appealing to 'yspryd y Frawdoliaeth' (the spirit of Fraternity), Hughes's deferential attitude in this letter highlights the perceived cultural superiority of the London Welsh.

Crucially though, Hughes had already aroused the interest of Thomas Jones of Corwen, and the Eisteddfod found itself a new champion who overshadowed Hughes in its subsequent history. Assuming the role of un-official secretary,[92] Jones also wrote to the Gwyneddigion after the eisteddfod in Llangollen.[93] At a meeting of the society's 'council' the Gwyneddigion agreed to send a silver medal to the next eisteddfod.[94] As soon as money was involved, the society, understandably, wanted control of proceedings. Deem-ing arrangements for the Corwen eisteddfod to be at too short notice, they committed to support the next one at Bala in September.[95] However, con-fident of the patriotic zeal of the Gwyneddigion, Jones had already advertised their patronage of the Corwen eisteddfod in the newspapers of the Welsh border.[96] Rather than embarrass both himself and the London Welshmen, Jones organized the Corwen eisteddfod single-handedly at his own expense,[97] and instead solicited the Vaughan family of Nannau for a medal for the main poet.[98] He also set the subjects for the impromptu *englynion*: the king's return to health; the queen; the Prince of Wales; William Pitt; Robert Vaughan, the heir of Nannau; Corwen bridge; Owain Glyndŵr (Owen Glendower); and (despite their failure to provide financial support) the Gwyneddigion Society.[99] Jones reported on the Corwen eisteddfod to William Owen Pughe ('Cofiawdwr' (Recorder or Secretary) of the Gwyneddigion), concluding that it had, in actuality, been two eisteddfodau: 'sef un dan Lywodraeth Clio, ar llall (mewn ystafell neillduol) tan lywodraeth Bachus' (that is, one under the Government of Clio, and the other (in a separate room) under the government of Bacchus).[100]

The eisteddfod in Bala (September 1789) was therefore the first to be held under the official patronage of the Gwyneddigion, 'i gyflawni amcanion y gymdeithas' (to fulfil the aims of the society).[101] By this, it is meant that the Gwyneddigion, offering a medal for the best strict-metre ode (*awdl*), not only privileged strict-metre verse over free-metre, but also established the eisteddfodic rubric: a set subject judged by a panel of adjudicators. Their role as arbiters of taste extended to setting guidelines for the main *awdl* competition and establishing Goronwy Owen's brand of native neoclassicism as a poetic blue-print. The subjects chosen for the main *awdl* competition and the less prestigious *cywydd* and *englyn* reflect a desire to uphold the bard's traditional role as remembrancer of the Welsh nation, while at the same time imbuing it with contemporary relevance. Set subjects include the life of man (Bala, September 1789), liberty (St Asaph, 1790), truth and the massacre of the bards (Denbigh, 1792), war (Dolgellau, 1794), 'The Love of our Country through the resurrection of the ancient Eisteddfod and customs of Wales' and 'the best Translation into Welsh, of Gray's Ode – The Bard' (Caerwys, 1798).

In this sense, the eisteddfodau are also good indicators of Welsh attitudes (at home and in London) to the French Revolution and its cultural legacy. One of the Eisteddfod's most enthusiastic supporters was David Samwell, an avid reader of the work of Paine who nonetheless had no wish to see Paine's ideas realized. On the second anniversary of the fall of the Bastille, he invited friends – 'Freedom's Sons' – to celebrate at the Crown and Anchor.[102] Such was Owen Jones's excitement in the aftermath of the Revolution that he retrospectively asserted liberty as the principal aim of the Gwyneddigion (est. 1770): 'Ie Rhydd-did mewn Gwlad ac Eglwys yw amcan y Gymdeithas' (Yes, the aim of the Society is Freedom in State and Church).[103] That Welsh bards were required to write an *awdl* on 'Liberty' ('Rhyddid') for the eisteddfod at St Asaph (1790) is perhaps the fullest expression of the society's approval of revolutionary ideals and, as Martin Fitzpatrick has observed, 'for a time, British radicalism and Welsh cultural revivalism seemed all of a piece'.[104] But despite this radical undertow, and no doubt in deference to their patrons, the Gwyneddigion steered the bards towards a safer loyalist approach. In a printed letter addressed to the eisteddfod in Bala they located the revolution in France within the ideological inheritance of the Glorious Revolution of 1688:

RHYDDID: Y Trysor gwerthfawrocaf ar wyneb daear; canys oddiwrthi y deilliau, ac arni y mae'n gobenyddu, y rhan fwyaf o ddedwyddwch dynol-ryw tû yma i'r bedd. Rhyddid a ffrwyna Drais a Gormes: y hi sydd yn bwrw ymaith gaddug Anwybodaeth ac yn dryllio rhwydau Gau-Athrawiaeth ac Ofergoelion, pa rai sydd yn gorthrymu, ac yn caethiwo pob cynneddfau da, perthynas i nattur Dyn. Rhyddid yw'r argaead gorau i amddiffyn ein meddiannau a'n breiniau, mewn Gwlad ac Eglwys; er mwynhau pa un y bu amryw wledydd yn llifeirio o waed; ac yn ei phlaid yr ymdrechodd ein hynafiaid yn ddewrwych dros rai cannoedd o flynyddau.[105]

(LIBERTY: The most valuable Treasure on the face of the earth; because the greater part of mankind's happiness this side of the grave emanates from, and rests upon liberty. Liberty curbs Violence and Oppression: it casts aside the darkness of Ignorance and shatters the traps of False Doctrine and Superstition, which oppress and enslave all good faculties in relation to the nature of Man. Liberty is the best bulwark to defend our possessions and our rights, in Country and Church; for in order to enjoy liberty, several countries have been flowing with blood; and our ancestors struggled valiantly in liberty's cause over hundreds of years.)

I have discussed elsewhere the cautious Burkean paeans to the British state by David Thomas and Walter Davies that won first and second prize, respectively.[106] William Jones of Llangadfan also composed an *awdl* 'i ryddid a thrais' (to liberty and oppression). It was not submitted for the competition, but since the wording of its title echoes the letter to the bards quoted above, it was probably composed with the St Asaph eisteddfod in mind. With its anti-Catholic and anti-clerical rhetoric it also answers the radical expectations of London-Welsh supporters of the French republic such as Owen Jones and David Samwell:

> Hoffi yr ydoedd offeiriadau
> Eu gwaith i wneud yn gaeth eneidiau,
> A'u cau yn dynnion mewn cadwynau,
> Yno i ymgadw mewn mygydau,
> Ac i arfeddyd gwag grefyddau
> A mwy o ddolur i'w meddyliau;[107]

> (Priests liked
> their work which was to make souls captive
> and lock them tightly in chains,
> there to hide in masks,
> and to practise false religions
> and to more pain in their minds).

Eisteddfod paraphernalia could also be politically charged. The medals at the eisteddfod at Corwen in May 1789 were engraved on one side with Cambria, 'and on the reverse side a Lion defending *British* Liberty, against Foreign Enemies'.[108] In contrast, those at St Asaph in 1790 were designed by the medallist of the First French Republic, Augustin Dupré, depicting Liberty wearing a Phrygian cap.[109] The eisteddfodic banners drawn by Thomas Jones were similarly imaginative, 'Yn 'r Eisteddfod nesa, mi a ddangosaf Rhyddid yn ei llawn flodau . . .' (In the next Eisteddfod I will reveal Liberty in full bloom).[110] However, as the oppressive political climate in Britain intensified from 1793 onwards, the subject matter and tone of eisteddfodic verse became increasingly concerned with expressing Welsh obedience to Church and king.[111]

The gorseddau of Edward Williams provide a radical counterpoint to the more staid eisteddfodic institution. While a Gorsedd (a bardic meeting) was

essentially the same thing as an eisteddfod, the loaded English cognates that
Williams himself used hint at its more subversive nature: convention, con-
gress, national assembly, voice conventional.[112] The Gorsedd was the public
face of Williams's bardic system, and the first was held in London, 21 June
1792, on Primrose Hill (where Toland's 'The Ancient Druid Order' was
established in 1714)[113] and was supported by a select few: Edward Charles,
Daniel Davies, John Jones, Thomas Jones (Bardd Cloff), William Owen
Pughe, and David Samwell.[114] In his collected poems, Williams gave an
account of this inaugural Gorsedd in the footnotes to a poem declaimed
there: 'Ode on the Mythology of the Ancient British Bards'.[115] These
'Jacobinistic' London gorseddau formed a parallel society for politically
engaged Welshmen living in London, much like other offshoot societies
such as the Caradogion. It is perhaps significant that William's gorseddau
begin, not only in a period of political ferment in London, but during a lull
in the support of the Gwyneddigion for the Eisteddfod in 1792. Two further
meetings were held in London in September and December of 1792, but
they subsequently fell prey to the caution of its London-Welsh supporters
in the increasingly repressive atmosphere following the outbreak of war with
France: only one Gorsedd was held the following year, 22 September 1793.
These events were, after all, politically daring (and, in some cases, treasonable),
voicing pacific, democratic and regicidal themes in both Welsh and English:
notably Williams's 'Ode on Converting a Sword into a Pruning Hook' and
'Breiniau Dyn' (Rights of Man), and Samwell's English ode to Rhita Gawr,
a murderous mythological Welsh giant famous for his cloak made with the
beards of kings and tyrants.[116] Williams returned to Glamorgan in spring
1795 and the gorseddau he held in the county between 1795 and 1798 lost
none of their radical energy in the face of repression and persecution,[117] as
in his denunciation of wars as 'the savage exploits of kings' and 'their demonic
genius',[118] and the vehement anti-clericalism of 'The priest's triads sung by
Iolo Morganwg in the summer solstice Gorsedd on Garth Mountain in
Glamorganshire 1797':

> Tri pheth a gâr fy nghalon:
> Heddychu rhwng cymdogion,
> > Cadw'r iawn rhag mynd ar goll,
> A chrogi'r holl 'ffeiradon.[119]

> (There are three things which are close to my heart:
> making peace between neighbours,
> preserving justice from getting lost,
> and hanging all the priests.)

The Gorsedd held at Dinorwig in 1799 in the company of David Thomas and a handful of his pupils was the last one that Williams arranged himself in Wales. It encapsulates the Welsh bardic nationalism's wide spectrum of political and religious ideology, in that Williams reprised his anti-monarchic '*cywydd* invoking peace',[120] while Thomas's bardic apprentice Griffith Williams (Gutyn Peris) wished long life and prosperity to the king.[121] The institution would not be revived until 1815, with its political import expunged, by Thomas Williams (Gwilym Morganwg) and a new generation of Welsh bards and neo-druids.

The Welsh and London-Welsh network alliance failed to maintain its early enthusiasm for the Eisteddfod and the patriotic venture lost momentum as the decade drew to a close. The reasons for this were circumstantial and personal, yet also indicative of deep divisions. Circumstances changed for the major protagonists in its organization. In 1795 Thomas Jones's work took him from Llanrhaeadr-ym-Mochnant to Bristol, where he felt out of touch with London and Wales. In London, the attention of the Gwyneddigion – Owen Jones and William Owen Pughe in particular – was more focused on their publication programme: *The Myvyrian Archaiology of Wales* alone cost the equivalent of £250,000 in modern currency and Jones had little spare cash for the Welsh bards.[122] In Wales, the plight of hard-up amateur poets remained an obstacle to attendance at eisteddfodau outside their immediate locality, but more significantly the poets there grew resentful of the way in which the Gwyneddigion dictated the terms and adjudication of competitions. William Jones of Llangadfan complained that the poets at Corwen had been rude to him and castigated their servility to the London Welsh: 'Tebyg eu bod yn ymfoneddigo o herwydd bod gwyneddigion Llundain yn ymarddelw a hi [=Awen]' (It is likely that they are becoming gentrified because the Gwyneddigion of London are championing her [=the Muse]).[123] Following his successes in the early 1790s, David Thomas was prohibited from competitions and, although he encouraged his protégés to compete, he retaliated by organizing eisteddfodau in Caernarfonshire in-dependently of the Gwyneddigion.

Conclusions

The initial stimulus may have come from within Wales and the financial and organizational structure from the London Welsh, but the narrative of the eisteddfodau sponsored by the Gwyneddigion demonstrates the thoroughly transformative agency of Wales's alliance of bardic and correspondence networks. Not only was the revived Eisteddfod the locus of network activity between Wales and London in the 1790s, but it was also one of its successes. The Eisteddfod is a narrative of engagement and participation in the public sphere. The same outlets that fostered internal communications in Wales and external communications with the London Welsh also served to publicize and validate its activities: eisteddfodic material was published in almanacs, anthologies, single-authored volumes, as well as in special Gwyneddigion publications. Despite the inevitable divisions that ensued, the experiment had many positive outcomes for Welsh literary culture in general. Building on the structures of the London-Welsh societies, Welsh bardic networks went on to develop their own associational culture in the form of literary societies. The early nineteenth century witnessed a flowering of these: those in north-west Wales were established largely under the influence of David Thomas, while those in south Wales were initiated by a network of literary parsons, with Walter Davies playing a prominent role. In turn, the literary parsons were responsible for the highly successful Regional Eisteddfod movement (Eisteddfodau Taleithiol; est. 1819) that evolved into the National Eisteddfod, still held in different regions of Wales each August. In both literal and figurative senses, then, the Welsh bards and London-Welsh societies successfully networked the nation.

Notes

[1] For imagined nationalist communities, see Benedict Anderson, *Imagined Communities: Reflections on the Origin and Spread of Nationalism* (revised edn., London, 2006).

[2] Prys Morgan, 'From a Death to a View: The Hunt for the Welsh Past in the Romantic Period', in Eric Hobsbawm and Terence Ranger (eds.), *The Invention of Tradition* (Cambridge, 1983), pp. 56–62.

[3] See chapters by William D. Brewer, Caroline Franklin, Michael J. Franklin and J. R. Watson in Gerard Carruthers and Alan Rawes, *English Romanticism and the Celtic World* (Cambridge, 2003).

[4] Cathryn A. Charnell-White, *Welsh Poetry of the French Revolution 1789–1805* (Cardiff, 2012).

[5] Prys Morgan, *The Eighteenth Century Renaissance* (Llandybïe, 1981).

[6] For Welsh forms of bardic nationalism, see Cathryn A. Charnell-White, *Bardic Circles: Personal, Regional and National Identity in the Bardic Vision of Iolo Morganwg* (Cardiff, 2007); eadem, *Welsh Poetry of the French Revolution*; Andrew Davies, '"Redirecting the Attention of History": Antiquarian and Historical Fictions of Wales from the Romantic Period', in Damian Walford Davies and Lynda Pratt (eds.), *Wales and the Romantic Imagination* (Cardiff, 2007), pp. 104–21; Shawna Lichtenwalner, *Claiming Cambria: Invoking the Welsh in the Romantic Era* (Newark,

2008); Sarah Prescott, *Eighteenth-Century Writing from Wales: Bards and Britons* (Cardiff, 2008).

[7] See Claude J. Summers and Ted-Larry Pebworth (eds.), *Literary Circles and Cultural Communities in Renaissance England* (London, 2000); Rebecca D'Monté and Nicole Pohl (eds.), *Female Communities 1600–1800* (Houndmills, 2000).

[8] This is particularly true of small bardic circles that included women and exponents of free-metre verse, see Cathryn A. Charnell-White (ed.), *Beirdd Ceridwen: Blodeugerdd Barddas o Ganu Menywod hyd tua 1800* (Barddas, 2005), pp. 37–9.

[9] Eiluned Rees, *The Welsh Book-Trade Before 1820* (Aberystwyth, 1988); *eadem.*, 'The Welsh Book Trade from 1718 to 1820', in *eadem* and Philip Henry Jones (eds.), *A Nation and its Books: A History of the Book in Wales* (Aberystwyth, 1998), pp. 61–92.

[10] A. Cynfael Lake, 'Sion Rhydderch a'r Eisteddfod', in Tegwyn Jones and Huw Walters (eds.), *Cawr i'w Genedl: Cyfrol i Gyfarch yr Athro Hywel Teifi Edwards* (Llandysul, 2008), pp. 35–58.

[11] David Davis, *Telyn Dewi* (Llundain, 1824), pp. iv–v. This also contains translations into Welsh of the work of Laetitia Barbauld, William Cowper, Thomas Gray, Alexander Pope and Isaac Watts.

[12] Damian Walford Davies uses the phrase 'reticular culture' to describe the interface of various political, literary and antiquarian discourses in the culture of the 1790s that form a network of allusions in literary works: *idem*, *Presences that Disturb: Models of Romantic Identity in the Literature and Culture of the 1790s* (Cardiff, 2002), pp. 4, 7.

[13] Jon Mee, *Conversable Worlds: Literature, Contention, and Community 1762 to 1830* (Oxford, 2011); Alex Benchimol and Willy Maley (eds.), *Spheres of Influence: Intellectual and Cultural Publics from Shakespeare to Habermas* (Oxford, 2007); Russell Gillian and Clara Tuite (eds.), *Romantic Sociability: Social Networks and Literary Culture in Britain, 1770–1849* (Cambridge, 2002).

[14] Ellis left his collection of manuscripts to Thomas upon his death in 1795.

[15] Geraint Phillips, *Dyn Heb ei Gyffelyb yn y Byd: Owain Myfyr a'i Gysylltiadau Llenyddol* (Caerdydd, 2010), pp. 98–9.

[16] See Dafydd Glyn Jones, *Un o Wŷr y Medra: Bywyd a Gwaith William Williams, Llandygái 1728–1817* (Dinbych, 1999), pp. 77–83.

[17] *HHSC*, pp. 258, 270.

[18] Charnell-White, *Welsh Poetry of the French Revolution*, pp. 17–18, no. 36.

[19] Thomas's immediate circle also included Hugh Evans (Hywel Eryri), Richard Jones (Gwyndaf Eryri), Robert Morris (or Robin Morus; Robin Ddu Eifionydd), Owen Williams (Owain Gwyrfai), and William Williams (Gwilym Peris).

[20] Cynan Evans-Jones, 'Tad Beirdd Eryri: Dafydd Tomos ("Dafydd Ddu Eryri") 1759–1822', *THSC* (1970), 6–23.

[21] A selection of their correspondence is reproduced in John Jones (Myrddin Fardd) (ed.), '*Adgof Uwch Anghof*: Llythyrau Lliaws o Brif Enwogion Cymru, Hen a Diweddar* (Pen y Groes, 1883).

[22] *Idem*, *Enwogion Sir Gaernarfon* (Caernarfon, 1922), pp. 23–4, 129–30, 150–2, 269–71.

162 CATHRYN A. CHARNELL-WHITE

23 Work by David Thomas, Thomas Edwards and others feature in Jonathan Hughes's second volume of poetry that was posthumously published, *Gemwaith Beirdd Awen Collen* (Croesoswallt, 1806).

24 Elizabeth Edwards, *English-Language Poetry from Wales 1789–1806* (Cardiff, 2013), *passim*.

25 *Y Greal, neu Eurgrawn, sef Trysorfa Gwybodaeth* . . . (Miscellany, or Magazine, that is Treasury of Knowledge; 1800).

26 In Cardiganshire, Ioan Siencyn (John Jenkin(s); 1716–96) was tutored by his father, a cobbler and Dissenting preacher. This kind of hereditary, familial dimension was also apparent in both professional and amateur bardic circles of medieval and early modern Wales: Dafydd Johnston, '*Canu ar ei fwyd ei hun': Golwg ar y Bardd Amatur yng Nghymru* (Abertawe, 1997), *passim*; Nia M. W. Powell, 'Women and Strict-Metre Poetry in Wales', in Michael Roberts and Simone Clarke (eds.), *Women and Gender in Early Modern Wales* (Cardiff, 2000), p. 139.

27 Brian Ll. James, 'The Welsh Language in the Vale of Glamorgan', *Morgannwg*, XVI (1972), 16–36; Charnell-White, *Bardic Circles*, pp. 85–7.

28 Poets that were members of the group included John Bradford of Betws, Edward Evan(s) of Aberdare, Dafydd Hopcyn of Coety, Dafydd Nicolas of Aberpergwm, Dafydd Thomas of Pandy'r Ystrad and William Roberts of Yr Ydwal, Llancarfan. The group may also have included Wil Hopcyn of Llangynwyd. See Ceri W. Lewis, 'The Literary History of Glamorgan from 1550 to 1770', in Glanmor Williams (ed.), *Glamorgan County History. Volume IV: Early Modern Glamorgan from the Act of Union to the Industrial Revolution* (Cardiff, 1974), pp. 535–639, 687–97.

29 G. J. Williams, *Iolo Morganwg – Y Gyfrol Gyntaf* (Caerdydd, 1956), p. 373; *CIM*, I, pp. 60–3, Siencyn Morgan to Iolo Morganwg, 30 November 1771.

30 For Williams's letter and *englynion*, see *CIM*, I, pp. 38–42, Iolo Morganwg to the publishers of *Trysorfa Gwybodaeth*, 25 February 1770. For the periodical, see D. Rhys Phillips, 'The "Eurgrawn Cymraeg" of 1770', *JWBS*, V, no. 1 (1937), 49–56.

31 'Annerch Iorwerth Morganwg', in Gwilym Howel, *Tymmhorol, ag wybrenol Newyddion, NEU ALMA[NAC] NEWYDD Am y Flwyddyn* . . . *1775* (Mwythig, [1775]), 31.

32 This sense of belonging is expressed by one of the Glamorgan grammarians, Rhys Morgan of Pencraig Nedd, in nine stanzas addressing Wales's bards printed in Siôn Rhydderch's almanac for 1734, *Newyddion oddiwrth y Ser; NEU ALMANAC* . . . *1734* (Mwythig, [1734]), 18–19. Morgan's work appeared in various almanacs between 1739 and 1792.

33 The Cymmrodorion part-financed Richards's dictionary: Charnell-White, *Bardic Circles*, p. 131, n. 47. Walters corresponded with Owen Jones and Edward Davies, see Phillips, *Dyn Heb ei Gyffelyb yn y Byd*, *passim*; Moira Dearnley, *Distant Fields: Eighteenth-Century Fictions of Wales* (Cardiff, 2001), p. 164. Richards is named as a corresponding member of the Cymmrodorion in 1762, as is Bradford: see *HHSC*, pp. 271, 266.

34 The first surviving letter between them is dated 25 January 1776: see *CIM*, I, pp. 109–13, Iolo Morganwg to Owen Jones, 25 January 1776.

35 Charnell-White, *Bardic Circles*, pp. 12, 16–18, 91–3.

36 *CIM*, I, pp. 159–64, Iolo Morganwg to Owen Jones, 10 July 1780.

37 For Williams's dealings with Evans, see ibid., pp. 140–2, Iolo Morganwg to Evan Evans, [?April 1779]; ibid., *III*, pp. 171–5, Iolo Morganwg to Taliesin Williams, 16–17 August 1813; Williams, *Iolo Morganwg*, pp. 378–87, 430–1.

38 NLW 13121B, p. 206.

39 William Owen [Pughe], *The Heroic Elegies and Other Pieces of Llywarç Hen* (London, 1792), p. xxxvii. Williams's ideas were first published in a sketch of Bardism in the introduction to this volume.

40 James E. Epstein, *Radical Expression: Political Language, Ritual, and Symbol in England, 1790–1850* (Oxford, 1994), p. 18; Mary-Ann Constantine, *The Truth against the World: Iolo Morganwg and Romantic Forgery* (Cardiff, 2007).

41 Mary-Ann Constantine, '"This Wildernessed Business of Publication": The Making of *Poems, Lyric and Pastoral* (1974)', in Geraint H. Jenkins (ed.), *A Rattleskull Genius: The Many Faces of Iolo Morganwg* (Cardiff, 2005), pp. 123–45.

42 The poetic responses to revolution of the Dissenting minister and grammarian Edward Evan(s) of Aberdare are edited and translated in Charnell-White, *Welsh Poetry of the French Revolution*, nos. 1–2.

43 Geraint H. Jenkins, *Bard of Liberty: the Political Radicalism of Iolo Morganwg* (Cardiff, 2012). See also Jon Mee, '"Images of Truth New Born": Iolo, William Blake and the Literary Radicalism of the 1790s', in Jenkins (ed.), *A Rattleskull Genius*, pp. 173–93; Davies, *Presences that Disturb, passim; idem.*, '"At Defiance": Iolo, Godwin, Coleridge, Wordsworth', in Jenkins (ed.), *A Rattleskull Genius*, pp. 147–72.

44 Charnell-White, *Welsh Poetry of the French Revolution*, no. 18; Mary-Ann Constantine and Elizabeth Edwards, '"Bard of Liberty": Iolo Morganwg, Wales and Radical Song', in John Kirk, Andrew Noble and Michael Brown (eds.), *Poetry and Song in the Age of Revolution. Volume I: United Islands? The Languages of Resistance* (London, 2012), pp. 63–76.

45 J. Pughe, curate of Cricieth, to Walter Davies in May 1794, quoted in Glenda Carr, *William Owen Pughe* (Caerdydd, 1983), p. 31.

46 *CIM*, II, pp. 226–9, Iolo Morganwg to Owen Jones, 5 October 1799; ibid., pp. 233–5, Iolo Morganwg to Owen Jones, 23 October 1799; Charnell-White, *Welsh Poetry of the French Revolution*, nos. 17–25.

47 Edwards, *English-Language Poetry from Wales*. An image of the broadside is available at *http://www.iolomorganwg.cymru.ac.uk/gwaith-trialbyjury.php*.

48 Martin Fitzpatrick, 'David Samwell: An Eventful Career', in *idem*, Nicholas Thomas and Jennifer Newell (eds.), *The Death of Captain Cook and Other Writings by David Samwell* (Cardiff, 2007), pp. 17, 29.

49 Davies, *Presences that Disturb*, p. 136.

50 See Geraint H. Jenkins, 'The "Rural Voltaire" and the "French madcaps"', in this volume.

51 See the politically inflected poetic exchange regarding peace between David Davis, Edward Williams and the Revd. Thomas Evans in Charnell-White, *Welsh Poetry of the French Revolution*, nos. 16, 24, 44.

52 William Vaughan of Corsygedol, Sir Watkin Williams Wynn II of Wynnstay and
    Sir Watkin Lewes all served the Antient Britons and the Cymmrodorion in various
    capacities and were famous enough to be satirized by the London press. See Peter
    Lord, *Words with Pictures: Welsh Images and Images of Wales in the Popular Press,
    1640–1860* (Aberystwyth, 1995), pp. 53–74.

53 Quoted in Glenda Carr, 'William Owen Pughe and the London Societies', in
    Branwen Jarvis (ed.), *A Guide to Welsh Literature c.1700–1800* (Cardiff, 2000),
    pp. 168–86.

54 Frank O'Gorman, *The Long Eighteenth Century: British Political and Social History
    1688–1832* (London, 2005), p. 4–5.

55 Murray Pittock, *Scottish and Irish Romanticism* (Oxford, 2008), pp. 235–58.

56 Peter Clark, *British Clubs and Societies, 1580–1800: The Origins of an Associational
    World* (Oxford, 2000).

57 *HHSC.*

58 Ibid., pp. 1–15; Emrys Jones, 'The Age of Societies', in *idem* (ed.), *The Welsh in
    London 1500–2000* (Cardiff, 2001), pp. 61–6; Prescott, *Eighteenth-Century Writing
    from Wales*, chapter 1.

59 *Constitutions of the Honourable Society of Cymmrodorion in London, begun in London
    in the month of September 1751* (London, 1755), p. 13.

60 Jones, 'The Age of Societies', pp. 74–81; *HHSC*, pp. 45–132.

61 Ibid., pp. 128–9.

62 E. G. Millward (ed.), *Cerddi Jac Glan-y-gors* (Barddas, 2003); J. B. Edwards, 'John
    Jones (Jac Glan-y-Gors): Tom Paine's Denbighshire Henchman?', *TDHS*, 51
    (2002), 95–112; Middleton Pennant Jones, 'John Jones of Glan-y-Gors', *THSC*
    (1911), 60–94; Marion Löffler, 'Cerddi Newydd gan John Jones, "Jac Glan-y-
    Gors"', *LlC*, 33 (2010), 143–50.

63 Phillips, *Dyn Heb ei Gyffelyb yn y Byd*; *idem*, 'Forgery and Patronage: Iolo Morganwg
    and Owain Myfyr', in Jenkins (ed.), *A Rattleskull Genius*, pp. 403–23.

64 Carr, *William Owen Pughe*; *eadem*, 'An Uneasy Partnership: Iolo Morganwg and
    William Owen Pughe', in Jenkins (ed.), *A Rattleskull Genius*, pp. 443–60.

65 Fitzpatrick, Thomas and Newell (eds.), *The Death of Captain Cook*; Martin Fitz-
    patrick, 'The "Cultivated Understanding" and Chaotic Genius o David Samwell',
    in Jenkins (ed.), *A Rattleksull Genius*, pp. 383–402.

66 J. Hubert Morgan, 'Edward Charles (Siamas Wynedd)', *Y Llenor*, X (1931), 25–34.

67 Some extant lists of full and corresponding members are reproduced as an appendix
    to *HHSC*, pp. 248–80.

68 William Jones's letters to Edward Jones are in NLW 168C, NLW 170C, NLW
    171E, NLW 323E, and NLW 1806E contains his letters to Walter Davies. See also
    Tecwyn Ellis, *Edward Jones Bardd y Brenin 1752–1824* (Caerdydd, 1957), pp. 25–6.

69 Among their publications are *Barddoniaeth Dafydd ab Gwilym* (1789), *The Heroic
    Elegies and Other Pieces of Llywarç Hen* (1792), *Cambrian Biography* (1803), *The
    Myvyrian Archaiology of Wales*, and the short-lived periodicals *Cambrian Register*
    (1795–6, 1818) and *Y Greal* (1807).

70 Thomas Jones, *At Gymdeithas y Gwyneddigion, Yr Awdl Hon i'ch Gwlêdd Flynyddawl
    . . .* (London, [1799]), p. 9. Appended to the poem in NLW, Mellon, 588 is a

printed poem by Edward Charles on the same occasion. For a nuanced discussion of Welsh writers and the British state, see Bethan Jenkins, 'Concepts of Prydeindod (Britishness) in 18th century Anglo-Welsh writing: with special reference to the works of Lewis Morris, Evan Evans and Edward Williams' (unpublished University of Oxford D.Phil. thesis, 2011).

[71] Cardiff 3.116, 'Brychlyfr Edward Charles', contains occasional and eisteddfodic verse, and poems of historical interest, as well as material regarding the societies' meetings, including songs and satirical speeches such as 'Bacchus's Creed', 'Charlie's Prophecy about Siôn Ceiriog', and 'John Jones of Glan-y-gors's favourite things'.

[72] NLW 21390E, p. 22; for more of Williams's ribaldry amongst the Gwyneddigion, see Cathryn A. Charnell-White, 'Women and Gender in the Private and Social Relationships of Iolo Morganwg', in Jenkins (ed.), *A Rattleskull Genius*, pp. 379–80. For extreme sexual sociability, see David Stevenson, *The Beggar's Benison: Sex Clubs of Enlightenment Scotland and their Rituals* (East Linton, 2001).

[73] Fitzpatrick, Thomas and Newell (eds.), *The Death of Captain Cook*, pp. 135–49; W. Ll. Davies, 'David Samwell's Poem – "The Padouca Hunt"', *NLWJ*, II, nos. 3–4 (1942), 144–52; Carr, 'An Uneasy Partnership', pp. 449–50. For the Madogwys, see Gwyn A. Willliams, *Madoc: The Making of a Myth* (London, 1979).

[74] For his poems denouncing the French after the execution of Louis XVI and the 'Democrats' tried for treason in 1794, see Charnell-White, *Welsh Poetry of the French Revolution*, nos. 31–2.

[75] Edward Charles (Antagonist), 'Golwg byr ar y llyfr a elwir Seren Tan Gwmmwl', *Y Geirgrawn*, I (1796), 16–21. Marion Löffler, *Welsh Responses to the French Revolution: Press and Public Discourse* (Cardiff, 2012), pp. 255–65.

[76] For the conventions of letter-writing, see Janet Gurkin Altman, *Epistolarity: Approaches to a Form* (Columbus, 1982); Rebecca Earle (ed.), *Epistolary Selves: Letters and Letter-Writers, 1600–1945* (Aldershot, 1999), pp. 1–12.

[77] Jones, *Enwogion Sir Gaernarfon*, pp. 23–4. In a letter dated 1800, Thomas Roberts informs John Roberts that he has nominated him as a corresponding member of the Gwyneddigion: see R. L. Griffiths, 'The contribution of certain Methodists from the area of Llyn and Eifion (Caerns.) to religious education and literature with special reference to the work of Siôn Lleyn (John Roberts, 1749–1817)' (unpublished University of Liverpool MA thesis, 1965–6), p. 214.

[78] Glyn M. Ashton, 'Arolwg ar Brydyddiaeth Gymraeg, 1801–25', *LlC*, 14, nos. 3 and 4 (1983–4), 239.

[79] Roberts's daughters lived in Wapping according to a letter to John Roberts (Siôn Lleyn) from Thomas Roberts, Llwynrhudol in 1800. Quoted in Griffiths, 'The contribution of certain Methodists from the area of Llyn and Eifion', p. 214.

[80] Despite the fact that professional guilds were less influential in this period, Jones joined the Salters' Company in 1784 in order to gain the right to vote and was not a member of his own profession's guild, the Worshipful Company of Skinners. Phillips, *Dyn Heb ei Gyffelyb yn y Byd*, pp. 13–14.

[81] Carr, *William Owen Pughe*, pp. 124–55; Patrick Thomas, 'Mr Pughe and the Poetess', *Cambria*, 11, no. 3 (2009), 28–30.

[82] For an edited and annotated version of Samwell's narrative, as well as his correspondence and selection of his Welsh and English poetry, see Fitzpatrick, Thomas and Newell (eds.), *The Death of Captain Cook*.

[83] Hywel Teifi Edwards, *The Eisteddfod* (Cardiff, 1990), pp. 4–10.

[84] Charnell-White, *Bardic Circles*, pp. 119–21.

[85] A selection are reproduced in G. J. Williams, 'Llythyrau ynglyn ag Eisteddfodau'r Gwyneddigion. A. Eisteddfod Corwen, Mai 12 a 13, 1789', *LlC*, I (1950–1), 29–47; *idem*, 'Llythyrau ynglyn ag Eisteddfodau'r Gwyneddigion. B. Eisteddfod y Bala, Medi 29 a 30, 1789', ibid., 113–25.

[86] For suspicions of cheating at the eisteddfodau of the 1790s, see Carr, 'William Owen Pughe and the London Societies', pp. 172–3.

[87] Siwan M. Rosser, 'Golwg ar ganu rhydd Jonathan Hughes, 1721–1805' (unpublished University of Wales M.Phil. thesis, 1998), p. 7; William Jones (ed.), *Llu o Ganiadau, neu gasgliad o garolau a cherddi dewisedig . . .* (Croesoswallt, 1798).

[88] Daniel Williams, *Beirdd y Gofeb* (Dinbych, 1951), pp. 60–2.

[89] Jones (ed.), '*Adgof Uwch Anghof*', p. 13, David Thomas to John Roberts, 17 January 1789.

[90] BL Add 9848, pp. 126a–128b, Jonathan Hughes to the Gwyneddigion Society, 25 February 1789.

[91] Loc cit.

[92] Williams, 'Llythyrau ynglyn ag Eisteddfodau'r Gwyneddigion. A,', 29.

[93] See the minutes for the meeting held 2 February 1789, BL Add 9848, p. 125a.

[94] Ibid., p. 125b, minutes for 2 March 1789.

[95] BL Add 14995, pp. 3a–4b, William Owen Pughe to Thomas Jones, May 1789; ibid., pp. 73a–76a, Thomas Jones to William Owen Pughe, 20 May 1789; NLW 13221E, pp. 439–42, Thomas Jones to Edward Jones, 3 August 1789.

[96] *Shrewsbury Chronicle*, 2 May 1789. See Williams, 'Llythyrau ynglyn ag Eisteddfodau'r Gwyneddigion. A.', 36.

[97] NLW 13221E, pp. 439–42, Thomas Jones to Edward Jones, 3 August 1789, suggests that Thomas Jones was reimbursed for costs incurred.

[98] The medal is no. 15 in Iorwerth C. Peate, 'Welsh Society and Eisteddfod Medals and Relics', *THSC* (1937), 293, 285–330.

[99] Cwrtmawr 35B, pp. 74–83; Cain Jones, *Tymmhorol, ac Wybrenol Newyddion, neu Almanac . . . 1790* (Mwythig, [1789]), 2–21.

[100] BL Add 14995, pp. 73a–76a, Thomas Jones of Corwen to William Owen Pughe, 20 May 1789.

[101] Ibid., pp. 3a–4b, William Owen Pughe to Thomas Jones of Corwen, May 1789. It also describes the rubric for the Bala eisteddfod.

[102] Cwrtmawr 35B, fly-leaf. See also *CIM*, I, pp. 389–90, David Samwell to Iolo Morganwg, [?July 1791].

[103] NLW 1806E, letter 665, Owen Jones to Walter Davies, 31 October 1789.

[104] Fitzpatrick, 'David Samwell: An Eventful Career', p. 29.

[105] BL Add 15024, pp. 367–9, a printed letter to the bards at the eisteddfod at Bala in 1789.

[106] Charnell-White, *Welsh Poetry of the French Revolution*, pp. 11–13, 36–8, nos. 34 and 41.

[107] Ibid,. no. 7, lines 102–7.

[108] NLW 1806E, letter 765, Thomas Jones of Corwen to Walter Davies, 29 July 1789.

[109] Peate, 'Welsh Society and Eisteddfod Medals and Relics', 293, 285–330.

[110] BL Add 15024, pp. 212a–213b, Thomas Jones of Corwen to William Owen Pughe, 7 October 1789.

[111] For a detailed discussion of the loyalist eisteddfodic output, see Charnell-White, *Welsh Poetry of the French Revolution*, pp. 31–9.

[112] Charnell-White, *Bardic Circles*, p. 119, n. 2.

[113] Stuart Piggot, *The Druids* (London, 1999), pp. 135–6.

[114] Walter Davies and Anna Seward are also named, but were probably initiated *in absentia*.

[115] Edward Williams, *Poems, Lyric and Pastoral* (2 vols., London, 1794), II, p. 193. See also Edwards, *English-Language Poetry from Wales*, no. 15.

[116] Edwards, *English-Language Poetry from Wales*, no. 7; Charnell-White, *Welsh Poetry of the French Revolution*, nos. 17–21; NLW 21398E, p. 29.

[117] See Charnell-White, *Welsh Poetry of the French Revolution*, nos. 22–4.

[118] Ibid., no. 24, lines 31, 34.

[119] Ibid., no. 23, lines 93–6.

[120] Ibid., no. 24.

[121] NLW 325E, p. 136.

[122] Phillips, *Dyn Heb ei Gyffelyb yn y Byd*, p. 239.

[123] NLW 1806E, letter 777, William Jones of Llangadfan to Walter Davies, 28 June 1789.

Radical adaptation: translations of medieval Welsh poetry in the 1790s

Dafydd Johnston

Recent studies of the early history of Welsh-English translation have focused primarily on the colonial relationship between Wales and England. Translators 'sought the approbation of the colonizer in an attempt to restore national self-respect and to assert an element of autonomy.'[1] M. Wynn Thomas has referred to the translations in Evan Evans's *Some Specimens of the Poetry of the Ancient Welsh Bards* (1764), as 'exercises in nation-building' which resulted in 'a carefully depoliticized cultural nationalism',[2] and the term 'bardic nationalism' has been used to describe the brand of literary patriotism popularized by Evans's seminal volume.[3] Whilst acknowledging that the post-colonial approach is essential for a broad understanding of translation from Welsh up to the twentieth century, this essay will contend that certain translators in the 1790s took advantage of the freedom of verse translation to engage with socio-political concerns which cut across issues of nationality and need to be seen in the context of the French Revolution and its aftermath.[4]

The upsurge of translation activity in the early 1790s was partly stimulated by another highly influential collection of source texts, *Barddoniaeth Dafydd ab Gwilym*, edited by two London Welshmen, Owen Jones and William Owen Pughe, and published within weeks of the fall of the Bastille in the summer of 1789. The contrast between this and Evans's *Specimens* is telling in several ways. *Specimens* is a scholarly trilingual volume which presents original texts and English prose translations of ten poems, mostly from the period of the independent Welsh princes in the twelfth and thirteenth centuries, accompanied by a Latin essay on the history of Welsh poetry, 'De Bardis Dissertatio'. These are exceptionally difficult texts in terms of both language and style, and Evans's careful translations provided an indispensable basis for later literary versions, such as those by John Walters (1782),[5] and that by Richard Llwyd discussed below. *Barddoniaeth Dafydd ab Gwilym* contains 261 poems thought to be the work of the great lyric poet of the fourteenth century, Dafydd ap Gwilym.[6] The language of these poems is not far removed from modern literary Welsh, and since it contains no translations the volume seems to have been intended for a Welsh-speaking audience, but on the other hand it has an English introduction sketching the poet's life and times, with a few translated extracts, which suggests an attempt to arouse interest in London literary circles. It was a book crying out to be translated, and translations of individual poems did soon appear, although no free-standing collection was published until 1834.[7]

A major contrast between the two volumes has to do with a fundamental change in Welsh culture in the fourteenth century. Prior to the Edwardian Conquest Welsh court poetry was closely associated with the struggle of the princes to maintain their independence under military pressure from the Normans, promoting a heroic ethic which went back to the earliest Welsh poetry by Aneirin and Taliesin in the sixth century. Evan Evans certainly succeeded in conveying the spirit of the originals in this respect, and seems to have delighted in shocking his readers with horrific details such as 'the flood of human gore gushed in streams down the knees'.[8] The same blood-thirsty glorification of martial prowess is evident in a translation by the Revd Richard Williams of Fron near Ruthin of a poem in praise of Owain Glyndŵr first published in Thomas Pennant's *Tours in Wales* in 1781, and republished in Edward Jones's *The Musical and Poetical Relicks of the Welsh Bards* (1784).[9] The original poem by Gruffudd Llwyd actually refers to Owain's exploits on behalf of the English crown in Scotland in the 1380s,[10] but the free translation portrays him as the scourge of the English which he later became:

> Loud Fame has told thy gallant deeds,
> In every word a Saxon bleeds;
> Terror, and flight, together came,
> Obedient to thy mighty name:
> Death, in the van, with ample stride,
> Hew'd thee a passage deep and wide.[11]

As that poem shows, the heroic ethic continued to be celebrated well after the Edwardian Conquest, but it was becoming increasingly anachronistic, and Dafydd ap Gwilym's poetry represented a turning point around the middle of the fourteenth century with its celebration of the peaceful arts of civility and the joys of love and the natural world, a shift in emphasis which would appeal to radicals who were opposed to war on principle, and also to many who suffered its consequences as the Napoleonic wars took their toll on the lives of the people of Britain.

Dafydd ap Gwilym's pivotal role in Welsh literary history is conveyed by William Owen Pughe in terms which draw on contemporary political discourse:

> Here it may be necessary to observe that the order of bards was considered as a branch of the constitution; and their poetry was the sacred repertory of history, agreeable to the direct injunction of the laws; and therefore it was requisite it should be, as we find it is, free from overcharged imagery which might be liable to obscure truth in the blaze of splendid fable. They generally did not deviate from this system, but considered it the principal object of their institution, until the dissolution of the order in that final catastrophe, the death of Dafydd ap Gruffudd, in the year 1283, which put a period to the independency of the ancient Britons. When that event took place, the bards were at liberty to follow the flights of their fancy; which of course produced a great revolution in their poetry . . . By the fall of the Cambro-British power, the original object being done away, to which the order of the bards had hitherto paid attention, their genius was left unrestrained, as has been before hinted, which caused a revolution in their poetry; and consequently this period gave birth to several new laws of versification and composition; which, though not capable of that great effect produced by the flowing and animated harmony of the old metres, were melodious, and congenial with the nature of the lighter subjects to which they were adapted.[12]

The term *revolution* is used here in its primary sense of a circular motion bringing about complete change, but the political sense is certainly implied by the claim that the bardic order was a 'branch of the constitution', and would have come readily to mind in a year when Britain had just celebrated the centenary of its Glorious Revolution of 1688, not to mention constitutional changes in France which were already being described as a revolution when this passage was written in the first half of 1789.[13] It is worth noting that liberty is seen here as a condition which produced a revolution rather than as an outcome achieved by it.

The question of the relevance of the French Revolution to *Barddoniaeth Dafydd ab Gwilym* can be approached in various ways, the most fundamental of which would be to pursue links between sexual freedom, as celebrated in Dafydd's sensual love lyrics, Rousseauian primitivism and political radicalism.[14] Here I shall focus on aspects evident in the early published translations, which were understandably concerned to project a 'respectable' image of the Welsh bard, although the thrill of licentiousness is never far from the surface.

At this point a key player in the formation of *Barddoniaeth Dafydd ab Gwilym* needs to be introduced. Edward Williams, better known as Iolo Morganwg, sent the two editors both biographical (mis)information and a total of fourteen new poems (which were actually his own compositions), all of which were included in the volume and substantially changed its character.[15] The main effect of this interference was to increase the role played by Glamorgan, and by the patronage of Ifor Hael in particular, in the poet's life and work. This has generally been seen as shameless promotion of Iolo's native region, but it was much more than that as well, involving socio-political ideals which were also highlighted in translations published by Iolo himself and by a fellow-member of the London Gwyneddigion Society, David Samwell.

The importance of translating Dafydd ap Gwilym for the development of Iolo's career as a poet is shown by the fact that his earliest published translation was printed in 1791 as a specimen to attract subscriptions to his collection *Poems, Lyric and Pastoral* (eventually published in 1794).[16] Entitled 'The Fair Pilgrim', it is a very expansive version of an original in which Dafydd ap Gwilym tells of a girl undertaking a pilgrimage from north Wales to St David's in order to do penance for having caused his death by her cruelty, and calls upon each of the rivers she must cross to allow her safe passage.[17] Iolo expands on the descriptions of the rivers to depict a Romantic landscape reflecting the emotions of the protagonists, and ascribes a virtuous benevolence to the girl which has no basis in the original. Several reviews of *Poems, Lyric and Pastoral* say that this translation is one of the best pieces in the collection – perhaps because it was part of the proposal?[18]

Poems, Lyric and Pastoral contains two other translations of poems by Dafydd ap Gwilym, one a complaint about a thunderstorm which disturbed his woodland tryst,[19] and the other a praise poem to Dafydd's patron Ifor Hael, entitled 'To Ivor the Liberal, on being presented by him with a pair of gloves'.[20] Iolo expands freely on the original again, and as in many of his forgeries he develops a core of genuine material into a new creation. This opening paragraph is based on a single couplet of praise for Ivor's generosity in the original Welsh poem:

> Thou Ivor, darling of the Muse,
> Who through the world thy fame pursues;
> Proclaims thy worth in ev'ry clime,
> Whilst rapture fills her lay sublime;
> And feels her thrilling soul expand,
> Whilst foster'd by thy bounteous hand.
> Thy ample gate, thy ample hall,
> Are ever op'ning wide to all;

And, warm'd in Heav'n, thy ampler mind
Dilates in Love to all mankind.
The Poor from thee with joy return,
They bless thy name, they cease to mourn;
And bid the God, who knew their grief,
Reward thy hand that gave relief.

The expansion on the theme of liberality is consonant with the depiction of Ifor in Dafydd ap Gwilym's seven surviving poems to him. Dafydd claimed to have given him the epithet 'Hael' (Generous/Liberal), by which he was known to later Welsh poets who frequently cited him as a model of the generous bardic patron. In that sense Iolo's 'darling of the Muse' is accurate, if anachronistic. As already noted, Dafydd's poems to Ifor represented a shift away from the former glorification of martial prowess towards a greater emphasis on the civilized virtues of the cultured court. The ideal of the paternalistic nobleman living peacefully on his country estate fitted well with Iolo's radical pacifism which blamed wars on the oppressions of a predatory aristocracy. The warrior Owain Glyndŵr, revived as a national hero by Thomas Pennant, seems to have represented the latter type of aristocrat for Iolo, judging by his marginal comment on a reference to bondsmen on Glyndŵr's estate: 'Slaves! Damn Owain with all his mock patriotism'.[21] Ivor's liberality constituted true patriotism as understood by republicans in that it extended to all classes of society. The medieval nobleman did indeed have a religious duty to offer charity to the needy, but the kind of high-minded universal philanthropy presented in Iolo's translation is clearly an Enlightenment ideal.

According to the biography which Iolo fed to the editors of *Barddoniaeth Dafydd ab Gwilym*, Dafydd and his married lover Morfudd were given shelter at Ivor's court to escape the vengeful wrath of her husband (a story made more credible by one of Iolo's forged poems in the body of the collection, as well as several genuine medieval poems of complaint against the Jealous Husband).[22] A more democratic version of the same story claimed that the men of Glamorgan acted collectively to free Dafydd from prison. This is the version which David Samwell recounted in a preamble to a poem sending the sun to Glamorgan,[23] which he translated in March 1790 and published in the *Gentleman's Magazine* in January 1791:

The following is a free translation, from the Welsh, of an ode of *Dafydd ab Gwilym*, a bard of great fame, who lived in the 14th century. He was a native of Cardiganshire; but, from the many favours he had received from the inhabitants of Glamorgan, he became particularly attached to that part of the Principality. In

this poem he invokes the Sun to visit that country with all the blessings of his
genial influence, in gratitude to his friends, for having liberated the poet from
confinement, into which he had been thrown for non-payment of a fine incurred
for criminal conversation with the wife of Cynvrig Cynin.[24]

Release from prison would have had particular resonance in the months
following the storming of the Bastille, and *criminal conversation*, a legal term
meaning an extra-marital affair, refers to notorious legislation used to restrict
the freedom of married women.[25] Glamorgan is thus represented as a place
of refuge for those who opposed the oppressive treatment of women as
chattels within marriage and asserted their right to choose their own sexual
partners, a region comparable to Le Valais at the foot of the Swiss Alps where
the lovers in Rousseau's *La Nouvelle Héloïse* enjoy freedom to fulfill their
hearts' desires.

David Samwell was a native of Denbighshire, and so his decision to
translate this particular poem cannot be seen as mere regionalist chauvinism.
In fact London is specified as the place of translation, and from that perspective
the translation can be seen as a celebration of Welsh republicanism, which
does seem to have flourished most strongly in Glamorgan, described by
Gwyn Alf Williams as a 'nursery of the democratic intellect' comparable to
Norwich or even Philadelphia.[26] Samwell's translation follows the original
much more closely than any of Iolo Morganwg's do, but nevertheless he
manages to convey contemporary ideals by quite minor changes. The sun
retains its primary significance of fertility and prosperity, as in the source
text, but its 'genial influence' also functions quite naturally as a symbol of
enlightenment. The objects of praise in the original are the landowning gentry,
minor aristocracy known as *uchelwyr* (literally 'high ones') in Welsh, but the
terminology of the translation and omission of some descriptors make it
possible to see the subjects of this passage as yeoman farmers and artisans:

> Great Sun, how wond'rous are thy ways!
> Through Ether dart thy warmest rays,
> Profusely strew thy blessings round;
> Let honey, vines, and corn abound;
> Through all her vales, for chieftains fam'd,
> And commons virtuous and untam'd,
> Those vales so eminently blest,
> Whose sons are brave, whose daughters chaste;
> Those vales, where hospitable fare
> Display th'industrious housewife's care,
> Where oft, by love and friendship borne,
> With wine and mead I fill my horn.[27]

The 'industrious housewife' corresponds to a fur-clad lady of leisure in the original, and 'commons' was the English term for the very social class which had just secured political representation in France.[28] The adjective 'virtuous' implies more than just moral goodness, retaining as it does much of the force of the Latin root *virtus*, 'manliness', and suggesting the virtues of republican Rome, defined by Simon Schama as: 'patriotism, fortitude, integrity and frugality'.[29] The original poem praised the noblemen of Glamorgan for their abundant patronage of the poets, but this translation and its preamble convey a sense of community, as implied by the key terms 'love and friendship' which suggest a collective good will and associational temper uniting the people. Samwell's translation is strongly reminiscent of the passage in Mary Wollstonecraft's *A Vindication of the Rights of Men* (1790) on the relief of the poor by 'the fostering sun of kindness, the wisdom that finds them employments calculated to give them habits of virtue', which goes on to declare that 'love is only the fruit of love', and offers a Rousseauian vision of self-sufficient farmers living in peace and harmony.[30]

Another early translation of Dafydd ap Gwilym published in London was one by David Davis in his review of *Barddoniaeth Dafydd ab Gwilym* in the *Analytical Review* for July 1790.[31] The fact that it was reviewed in a metropolitan journal known for its radical sympathies is an indication of the readership which the publishers of the volume were targeting. And David Davis of Castellhywel in Ceredigion was an ideal reviewer, a classical scholar and accomplished poet who had translated Pope, Addison and Gray into Welsh and wrote poems welcoming the French Revolution. His assured review shows no sign of the subaltern inferiority which one might expect from a rural Welsh schoolmaster. Republican Rome is again invoked by the quotation of a line from Horace's ode to the great literary patron Maecenas, *et praesidium et dulce decus meum* (both my protector and my sweet glory) to describe Ifor Hael, placing Welsh poetry in the mainstream of the European classical tradition.[32] But the main emphasis of the review is on the metrical complexity of Dafydd ap Gwilym's poems, and on this topic Davis seems torn between Classicism and Romanticism. On the one hand he is at pains to show that the elaborate embellishments of *cynghanedd* are not unique to Welsh, quoting examples in English, Latin and Greek, whilst on the other hand he is clearly uneasy that Welsh poets voluntarily subjected themselves to such strictures, and speaks of the language being 'tortured' by the strict metres. He seems to have considered Dafydd ap Gwilym as a poet whose inventive imagination struggled to overcome such constraints:

> Gwilym's fruitful invention, aptness, and variety of similes, will always be admired by those who can understand the original; and the literati of Europe would be

surprized at his mighty strides towards Parnassus, if they could but conceive the unrelenting, worse than *Bastilian* shackles of Welsh prosody, in which he gained every inch of ground.[33]

The reference to the Bastille would have been particularly telling in the month when Parisians staged elaborate ceremonies to celebrate the first anniversary of the fall of that infamous symbol of oppression. The figurative use of the prison to represent artistic constraint places Dafydd ap Gwilym in the role of heroic Jacobin, and it might be compared with a similar usage by Thomas Paine in his *Rights of Man* (1791) of a man with a title: 'He lives immured within the Bastille of a word and surveys from a distance the envied life of man.'[34]

Despite Davis's ambiguous attitude towards the Welsh strict metres, he went to considerable lengths to demonstrate the mechanics of *cynghanedd* in the first four lines of the translation which concludes his review, using italics to indicate the correspondences:

> *Hist! I heard* but *yesterday*
> *In* a *loud* and *solemn lay*,
> *Thrice a great* and *hideous groan*,
> O! the *doleful mournful moan*.[35]

The poem translated is an elegy to a Cardiganshire nobleman, Rhydderch ab Ieuan Llwyd, whose descendants were still prominent at Gogerddan in Davis's time, but the text also demonstrates the rhetorical pathos of Welsh verse, and when unconstrained by metrical showmanship presents in Rhydderch an enlightened and benevolent aristocrat not dissimilar to Iolo Morganwg's projection of Ivor Hael:

> Ah! that beauty, valour, youth,
> Grac'd with learning, friendship, truth,
> And the brightest talents, fell
> To so dark and narrow a cell!
>
> As the brave and valiant knight,
> Tho' tenacious of his right,
> Was forgiving, gen'rous, kind;
> Grace and mercy may he find.[36]

For Welsh democrats in the early 1790s Dafydd ap Gwilym's life and work represented an ideal of literary freedom supported by enlightened patronage.

The radical idealization of the Welsh bardic order is set out in its most extreme form in William Owen Pughe's preface to his translations in *The Heroic Elegies and Other Pieces of Llywarç Hen*.[37] Heavily influenced by the theories of Iolo Morganwg as proclaimed in the Gorsedd (bardic convention) held in London in 1792, the preface sets out the principles of 'the Institution of Bardism, amongst the *Cynmry*, a system embracing all the leading principles which tend to spread liberty, peace and happiness amongst mankind'.[38] The 'perfect equality of its members' was a key tenet of the bardic order, as was transparency or 'publicity of their actions' and 'the free investigation of all matters contributing to the attainment of truth and wisdom'.[39] The poetry associated with the figure of Llywarch Hen (and thought to have been composed by him) was valued for its supposed antiquity and primitive qualities, and its gnomic style served to exemplify the rationality of Bardism, with high-minded statements such as 'Reason is the fairest light for man'.[40] These translations also had a contemporary political significance in that the original texts foreground the suffering caused by war, and can even be seen as critical of the heroic ethic.[41] The Christian morality of the original texts was easily given a radical slant in translation, such as 'Accustomed is the violent to oppress',[42] and 'Against oppression there will be an outcry'.[43] In 1799 Pughe published a prose translation of Dafydd ap Gwilym's 'Invocation to the Wind' in the *Monthly Magazine* (one of a series of contributions on Welsh literature by him under the pseudonym 'Meirion'), which portrays the wind as a being free from all constraints including the power of law, and uses the prison as a metaphor for the poet's condition: 'My country and its blessings are a prison to me'.[44]

The second edition of Edward Jones's *The Musical and Poetical Relicks of the Welsh Bards* published in 1794 includes an anonymous translation of one of the most remarkable Welsh poems of the later Middle Ages, Dafydd ab Edmwnd's elegy for the harpist Siôn Eos who was hanged for murder after trial under English law in Chirk about 1450.[45] Under the Welsh law of Hywel Dda his life would have been spared, and the elegy is an impassioned protest against the principle of capital punishment, as well as a lament for the loss inflicted on Welsh culture:

Indignation fires my breast, that the severe laws of *Chirk* should deprive music of its *Nightingale*! O thou revengeful tribunal! – thou bribed court! Why hadst thou not tried the warbling chorister, by the impartial laws of *Howel*? When the court of Westminster adopted the rigid sentence, penance nor any other punishment could mollify, nor interfere with thy refractory verdict. The jury, with one united voice (O Heavens!) consented his death.[46]

In the year of the London Treason Trials the claim that the ancient laws of Wales were more impartial and humane than those of England had radical implications, comparable to the words of John Martin and Thomas Hardy, two of the accused, in an address to the London Corresponding Society in January 1794: 'We must have redress from our own laws, and not from the laws of our plunderers, enemies, and oppressors.'[47]

The final translation to be considered, Richard Llwyd's 'Ode of the Months', dating from the very end of the decade, may appear at first sight to be the most nationalistic in spirit, presenting the figure of the bard and his patron as heroic victims of imperialist oppression.

Richard Llwyd (1752–1835), known also as the 'Bard of Snowdon', was a self-educated antiquarian scholar from Anglesey who lived for the last twenty-eight years of his life in Chester. He published three volumes of poetry in English, beginning with the topographical poem *Beaumaris Bay* published in 1800, the footnotes to which are twice as long as the text, containing numerous translated extracts from Welsh poetry.[48] Amongst his earliest works are verse translations of two medieval Welsh poems published in the *Chester Chronicle* in July and August 1790, one Llywelyn Goch's famous elegy to Lleucu Llwyd which would have appealed to the Gothic taste for love and death, and the other a eulogy by Llygad Gŵr to Llywelyn the Last Prince of Gwynedd (d. 1282).[49]

Llwyd made no direct statement of his political views, but one indication is his long and close association with the *Chester Chronicle*, a newspaper with openly radical sympathies which had a wide circulation in north Wales.[50] Some passages in his published work, such as criticism of slavery both medieval and contemporary in *Beaumaris Bay*, indicate that he held liberal views.[51] In January 1791 the *Chester Chronicle* published an anonymous 'Ode for the New Year' celebrating the progress of freedom from Britain to America and France:

> Hence the glorious theme was sung,
> Hence her fields and vallies rung,
> The sounds her torrents still retain,
> And tell it to the ambient main!
> Triumphant Thames proclaims it far,
> Responsive roars the Delawar;
> Old Ocean pleas'd returns the strain,
> And pours it on the polish'd Seine.
>
> Hail, all hail, the godlike ray
> That sparkles, kindles into day;

Gallia feeds the gen'rous flame,
Soars, to raise the human name,
Spurns a tyrant's mad decrees,
Nor rears a myriad for one fiend's caprice.[52]

The poem was republished and attributed to Llwyd by a certain 'Meirionydd' in the *Gentleman's Magazine* in April 1792 (apparently without Llwyd's consent), and a revised version entitled 'Ode to Freedom' was included in Llwyd's *Poems* of 1804.[53] That version omitted all reference to France, presenting freedom as a purely Anglo-American endeavour. The omission may well reflect disillusionment with the French Revolution as a result of the events of 1793–4, but fear of reprisal at a time when Britain and France were at war should not be discounted.[54]

Although a despiser of despots, Llwyd was no Jacobin. He seems to have regarded the independent Welsh princes as a model of the Whig ideal of paternalism by a benevolent aristocracy, and his free translation of the eulogy to Llywelyn inserts a reference to the relationship between the prince and his people which creates an impression of democratic will: 'Prudence marks Llewelyn's sway, / A grateful people pleas'd obey'. The dedication of this poem to Lady Penrhyn, wife of the Caernarfonshire slate-quarry owner and an alleged descendant of Llywelyn, indicates Llwyd's desire for continuity of this harmonious relationship and the value he placed on the benign effects of commerce.[55] Similarly, 'Ode of the Months' is dedicated to Sir Thomas Mostyn, Member of Parliament for Flintshire, a descendant of Sir Gruffudd Llwyd's eldest daughter.

'Ode of the Months' was first published in Llwyd's collection *Poems, Tales, Odes, Sonnets, Translations from the British* of 1804, but a quotation from it in a footnote to *Beaumaris Bay* indicates that he was working on the translation at least as early as 1800.[56] It is a free version of 'Awdl y Misoedd' (as the source text is entitled in the Red Book of Hergest), which expands the 62 lines of the original to 154 octosyllabic lines. 'Awdl y Misoedd' is one of two poems composed by Gwilym Ddu of Arfon in response to the imprisonment of Sir Gruffudd Llwyd in Rhuddlan castle in 1317 following a failed rebellion against English rule in north Wales, in which the poet laments the absence of his patron and the leader of the people of Gwynedd.[57] Like all the court poetry of this period the text is extremely difficult due to its archaic language and allusive style, and Richard Llwyd clearly based his translation on the literal prose version by Evan Evans in his *Specimens*. Evans follows the original faithfully until his very last sentence, where the rhetorical question is his own addition and the use of the first person plural implies a figurative interpretation of the prison as a symbol of national oppression: 'We are confined in a close prison by a merciless unrelenting enemy; and what avails a bloody and brave contest for liberty.'[58]

Evans's prefatory note to his translation places the poem in the context of 'that inhuman massacre of the Bards made by that cruel tyrant Edward the First, which gave occasion to a very fine Ode by Mr. Grey'.[59] The story of the massacre of the Welsh bards by Edward I after the conquest of 1282 first appeared in Sir John Wynn's *History of the Gwydir Family* (written after 1580, and circulated in manuscript until publication in 1770), where it seems to have been invented in order to explain the absence of fourteenth-century praise poetry to Wynn's ancestors. It was taken up by Thomas Carte in the second volume of his *General History of England* (1750), which was the source for Thomas Gray's 'The Bard' (1757).[60] As Evans's note indicates, it was evidently Gray's influence that stimulated him to associate Gwilym Ddu's poem with the story of the massacre of the bards, although, as Evans acknowledges, the poet 'had the good luck to escape Edward's fury' (Edward I having died in 1307).[61]

Gray's 'The Bard' was an early instance of Gothic medievalism which influenced the way the Welsh read their own literary history, as well as the way painters depicted Welsh landscapes.[62] The myth of the massacre of the bards gained a new lease of life in the 1790s as Edward became a hate-figure for Welsh republicans, archetype of the tyrannical imperialist monarch. 'Cyflafan y beirdd trwy orchymyn Iorwerth y Cyntaf' (The massacre of the bards by order of Edward I) was the set subject for the *awdl* competition at the Gwyneddigion eisteddfod held at Denbigh in 1792, and at the eisteddfod of 1798 a prize was offered for the best translation into Welsh of 'The Bard'. In a note in *Poems, Lyric and Pastoral* Iolo Morganwg merged the story with his Jacobin interpretation of bardic history, and also made it slightly more credible by allowing for the survival of some of the bards (as would have been evident to anyone familiar with fourteenth-century Welsh poetry):

> *Edward the Bardicide*, surnamed Longshanks, had caused many of the *Bards* to be massacred, and all were *severely restricted in the exercise of their ancient functions*. They were *Sons of Truth and Liberty*, and of course offensive to that age of *tyranny* and *superstition*, but the *Welsh* would not suffer them to be exterminated.[63]

And in a letter to William Owen Pughe in May 1798 Iolo made a connection between the massacre and contemporary persecution of radicals which anticipates the use that Richard Llwyd made of the story: 'We (the Bards of Glamorgan) have been as severly persecuted by Church and Kingists as our glorious predecessors were by Edward the Bardicide'.[64]

In a note in *Beaumaris Bay* Llwyd defends the veracity of the story of the massacre of the bards: 'Of late it has become fashionable to doubt this, among other historical facts: but what is to become of the testimony of Sir John Wynn, and the strains of the sufferers?'[65] But like Iolo Morganwg, Llwyd was doubtless well aware that not all the bards were exterminated, and in 'Ode of the Months' the bards are not massacred but silenced:

> O! Thou, decreed a world to save,
> Where can I rest, but in the grave,
> Where can I pass the hours of pain,
> Forbid even sorrow's soothing strain;
> Forbid by foes, whose breasts are steel,
> To pour to heaven the pangs we feel.[66]

A footnote on the second instance of 'forbid' in this passage quotes from a fifteenth-century poem by Dafydd Llwyd of Mathafarn to Owen Tudur, grandfather of Henry VII, 'Gwyddom dewi a goddef' (we know to suffer, and to be silent), as evidence that the repression of the bards continued 'even so late as 1480' – i.e. up to the Tudor union of England and Wales.[67] This theme of repression is reinforced in the translation by a strain of imagery associating the prison with the grave: Gruffudd's empty hall is 'chill as the cells that hold the dead'.[68] And as already implied by Evan Evans, the prison becomes an image for the condition of a subject people, here invoked with a gothic frisson of horror as a living grave:

> Oppression's plan at length succeeds,
> At every pore, my Country bleeds;
> No ray of hope pervades our woes,
> No trait of mercy, marks our foes;
> And Britains's sons, in vain, are brave,
> Immur'd within a living-grave![69]

'Immur'd' is particularly suggestive in evoking the castle walls (*mur* in Welsh, from the Latin *murus*), lasting memorials of oppression in the Welsh landscape, as Richard Llwyd wrote in *Beaumaris Bay*, a passage which calls to mind the trade in models and souvenirs made from the stones of the Bastille:[70]

> Here earth is loaded with a mass of wall,
> The proud insulting badge of Cambria's fall,
> By haughty Edward rais'd; and every stone
> Records a sigh, a murder, or a groan.

> The Muse of Britain, suff'ring at its birth,
> Exulting sees it crumbling to the earth.[71]

Richard Llwyd would have us suppose that Sir Gruffudd 'ended his days in the castle of Rhuddlan', although in fact he is known to have been released from prison in 1318 and to have resumed his service to the English crown (much to Gwilym Ddu's satisfaction no doubt, since the essential purpose of the original poem was to effect his release).[72] But it is the fate of the bard which is of central importance to the translation, in a concluding paragraph which corresponds to nothing in the original, and owes a good deal to Gray:

> Affliction wild, with piercing cry,
> And dark Despair, with downcast eye;
> The manly Mind, that scorns to speak,
> The indignant Heart, that swells to break;
> All agonize my breast to close,
> At once – existence and its woes![73]

However, despite the similarity to Gray's poem in that both end with the death of the bard, the manner of their deaths is significantly different. Eloquent denunciation is the keynote of 'The Bard' from the opening curse, "Ruin seize thee, ruthless king!", to the triumphant valediction which precedes the bard's spectacular suicide:

> 'Enough for me: with joy I see
> The different doom our Fates assign.
> Be thine Despair, and scept'red care,
> To triumph, and to die, are mine.'
> He spoke, and headlong from the mountain's height
> Deep in the roaring tide he plung'd to endless night.[74]

In contrast to this defiant loquacity, it is precisely the burden of unspoken emotion which causes the death of the bard in 'Ode of the Months', although it is unclear whether his silence is self-willed or imposed by political repression as the narrative would have it. The ambiguity is perhaps deliberate in order to preserve a sense of dignity like Gray's bard who has control over his own destiny – 'The manly Mind, that scorns to speak'.

Richard Llwyd maintains the persona of the fourteenth-century bard throughout this translation, but in these lines which expand on a passing reference to a sixth-century poet the blurring of temporal perspective may suggest a contemporary political relevance:

Like Dunawd's Bard, whose plaintive tongue,
The woes of other times has sung;
So I, on recent sorrows dwell,
And sad, my Country's troubles tell.[75]

Footnotes offered a means of paratextual comment, and explicit contemporary reference is made in a note on the flowers adorning the graves of the Welsh warriors who gave their lives for their country. Llwyd quotes, 'Unfading blooms on the grave of the hero, the garland prepared by his country',[76] and then departs completely from the explanatory function of the footnotes to make this comparison:

> Such also, was the sentiment engraved on the pedestal of a column of Norwegian marble, and placed by the gratitude of the Danish nation, on the grave of her brave sons who fell in the bombardment of Copenhagen, by the British fleet, April 2, 1801; and that breast can have little of liberality that would confine the Virtues to the limits of his Country.[77]

This refers to Nelson's victory over the Danish fleet which was supporting France's attempt to impose a blockade on Britain. The implied parallel between Wales and Denmark as small nations suffering oppression by an imperial power was a particularly bold one at a time when war was exerting considerable pressure for unity within Britain. However, it would be a mistake to confine the political significance of Llwyd's translation to the kind of 'bardic nationalism' which inspired Evan Evans to translate the poem. Llwyd certainly admired patriots who were prepared to sacrifice their lives for their country, but armed resistance to English oppression belonged to the distant past, and its only contemporary relevance was as inspiration, for the militia in particular, to defend Britain's shores against the threat of foreign invasion in the anxious years following the Fishguard landing of 1797.

Contemporary relevance of a much more challenging and potentially dangerous kind is to be found in the silencing of the bard in Llwyd's translation. This can be seen to relate to the suppression of radical and oppositional voices in Britain following the 'Gagging Acts' of 1795 which extended the definition of treason to include speaking and writing. The resultant repression and intimidation are well known in the British context, but it is worth noting some instances relating to publishing in Wales which would have been of particular concern to Richard Llwyd.[78] Perhaps his earliest personal experience would have been the threat of assassination received by his friend William Cowdroy, editor of the *Chester Chronicle*, in November 1794 from a 'Detester of all Democrats'.[79] Morgan John Rhys, the radical Baptist preacher and editor of the journal *Cylch-grawn Cynmraeg*, is said to have emigrated to America in order to avoid arrest in Carmarthen in 1794. Another radical Welsh journal, *Y Geirgrawn*, edited by David Davies of Holywell and printed in Chester, ceased publication abruptly in 1796, apparently because of harassment by the authorities. And most disturbing of all, the Unitarian minister Tomos Glyn Cothi, editor of another short-lived journal, *Y Drysorfa Gymmysgedig*, was imprisoned for two years in August 1801 for singing seditious songs.[80] This imprisonment would surely have had particular resonance for Richard Llwyd at the very time he was working on 'Ode of the Months'. Such cases would have made him acutely aware of the intolerable pressures on liberal writers, and I suggest that he chose to translate this poem in order to express his concern about 'recent sorrows'. Translation of a historical text was a means for Llwyd to engage indirectly with a contemporary issue which he seems to have been unable to confront openly in his own voice. Despite the inherently nationalistic force of the Welsh source text as transmitted by Evan Evans's prose translation, and of the related myth of the massacre of the bards, Llwyd's adaptation of them can be seen to cut across the polarities of nationality, making common cause between silenced voices on both sides of the border.

The 1790s formed a brief window in which creative translation was a means of transforming a newly rediscovered literary inheritance to construct an original Welsh radicalism which anticipated contemporary concerns. Modern scholarship has revealed the liberties taken by some of the translators, and their work, if known at all, has been mostly discounted as perversion of the genuine tradition. It is surely time now to place these translations alongside other texts which express Welsh responses to the French Revolution.

Notes

[1] Rhian Reynolds and M. Wynn Thomas, 'Introduction', in S. Rhian Reynolds (ed.), *A Bibliography of Welsh Literature in English Translation* (Cardiff, 2005), p. xiv. Some of the translations discussed in this paper have come to light since the compilation of this bibliography.

[2] M. Wynn Thomas, *Corresponding Cultures* (Cardiff, 1999), p. 118.

[3] See Sarah Prescott, *Eighteenth-Century Writing from Wales: Bards and Britons* (Cardiff, 2008), pp. 57–83, following Katie Trumpener, *Bardic Nationalism: The Romantic Novel and the British Empire* (Princeton, 1997). On the context to Evans's work, see Ffion Llywelyn Jenkins, 'Celticism and Pre-Romanticism: Evan Evans', in Branwen Jarvis (ed.), *A Guide to Welsh Literature c.1700–1800* (Cardiff, 2000), pp. 104–25.

[4] On the indistinct boundaries between translation, adaptation and original com-position, particularly where verse translations were published in collections of

original poems, see Matthew Reynolds, 'Principles and Norms of Translation', in Peter France and Kenneth Haynes (eds.), *The Oxford History of Literary Translation in English Vol. 4 1790–1900* (Oxford, 2006), pp. 61–82, at pp. 75–6.

5   John Walters, *Translated Specimens of Welsh Poetry in English Verse* (London, 1782); see Prescott, *Eighteenth-Century Writing from Wales*, pp. 114–20.

6   For an online edition of Dafydd ap Gwilym's poetry with English translations, see *http://www.dafyddapgwilym.net*.

7   Arthur James Johnes (Maelog), *Translations into English Verse from the Poems of Davyth ap Gwilym* (London, 1834). See Dafydd Johnston, 'Early Translations of Dafydd ap Gwilym', in Alyce von Rothkirch and Daniel Williams (eds.), *Beyond the Difference: Welsh Literature in Comparative Contexts* (Cardiff, 2004), pp. 158–72.

8   Evan Evans, *Some Specimens of the Poetry of the Ancient Welsh Bards* (London, 1764), p. 18.

9   Edward Jones, *The Musical and Poetical Relicks of the Welsh Bards* (London, 1784), pp. 21–4.

10   Rhiannon Ifans (ed.), *Gwaith Gruffudd Llwyd a'r Llygliwiaid Eraill* (Aberystwyth, 2000), poem 11.

11   Edward Jones, *Musical and Poetical Relicks*, p. 24.

12   Owen Jones and William Owen Pughe, *Barddoniaeth Dafydd ab Gwilym* (London, 1789) (*BDG*), pp. xxviii–xxix.

13   Pughe's introduction is dated 1 July 1789. For examples of 'revolution' used by Richard Price with reference to events in France in 1784 and early July 1789, see Paul Frame and Geoffrey W. Powell, '"Our first concern as lovers of our country must be to enlighten it": Richard Price's Response to the French Revolution', in this volume, and with reference to America in 1785, see Caroline Franklin, 'Wales as Nowhere: The *Tabula Rasa* of the "Jacobin" Imagination', also in this volume.

14   I have explored these themes in '*Barddoniaeth Dafydd ab Gwilym* 1789 a'r Chwyldro Ffrengig', *LlC*, 35 (2012), 32–53.

15   See Mary-Ann Constantine, *The Truth Against the World: Iolo Morganwg and Romantic Forgery* (Cardiff, 2007). Two of the forged poems are in the body of the collection (nos. LXX and LXXX) and the other twelve in an appendix.

16   See *eadem*, '"This Wildernessed Business of Publication": The Making of *Poems, Lyric and Pastoral* (1794)', in Geraint H. Jenkins (ed.), *A Rattleskull Genius: The Many Faces of Iolo Morganwg* (Cardiff, 2005), pp. 123–45, at p. 128). Two printed versions are preserved amongst Iolo's papers in NLW 21392F, one part of a proposal for the volume, and the other a separate twelve-page booklet, both published by S. Hazard of Bath in 1791. The booklet is said to be the third edition, as is the copy in the BL. The translation in the booklet is a revised version of that in the proposal, and corresponds closely to that in *Poems, Lyric and Pastoral* (2 vols., London, 1794), I, pp. 74–84. The proposal quotes the opening couplet in Welsh which is in fact a back-translation from Iolo's English bearing no relation to the original.

17   'Pererindod Merch', *http://www.dafyddapgwilym.net*, poem 129.

18   *Gentleman's Magazine*, 64, part 2 (1794), 1113; *Monthly Review*, 13 (1794), 406; *Critical Review* (1794), 170.

[19] Williams, *Poems, Lyric and Pastoral*, II, pp. 20–2. The Welsh original is not now considered to be the work of Dafydd ap Gwilym.

[20] Ibid., I, pp. 192–8; for the original text and English translation, see *http://www. dafyddapgwilym.net*, poem 15. See further Damian Walford Davies, '"At Defiance": Iolo, Godwin, Coleridge, Wordsworth', in Jenkins (ed.), *A Rattleskull Genius*, pp. 147–72, where it is argued that Iolo's translation influenced Wordsworth (pp. 169–72).

[21] BL Add 14970, 95a (written in 1800); for an edition and translation of the original text, see Dafydd Johnston (ed.), *Iolo Goch: Poems* (Llandysul, 1993), poem 10, line 71.

[22] Iolo's forgery is poem LXXX in *BDG*.

[23] According to its most recent editor the original poem is not the work of Dafydd ap Gwilym, but rather that of a later fourteenth-century poet, Gruffudd Llwyd. See Ifans (ed.), *Gwaith Gruffudd Llwyd*, poem 9.

[24] *Gentleman's Magazine*, 61 (January 1791), 69–70. The same translation was re-published with minor changes in John Croft (ed.), *Scrapeana: Fugitive Miscellany* (York, 1792), pp. 268–71, and again by Edward Jones in the second edition of his *Musical and Poetical Relicks of the Welsh Bards* (London, 1794), together with a translation of a short love poem, 'Ode to Morvydh', pp. 43–4.

[25] See Caroline Franklin, *Mary Wollstonecraft: A Literary Life* (Basingstoke, 2004), pp. 180–2.

[26] Gwyn A. Williams, *Madoc: the Making of a Myth* (Oxford, 1987), pp. 98–9.

[27] *Gentleman's Magazine*, 61, 70.

[28] The Welsh word translated by 'commons' is *gwerin*, originally meaning just 'people', which provided the root of new terms coined in this period such as *gweriniaeth* and *gwerinlywodraeth* for republic and democracy.

[29] Simon Schama, *Citizens: A Chronicle of the French Revolution* (London, 1989), p. 142.

[30] Mary Wollstonecraft, *A Vindication of the Rights of Men, in a Letter to the Right Honourable Edmund Burke*, ed. Janet Todd (Oxford, 1994), p. 58. On the harsh realities of life for the rural poor, see Geraint H. Jenkins, 'The "Rural Voltaire" and the "French madcaps"', in this volume.

[31] 'David ab Gwilym's *Poems*', *Analytical Review*, 7 (July 1790), 295–9. The review is anonymous, but David Davis can be confidently identified as the author on the basis of both references in Iolo Morganwg's letters to him as reviewer of the volume (*CIM*, II, pp. 451 and 456), and the fact that the translation in the review was subsequently published in Davis's collection *Telyn Dewi* (London, 1824), pp. 151–2.

[32] Horace, *Odes*, Book I, poem 1, line 5.

[33] *Analytical Review*, 7, 296.

[34] Mark Philp (ed.), *Rights of Man, Common Sense and Other Political Writings* (Oxford, 1995), p. 132.

[35] *Analytical Review*, 7, 298. *Hist* was changed to *Yes* in *Telyn Dewi*.

[36] *Analytical Review*, 7, 299. For the original and English translation, see *http://www. dafyddapgwilym.net*, poem 10.

37 The volume is dated 1792, but Glenda Carr has argued convincingly in *William Owen Pughe* (Caerdydd, 1983), p. 54, that it was actually published sometime in the first half of 1793.

38 William Owen [Pughe], *The Heroic Elegies and Other Pieces of Llywarç Hen* (London, 1792; see note 37), p. xxiv. See further Cathryn Charnell-White, *Bardic Circles: National, Regional and Personal Identity in the Bardic Vision of Iolo Morganwg* (Cardiff, 2007), pp. 21–4.

39 Owen [Pughe], *Heroic Elegies*, pp. xxvi–xxvii. A creative translation in a footnote on p. xxvii has the twelfth-century court poet Prydydd y Moch craving the Maker of the sun and moon for the 'intellectual light' of bardic inspiration.

40 Ibid, p. 109 (translating 'Tecav canwyll pwyll i ddyn').

41 See A. O. H. Jarman, 'The Heroic Ideal in Early Welsh Poetry', in Wolfgang Meid (ed.), *Beiträge zur Indogermanistik und Keltologie* (Innsbruck, 1967), pp. 193–212.

42 Owen [Pughe], *Heroic Elegies*, p. 21 (translating 'Gnawt taer i dreisiaw').

43 Ibid. p. 69 (translating 'Gnawt rhag traha tra llevain').

44 *Monthly Magazine*, 8 (August 1799), 542–3. See Damian Walford Davies, 'Pwy yw 'Meirion' y *Monthly Magazine*?', *LlC*, 21 (1998), 182–8, which also notes another translation by 'Meirion' of a Dafydd ap Gwilym poem, 'The Invocation of St. Dwynwen', in the *Monthly Magazine*, 2 (July 1796), 448–9. The source text for the poem to the wind, *BDG*, LXIX, does not make any specific reference to prison.

45 Edward Jones, *The Musical and Poetical Relicks of the Welsh Bards* (2nd edn., London, 1794), pp. 44–6. For the original poem, see Thomas Parry (ed.), *The Oxford Book of Welsh Verse* (Oxford, 1962), pp. 138–41, and for a translation, see Joseph P. Clancy, *Medieval Welsh Poems* (Dublin, 2003), pp. 332–4. It is interesting to note that William Jones, Llangadfan, assisted Edward Jones in gathering material for his collection, see Jenkins, 'The "Rural Voltaire" and the "French madcaps"'; could he perhaps have been responsible for this anonymous translation?

46 Jones, *Musical and Poetical Relicks* (1794), p. 45.

47 Quoted by Nancy E. Johnson in 'Fashioning the Legal Subject: Narratives from the London Treason Trials of 1794', *Eighteenth-Century Fiction*, 21, no. 3 (2009), 413–43, at 433.

48 The posthumous *Poetical Works of Richard Llwyd* (Chester, 1837), with a memoir by Edward Parry which is the only published source for Llwyd's life, contains *Beaumaris Bay* and all of *Poems, Tales, Odes, Sonnets, Translations from the British* (1804), as well as some previously unpublished poems, but not *Gayton Wake* (1804).

49 *Chester Chronicle*, 16 July and 13 August 1790. Both were based on prose versions by Evan Evans; the former in manuscript (see D. Silvan Evans (ed.), *Gwaith y Parchedig Evan Evans* (Caernarfon, 1876), pp. 150–2), and the latter in Evans, *Some Specimens of the Poetry of the Ancient Welsh Bards*, pp. 38–44.

50 See the selection of texts from the *Chester Chronicle* in Marion Löffler, *Welsh Responses to the French Revolution: Press and Public Discourse 1789–1802* (Cardiff, 2012), pp. 137–71, which includes anti-war poems and a critical report of burnings of effigies of Thomas Paine.

[51] Richard Llwyd, *Beaumaris Bay* (Chester, 1800), pp. 25–8.

[52] *Chester Chronicle*, 7 January 1791.

[53] See Elizabeth Edwards, *English-Language Poetry from Wales 1789–1806* (Cardiff, 2013), pp. 72–4.

[54] On the difficulty of identifying motivations for changes in attitude towards the French Revolution in the later 1790s, see Kenneth R. Johnston, 'Whose History? My Place or Yours? Republican Assumptions and Romantic Traditions', in Damian Walford Davies (ed.), *Romanticism, History, Historicism. Essays on an Orthodoxy* (London, 2008), pp. 79–102.

[55] A footnote to Llwyd's translation of 'Elegy on Evan the Thatcher' (*Poems, Tales, Odes, Sonnets, Translations from the British* (Chester, 1804), pp. 22–9) praises Lord Penrhyn, 'this publick spirited nobleman', for the contribution his slate quarries had made to the economy of the region.

[56] Llwyd, *Beaumaris Bay*, p. 29. For the full text of 'Ode of the Months', see Edwards, *English-Language Poetry from Wales*, pp. 224–33.

[57] The text is edited by R. Iestyn Daniel in N. G. Costigan et al., *Gwaith Gruffudd ap Dafydd ap Tudur, Gwilym Ddu o Arfon, Trahaearn Brydydd Mawr ac Iorwerth Beli* (Aberystwyth, 1995), poem 7, 'Moliant Syr Gruffudd Llwyd ap Rhys ap Gruffudd o Dregarnedd'. On the historical background, see J. B. Smith, 'Gruffudd Llwyd and the Celtic Alliance', *BBCS*, 26 (1974–6), 463–78, and Morgan Thomas Davies, 'The Rhetoric of Gwilym Ddu's *Awdlau* to Sir Gruffudd Llwyd', *Studia Celtica*, XL (2006), 155–72.

[58] Evans, *Some Specimens of the Poetry of the Ancient Welsh Bards*, p. 50.

[59] Ibid., p. 45.

[60] See Prescott, *Eighteenth-Century Writing from Wales*, 63–70.

[61] Evans, *Some Specimens of the Poetry of the Ancient Welsh Bards*, p. 46.

[62] See Prys Morgan, *The Eighteenth-Century Renaissance* (Llandybïe, 1981), pp. 120–1; Peter Lord, *The Visual Culture of Wales: Imaging the Nation* (Cardiff, 2000), pp. 113–15.

[63] Williams, *Poems, Lyric and Pastoral*, II, p. 223. It is worth noting that the credibility of the story was already bolstered by the fact that the list of poets in John Davies's authoritative *Dictionarium Duplex* (1632) gives the floruits of the two major poets of the fourteenth century, Dafydd ap Gwilym and Iolo Goch, as 1400.

[64] *CIM*, II, p. 85, Iolo Morganwg to William Owen Pughe, 12 May 1798.

[65] Llwyd, *Beaumaris Bay*, p. 15.

[66] *Idem, Poems*, p. 54.

[67] The note in *idem, Beaumaris Bay*, p. 15, quotes to the same end from the elegy to the poet Gruffudd Llwyd by Rhys Goch [Eryri] in the early fifteenth century, 'Y goreu Bardd a waharddwyd (The best of Bards is interdicted)'.

[68] *Idem, Poems*, p. 60.

[69] Ibid., pp. 63–4. See Elizabeth Edwards, 'Confined to a Living Grave: Welsh Poetry, Gothic and the French Revolution', in Marion Gibson, Shelley Trower and Gary Tregidga (eds.), *Mysticism, Myth and Celtic Identity* (London, 2012), pp. 87–98.

70   Schama, *Citizens*, pp. 344–53. Cf Paine's 'immured within the Bastille of a word' quoted above.

71   Llwyd, *Beaumaris Bay*, pp. 13–15.

72   *Idem, Poems*, p. 48.

73   Ibid., p. 64.

74   Thomas Gray, *The Bard*, III, 3, lines 139–44.

75   Llwyd, *Poems*, p. 55.

76   The source of these words has not been identified, and it may well be a paraphrase rather than a direct quotation.

77   Ibid., p. 57.

78   A useful summary of the main events in England and Scotland is given by Kenneth R. Johnston, 'Whose History?', pp. 83–4.

79   Löffler, *Welsh Responses to the French Revolution*, pp. 145–6.

80   On the three journals and their editors, see ibid., pp. 28–30; on Tomos Glyn Cothi's imprisonment, see Marion Löffler, 'The "Marseillaise" in Wales', in this volume, and Geraint H. Jenkins, '"A Very Horrid Affair": Sedition and Unitarianism in the Age of Revolutions', in R. R. Davies and *idem* (eds.), *From Medieval to Modern Wales: Historical Essays in Honour of Kenneth O. Morgan and Ralph A. Griffiths* (Cardiff, 2004), pp. 175–96. See also Geraint Jenkins's account of the harassment of William Jones, Llangadfan, at this time: Jenkins, 'The "Rural Voltaire" and the "French madcaps"'.

'Brave Republicans': representing the Revolution in a Welsh interlude

FFION MAIR JONES

As usual in times of political upheaval, the theatre in Britain was subject to rigorous processes of censorship following the outbreak of the Revolution in France.[1] Even though the Britain of the 1790s retained a strong cultural theatricality, political discourse was largely shifted from the theatre itself into other domains. It has been suggested that, in the English-speaking world, the greatest drama of the decade was played out between Edmund Burke's *Reflections on the Revolution in France* (1790) and Tom Paine's *Rights of Man* (1791, 1792).[2] In Wales likewise, drama increasingly resided in the confrontations of opinion carried out on the pages of journals and printed pamphlets, and scholars have pointed to the late years of the eighteenth century and the early 1800s as a period of demise for the popular Welsh dramatic genre known as the *anterliwt* (interlude).[3] The discovery of a printed text of a Welsh play responding directly to the Revolution, however, shows that the genre may have been more adaptable to change than has previously been recognized.[4] *Gwedd o Chwaraeyddiaeth, sef Hanes Bywyd a Marwolaeth Brenhin a Brenhines Ffraingc* (A Form of Drama, namely the Story of the Lives and Deaths of the King and Queen of France) is the work of a little-known author named Hugh Jones of Glanconwy in Denbighshire.[5] It is a unique contribution to the dramatic literature of the decade: freed from the constraints of censorship which bedevilled 'legitimate' forms of theatrical activity in the English language during the 1790s, the fact that it was printed has protected it from the oblivion to which popular theatrical activity generally fell. This chapter provides an introduction to Jones's text, placing it in the context both of contemporary debates on the Revolution and of British drama of the period, including the genre of the Welsh interlude itself.

* * *

The gradual decline of the Welsh interlude between the second half of the
eighteenth century and the first quarter of the nineteenth century has often
been accounted for by scholars as the result of the conflict between traditional
forms of merriment and an increased religiosity within Welsh life, particularly
as Methodism took hold in the north of the country.[6] Methodism comes
out as winner of the confrontation: conversion narratives show how stout
adherents of a traditional way of life, which included interlude-playing and
attendance at performances, immediately rejected this pastime upon seeing
the light of a new faith.[7] A tale from Caernarfonshire c.1807 shows how the
two contrasting performance genres of interlude and Methodist sermon
could sometimes come into direct conflict, to the detriment of the older
tradition. A Methodist meeting was scheduled for two o'clock on Ascension
Thursday that year, or thereabouts, at Pentir near Bangor, at exactly the
same hour as a group of players intended to stage an interlude. One of the
preachers prayed for 'failure upon the playing. And in those minutes God
observed the crowd and broke the stage, and the player called the fool was
injured, and so was all frustrated for that day; yeah, and for ever, since this
was the last meeting [of players] held there.'[8] While Methodism threatened
the survival of the genre in Wales, the interlude found support and appre-
ciation within London-Welsh circles, whose members were largely hostile
to the enthusiasm of evangelical religion. When Thomas Edwards (Twm
o'r Nant) staged a play at the Bala eisteddfod arranged by the London-Welsh
Gwyneddigion Society in September 1789, he received the unadulterated
praise of David Samwell, who sent in a report to the *Gloucester Journal*
extolling Twm as 'the Welsh Shakespear'.[9] Speaking metaphorically, Samwell
claimed that Twm had 'composed several sermons which have been delivered
from the Welch pulpit to the great benefit and edification of his countrymen',
indicating how this popular tradition within Welsh theatrical life was
increasingly endowed with moral weight and substance, or at least portrayed
as capable of rivalling the forces of Methodism. In 1791 Edward Charles, a
vitriolic critic of ad hoc Methodist preaching, staged Twm's *Tri Chryfion
Byd* for the Gwyneddigion Society at the Seven Stars tavern near London
Bridge.[10] The actors included Daniel Davies, Peter Davies, the radical Welsh
pamphleteer John Jones (Jac Glan-y-gors), and Charles himself.[11] G. G.
Evans has accounted for this upsurge of interest by noting the fascination of
contemporary Welshmen with the relics of antiquity, an argument which
is largely substantiated by comments on the genre in the *Cambrian Register*,
an English-language and London-produced journal relating to Welsh culture,
literary and historical.[12] The first volume, published in the mid-1790s, states

that interludes 'have been a very general entertainment, at particular seasons of the year, at least from the beginning of [the seventeenth century]'; whereas a commentator in the third volume of 1818 goes a step further, arguing that, although usually the work of 'the inferior Welsh Bards', they are of 'Trojan origin'.[13] The nature of this attention to the genre is a sure indication of its decline: the Welsh interlude was entering a 'museum' or antiquarian phase in its existence which signalled its end as a vivid and viable performative art form.[14]

The decline of the interlude may also be seen as the effect of the increased literacy of Welsh audiences during the latter part of the eighteenth century.[15] Twm o'r Nant, one of the most renowned interlude writers, published six plays during his career, but his final composition was not in any sense a performable drama. *Bannau y Byd, neu Greglais o Groglofft* (1808), a lengthy poem which includes dialogue between the 'Bard' and the allegorical figure of 'Truth' ('Bardd' and 'Gwirionedd'), is clearly aimed at a literate audience in an age where, its author noted, there is 'so much movement towards printing books and learning to read . . . compared to earlier times'.[16] Twm's comments give some credence to G. G. Evans's account of the final days of the genre, an account which emphasizes the negative effect upon the interlude of the momentous events of the French Revolution and the new ideas which spread in its wake, effecting a sea-change throughout European society.[17] Yet Evans under-represented the potential of the genre to engage with political ideas spread through the printed word, much less with the idea of the Revolution head-on. The anonymous 1784/5 interlude adaptation of Sir William Jones's reformist pamphlet *The Principles of Government, in a Dialogue between a Scholar and a Peasant* (1782) had already shown very clearly that the supposedly moribund folk-drama could still be considered a useful vehicle for the propagation (and translation into Welsh) of new and potentially subversive ideas.[18] The fact that Evans did not know of Hugh Jones's *Gwedd o Chwaraeyddiaeth*, which takes its action directly from events in France, meant that he was unable fully to appreciate how the interlude might work with ideas current in the sphere of the printed word to create a performable play. Jones's text, almost immaculately presented by Ishmael Davies, in contrast with many earlier eighteenth-century printed interludes, shows signs of adherence to both the world of print and to the oral and performance culture of popular drama. Its main themes closely interact with the concerns of contemporaries as recorded in printed media including journals, almanacs and pamphlets, and its incarnation as a printed text shows an effort to authenticate the events presented in the play with factual information. For example, Louis's name is glossed as 'Lewis Capet, sef Brenin Ffrainc' (Louis Capet, namely the king of France), and the date of his execution, 'yn y flwyddyn 1793' (in the year 1793), is added to the stage directions. Information regarding 'rheolwyr y deyrnas' (the rulers of the kingdom, following the fall of the Bastille) is likewise added to the material, as if the dramatist were at pains to communicate his understanding of the changes in the manner of ruling France between *ancien régime* and Revolutionary days. An *englyn* summarizing the anti-popish animus of the play appears on the title page and a stanza asking for God's blessing upon George III and his subjects appears to have been added to the text of the play proper at the end, thus framing the material and providing a spur to reflection on its contents.[19]

In spite of these features, the printed text also points to the fact that this is a performable work. Hugh Jones's preface to 'my fellow-countrymen' ('fy nghydwladwyr') describes it simply as the 'work of my youth' ('fy llafurwaith yn fy ieuenctid'), a typical line for printed interlude-makers' apologias, yet hardly one that resounds with credibility in view of the fact that the text cannot have been composed more than five years earlier, at the most conservative estimate.[20] The fact that the author relegates the composition of the work to his youth does not prove that it was once performed; yet it suggests that it had pre-print culture origins, where it may have circulated – and in what better or more likely manner than through performance? – in circumstances where scrutiny of rhyme and metre would have been of less importance.[21] In view of the relative shortness of the period between the possible composition of the play and its printing it may even be the case that Hugh Jones, like Twm o'r Nant, decided to print the work as it was reaching the end of a successful run of performances: Twm noted in his autobiography, 'When I was about to give up playing them, I would print them; and they sold well and made good money.'[22] The printed text includes a list of the interlude's characters, divided into three groups to facilitate the presentation of the drama by three players only – a factor which would have counted a great deal to the players, since greater income was to be had from plays with fewer actors.[23] In content, it mirrors many of the conventions apparent in the extant body of Welsh interludes, both printed and manuscript, including dancing by the fool in the opening section; a formal summary of the plot by the 'Traethydd' (Narrator); acrimonious interaction between characters as they enter the stage; references to members of the audience (some possibly naming characters known in Hugh Jones's locality); a demand by the fool upon one exit to be reminded by a ringing bell of the time to re-enter the stage; and as many as eight songs to be sung to popular tunes of the day. The fool's fake phallus – which is a traditional feature of the interludes, and probably has its origins in ancient fertility rites – is not very prevalent, but one reference by the fool to his 'cala' (penis) is perhaps enough of a nod to this tradition in the later eighteenth century, by which time interlude writers were increasingly shunning this requirement of the genre.[24] Moreover, the audience are participants in this play and thus critical to its success. As the much maligned character of the Pope makes a dash for it through the crowd at the end of the interlude, they are encouraged to restrain him so that the fool can 'mob' him. Their involvement can be said to mirror Gillian Russell's sense of a 'newly proclaimed sovereignty of the people' within British theatrical culture of the 1790s.[25] In the most prominent London and provincial theatres, the Revolutionary decade saw the erosion of the traditional division of audiences into groups depending on their social status, thereby legitimizing wider participation in the theatrical world. Russell notes the popularity of large-scale pantomimes to celebrate military and naval victories, or patriotic reviews by the monarch, such as that which took place in Portsmouth in 1797. The latter was commemorated in a play by Andrew Franklin which emphasized the presence of a crowd of loyal supporters who had turned out to greet George III on the occasion.[26] Even in the context of the theatre of loyalism, therefore, the representation of mass participation, and the performing of plays on contemporary themes to mass audiences, was a feature of the drama of this decade.

The choice of material for dramatization is very ambitious and, in the context of British drama of the decade, rather unexpected. The play offers a summary of the iniquities of *ancien régime* France, ruled by a tyrannous Catholic king and his queen. It then depicts the upsurge of protest against them on Bastille Day, 1789, the incarceration, trials and executions of Louis and Marie Antoinette, together with the new rule of the republicans and their war efforts against other major European powers. Whereas Russell notes that contemporary English theatre showed a liking for 'theatre that communicated the topical immediacy of what was happening in France', with the exception of a score of Bastille pantomimes staged in the summer of 1789, she claims that a printed play by Coleridge and Southey, not intended for performance, was 'the only play of the decade . . . to deal directly with events in France'.[27] The ambitious chronological scope of the interlude suggests Hugh Jones's fascination with developments in France and his wish to record and to analyse them.[28] Whereas stringent censoring policy may have conditioned the choices made by dramatists writing within the jurisdiction of the examiner of plays, John Larpent, Hugh Jones was clearly oblivious to any danger of upsetting the status quo. Larpent nervously banned a play by Edmund Eyre which depicted the sufferings of Marie Antoinette, clearly considering 'the mere spectacle of European royalty being represented on stage as the subject of popular persecution and domestic distress . . . sufficient to ban the play on the grounds of its appearing to be some kind of advocacy by materializing regicide on English playboards'.[29]

Hugh Jones's representation, unlike Eyre's, owes nothing to the pathos of
the depiction of the French queen's sufferings found in Burke's *Reflections
on the Revolution in France*. Rather, his play crushes all her dignity, producing
a portrayal of her execution on stage in a manner which closely approaches
the farcical. Lead onto the stage by the fool, Marie Antoinette is accused of
being the cause of the war and is denied any sympathy whatsoever:

> *Y Frenhines*: Ow! Fy mhlant sydd yn ddiswcwr!
>
> *Dic*: Hidiwch monynt – hwy dawent â'u dwndwr,
> 'Ran rydym ni am ladd eich plant
> A'u taflu i bant yn bentwr.
>
> *Y Frenhines*: Ow! Rhowch bardwn i frenhines!
>
> *Dic*: Tewch â'ch dwndwr, da fy meistres.
> Gorwedd yma yn un rhol
> Ar dy fol, hen fules.
>
> Wel, mi ro' i ti ddyrnod dibris
> Er dy fod yn wraig i Lewis;   *Torri ei phen*
> Dyna ei phen hi, yn ddi-gêl,
> O danodd fel pêl denis.

> (*Queen*: Oh! My children have no succour!
>
> *Fool*: Have no care for them – they will stop their noise
> for we intend to kill your children
> and throw them away in a heap.
>
> *Queen*: Oh! Pardon a queen!
>
> *Fool*: Be quiet, my good mistress.
> Lie down here curled up
> on your stomach, old ass.
>
> Well, I'll give you a reckless blow,
> even though you are Louis's wife;   *Cuts off her head*
> there is her head for all to see,
> down below like a tennis ball.)

Linda Colley has argued that Burke's portrayal of Marie Antoinette's sufferings had widespread appeal in Britain.[30] Its sentiments are echoed in a Welsh
ballad by Richard Roberts, published in 1794.[31] Roberts captures the pathos
of the queen's situation, painting a vivid picture of her sufferings during her

incarceration and at her trial and execution, and appealing to the humanity of listeners and readers who have children of their own as they hear of her woes as a mother. The ballad mentions without a hint of criticism the queen's attempts to finance the war against France by sending money surreptitiously to her brothers, two successive Austrian emperors during the period of her tribulations. This, of course, was a damning course of action in the eyes of the leaders of the Republic, and surfaced during her trial as one of the major transgressions of which she was accused. Hugh Jones most probably shares Roberts's unawareness of the controversial nature of Marie Antoinette's relations with major European heads of state. Although he accuses her of causing the war, the accusation is less likely to be grounded in an awareness of the political turmoil of Revolutionary France than based on the traditions to which the Welsh popular genres of ballad and interlude subscribe. Siwan M. Rosser has shown the dichotomy of perceptions of women in the balladry of eighteenth-century Wales.[32] Whereas Richard Roberts emphasizes the vulnerability of the victimized Marie Antoinette, playing on the theme of the virtuous maiden (who in this case has metamorphosized into a matron), Hugh Jones casts her in the guise of the deceiving, scheming female, whose behaviour is immediately understandable in view of her descent from Eve, the first temptress and the cause of man's fall from grace.[33] Contemporary international news is thus filtered through the channels familiar to a popular, regional audience, and recast in terms which make sense to them.

The decision to represent Marie Antoinette's sufferings in an unsympathetic light is based upon Hugh Jones's overall understanding of the Revolution. Like that of a 'Cofrestr o amryw bethau hynod' (A register of various remarkable things) found in a 1795 almanac, Jones interpreted the fall of the French monarchy as a case of 'France casting away the papist yoke' ('Ffraingc yn bwrw ymaith yr Iau Babaidd').[34] There was some justification for doing so. Even in France itself the ferociousness of the attack on the Catholic Church and its clergy meant that the overthrow of the *ancien régime* was, in some circles, considered 'a Protestant plot'.[35] In 1793/4, the French dramatist P. Sylvain Maréchal published a play which depicted the overthrow of the kings of Europe, accompanied by the Pope. Several tyrants, who include George III, are brought to an island by a group of sans-culottes, representing the nations of Europe. Ravenous and squabbling, they are engulfed when a volcanic mountain on the island erupts at the end of the play.[36] The play, performed in the Théâtre de la République, is described as a 'prophétie' (prophecy) and displays the twin development of anti-monarchism and anti-popery within republican thought. Its projection of actions onto the future emphasizes the sense of the incompleteness of the Revolution at this stage in time. Hugh Jones's play is likewise prophetical, since it adjuncts to a broadly historical narrative of the events of 1789–c.1793 a final scene in which the Pope is attacked by both actors and crowd and seemingly outlawed. The foretelling of the downfall of papism was a feature of some liberal and Dissenting works composed during the eighteenth century. Richard Price, writing in 1759, predicted 'a time when popish darkness and oppression shall be exceeded by universal peace and liberty'.[37] Thirty years later, in his controversial sermon, *A Discourse on the Love of Our Country* (1789), he advocated the greater 'enlighten[ment]' and 'illumination' of mankind as a means of 'hasten[ing] the overthrow of priestcraft and tyranny'.[38] Morgan John Rhys included in the third number of his *Cylch-grawn Cynmraeg*, a new venture in Welsh journal publication, an adaptation of *The Signs of the Times: or the overthrow of the Papal Tyranny in France, the Prelude of Destruction to Popery and Despotism, but of Peace to Mankind* by the English Baptist James Bicheno.[39] Rhys had paved the way for the inclusion of Bicheno's work in earlier numbers of the *Cylch-grawn*. The first number claimed that 'it is likely that papism has been dealt a mortal wound' in France and suggested that it was unlikely that the Pope's authority should last much longer.[40] Anticipating the association between the second beast of the Book of Revelation and the French monarchy made in his rendition of Bicheno's work, Rhys maintained that 'the kings of France have been faithful servants of the Pope, and have caused the blood of thousands of Protestants to flow through their streets'.[41] Although he conceded that Louis XVI was not a tyrant to the same degree as his ancestors, Rhys believed that his execution was a punishment for the sins of his fathers:

> Er i Lewis yr unfed ar bymtheg, farw yn Bapist ffyddlon, etto yr oedd yn fwy tyner na nemmawr o'i hynafiaid, yn neillduol y gormeswr gwaedlyd Lewis y XIV. Wrth sylwi ar draws-lywodraethwyr yn gyffredin, gwelwn fod rhyw farn yn dilyn eu tylwyth, ïe, weithiau ymhellach na'r drydedd a'r bedwaredd genhed-laeth. – Mae llin âch y gormeswr Charlemagne, yn Ffraingc, a'r Stuarts yn Mrydain, yn ddigon i brofi hyn.[42]

> (Although Louis the Sixteenth died a faithful papist, yet he was more lenient than many of his ancestors, specifically the bloody oppressor Louis XIV. When we observe tyrants in general, we see that some kind of judgement pursues their family, yeah, sometimes further than the third and the fourth generation. The progeny of the oppressor Charlemagne in France and the Stuarts in Britain, is sufficient to prove this.)

Hints of this point of view colour even the most conservative and sympathetic portrayals of Louis XVI's execution printed contemporaneously in the Welsh language. Edward Charles included the following lines in a poem highly critical of the regicide French:

> Och, alaeth! pan ddymchwelodd, och y fi!
> Pawb o'r un stori a'i di'styrodd;
> Ei ddeiliaid a ddialodd, creulondeb,
> Ger bron ei wyneb a enynnodd.[43]

> (Alas, the sorrow when he fell, woe is me!
> Each one for the same reason despised him;
> his subjects wreaked vengeance; cruelty
> flared up before him.)

The notion of retaliating or avenging subjects presupposes a justification for vengeance; the suggestion that 'Each one for the same reason despised him' shows the isolation of a man against whom stringent action may have seemed inevitable. A ballad by Richard Roberts, sympathetic to the king's plight as to his wife's a few months later, contains what may be seen as a comparable recognition that Louis XVI was in some respect guilty. There is considerable ambiguity in the interpretation of the following two lines, which perhaps suggest that the now-deceased king of France (or perhaps one of his predecessors in the office) instigated some kind of violent and vengeful action against his own people:

> Fe aeth brenin Ffrainc yn anghytûn
> I roi dial hy ar ei deulu'i hun . . .[44]

> (The king of France went contentiously
> to effect a bold vengeance upon his own family . . .)

These nuances, however, only fleetingly surface in poems otherwise full of condemnation of the French, described by Edward Charles as 'gwermod y gwŷdd' (wormwood of the woods). Rhys was thus not unjustified in maintaining that 'Many, in mentioning [Louis's] death, forget the Bastille.'[45] Hugh Jones ensures that no one can forget Louis's behaviour and attitude towards his people. He is well served in this by the interlude tradition of setting characters upon the stage to brag of their own prowess, before the fool (a stock character) interrupts to challenge their flattering view of themselves.[46] Self-congratulatory songs, sung to popular tunes, restate their bravado, as when Louis and his wife sing with satisfaction of their own dominance over their people. After a digression to reveal the parallel iniquities of a typical

popish priest, who sells indulgences to murderers and adulterers, Jones
displays the level of persecution suffered by Protestant heretics in Catholic
France, as meted out by a 'Justice', with the king's approval. As in *Cylch-
grawn Cynmraeg*, no specific instance of persecution is named, although it
seems fair to assume that the horrific massacre of the Huguenots in 1572
may well lie behind the general condemnation of the anti-heretical violence
of the French crown.[47]

   The interlude provides a consistently damning account of the lives of
Louis XVI and Marie Antoinette, unusual in comparison with other extant
theatrical work of the decade. Gillian Russell has argued against 'binary'
models of cultural production, separating the metropolitan and the provincial,
the legitimate and the illegitimate, for the theatre of this period, and has
shown how (often impoverished) strolling actors adopted city fashions in
theatrical work to their own needs as they travelled around the country.[48]
Since there is little evidence for the kind of play on a chronological plan
which the interlude represents in the legitimate and metropolitan culture
of the decade, it is unlikely that Hugh Jones's play was an adaptation of
theatrical work in London or other prominent towns or cities. It remains a
possibility that the anti-popery of the work was inspired by traditional
theatrical practices such as pope burnings, which originated in Tudor times
but continued to be played out into the eighteenth century.[49] Evidence for
such pageantry in Wales is not easily found, however, and it is difficult to
build up a picture of a theatrical anti-Catholic popular tradition in eighteenth-
century Wales. In the context of the Welsh interlude, a 1735 drama represents
the figure of a priest of 'the old faith' ('yr hên ffydd') on stage, as part of the
machinery to ensure the downfall of the miser, an unpopular fellow whose
grudging ways deny his young daughter the opportunity to marry her dashing
lover.[50] The priest is in fact one of the play's two fools in disguise. He cajoles
the miser and supports his campaign against his daughter's marriage by
offering to give her a sermon such as will 'make her weep or sadden until
her heart almost melts at the root'.[51] Such a promise earns him the miser's
trust, but it is dashed as the second fool, in the guise of the Devil ('Y Gwr
drwg'), enters the stage, reveals the worthlessness of the old man's trust in
the popish priest, and bullies him into submitting to his daughter's marriage
and to granting her a handsome dowry. Popery is revealed in this episode
as a recourse for credulous sinners, the fake devil claiming to have won the
fake priest over to his cause many years ago.[52] Such a representation of the
Catholic figure of the priest, whilst not flattering, does not suggest any real
sense of a fear of Catholicism: it is, precisely, an 'old faith', to which only
a few misguided and foolish people will superstitiously adhere. The fool's
ability to 'play' with it endows it with a sense of relative harmlessness, a

feature strongly at odds with the portrayal of Catholic France found in Hugh Jones's interlude sixty years later.

Welsh balladry of the eighteenth century, conversely, contains numerous references to the iniquities of popery. Linda Colley's influential thesis regarding the Protestant unity of the constituent parts of Great Britain during the long eighteenth century, in the face of the Catholic European threat, resonates within the works of Welsh ballad writers. Anti-popish sentiment surfaces in particular during periods of war. Ballads celebrating the establishment of militia units in certain Welsh counties during both the Seven Years' War (1756–63) and the American War of Independence (1775–83) aim to arouse their audiences in favour of armament by drawing attention to the despicability of popish tradition and rule.[53] Only rarely does the Catholic threat seem to belong on British soil proper. A ballad by Richard Davies, entitled 'Marwnad y Merthyron' (An Elegy for the Martyrs), depicts the history of Protestant martyrs. With an insecure grasp of the history of persecution, Davies mentions as hot spots for the burning of Protestant heretics the reigns of Edward (VI, reigned 1547–53), under whom, in fact, the Reformation instigated by his father, Henry VIII, continued and, more appropriately, Mary (reigned 1553–8).[54] His glance across the Channel to persecution in France by 'Lewis yr ailfed ar bymtheg' (Louis XVII) – possibly an error for the Catholic arch-enemy of Britain, Louis XIV – also displays uncertain knowledge of the facts, even while it may point to the 1790s as a possible date for the composition of the ballad, since it was then that the Dauphin Louis Charles became known by the title Louis XVII.[55] In view of the existence of anti-Catholic diatribe within Welsh balladry it remains a possibility that Hugh Jones's anti-papism was, at least in part, inspired by popular attitudes.

We have seen that, for John Larpent, the examiner of plays, even a sympathetic rendition of the sufferings of the French queen on stage was cause for consternation. Attacking the French monarchy had ramifications for perceptions of the British monarchy and for the institution of monarchy in general in a world where Painite republicanism evidently held such widespread appeal. Differentiating between a corrupt, Catholic monarchy in France and a benign, just monarchy in Britain, while problematic to people of higher social rank such as Larpent, was not necessarily so unfeasible a task among the lower orders. The illegitimate Bastille pantomimes of 1789, even while they celebrated the end of an oppressive regime in France, all had 'noticeably loyalist endings', with scenes of 'beautiful decoration representing Britannia seated in a triumphal car, holding transparent portraits of the *King and Queen of Great Britain*'.[56] Hugh Jones's play makes frequent reference to the British monarchy's virtue, not simply at the end, where a loyal song on 'God Save the King' is sung, but at intervals throughout the play.[57] Dic, the play's fool, contrasts the availability of the Scriptures to all in Britain with the constraints put upon the French people, to whom they are 'Locked up (it is pure shame!) / in Latin' ('A'u cloi nhw i fyny (mae'n gywilydd noeth!) / Yn Lading'). Elsewhere he argues that 'George, gracious king of England, / seeks freedom for all his subjects' ('mae Siôr, Brenin Lloegr dirion, / Yn erchi rhydd–did i'w holl drigolion'), this again in contrast to the situation in France. A further exchange relating to the comparison between the corrupt Capet monarchy and the benign Hanoverian equivalent in Britain runs like this:

> *Y frenhines*: Pwy oedd hwn yma, fy arglwydd frenin,
> Oedd yn siarad mor dra chethin?
>
> *Lewis*: Neb ar dwyn, rwy'n deud yn dyner,
> Ond gwas a ffŵl i frenin Lloegr.
>
> *Y frenhines*: Yn wir, mae Siorsyn, brenin Lloegr,
> Yn rhy feddal ym mhob mater;
> Gado'i ddeiliaid dan ei ddwylo
> Yn rhydd bob egwyl braidd i bigo.
>
> (*Queen*: Who was that, my lord king,
> who was speaking so very hideously?
>
> *Lewis*: Nobody, clearly, I say gently,
> but a servant and a fool to the king of England.
>
> *Queen*: Indeed, George, the king of England,
> is too soft in every matter;
> leaves his subjects under his hands
> free at almost every instance to sting.)

Although the condemnation of George III, coming from the mouth of the corrupt and tyrannous French queen, is clearly more praise than anything, the designation of the fool as an instrument for 'stinging' suggests the wider compass of the play's critique. For although the interlude's most damning commentary is indisputably aimed at the Catholic French regime, in its latter sections the play moves on to offer a highly sympathetic portrayal of the new republic. Hugh Jones goes yet a step further by highlighting specific areas of contention directly relating to the situation at home in Britain. He considers Britain's war policy, the reception given to popish émigrés from France in Britain, and the alleged sale of British wheat to France by wealthy landowners. The nature of two of these attacks is now considered.

The expression of a hope for peace is widespread in the Welsh balladry of this period, but is usually accompanied by protestations of loyalty to king and country and as such is more a case of longing for the end of hostilities than an effort to stir anti-war sentiment.[58] Although the interlude also initially only offers a general plea for peace in this vein, it later boldly attributes a discussion of British war policy to one of the French republicans, who argues that Britain went to war for very dubious reasons:

> Dyma yr achos, yr ydwy' yn meddwl,
> Oedd iddynt godi mewn cythryfwl,
> O ran mae yn Lloegr fyrdd yn pesgi,
> Yn fawr eu truth, wrth fwyta trethi.

> Ac nid oedd ganddynt ddim i'w wneuthur
> Ond gyrru'r Duke of York a'i sawdwyr,
> Gan feddwl cael ein lladd o'n cyrrau
> Er siampl noeth i'w deiliaid nhwythau.

> Er bod yn Lloegr gyfraith addas
> Mewn cadarnwch yn y deyrnas,
> Eto, er hyn, mae'r dynion gwaela'
> Yn cael eu gwasgu hyd yr eitha'.

> A dyna'r peth wnaeth iddynt ofni,
> Os nyni a wna feistroli
> Y gwna eu deiliaid hwythau dyrru
> I'w lladd i gyd, fel maent yn haeddu.

> (This was why, I believe,
> they rose up in tumult,
> since there are scores in England fattening themselves,
> great their deceit, by consuming taxes.

> And there was nothing they could do
> save send the Duke of York and his soldiers,
> intending to kill us all
> as a plain example for their own subjects.

> Although there is a worthy law in England,
> steadfast within the kingdom,
> yet, in spite of this, the poorest men
> are ground down to the utmost.

And this is what made them fear
that, if we should prevail,
their own subjects should amass
to kill them all, as they deserve.)

The speaker's clear suggestion is that sending men to war is the English ruling class's way of maintaining its grip on power, a highly contentious point of view with clear radical dimensions. The reference to the scores who are fattening themselves on taxes may reflect sentiments expressed in Richard Brinsley Sheridan's House of Commons speech of 21 January 1794, which was reproduced in *Cylch-grawn Cynmraeg* shortly afterwards. Sheridan is said to have suggested that 'All the gentry who come forward to support this wonderful war are to have a part of the taxes . . .'[59] The fact that these sentiments are balanced by a typically Nonconformist affirmation of the essential goodness of the British constitution may suggest that Hugh Jones writes from a conscious religio-political standpoint, and is not simply venting his wrath in a haphazard way.[60] Nonetheless, our ignorance of his political and religious affiliations, outside the evidence offered in the interlude text and the seven poems in his name, means that caution must be shown before attributing radical views to him too decisively.

The possibility that Hugh Jones's anti-war diatribe originated in his reading of *Cylch-grawn Cynmraeg* is supported by the fact that a second line of attack in the interlude against the British status quo also has a precedent in that magazine. The journal staged a critique of the British establishment's sympathetic attitude to the plight of Catholic priests following the establishment of the Civil Constitution of the Clergy in 1790. 'Lately', argued a writer in the fourth issue, 'it is a ritual to pray for the popish priests, although we have to swear that their doctrine of trans-substantiation is a damnable heresy: if they are well fed (as I hear they are) their most holy [priest], the Pope, may release this country from the sin of perjury.'[61] The appendix to the same number of the journal wryly noted:

Y mae'r Pab yn dywedyd (nid heb achos) fod gantho well gobaith am y deyrnas hon nag a fu erioed . . . Y mae'r Esgobion a'r Offeiriaid Protestanaidd, o'r diwedd, yn cyfaddef mai eu hanwyl frodyr yw'r offeiriaid pabaidd, er eu bod yn ol cyfraith Loegr yn gorfod tyngu mai heresi ddamniol yw eu crefydd; ïe mae un o'r Esgobion hyn* [*Dr. Horsley] wedi myned mor belled a dywedyd mai'r Papistiaid yw ei frodyr, ac nad yw'r Ymneillduwyr yn y deyrnas hon ddim yn deilwng i'w galw'n frodyr.[62]

(The Pope says (not without reason) that he has better hope for this kingdom than ever . . . The Protestant bishops and priests acknowledge at last that the popish priests are their dear brothers, although they are obliged according to the law of England to swear that their religion is a damnable heresy. Indeed, one of these bishops★ [★Dr Horsley] has gone as far as to say that the papists are his brothers and that the Dissenters in this kingdom are not worthy of being called brothers.)

This perception that Anglicans and French Catholics are all one is a sardonic means of attacking Church-and-king factions on the pages of *Cylch-grawn Cynmraeg*. Indeed, as Hywel Davies has pointed out, the term Antichrist in both Bicheno and Rhys's work is made 'to apply equally to the Established Anglican Church and Erastian concept of the state . . . as to the Popish tyranny in France'.[63] It is not so clear in the case of the interlude that attacking the papacy and Catholicism in France is an indirect means of attacking either the British state or its Established Church. The play's angry reference to the arrival of émigrés in Britain centres on the evils committed by Catholics within British history (presumably during the reign of Mary), a fact which suggests a fear of 'real' Catholic influence rather than an attempt to muddy the waters and suggest the Catholic sympathies of the élite.[64] Moreover, lack of knowledge of the author's life and background must again be a mitigating factor in any interpretation.

In an exchange between the characters of Louis XVI and the fool at the beginning of the interlude, the latter concedes:

> Bûm minne'n darllain hanes pabistiaid
> Tan chollais agos lewyrch fy llygaid,
> A dal sylw, fel roeddwn lob,
> Ar eu crefydd ym mhob crafiad.

> (I too once read the history of the papists
> until I almost lost the lustre of my eyes,
> and took note, idiot that I was,
> of their faith in every touch.)

Locating the work which Jones read is not an easy task, but it remains the case that his reliance on printed sources and the interaction of his thought with material found in them is one of the most striking features of his work. Long gone was the practice of using legendary basis for interlude stories, prevalent in plays composed earlier in the eighteenth century.[65] This is a play which engages with its own historical moment in time, absorbing the

excitement of participation in the culture of print. There is no doubt that
it was designed for performance (and may well have been performed). It
seems particularly apt, however, that Hugh Jones later surrendered it to the
hands of the printer Ishmael Davies, so that it could feed back into the stream
of print culture.

It is almost inconceivable that a similar play could have been printed in
English c.1798. Although the broad outline of the text centres on a fierce
hatred of Catholicism which is viewed as the iniquity of a foreign monarchy,
the play also offers a direct criticism of aspects of the behaviour of the British
ruling class. In the context of the current interest within British scholarship
in teasing out the varied responses to the French Revolution within the
regions and among the nations of the British Isles, it offers a unique perspective
on responses in Wales. Not only does it testify to interaction between a
rapidly expanding culture of print and a traditional native performance genre,
it also, in its apparent unawareness of its own daring, demonstrates the
remarkable aloofness and dissociation of this Welsh world from standard
responses in mainstream British culture.

Notes

[1] See David Worrall, *Theatric Revolution: Drama, Censorship, and Romantic Period
Subcultures 1773–1832* (Oxford, 2006); Gillian Russell, 'Revolutionary Drama',
in Pamela Clemit (ed.), *The Cambridge Companion to British Literature of the French
Revolution in the 1790s* (Cambridge, 2011), pp. 175–89. Worrall's study shows
that impoverished itinerant players, although able to avoid state censorship proper,
were subjected to suppression by local communities, often headed by Methodists,
and as vagrants and debtors during the period with which his study is concerned.
Worrall, *Theatric Revolution*, pp. 237, 239–40. Specifically on popular metropolitan
and rural dramatic activity in England and Scotland, drawing on testimony from
the 1790s to 1818, see Gillian Russell, 'Keats, Popular Culture, and the Sociability
of Theatre', in Philip Connell and Nigel Leask (eds.), *Romanticism and Popular
Culture in Britain and Ireland* (Cambridge, 2009), pp. 194–213.

[2] Russell, 'Revolutionary Drama', pp. 176–7.

[3] The Welsh periodicals *Cylch-grawn Cynmraeg* (1793–4) and *Y Geirgrawn* (1796)
provided a forum for a lively discussion of Welsh pamphlet literature, notably
John Jones's *Seren Tan Gwmmwl*. Edward Charles's *Epistolau Cymraeg, at y Cymry*
were also originally intended for the periodical press. See Marion Löffler, *Welsh
Responses to the French Revolution: Press and Public Discourse 1789–1802* (Cardiff,
2012). On the decline of the interlude, see G. G. Evans, 'Henaint a Thranc yr
Anterliwt', *Taliesin*, 54 (1985), 14–29, and E. Wyn James, 'Rhai Methodistiaid
a'r Anterliwt', *Taliesin*, 57 (1986), 8–19.

4   Although listed in Eiluned Rees's comprehensive bibliography, *Libri Walliae*, the play eluded the attentions of scholars of the genre, failing to appear in G. G. Evans's list of interlude texts. See Eiluned Rees, *Libri Walliae: A Catalogue of Welsh Books and Books Printed in Wales 1546–1820* (2 vols., Aberystwyth, 1987), I, p. 362; G. G. Evans, 'Yr Anterliwt Gymraeg', *LlC*, I, no. 2 (1950–1), 83–96.

5   See the forthcoming edition of the interlude: Ffion Mair Jones (ed.), *Y Chwyldro Ffrengig a'r Anterliwt: Hanes Bywyd a Marwolaeth Brenin a Brenhines Ffrainc*. This charts Jones's career as a ballad writer and poet, and includes the seven additional poems that can safely be attributed to him. All quotations from the interlude in this chapter are from this edition.

6   'North Wales is now as Methodistical as south Wales and Southwales as hell.' These comments by Edward Williams (Iolo Morganwg) in a letter of 1799 are a colourful indication of the extent to which Methodism had taken the whole of Wales by storm by the end of the eighteenth century. *CIM*, II, p. 197, Iolo Morganwg to William Owen Pughe, 10 July 1799. On the connection between Methodism and the decline of the interlude, see Evans, 'Henaint a Thranc yr Anterliwt'; and James, 'Rhai Methodistiaid a'r Anterliwt'.

7   Examples include the famous Welsh Methodist hymnologist Ann Griffiths of Dolwar Fach in Montgomeryshire. See James, 'Rhai Methodistiaid a'r Anterliwt', 16–19.

8   'aflwyddiant ar y chwareu. Yn y mynydau hyny fe edrychodd duw ar y fintai honno, a thorodd yr esgynlawr, ac anafwyd y chwareuwr a elwid ffŵl, ac felly dyrysodd y cwbl am y diwrnod hwnnw, ie, am byth hefyd, oherwydd hwn oedd y cyfarfod olaf a fu yno.' W. Hughes (Proscairon), *Y Drysorfa* (1839), 148; quoted in R. O. Roberts, 'Crefydd ac Addysg yn Ardal Pentir a Rhiwlas ger Bangor, 1750–1900. Rhan 1', *Caernarvonshire Historical Society Transactions*, 58 (1997), 82.

9   Cecil Price, *The English Theatre in Wales in the Eighteenth and Early Nineteenth Century* (Cardiff, 1948), pp. 54–5, 182.

10   For examples of Charles's critical comments regarding Methodists and Methodism, see Edward Charles (Siamas Wynedd), 'Y Pregethwyr Bol Clawdd, A'r Teiliwr Bongleraidd', *Cylch-grawn Cynmraeg*, III (August 1793), 198–201; *idem, Epistolau Cymraeg, at y Cymry* (Llundain, 1797), no. 1, pp. 7, 23; no. 5, pp. 32–3.

11   Evans, 'Henaint a Thranc yr Anterliwt', 16.

12   Ibid.

13   *Cambrian Register*, I (1795), 426; ibid., III (1818), 99.

14   Cf. comments on the decline of the 'female warrior' motif within English-language balladry in Dianne Dugaw, *Warrior Women and Popular Balladry 1650–1850* (Cambridge, 1999), pp. 65–90.

15   Literacy rates in Wales were raised by the efforts of several religious societies to teach adults and children to read Welsh from the latter part of the seventeenth century onwards. Among the most influential were Griffith Jones's Circulating Schools (1731–79), which greatly aided in bringing about the 'beginning of a breakthrough to mass literacy' by the end of the eighteenth century. Eryn M. White, 'Popular Schooling and the Welsh Language 1650–1800', in Geraint H.

Jenkins (ed.), *The Welsh Language before the Industrial Revolution* (Cardiff, 1997), pp. 317–41.

[16]   'cymaint o gynhyrfiad i argraphu llyfrau a dysgu darllen . . . o ragor yr amseroedd aeth heibio.' I. Foulkes (ed.), *Gwaith Thomas Edwards (Twm o'r Nant)* (Liverpool, 1874), p. 214.

[17]   Evans, 'Henaint a Thranc yr Anterliwt', 27.

[18]   Sir William Jones's text (which was circulated by the Society for Constitutional Information) and the Welsh interlude adaptation are discussed by Michael J. Franklin, 'Sir William Jones, the Celtic Revival and the Oriental Renaissance', in Gerard Carruthers and Alan Rawes (eds.), *English Romanticism and the Celtic World* (Cambridge, 2003), pp. 20–37. On the authorship of the interlude, see A. Cynfael Lake, 'Rhai Ystyriaethau Pellach Ynghylch Awduraeth *Yr Anterliwt Goll*', *NLWJ*, XXVII, no. 3 (1992), 337–49.

[19]   Cf. this device as a function of marginalia to printed sources. Heather Jackson, *Romantic Readers: The Evidence of Marginalia* (London, 2005), p. 256; Ffion Mair Jones, '*The Bard is a Very Singular Character': Iolo Morganwg, Marginalia and Print Culture* (Cardiff, 2010), pp. 123–5.

[20]   Since the execution of Marie Antoinette takes place at the latter end of the play, references to hostilities between France and Britain may well relate to the earliest months of the wars. The text mentions the Duke of York's Flanders campaign and the French invasion of Holland and (most probably) the Austrian Netherlands (Belgium), all of which had taken place during 1793 (although they continued into the following years, too). For another example of an apologia in a printed interlude, see Dafydd Glyn Jones, 'Thomas Williams yr Anterliwtiwr (1689–1763)', in *idem*, *Agoriad yr Oes: Erthyglau ar Lên, Hanes a Gwleidyddiaeth Cymru* (Talybont, 2001), pp. 120, 141.

[21]   Hugh Jones's apologia centres wholly on the fear of criticism of his prosody. There is no indication that he considered the content of his interlude in any way controversial.

[22]   'Mi a fyddwn yn arfer, pan ym min troi heibio chwarae, mi a'i hargraffwn, ac i gwerthwn; a gwerth hwylus oedd arnynt, a thâl da oddiwrthynt'. G. M. Ashton (ed.), *Hunangofiant a Llythyrau Twm o'r Nant* (Caerdydd, 1948), p. 37.

[23]   Ibid.

[24]   Evans, 'Yr Anterliwt Gymraeg', 91.

[25]   Russell, 'Revolutionary Drama', p. 176.

[26]   Ibid., p. 185.

[27]   Ibid., p. 183. For London Bastille plays and dramas celebrating the Fête de la Féderation, see Worrall, *Theatric Revolution*, pp. 91–9. For material on these and other Revolution-related topics delivered in Dublin, see John Hall Stewart, 'The French Revolution on the Dublin Stage, 1790–1794', *The Journal of the Royal Society of Antiquaries of Ireland*, 91, no. 2 (1961), 183–92. At least one of the productions named in Stewart's article was later transferred for staging in Liverpool, not very far from audiences located in north-east Wales.

[28]   An obvious precedent in the Welsh interlude tradition is Huw Morys's interlude on the seventeenth-century British Civil Wars, which covers a twenty-year period.

See Huw Morys, *Y Rhyfel Cartrefol*, ed. Ffion Mair Jones (Bangor, [2008]); *eadem*, 'Huw Morys and the Civil Wars', *Studia Celtica*, XLIV (2010), 165–99.

29 Worrall, *Theatric Revolution*, pp. 129–30.

30 Linda Colley, *Britons: Forging the Nation 1707–1837* (New Haven, 1992), pp. 266–7, 269–70.

31 Ffion Mair Jones, *Welsh Ballads of the French Revolution 1793–1815* (Cardiff, 2012), no. 7.

32 Siwan M. Rosser, *Y Ferch ym Myd y Faled: Delweddau o'r Ferch ym Maledi'r Ddeunawfed Ganrif* (Caerdydd, 2005), pp. 13–15.

33 Ibid., pp. 10, 11, 144.

34 *Cyfaill Brawdol* (Dublin, 1795), 24. For an anti-Catholic interpretation of the Revolution in pamphlet literature, see John Owen, *Golygiadau ar Achosion ag Effeithiau'r Cyfnewidiad yn Ffrainc* (Machynlleth, [1797]).

35 William Doyle, *The Oxford History of the French Revolution* (2nd edn., Oxford, 2002), p. 138.

36 P. Sylvain Maréchal, *Le Jugement Dernier Des Rois, Prophétie en un Acte, en prose . . . Jouée sur le Théâtre de la République, au mois Vendemiaire et jours suivant L'an second de la Républiqe Francaise* (The Last Judgement of the Kings, a Prophecy in one Act, in prose . . . Played at the Theatre of the Republic, in the month of Vendemiaire and on subsequent days in the second year of the French Republic) (Paris, 1793/4).

37 Clement Fatovic, 'The Anti-Catholic Roots of Liberal and Republican Conceptions of Freedom in English Political Thought', *Journal of the History of Ideas*, 66, no. 1 (2005), 37–58, esp. 51. Fatovic quotes from 'Britain's Happiness, and the Proper Improvement of it', in D. O. Thomas (ed.), *Price: Political Writings* (Cambridge, 1991), p. 12.

38 Richard Price, 'A Discourse on the Love of Our Country', in Thomas (ed.), *Price: Political Writings*, p. 182.

39 Hywel M. Davies, 'Morgan John Rhys and James Bicheno: Anti-Christ and the French Revolution in England and Wales', *BBCS*, XXIX, part I (1980), 111–27.

40 'y mae'n debyg fod Pabyddiaeth wedi cael ei farwol glwyf yno'; 'Tebygid na phery awdurdod y Pab ddim yn hir.' *Cylch-grawn Cynmraeg*, I (February 1793), 56.

41 'mae brenhinoedd Ffraingc wedi bod yn weision ffyddlon i'r Pab, a chwedi peri i waed miloedd o'r Protestaniaid redeg trwy eu heolydd.' Ibid.

42 Ibid.

43 Edward Charles, 'Ar Farwolaeth Lewis yr Unfed ar bymtheg Brenin Ffraingc, yr hwn y torrwyd ei Ben yn gyhoeddus, yn Ninas Paris, ar yr 21 o fis Ionawr, A.D. 1793, drwy archiad y Gymmanfa Giwdawdol' (Upon the Death of Louis the Sixteenth, King of France, who was publicly beheaded in the City of Paris, on 21 January AD 1793, by command of the National Assembly), ibid., II (May 1793), 111.

44 Jones, *Welsh Ballads of the French Revolution*, no. 3.

45 'Y mae llawer, wrth son am ei farwolaeth yn anghofio'r Bastile.' *Cylch-grawn Cynmraeg*, III, 173.

46　One such example, involving the figure of a king, is found in Twm o'r Nant's interlude, *Pedair Colofn Gwladwriaeth*. Glyn Ashton (ed.), *Anterliwitiau Twm o'r Nant: Pedair Colofn Gwladwriaeth a Cybydd-dod ac Oferedd* (Caerdydd, 1964), pp. 4–5.

47　Davies, 'Morgan John Rhys and James Bicheno', 114; Fatovic, 'The Anti-Catholic Roots', 41.

48　Russell, 'Keats, Popular Culture, and the Sociability of Theatre'.

49　Colin Haydon, *Anti-Catholicism in Eighteenth-Century England* (Manchester, 1993), pp. 33–7. For the way in which English medieval Catholic drama was Protestantized following the Reformation, see Rainer Pineas, *Tudor and Early Stuart Anti-Catholic Drama* (Nieuwkoop, 1972).

50　Richard Parry, 'Cyndrigolion y Deyrnas Hon', in Ffion Mair Jones, 'Pedair Anterliwt Hanes' (unpublished University of Wales PhD thesis, 2000), pp. 509–659.

51　'bô hi'n wylo neu bruddo braidd / na thoddo gwraidd ei chalon.' Ibid., p. 555.

52　'mi ynilles o ers llawer Blwyddyn.' Ibid., p. 556.

53　Anon., 'Cerdd newydd, sef y Militia yn canu ffarwel i'w gwlad, yr hon a genir, a'r Tempest of War' (A new song, namely the militia singing farewell to their country, which is sung on 'Tempest of War') (Amwythig, 1761; JHD 876ii); Ellis Roberts, 'Cerdd ar "Frynie yr Werddon" o glod i'r milisia Cymru, sy yn ddychryn i'n gelynion' (A song on 'The Hills of Ireland' in praise to the militia of Wales, who frighten our enemies) (Wrecsam, [?1778]; JHD 289i). Both are discussed in Ffion Mair Jones, '"A'r ffeiffs a'r drums yn roario": Y Baledwyr Cymraeg, y Milisia a'r Gwirfoddolwyr', *Canu Gwerin*, 36 (2011), 23–5, 28, 29.

54　See *ODNB* s.n. Mary I (1516–58); Edward VI (1537–53).

55　The ballad is undated, but was printed in the eighteenth century and by Ishmael Davies, Trefriw, active as a printer from 1785. See John Davies, *A Bibliography of Welsh Ballads Printed in the Eighteenth Century* (London, 1911), no. 423.

56　Worrall, *Theatric Revolution*, p. 93, quoting the observations of a French onlooker; Russell, 'Revolutionary Drama', pp. 179–80.

57　Note that the words to the final song of the interlude require a 'God Save the King' tune closely resembling the current British national anthem, rather than the traditional Welsh song, designated 'God Save the King the old way'. Many other 'God Save the King' ballads during the decade were sung to the latter version of the tune. See Jones, *Welsh Ballads of the French Revolution*, pp. 361–2.

58　See for example ibid., nos. 15, 19, 26, 27, 29.

59　'Y mae'r holl fonedd a ddelo ymlaen i gynnal y rhyfel ogoneddus hon, i gael rhan o'r trethi . . .', *Cylch-grawn Cynmraeg*, IV (January–February 1794), 279–80.

60　'Os oes yn Lloegr rai'n gormesu, / Ceir chware teg mewn rhan er hynny; / 'Dydyw'r gyfraith yno'n gofyn / Gwneuthur cam ag un cardotyn. / Ceiff yno bawb y Bibl sanctaidd / Yn eu hiaith i fyw'n Gristnogaidd; / Ond llawer iawn o waed a gollwyd / Yno, cofiwn, cyn y cafwyd' (If there are some oppressors in England, / there is partial fairness too; / the Law there does not require / that any beggar should be mistreated. / Everyone there is given the Holy Bible / in their language to live in a Christian manner).

61　'yn ddiweddar, y mae'n ddefod i grefu dros yr offeiriaid Pabaidd, er ein bod yn gorfod tyngu bod eu hathrawiaeth o draws-sylweddiad yn heresi ddamniol: os porthir hwy'n dda (fel yr ydwyf yn clywed eu bod yn cael) o bossibl y bydd i'w sancteiddiolaf, y Pab, i ryddhau'r wladwriaeth hon oddiwrth y pechod o annudonedd.' *Cylch-grawn Cynmraeg*, IV, 256.

[62] Ibid., appendix, 13.

[63] Davies, 'Morgan John Rhys and James Bicheno', 114.

[64] On the strength of 'Folk memories of Marian burnings' within the popular imagination in early modern England, see Haydon, *Anti-Catholicism in Eighteenth-Century England*, p. 6.

[65] See for example 'Llur', an interlude on the story of King Lear, probably composed during the mid-eighteenth century. The anonymous author almost certainly had to rely on his memory of the story, a fact suggested by his confusion regarding some of the characters' names. Jones, 'Pedair Anterliwt Hanes', pp. 660–890.

Engraved by J. Holloway from the Original Painting

M.rs Piozzi.

Publish'd by J. Sewell Cornhill 1786.

Figure 8. 'Mrs Piozzi', engraving by Thomas Holloway, 1786,
after a painting of 1781 by Robert Edge Pine.

'A good Cambrio-Briton': Hester Thrale Piozzi, Helen Maria Williams and the Welsh sublime in the 1790s[1]

JON MEE

From at least the time of Thomas Gray's 'The Bard', eighteenth-century literary culture in English witnessed a developing interest in the Welsh sublime. This interest was partly to do with landscape, for obvious reasons associated with Snowdonia, but almost equally important were antiquarian ideas of the bards and Druids of the Celtic past. Within this last complex of associations, identification between Wales and 'liberty' was very strong. From Gray to William Blake, at least, whose lost painting 'The Ancient Britons' seems to have been indebted to Gray as well as to the researches of Welsh antiquarians like William Owen Pughe, this 'liberty' was associated with resistance to the imposition of foreign empire.[2] Damian Walford Davies has unpacked many of these complex associations brilliantly from the perspectives of those sympathetic to reform, but in this chapter I would like to take a different political tack by looking principally at Hester Piozzi's writing about Wales.[3] Nearly all the writing Piozzi published in the 1790s was explicitly anti-Jacobin, but in her letters and unpublished journal, known as the *Thraliana*, tensions appear within her loyalty to the British state. These include her relations with another woman writer who could have claimed a Welsh heritage, Helen Maria Williams. Appalled by the personal and political conduct of Williams, Piozzi broke off their correspondence in 1793, but continued to harbour the sense of a deeper connection based on the idea of a quality of emotional freedom Piozzi identified with Wales.

Of all the writing Piozzi published in the 1790s, the most obviously opposed to the French Revolution was her short pamphlet *Three Warnings to John Bull* (1798), which urged national unanimity in defence of government; proper regard for the national religion; and the amendment of manners. This defence of what are presented as British values tends to appear even where her topic, as in *British Synonymy* (1794), would seem to have little or nothing to do with politics, but, in her unpublished writing, Wales – as opposed to England – often appears as a place liberated *from* political questions. Furthermore, while confident that Wales would loyally resist the radical influences she perceived as emanating from France – a conservative revision of the foreign-invasion trope at the heart of the discourse of the Welsh sublime – the birthplace is also valued in her unpublished journals and letters precisely because it is distinct from English literary culture. Gender, I would argue, played a large if complex part in these contradictions. Piozzi had fought hard to create an authority for herself in literary culture from at least the 1770s, but she was never quite accepted, even when writing in defence of the British state. For Piozzi, Wales was associated with her sense of outsider status in relation to London's literary élite; especially after her marriage to the Italian musician Gabriele Piozzi in 1784 caused widespread scandal in fashionable London society. Even the 'effusion of pure British loyalty' of *Three Warnings to John Bull* might be perceived as less a simple identification with the status quo than a prophecy imbued with a sense of corruption threatening the established order from within.[4]

Hester Lynch Thrale Piozzi was the scion of a Welsh gentry family of diminishing means but grand lineage. She was, says her most recent biographer, 'inordinately proud of her Welsh ancestry'.[5] Piozzi was born in 1741 near Pwllheli in Caernarfonshire to Hester and John Salusbury, both of whom claimed descent from Catrin of Berain, known as *Mam Cymru* because of the number of families who associated themselves with her name. The Salusbury family estate, Bachegraig, was heavily mortgaged by the time Hester was born, and her father's financial recklessness ensured she spent much of her childhood being passed around relatives, mainly in Wales and London. What she did acquire was a more liberal education than many daughters of the gentry. As early as 1762, she published 'An American Eclogue – imitating the Style of Fingal' in a newspaper, but, not least because of the family's financial situation, marriage became a more pressing issue than any literary ambitions.[6] In 1763, encouraged by her uncle, who called the financial shots, she married Henry Thrale, a wealthy brewer, later MP for Southwark, more given to fox-hunting than erudition. The Thrales divided their married life primarily between a house conjoint with the brewery in Southwark and the more suburban elegance of the villa at Streatham Park, just outside London.

Somewhat against her husband's inclinations, Hester began to exert her literary aspirations by turning Streatham Park into a salon. Most famously it became a home-from-home for Samuel Johnson, who had been introduced to Thrale by the Irish playwright Arthur Murphy in 1765.[7] Although Johnson seems particularly to have appreciated being a member of the family, enjoying the domestic comforts of Streatham, members of his Literary Club, including Edmund Burke, Oliver Goldsmith and Sir Joshua Reynolds, sometimes visited with him. In the 1770s Reynolds was commissioned to provide a series of portraits of these and other literary luminaries for the library at Streatham. *Not* numbered among those Reynolds painted was James Boswell, who from early on developed a rivalry with Piozzi over Johnson that turned into open warfare after their hero's death.[8] By 1784, when Johnson died, Hester was becoming an influential player in British literary culture, even if she had still published little herself. In an age of literary clubs and informal coteries, Streatham Park had become 'one of the most influential, the most active, and the most cosmopolitan both in its composition and tendencies'.[9] She set about cementing this position after Johnson's death by compiling *Anecdotes of Johnson* (1786) and *Letters to and from the Late Samuel Johnson* (1788). Always envious of her relationship with Johnson, Boswell launched a campaign against Piozzi, representing her as a heedless female interloper in the serious business of memorializing Johnson. He conceived his *Life of Johnson*, eventually published in 1791, as a masculine riposte to her feminine chatter. Aware that he was at work in a very competitive field, Boswell also ruthlessly exploited the scandal that surrounded Hester's decision to marry the Italian musician Gabriele Piozzi after Thrale's death.[10]

All of those involved in the Johnson industry that sprang up after his death, including Boswell, were guyed in the press, but as a woman presuming to manage the reputation of a writer thought to represent the heroic ambition of British literary culture, Piozzi was particularly vulnerable to mockery, especially as her work centred on the domestic details of life at Streatham, easily parodied as the female confusion of gossip with solid conversation.[11] The *Monthly Review*'s account of *Anecdotes of Johnson*, for instance, reported the frustration of its expectation of 'learned observations, with moral reflections, and profound disquisitions'.[12] Furious at being side-lined in Piozzi's published accounts of her relationship with Johnson, Boswell joined in the sport of baiting her, but her former allies among the Bluestockings associated with Elizabeth Montagu and friends were not much more support-ive. These former friends Piozzi came to see as 'a Coterie of my unprovoked Enemies.'[13]

In fact, Piozzi's relationship with this circle had always been somewhat ambivalent. She acknowledged Montagu's power in the literary world, and attended and enjoyed her assemblies, but she also competed with them, if indirectly, by offering Streatham as a more self-consciously informal and affective space for conversation to flow around. 'Mrs. Montagu's Bouquet is all out of the Hot-house', she once wrote, 'mine out of the Woods & Fields

& many a Weed there is in it.'[14] Piozzi's Welshness played its part in her self-understanding as a more natural and less artificial literary personality than Montagu's West-End glamour. In 1781, she wrote out in her journal 'the Characters of the People who are intended to have their Portraits hung up in the Library here at Streatham'.[15] Of Sir Joshua Reynolds's painting of her as a smooth society hostess, she wrote:

> In Features so placid, so smooth, so serene,
> What Trace of the Wit – or the Welch-woman's seen?
> Of the Temper sarcastic, the flattering Tongue,
> The Sentiment right – with th' Occasion still wrong.
> What Trace of the tender, the rough, the refin'd,
> The Soul in which all Contrarieties join'd?[16]

For Hester Piozzi this idea of herself as an untamed 'Welch-woman' remained an important part of her self-definition, especially in the face of the acrimony sparked by her remarriage in the 1780s, but it had been present earlier, for instance, in her responses to the Welsh landscape on the 1774 tour she undertook with Johnson and Henry Thrale after she inherited Bachegraig.

The journal of the tour records her delight at the untamed Welsh landscape. Sir Rowland Hill's estate, for instance, pleased her because it was 'lofty, craggy, woody, not fringed with bushes to conceal its barrenness, but ornamented with timber trees of a considerable height and size'.[17] She thrilled even more at her visit to Rhuddlan castle:

> Wild in its situation, rude in its appearance, the haunt of screaming gulls and clamorous rooks, a magazine below it which serves as a beacon to ships liable to suffer distress in their dangerous passage across the Irish Seas. Barren rocks rising on one side and the sea roaring on the other fill the mind with poetical imagery. Images of captivity, courage, or desperation.[18]

Sometimes the ruggedness seemed more terrifying than delightful, at least from the perspectives of her 'English' experience:

> The look from the windows, however, soon reminds you of the distance from any English habitation. The mountains rising on your right hand fatigue the eye with looking upward, and the sea, stretched out before you, tire it equally with looking forward upon total vacuity . . . This is indeed a retreat from the World which seems wholly excluded, and in effect it is so, by mountains and by sea. The distance one is at from all relief if an accident should happen fills one with apprehension, and when I have surveyed the place of my nativity, I shall be glad to return to a land fuller of inhabitants.[19]

She was frustrated by the failure of Johnson and Thrale's English tastes to share her enthusiasm for the landscape. In the 1780s the response to her remarriage and the battle with Boswell over Johnson's reputation gave her all the more reason for ambivalence about England's polished circles and to feel the attractions of a 'retreat from the World'. Her journal recorded her sense that Italians were 'less spurning of the common Ties of Nature'. Reflecting on her treatment at the hands of her former Bluestocking associates – 'Charming Blues! Blue with Venom I think' – and estrangement from her daughters with Thrale, she judged the English 'too much civilized. They had refined away original Feelings strangely'.[20]

Partly to distance herself from the reaction against her marriage, she had left on a European tour soon afterwards. In general, she found little relief among other expatriates, but did make a few friends among them, including the Greatheed family: 'All the other English I have seen, disgusted me for one Reason or another; except perhaps Mr. Merry, who we saw a great deal of at Florence.'[21] With Bertie Greatheed, Robert Merry, and the other 'Della Cruscans', as they became known, she collaborated on a volume of poems, published as The Florence Miscellany (1785), celebrating Italian liberty and freedom of the feelings from the constraints of the respectable English society that was condemning her remarriage back in London.[22] She also decided to write up her travel experiences for publication as Observations and Reflections made in the Course of a Journey through France, Italy, and Germany (1789). Across the two volumes of Observations, she developed a distinctively conversational style, where her response to the landscapes she encountered was freely mediated through her own sensibility. Mary Wollstonecraft noted the originality of what Piozzi was doing, although she judged the style 'too full of colloquial expressions' and 'those childish feminine terms, which occur in common novels and thoughtless chat':

These travels are very desultory, and have all the lax freedom of letters without that kind of insinuating interest, which slightly binds a nosegay of unconnected remarks, and throws a thin, but graceful veil over egotism; the substitution of one for I, is a mere cobweb.[23]

From Wollstonecraft's perspectives the liberties taken here were not rational, but too much like fashionable chit-chat that she believed allowed reviewers to under-estimate female talents. For Piozzi, however, this style seems to have been part of her gendered valorization of the affections against what she believed to be artificial constraints of polished circles.

When her Anecdotes of Johnson (1786) was about to appear in London, she wrote to Samuel Lysons from the Continent to celebrate the fact that the volumes would show her to be *'alive and at Liberty'*.[24] On her return to England in 1787, faced with continuing hostility from her former friends, she set about making Streatham a centre of literary sociability again. Many of those involved were new-found allies, including Sarah Siddons the actress, and quite a few of them were noticeably reform-minded in their politics. Various literary aspirants, who considered her an important cultural broker, including Merry and the other Della Cruscans, courted her. She also developed a friendship with Helen Maria Williams, almost certainly via the Glaswegian medic Dr John Moore. Merry, Moore and Williams were among those in this set who combined an investment in freedom of emotional expression with hope for changes in the political order. For Piozzi, this association between affective and political freedom was problematic to say the least. The freedom she often associated with a Welsh wildness against English manners was not to be disaffiliated from a commitment to the British state, even if it was to make for a particularly painful break with Williams.

Piozzi seems to have become friendly with Helen Maria Williams in 1789.[25] She identified with her as a woman of feeling 'whose pensive Look and loveliness of manner engages every one's Affection while her Talents render her extremely respectable'.[26] Despite this affinity in sensibility, the question of respectability was to haunt their relationship, perhaps more even than their political differences. Both women also had a Welsh heritage. Williams was the daughter of a Scottish mother and a Welsh father.[27] Her father died before Helen Maria and her sister Cecilia could know him, but the two daughters were taught to value their Welsh ancestry. Williams never made much of the Welsh connection herself. She and her sister were brought up in the Presbyterian tradition of their mother, first in Berwick-upon-Tweed, then in London, where the family became members of Andrew Kippis's congregation. Encouraged by Kippis and later Moore, as well as by Montagu and Anna Seward, Williams had already established herself as a major writer by the time Piozzi met her. *Edwin and Eltruda* was published in 1782, followed by the epic *Peru* (1784), and *An Ode on the Peace* (1783). *Poems* (1786) cemented her position before the public as a major poet of sensibility.[28] When in May 1789 Piozzi recorded her glee at female cultural ascendancy – 'How the Women do shine of late!' – Williams was the literary example she gave.[29]

Like many other women writers in the 1780s, both Piozzi and Williams had benefited from a degree of encouragement from Elizabeth Montagu, but their idea of sensibility was at odds – perhaps for generational reasons – with the style associated with her assemblies.[30] At the literary gatherings Williams hosted over 1789–91, the atmosphere was more informal and also more politically progressive. Take this exchange from April 1791 between

Samuel Rogers, William Seward, and Robert Merry (to whom Williams may have been introduced by Piozzi). During a discussion of Montagu, Seward described her as a 'composition of art' that mocked guests at her assemblies behind their backs. Smartly picking up on the allusion to Tom Paine's attack on Edmund Burke in *Rights of Man*, Rogers retorted: 'the genuine soul of nature has forsaken her'.[31] The entire conversation is informed by the fact that 'Mrs. Montagu . . . entertains all the aristocrats', as Anna Laetitia Barbauld, whom Williams invited to tea with Piozzi in 1790, put it in a letter to her brother.[32] Although Piozzi did not share the politics of Williams and her friends, their sentiments echo her sense that Montagu was 'vainer of the Quality Friends gracing her Apartment, than of the Wits who followed humbly in her Train.'[33]

If Williams probably thought herself as a citizen of the world, there is at least one place she did celebrate the Welsh sublime in print, if somewhat ambivalently.[34] In the 1792 edition of her *Letters from France* Williams published a verse epistle 'To Dr. Moore, in answer to a Poetical Epistle written by him, in Wales, to HELEN MARIA WILLIAMS'.[35] I have not been able to trace Moore's poem to Williams, possibly it never appeared outside their private correspondence, nor, therefore, the terms of its celebration of Wales, but her poem's opening invocation of 'the landscapes of my native isle' culminates in an allusion to the wildness associated with the Welsh sublime:

> WHILE in long exile far from you I roam,
> To sooth my heart with images of home,
> For me, my friend, with rich poetic grace,
> The landscapes of my native isle you trace;
> Her cultur'd meadows, and her lavish shades,
> Her winding rivers, and her verdant glades;
> Far, as where frowning on the flood below,
> The rough Welsh mountain lifts its craggy brow:
> Where nature throws aside her softer charms,
> And with sublimer views the bosom warms.[36]

Despite the association of Wales with a form of sublime truth deeper than 'softer charms', the mention of 'exile' in the first line doesn't quite provide the contrast loyalist British readers – like Piozzi – may have expected. Writing from France, Williams is setting up a contrast between two kinds of liberty. The revolution in France is defined in terms of the beauty of its new social compact:

> ... where Autumn yields
> A purple harvest on the sunny fields;
> Where, bending with their luscious weight, recline
> The loaded branches of the clust'ring vine;
> There, on the Loire's sweet banks, a joyful band
> Cull'd the rich produce of the fruitful land;[37]

This beautiful freedom is contrasted with Gothic authority and 'abuse, / Sanctioned by precedent.' France is a 'renovated shore', and from its visionary destruction of the Gothic authority of precedent a new form of the sublime suddenly seems to emerge:

> While, rising from the hideous wreck, appears
> The temple thy firm arm sublimely rears;
> Of fair proportions, and of simple grace,
> A mansion worthy of the human race.[38]

This 'new era in the storied earth' is most obviously being contrasted with Burkean ideas of the authority of precedent, but there are also implications for the ruggedness of the Welsh sublime as it appears at the beginning of the poem, which seems to have more in common with the poem's description of Gothic authority than the proportions of the republican sublime Williams sees as emerging from the Revolution. At this point, the poem turns back to Moore:

> ... whose warm bosom, whose expanded mind,
> Have shar'd this glorious triumph of mankind.[39]

Moore himself had begun to express doubts about the French experiment from around 1791, although Piozzi, for one, continued to think of him as at least harbouring democratic sympathies.[40] Williams's poem might be read as an assertion of her continuing faith in the sublime potential of France against his doubts. Although it ends with a tearful recollection of her 'vacant place' in the 'social circle' (which, of course, had included Piozzi as well as Moore), the poem itself does not place her present situation in Paris as inferior to her former situation in London, or, for that matter, Wales.[41]

   Williams's nostalgia for her literary friends in Britain often formed a part of her correspondence with Piozzi. In October 1791 she assured her friend, 'nor do I feel any pleasure from the Democrats which at all compensates to my heart from this cruel separation from my friends at home', but even when she acknowledged the increasing turbulence of the French scene from late 1792, she was reluctant to weigh British liberty higher in the scale than the French experiment. Piozzi was exasperated by what she perceived as political disloyalty, but their correspondence continued longer than might have been expected if one judged only from Piozzi's published anti-Jacobin writings. Piozzi usually identified Williams as 'Scotch' in her journals, especially when explaining their political differences. In December 1790, for instance, she explained *Letters from France* in terms of her friend's Scottish upbringing:

Helen Williams's little Democratical Book is a mighty pretty Thing, but the Aspersions in it upon the English for hardheartedness towards the Poor, are cruel & unjust. No Nation is so generous as ours – so charitable none! But She is a *Scotch* Woman, & feels herself influenced by natural prejudices in favour of France.[42]

Piozzi would have found it difficult to square these '*Scotch* . . . prejudices' with her idea of Welshness, except there are hints in her journals and letters of seeing a deeper affinity between the nations on the basis of a shared position outside polished English manners. In December 1789, for instance, she had noticed a parallel between the Scottish and Welsh in terms of senti-ment:

In Scotland & Wales there seems to be much Affection, & much hatred of Course: much Sentiment one may call it. – They have little to do, & cultivate such Refinements of Character for Amusement.[43]

If the phrasing suggests an anthropological position outside what she is describing, what she says about Scotland and Wales coincides with the qualities she thought she had as a 'Welch-woman'. Piozzi always felt the attraction of this quality of affect, usually defined against metropolitan manners, a quality she saw herself as sharing with Williams, even if she never recognized her friend's Welsh heritage.

Piozzi's idea of the proper role of the republic of letters was increasingly patriotic in the 1790s, but never comfortable with what she perceived as rigid aristocratic hierarchy. On her return from the Continent, she had encouraged an array of talents – Williams included – based on an idea of British liberty as meritocratic: 'Talents & Conduct are sufficient to draw mean Birth & original Poverty out of the Shades of Life, & set their Merit to ripen in the Sun.'[44] Despite their political differences, she continued to see some hope for redemption of the woman of feeling in Williams. Piozzi wrote to the clergyman Leonard Chapellow in 1791, as Williams was about to return to France, that she hoped her friend would 'come back a better Patriot than She goes away – a better or a more amiable *Woman* can She not be'.[45] Against this delight in the amiable woman, Piozzi struggled with questions of female virtue that can only have been made acute by the response to her own remarriage. Piozzi at the same time both identified with a culture of feeling that imagined itself as freer than English society, and desperately worried about the security of her place in relation to the metropolitan élite. After Williams briefly visited her on a trip home in the summer of 1792, Piozzi was alarmed to discover that the man she had brought with her, John Hurford Stone, was still married to another woman. On 15 September, she wrote to their mutual friend Penelope Sophia Pennington, alarmed at Williams's conduct, but also at how she herself would be viewed for entertaining the couple:

> Helena Williams should mind who she keeps Company with – so indeed should Hester Piozzi: that fine Man She brought to our house lives in *no* Emigrant's Hotel at Paris but a common Lodging, in a Place where Numbers lodge: he carried *no* Wife over with him, nor *no* Children, they are left at Hackney I am told – her Mother and Sister are at Montreuil.[46]

From this point on the correspondence between the two women became increasingly strained, until Piozzi broke it off completely, despite the best efforts of Pennington to bring them together.

Williams wrote to Piozzi from her sick-bed in Paris on 12 December 1792, anxious about the oncoming trial of Louis XVI, and hurt by a coldness in her friend's correspondence (now lost). She begged Piozzi to put their political differences aside and wrote warmly of her memories of Streatham Park, but something of a barb appears when she came to the question of patriotism:

> I am not indifferent about the tranquility & welfare of my country. I do not wonder that with your fortune & Streatham Park, you prefer England to all other countries – people who like ourselves have but a small pittance are glad to go & pitch their tent where that pittance affords more ease and comfort.[47]

Piozzi chose to ignore the barb; at least she seems to have replied. On 22 May 1793 she complained to Pennington 'none of us hear a Word from Helena Williams'. Then in July she did hear from Williams, a letter that describes her fears under the Terror, where 'instead of the dear voice of friendship and the sweet song of the Muses here I am listening to the dismal sound of the tocsin'.[48] Moved by what she read, Piozzi nevertheless decided to discontinue the correspondence:

Poor Soul! She adverts to our Felicity at Streatham Park, and says how happy we all are here . . . while she listens only to the Sound of the Tocsin' But she says 'God keep her in personal safety! Meantime I will not write to her; She has given me Directions . . . I will not help those forward who are doing, or trying to do Mischief.[49]

Faced with Piozzi's unresponsiveness, Williams wrote again in 1794, providing news of Robespierre's death and begging for reconciliation. Despite the conviction she had expressed to Pennington the previous year, Piozzi confided to her journal that she was sorely tempted to reply:

tis just two Years since She wrote last, & beg'd an Ans[r] but I was then fretting about Cecilia Thrale's Health & thought little of any other Concern but that. I had however discretion enough not to correspond with a profess'd Jacobine resident at Paris, tho' She requested a Letter very sweetly indeed, & with much appearance of true Regard for *me*: . . . but now She is escaped from Paris poor Soul! I think I may congratulate her on her having had Power & Will to leave the Wretches:– but I fear *Reputation* has been left behind somehow – I *fear* so: tho' perhaps no real harm has been done . . . I think I will send a Letter.[50]

Here their relationship and how it is perceived seems more important than ideological differences with Williams as such. A note in Piozzi's journal explains that she did not eventually reply only because her husband would not allow it. Piozzi became an increasingly fervent supporter of Church and king after 1789, but her patriotism was not simple nor was her position as a literary woman within the English élite quite as comfortable as Williams had implied.

If *Thraliana* suggests that Piozzi was far from secure in her anti-Jacobin hostility to Williams, then throughout her journals and letters of the 1790s there is also a strand that reiterates the idea that she felt most at home not in Streatham Park but in Denbigh and then, especially, in her home from 1795, the new-built house on the Bachegraig estate, Brynbella: '*My own house*; my new beautiful Residence built for me in my own lovely Country, by the Husband of my Hearts Choice, never was so Charming a spot, never ought there to be so grateful a Creature as I.'[51] The new house was bound up with Piozzi's desire to be '*alive and at liberty*', but her desire for autonomy was always in tension with a need for recognition within metropolitan circles. The very ungrammatical awkwardness of the Welsh-Italian hybrid suggests something of the contradictions of her self-understanding. Writing loyally in defence of the British state, calling on a unanimous effort against French atheism, she nevertheless continually hankers for a place of autonomy retired from the world. In 1795, soon after moving into the new house, she described herself as 'a good Cambrio-Briton, as I hope, and properly Zealous for my Countrys Glory'. She had been reading two tracts on Welsh royal genealogy, and acknowledged 'I have lived too long in England not to laugh when reading of Madog and Fadog and Cywrie.'[52] She places herself as somewhere in-between English and Welsh perspectives. She never lost her taste for gossip and news about fashionable circles, but Wales for Piozzi represented an increasingly important refuge both from literary society in London and her growing sense of a world heading for destruction. Early in the New Year, she wrote to the clergyman George Horne about his Millenarian pamphlet *Antichrist in the French Convention* (1796). Her reading of events in the wider world, often with more than a tinge of anti-Catholicism, predated the French Revolution in *Thraliana*. Anti-Catholicism coloured, for instance, her response to the Regency crisis of 1788–9, especially Mrs Fitzherbert's role in it, but the Millenarian tendency strengthens once she starts to see events in France as signs of the end of the old order: 'the Sea & the Waves literal & figurative are roaring away, & the French are advancing in Italy with rapid strides – *how & when will it End*?'[53]

Wales is not described as free from turmoil, she noted various popular disturbances and a translation of *Rights of Man* into Welsh, but its landscapes are consistently described in terms of a sublimity that transcends the conflict in France and the superficialities of London life.[54] In 1789, for instance, *Thraliana* described her pleasure at finding her second husband liked Wales much better than her first:

> It is a heavenly Country: I think the Cumberland Lakes, & Westmoreland Mountains, far below our sweet vale of Llywydd for Beauties of Scenery; nor do I recollect ought upon the Continent superior to the variety exhibited in the Views from Garthvino; or the great Burst from the rough Top of Bryn Dymerchion.[55]

The decision to make Brynbella her home was not a sudden one, nor did she completely withdraw from Streatham Park and the metropolitan circles associated with it. Wales for Piozzi in this regard seems to have represented a very specific kind of freedom, part of Britain but outside the literary bustle and even her own anti-Jacobin publications that issued from it:

> We have *here* only the Echo of those noisy Contests which I think will never have done shaking poor harassed Europe, and here we shall pass the remainder of our nearly finished Century if it please God – only going for a little hot water to Bath in the dead winter Months.[56]

The final qualification hints at the way Piozzi never entirely cut herself off from her love of literary gossip and news about the world. The previous month she had complained to Leonard Chappelow: 'My great Dependance is on You for *News: Scandal* I shall purvey from other Quarters; I never can get you to tell even true Tales of *Ladies*.'[57] Piozzi wanted to know what was going on and play a role in public culture, but she increasing wrote from a sense of Wales as secure from the greater chaos around her, on the Continent especially, but also in London. In 1796, about to set out again for Streatham, she complained at leaving behind Brynbella's 'Majestic View of Nature . . . lovely in the gay Season, sublime in the severe one.'[58] Before her lay only a prospect of a literary world where 'Books come out every day to prove Depravity of Manners or Perversion of Talents so as to fright one from delighting in one's *Humanity*.'[59]

This perspective can only have been reinforced by the lack of enthusiasm for her loyalist works received in the metropolitan press. 'The constant struggle for social recognition', as James Clifford put it, 'while it had proved partly successful, was becoming wearisome.'[60] William Gifford, for instance, insisted on reading her work in a Della Cruscan circumstance long after she had broken with Merry, dismissing *British Synonymy* as a book written in 'a jargon long since become proverbial for its vulgarity'.[61] In 1801 her Millenarian perspective on the times culminated in the two volumes of *Retrospection; or a Review of the Most Striking and Important Events, Characters, Situations, and their Consequences, which the Last Eighteen Hundred Years have Presented to Mankind*. Wales is pictured as remaining firm in its defence of Christian values against the incursions of French atheism at the Fishguard landing of 1797: 'There the bold Cambrians, nothing intimidated by this extraordinary stroke of policy, applied the remedy of ready valour.' There is a pointed contrast with events in Ireland the following year: 'a theatre of civil blood-shed and religious war'.[62] Metropolitan reaction remained lukewarm to the mix of Millenarian foreboding with Piozzi's informal style. Even the relatively favourable review in the *British Critic* could only say that the book contained 'good sentiments' marred by the dismissive epithet 'chit–chat language'.[63] Piozzi's loyalty was seen as vitiated by an informality that the dismissive 'chit–chat' identifies with a fashionable femininity.

Piozzi's *Three Warnings* imagined a moral rearmament for the entire nation: 'Those who cannot fight must write for their country: *all* must join, all must agree.'[64] Recent work on conservatism in the period has emphasized the contradictions surrounding the populist loyalism of the 1790s and the anxieties it created in those who thought the people should obey but not exactly participate.[65] Piozzi's published loyalist writing seems to have elicited similar responses, suspicious of any claim that those outside the magic circle of the masculine élite could do much to save the State. The response reinforced her own tendency to think of herself as a 'Welch-woman'; her Cambro-Britishness only halfway to be accepted as part of a properly British order. Piozzi's desire to contribute to an anti-French unanimity, like her desire to keep in touch with fashionable gossip and news, often sits uncomfortably with her sense of Wales as a special place above and beyond such concerns. 'I want to get rid of Streatham Park', she wrote in 1798, '& come home here to lay my Bones with my old ancestors.'[66] Her desire to secure a place respectably within the established order ensured she broke with Helen Maria Williams, but she seems to have retained a sense of her as a fellow-countryman, if not in terms of a Welsh identity she never acknowledged, at least in terms of a kinship within a structure of feeling.

Even after political differences caused her to break off their relationship, Piozzi retained a hope that Williams would return to the fold. In July 1803, she told Pennington:

> If Helen Williams – ever lovely, and once *so* beloved! is looking towards England now in Preference of France, it is a great Testimony to our Island's Felicity and Honour – for such Suffrage is not mean, and Helena has had experience of *both Nations*.

For her part, when Piozzi died in 1822 Williams tried to make sense of these contradictions, continuing to see a potential in this 'heart' that could never quite let go of its anxieties about its place in English society:

> I shall always love her memory, tho' she never forgave me for coming to France, and severed me from her affections because we differed in politics. If she could have known all I have suffered amid the convulsions of states, her good-natured heart would have been more disposed to pity rather than condemn.[67]

What Williams could not know for sure, although Pennington may have told her, was that Piozzi seemed to have hesitated, in private at least, for a very long time between pity and condemnation.

Notes

[1]   This chapter has benefited greatly from Felicity Nussbaum and Deborah Kennedy generously sharing their knowledge of Piozzi and Williams with me. I would like to extend my grateful thanks to them, and to John Hodgson of the John Rylands Library at the University of Manchester, for their help with a faulty transcription.

I am also grateful to the Library for permission to quote from the Thrale-Piozzi papers.

2   See the discussion in Jon Mee, *Dangerous Enthusiasm: William Blake and the Culture of Radicalism in the 1790s* (Oxford, 1992), pp. 75–120.

3   See Damian Walford Davies, *Presences that Disturb: Models of Romantic Identity in the Literature and Culture of the 1790s* (Cardiff, 2002).

4   Hester Lynch Piozzi, *Three Warnings to John Bull, before he Dies* (London, 1798), p. 27.

5   Ian McIntyre, *Hester: The Remarkable Life of Dr. Johnson's 'Dear Mistress'* (London, 2008), p. 3.

6   Ibid., p. 33

7   Ibid., pp. 45–7.

8   Ibid., p. 54. For a detailed account of the relationship, see Mary Hyde, *Impossible Friendship: Boswell and Mrs. Thrale* (Cambridge, 1972).

9   A. M. Broadley, *Doctor Johnson and Mrs. Thrale: Including Mrs. Thrale's Unpublished Journal of the Welsh Tour Made in 1774* (London, 1910), p. 119.

10   See the accounts in McIntyre, *Hester*, pp. 223–42, and Hyde, *Impossible Friendship*, pp. 68–171.

11   This issue is explored at length in Jon Mee, *Conversable Worlds: Literature, Community, and Contention, 1780–1830* (Oxford, 2011).

12   *Monthly Review*, 74 (1786), 374. Piozzi copied the review into her journal. See *Thraliana: The Diary of Mrs. Hester Lynch Thrale (Later Mrs. Piozzi) 1776–1809* (2 vols., Oxford, 1951), II, p. 704.

13   Piozzi, *Thraliana*, II, p. 728, entry for 5 February 1789.

14   Quoted in James L. Clifford, *Hester Lynch Piozzi (Mrs. Thrale)* (2nd edn., Oxford, 1952), p. 153, from a note on a card at John Rylands Library, Thrale-Piozzi Papers, 629.

15   Piozzi, *Thraliana*, I, p. 470.

16   Ibid., I, p. 47.

17   Broadley, *Welsh Tour*, p. 179.

18   Ibid., p. 188.

19   Ibid., p. 201.

20   Piozzi, *Thraliana*, II, pp. 728 and 739, February and April 1789. The first quotation is in a passage reflecting on the hostility of her former friends among the Blue-stockings.

21   Ibid., I, p. 640.

22   See McIntyre's account, *Hester*, pp. 219–20, which rightly suggests Piozzi would have been more alert to the political connotations of the project than is often allowed.

23   *Analytical Review*, 4 (June 1789), 142–6, and 4 (July 1789), 301–6. Quotation from 301.

24   Edward A. Bloom and Lillian D. Bloom (eds.), *The Piozzi Letters: Correspondence of Hester Lynch Piozzi, 1784–1821 (formerly Mrs. Thrale)* (6 vols., London, 1989–2002), I, p. 168 [21 September 1785].

[25] See the letters to Penelope Sophia Pennington (née Weston) of 10 July and 2 November 1789, where Piozzi asks to be remembered to Williams, *Piozzi Letters*, I, pp. 302, 327. The two friends came to stay at Streatham soon afterward. See ibid., I, p. 342, Piozzi to Charlotte Lewis, 8 December 1790.

[26] Piozzi, *Thraliana*, II, p. 794.

[27] Charles Williams, some time secretary in the War Office, was descended from an old Welsh family, which counted John Williams of Aberconwy, seventeenth-century archbishop of York, among its luminaries. See Deborah Kennedy, *Helen Maria Williams and the Age of Revolution* (London, 2002), pp. 22–3.

[28] For a full account of Williams's literary career in the 1780s, see Kennedy, *Helen Maria Williams*.

[29] Piozzi, *Thraliana*, II, p. 748.

[30] Kennedy, *Helen Maria Williams*, p. 27.

[31] P. W. Clayden, *The Early Life of Samuel Rogers* (London, 1887), p. 173. The person Montagu is supposed to have mocked was the Welshman Richard Price, whose religious and political views this company would have been particularly quick to defend against Montagu's perceived sense of aristocratic superiority.

[32] 'To John Aikin, Hampstead, 1791', in Lucy Aikin (ed.), *The Works of Anna Lætitia Barbauld, with a Memoir by Lucy Aikin* (2 vols., London, 1825), II, p. 159. Williams invited Piozzi to tea with Barbauld in February 1790. See Kennedy, *Helen Maria Williams*, p. 54.

[33] Piozzi, *Thraliana*, II, p. 1092.

[34] Williams was proud of her Scottish associations. Moore had introduced her to Robert Burns, with whom she briefly corresponded. In 1787 she assured him 'the dialect has been familiar to me from infancy; I was therefore, qualified to taste the charm of your native poetry, and as I feel the strongest attachment for Scotland, I share the triumph of your country in producing your laurels.' An awareness of her Welsh affiliation may, however, be glimpsed later in the same letter, when she tells Burns she was writing from a house where she believed Gray had written 'The Bard' in its 'little study'. Quotations from Kennedy, *Helen Maria Williams*, pp. 38–40. Piozzi copied verses Moore wrote to Williams on this idea into *Thraliana*, II, pp. 791–2.

[35] Helen Maria Williams, *Letters from France, in the Summer of 1790* (2 vols., London, 1792), II, pp. 10–13. The second volume, *Letters from France: containing many New Anecdotes etc*, published by the Robinsons, appeared for the first time in 1792 with the third edition of volume one (published by the more fashionable Thomas Cadell of the Strand). Williams had published a different epistle to Moore in her *Poems* (1786).

[36] *Idem, Letters from France*, II, p. 10. It is worth noting that on 13 December 1790, Piozzi wrote out in her journal, *Thraliana*, II, pp. 792–3, a verse epistle to Moore's son from south Wales that she found 'so very flattering to us Welch Folks'. The poem to Williams was probably written on the same trip and presumably contained sentiments equally flattering to Wales.

[37] Williams, *Letters from France*, II, p. 10.

[38] Ibid., II, p. 12.

39 Ibid., II, p. 13.
40 In November 1796 Piozzi wrote of the 'dubious Moore' that his novels showed that he 'loves a little Democratic Doctrine in Religious as in Political Speculations: & leans towards the Infidel Side on every Argument, on every Occasion'. *Thraliana*, II, p. 1796.
41 Williams, *Letters from France,* II, p. 13.
42 Piozzi, *Thraliana*, II, p. 790.
43 Ibid., II, p. 750.
44 Ibid., II, p. 62.
45 *Piozzi Letters*, I, pp. 348–9, Piozzi to the Revd Leonard Chappelow, 23 February 1791.
46 Ibid., II, p. 68, 15 September 1792.
47 John Rylands Library, Piozzi-Thrale Papers, 570.
48 Ibid., 29 July 1793.
49 *Piozzi Letters*, II, pp. 135–6, 10 August 1793.
50 Piozzi, *Thraliana*, II, pp. 894–5.
51 Ibid., p. 941.
52 Ibid. p. 946.
53 Ibid., p. 951. For Piozzi's attitude to Fitzherbert, see the journal entry for 20 November 1788: 'the Prince's Character makes his Elevation to power extremely perilous to the State; his Connection with a Catholic Lady increases our peril . . . for She will seize the first Moment of his Returning Virtue or decaying Powers to teach him the intolerant Principles of Popery', ibid., pp. 722–3.
54 In autumn 1794, responding to reports that there had been an attempt to assassinate George III, Piozzi wrote in her journal: 'The King-killers are here among us they say: not *here* at Denbigh, but dispersed through London', ibid., p. 896. At the end of October, she was reading strange climactic conditions in Wales as a sign of more general turmoil. Reporting on a Welsh translation of *Rights of Man*, she planned to get Hannah More's counter-revolutionary tracts translated into Welsh as 'Antidotes', ibid., p. 898; yet, reporting on a disturbance in Denbigh in December, she still wants to hold out a contrary view of Wales as innately different: 'Low people here in North Wales are eminently gentle, grateful & kind', ibid., p. 910.
55 Ibid., p. 750.
56 *Piozzi Letters*, II, p. 129, Piozzi to J. C. Walker, 8 October 1799.
57 Ibid., III, p. 127, Piozzi to the Revd Leonard Chappelow, 25 September 1799.
58 Piozzi, *Thraliana*, II, p. 971.
59 Ibid., p. 972.
60 Clifford, *Hester Lynch Piozzi*, p. 375.
61 William Gifford, *The Mæviad. By the author of the Baviad* (London, 1795), p. v.
62 Hester Lynch Piozzi, *Retrospection; or a Review of the Most Striking and Important Events, Characters, Situations, and their Consequences, which the Last Eighteen Hundred Years have Presented to Mankind* (2 vols., London, 1801), II, pp. 526–7.
63 *British Critic*, 19 (April 1802), 355–8.
64 Hester Lynch Piozzi, *Three Warnings*, p. 36.

[65]   See esp. Kevin Gilmartin, *Writing Against Revolution: Literary Conservatism in Britain 1790–1832* (Cambridge, 2002).

[66]   Piozzi, *Thraliana*, II, p. 993.

[67]   Quoted in Oswald G. Knapp (ed.), *The Intimate Letters of Hester Piozzi and Penelope Pennington, 1788-1821* (London, 1914), p. 358.

What is a national Gothic?

MURRAY PITTOCK

To judge by the explosion of criticism in the last thirty years, the Gothic
has become one of the most central of literary genres to scholars of the
Romantic era. It has become associated with – and reinforced by – the
direction of many other readings which have also become prominent since
the 1970s. Gender studies, psychoanalytic criticism, post-colonialism and
the deconstruction of metaphysical truth are all intertwined to a greater or
lesser degree with critical evaluation of the Gothic. The identification of
Enlightenment theory's role in certain of the subsequent assumptions of
colonialism has enabled Gothic's role as a 'challenge to Enlightenment
notions of rationality' to draw 'the attention of postcolonial critics', while
Gothic can also be seen as working to obstruct the Enlightenment Science
of Man's ability to chart human subjectivity completely, and thus to provide
an escape from the culture of Foucault's *Surveillir et Punir* (1975).[1] Insofar as
it represents a world which is, in David Punter's words, 'not available to
the normal processes of representation',[2] Gothic evades the prison-house
of concept and language which characterizes the universalizing claims of
'discipline' in all its many senses in particular, and of rationality in general.
Bourgeois and suburban Gothic, from John Carpenter's *Halloween* (1978)
to J. K. Rowling's violation of Harry Potter's humdrum middle class home
portrayed so ably in the sequence of films which accompany the best-selling
novels, likewise overturns rationality, conventionality and all their expectations. In remaining inescapably unplaced, while paradoxically inhabiting a
locus which presents an intensified sense of place, the Gothic defies charts
and theories alike. How then can there be a national Gothic, a reduction
to quotidian politics of a genre which could be argued to have developed
to compensate its readership for the tyrannical centrality of rationality and

the human subject, which to many theorists of nationalism, underpins in its turn the development of modern nationality itself?[3]

Given Romanticism's interrogation of aspects of Enlightenment universalism on behalf of the local and particular, it may seem strange that more has not been made of the *locus amoenus* or indeed *locus horribilis*, the stress on particularity and place in some aspects of the Gothic, and the lack of conformity of such places to the general laws of nature. There have been some efforts to identify 'national Gothic' tropes as reflecting political anxieties, most notably perhaps in the identification of Ascendancy Gothic, with its stress on the Big House as a locale of imprisonment, threat or decay in Ireland, identified by Jarlath Killeen, Luke Gibbons and others, and exemplified in books such as Charles Maturin's *Melmoth the Wanderer* (1820), Elizabeth Bowen's *The Last September* (1927) and – humorously – in John Banville's *Birchwood* (1973). Gibbons in particular notes – as can also be seen in Scott's fiction and Welsh Gothic writing – the importance of the 'Celtic sublime', landscapes of terror linked to deeds of violence, themselves the expressions of discontent by elements of the peripheral nations of the British Isles, which erupted in armed resistance several times between 1689 and 1798.[4] The role the national landscape plays in Scottish, Irish and to a lesser extent Welsh fiction, is one which is often displaced abroad or into a more remote historical time period in their English counterpart, though one must be cautious of over-generalizing. Nonetheless, the relatively recent past is much more insistent in Scottish or Irish (and to an extent Welsh) historical or Gothic writing: *Castle Rackrent, Melmoth the Wanderer, The Bride of Lammermoor, Confessions of a Justified Sinner, Farewell, Miss Julie Logan, Carmilla, Dracula, Ellen, Countess of Castle Howel*. The model of 'sixty years since' or even more recent time is less evident in the historical and Gothic novels of the era before Scott: Anne Stevens's list of historical novels from this period reveals that some 66 are set in the ancient world, Continental Europe or medieval ('Gothic') England, with only 13 set in the modern era. In other words, the Catholicism or feudalism discarded by progress is less likely to disturb the reflections of modernity in English fiction of this type in the Romantic era than it is in fiction from the 'peripheral' nations of the British Isles, in Scotland and Ireland in particular. The Welsh case is – as we shall see – notably interesting for a number of reasons. The ambivalent relationship of Wales to Britain (were the Welsh not the first Britons, and therefore the most British?), the early rejection of Catholicism right across much of Wales, the relative lack of Jacobite support outside the gentry, and the absence of national or quasi-national armed struggle against incorporation into the empire state (as with Scotland in 1715 and 1745, Ireland in 1689 and 1798, and even the north of England in 1536 and 1569) abraded the severity of history's defeats and the power of tropes used elsewhere.[5] In addition to this, English (and the genres of its fiction and poetry) stood at a greater distance from the key role language had in Welsh identity than was the case in Scotland or Ireland by 1800.

In the British Isles subordinated or compromised national identities are clearly very important, and they are also linked to the nature of the return of the repressed in certain Gothic texts, 'the disturbing return of pasts upon presents', where supernaturalism is associated with native, Catholic or dynastic claims, and its defeat a 'disavowal of past forms of power' in Fred Botting's terms.[6] Perhaps the exiguousness of these dimensions of Gothic criticism outside Ireland is yet another sign of literature, culture and history's failure to take the defeated alternative cultures of the eighteenth century seriously enough, most notably of course Jacobitism: even as late as M. R. James's *Ghost Stories of an Antiquary* in the early twentieth century, it is typically the late Stuart past which is revenant. The obvious allusions of *The Castle of Otranto* (1764) to usurpation and the weight of the rejected past are not often read in a way that one would have thought might suggest itself to anyone who considered the lifelong obsession of Sir Robert Walpole with the threat of Jacobitism, or his son's interest in a tamed and domesticated Gothic décor, which, like the Duke of Argyll's newbuild late 1740s Gothic at Inveraray castle, incorporated signature elements of the way of life its owner had defeated. Markman Ellis wisely notes that *Otranto* is 'a defence of Protestantism and British liberty' and 'celebrates the overthrow of a tyrant',[7] but does not pursue the obvious link with the defeat of the Jacobite cause very far. Yet the anxiety of that repressed past and its alternative route not taken surely sounds a very insistent, if often displaced, note throughout a wide variety of fiction. The Jacobite army of 1745 marched from a sublime landscape, and were characterized as Catholic banditti with voracious sexual appetites and barbaric habits, including cannibalism: so the obsession of the Gothic with sublime landscape, unpleasant papists, wild men and banditti forms a reinscription of the propaganda priorities of the Jacobite era. Given that Jacobites fought to defend Irish and Scottish native rights, their somewhat different role in national Gothics outwith England is also foreshadowed by the history of the first half of the eighteenth century.

Luke Gibbons has argued that in Ireland the Protestant Ascendancy incorporated subdued architectural signs of the past into their buildings in the wake of the 1798 Rising,[8] and this could be read in a similar vein to the Campbell architecture at Inveraray, part of a legacy of incorporated sympathy which had turned into one of incorporated repression.[9] In both cases the past is revisited to obtain the security of the knowledge of its defeat. The rejection of Catholicism which is so central to early Gothic writing (*pace*

Maria Purves's recent arguments) is surely linked – and in some cases, demonstrably so – to the rejection of a Catholic dynasty and all its works, which of course included the defence of Irish and Scottish parliamentary rights and native identities.[10] It was not for nothing that Irish and (despite its wide-spread Presbyterianism) Scottish native identities became closely linked to supernatural beliefs and practices in fiction. In more explicitly religious terms, just as William Robertson's historiography domesticated the Catholic Stuart past as pathetic not politic, so William Beckford's Catholic décor at Fonthill Abbey was that of 'an Amateur, a Dilettante, a Connoisseur . . . but no Professor' of Catholicism.[11] In such domestication, the escapist dimension of Gothic was also the means of its successful use as a tool of repression, of discipline. Costumed Catholicism, sentimental Jacobitism, recreational titillation, were alike means of imposing the repression of what – in allowing its return under restricted generic signs and narrative lines – authors were permitting their readership to both enjoy and escape. Much Gothic writing was, in Frederic Jameson's terms, a 'social contract' between a 'writer and a specific reading public', a public who understood the terms on which the repressed will be enabled to return, and their limits. Terror was the distance by which repressed alterity was displaced, either of space or time; horror the gore of its revenant escape from displacement. Yet all took place within the dimensions of 'a consumer item, available to all' on the book market, which found in Ann Radcliffe's *The Mysteries of Udolpho* (1794) its 'first "bestseller"'.[12] Radcliffe's vision of brutal patriarchy in her earlier fiction helped to domesticate the (Stuart) tyrant of *Otranto* for a wider range of readers. The preface to Matthew Lewis's *Monk* (1796) knowingly writes of the remaindering, mouldering and decay of the physical text in which his story is contained: the Gothic tale will never escape its boundary on the page. In life the book confines it; in death it decays with the book, 'In some dark dirty corner thrown, / Mouldy with damps, with cobwebs strown, / Your leaves shall be the bookworm's prey.' A grisly embrace indeed, but in the end one controlled by modern commercial society, which thus allows Gothic to exist only insofar as it supplies a market created and maintained by the very society that produces the books which sell the titillating tale of rebellion against the values the majority of its readers share.[13]

At times Gothic criticism reinscribes that contract rather than renegotiating it. The shift in 'Gothic' space in English fiction from northern to southern Europe occurs at just the time when Enlightenment stadial historiography was modelling the growth of Germanic liberties as the cultural – if not racial – original of stadial development towards commercial modernity. This was the 'good Gothic', ally of rationality, liberty and its universal claims; its opposite, the decayed and irrational Gothic, was often displaced either to the Catholic south, the remote and therefore feudal and Catholic native past, or the Celtic fringe.[14] Just as 'liberty' was seen as the preserve of the northern Goths, so 'slavery' was the fate of southern Catholics, who – like the Orientals who also formed an important element in the subject matter of Gothic – had allowed themselves to be seduced by irrational elements (superstition, mystique, effeminacy) into an abandonment of manly freedoms. In the nineteenth century, Daniel O'Connell's movement in Ireland made much of Irish slavery as a British metaphor for its Catholicism, and sought in its public displays to reverse its assumed categories.[15]

In Gothic writing from Ireland, Scotland and, to an extent, Wales, things can be different. The 'disparate discursive structures we perceive in the Gothic' are more likely to evade the bounds set for them,[16] and the heteroglossic hierarchy which allots Gothic supernaturalism only a bounded space to display its narrative function is sometimes successfully challenged by the very tropes it chooses, and its use of language. I will be examining these, and their relationship to English Gothic, in more detail as this chapter progresses.

What Stiofán Ó Cadhla has identified as 'asymmetrical power relationships . . . expressed by the partial and selective processes of translation' is key to English Gothic insofar as it is a genre written from outside its subject: Italian monks, abductors, jailers, tyrannical foreign noblemen, Catholics and debauchees are seldom its authors.[17] In that sense the controlled anxiety Gothic permits about the revenant past is contained by the power relationships of metropolitan speech, expectation, value, and above all, consciousness of victory. Power enables the definition of space, and with it attribution of typicality to the nature, culture, beliefs 'or religion of the people' who occupy it. Gothic written from outside, which, for example, stresses the 'power and decline, sublimity and decay' of a ghost-train version of the grand tourist's Italy, enervated from Roman splendour into Catholic corruption, can be, because of the stereotypical representation of its anxieties and their composition in an unfamiliar space, ultimately less threatening than Gothic which operates from within known and adjacent histories or spaces. As Henry Tilney says in *Northanger Abbey*:

Dear Miss Morland, consider the dreadful nature of the suspicions you have entertained. What have you been judging from? Remember the country and the age in which we live. Remember that we are English, that we are Christians. Consult your own understanding . . . Does our education prepare us for such atrocities? Do our laws connive at them? Could they be perpetrated without being known, in a country like this . . .

Tilney claims that the Gothic is impossible in contemporary England, and even though the 'neighbourhood of voluntary spies' he cites as part of that modernity casts a shadow, and though General Tilney is a homegrown version of the Radcliffian patriarchal tyrant of *A Sicilian Romance*, ultimately Henry is right, for the book is a comedy, and the General's feudal pride doomed to defeat. Regency England has neither the identity ('Remember that we are English, that we are [Protestant] Christians') nor the environment to sustain the Gothic, which is ultimately a foreign, displaced and imagined space modern English people occupy for their own amusement or titillation on the way to the consideration of maturer subjects.[18]

Thus English Gothic writing often inscribes itself in an alien space which can be both more freely imagined and more securely strait-jacketed into stereotype. Matthew Lewis does not even have to nod at the Black Legend to be secure of his readers' reaction to lines such as 'a city where superstition reigns with such despotic sway as in Madrid', while Ann Radcliffe puts it even more directly:

> At intervals, indeed, the moon, as it passed away, shewed, for a moment some of those mighty monuments of Rome's eternal name, those sacred ruins, those gigantic skeletons, which once enclosed a soul whose energies governed the world.[19]

These views of Rome and Madrid are heightened versions of the conventional representations of the Spain of the Inquisition (still of course formally constituted when Lewis wrote) and the Italy of the Grand Tour, a site of decayed greatness which both warned of the enervating power of Catholicism to a manly and successful civilization (stressed in particular in Gibbon's *Decline and Fall of the Roman Empire*) and acted as a monitory warning to future empires of what might lie in store. The 'self-fashioning against a Continental and Catholic other' which plays such a key role in English Gothic depends on reversing the trend of using imagined outsiders as a critique of English culture (as in *Gulliver's Travels* or Goldsmith's *Citizen of the World*, themselves of course both written by outsiders) in order to dispose of the contemporary political, and historical Catholic and dynastic threat, by confining it in stereotype or subjecting its potential revenance to aesthetic space at the expense of political space. Thus the heaviest use of Gothic tropes is characteristic of English Gothic: wandering Jews and bleeding nuns, cloisters and their secrecy, spying and transgressions are part of a furniture of xenophobia which builds high walls between the aesthetic and political. Once domesticated as an English tale, the Gothic threat is reduced to the dimensions of an aesthetic object, the book, and its aesthetic subject, the story. What happens to a young virgin in Spain happens to a story of one in England: the past is confined in a page, its threat become an amusement, its terrors reduced to the loss of novelty. Not every text fits this paradigm – *Caleb Williams* certainly does not for example – but even here, 'Falkland' and 'Tyrrell' are the displaced names of one of the most pro-Stuart and later pro-Jacobite of all noble families, and the alleged accidental assassin of William II Rufus. Even in Godwin's contemporary politics, the displaced past lurks.[20]

In the case of Irish Gothic writing, what has been identified by Joep Leerssen as 'auto-exoticism' compromises the detachment into dominance of Ascendancy writers embedded in a culture they simultaneously wished to adopt and distance themselves from.[21] In writing Gothic, it can be argued that what begins to create a 'national Gothic' is inherent in the nature of the compromises these writers have to make to disguise – or appear to embrace – the fact of their closeness to the particularity of what they evoke, not only in imagination, but through daily life also.

Ó Cadhla has charted how 'the lament for the dead, often called the Irish cry by the surveyors, is a recurrent sign of the indigenous culture' in the records of the Ordnance Survey in the 1820s and 1830s: when this disappears, it is seen by Anglophone commentators as 'a sign of improvement' (Ó Cadhla, *Civilizing Ireland*, p. 140). Here the historical record indicates a struggle between national particularism and Enlightenment universalist practice based on metropolitan value ('improvement'). It is surely no coincidence that the '*caoine*', or keen for the dead, is a core feature of Irish texts with Gothic features: Claire Connolly sees it as a central trope of Irish writing in the Romantic era.[22] Death and its ceremonies are central to the difference and threat of Catholic Ireland: their public nature and loudness mark the place of the dead in the community and imply that they can hear. The wake is a threshold, and if the native community controls the threshold, they control passage and return remains possible. The revenant native leadership, the Carmillas or the Fenian vampire bats identified by Luke Gibbons in the periodical press, can always threaten to re-cross that threshold as long as their allies hold it open.

Connolly has begun to point out the dimensions of that struggle for control, where the growing Anglican ownership of Catholic graveyards and the prevention of Catholic priests consecrating new ones were seen as an 'insult and outrage to the dead'. Wakes could even be seen as heralding radical conspiracies, in much the same way as the rising of the moon symbolized the moment when the Irishman in breach of curfew was beginning to go about his real business, both radical and demoniacal: the 'monstrously uncanny tinge' of Jacobinism, the iconography of which has been detected by critics such as Ellis in English Gothic writing, here acquires a native – and active – Irish tinge. This tinge, though, is all the more powerful because its radicalism is bound to soil and language, not the *montagnard* ideology of Robespierre and Saint-Just. This can be seen in the *caoine*: the 'denial of reciprocity between living and dead' which underpins the attack on wakes is a version of Burke's 'monstrous society', the revolutionary society that forgets its intergenerational obligations. The British power that repressed Irish revolutionary Jacobinism in the 1790s thus becomes a spiritual and moral Jacobinism which invites the return of the repressed to reforge the link between generations so ruthlessly broken by the rule of the stranger.[23]

At the heart of any exploration of the national Gothic stands Cliff Siskin's claim that 'ideas are always in genre; they are never unmediated'.[24] Part of that mediation is, as I have argued in *Scottish and Irish Romanticism*, that the inflection of genre is one of the five key means by which a national literature is created.[25] To take only three Irish examples, by the time John Keegan Casey wrote 'The Rising of the Moon' in the 1860s, 'the banshee's lonely croon' was the signal for the 'murmurs' of rebellion to sound along the valleys, while Irish rebellion 'at the rising of the moon' (given the traditional nocturnal meetings of Irish rebel groups) was a functioning cultural cliché on which the song could draw, as was the 'beloved green's association with the nation in revolt, but also the fairy and supernatural world. Green is the fairy colour, and so it is no surprise that 'the orange will decay' when the Sean-Bhean Bhocht arrives in favour of 'our own immortal green', or that *aisling*-style encounters with nineteenth-century examples of the *speirbhean* (the sky woman of the *aisling*) cross the threshold repeatedly between live politics and dead memorialization, memory and revenance. Genre and the embedded tropes which signal its manifestation or hybrid presence were important mediators of national Gothic, and they were arguably most important and most developed in the context of Irish Gothic writing.[26]

The importance of the female personification of the nation – present in Scotland, but to a lesser extent – was important in Irish Gothic. Women are often seen in cultures under siege as the chief custodians of tradition, and their centrality in Irish wakes and funeral rites clearly inserted them into the debates above. As Vera Kreilkamp has argued, Mortimer's perception of 'the beautiful Glorvina as a "horrid spectre"' in *The Wild Irish Girl* (1806) is a 'return of the colonial repressed to the imperial British subject' of the kind 'postulated by recent critical formulations of a Protestant Gothic tradition in Irish fiction'. It is also, however, a depiction of the gendered guardianship of national existence.[27]

If figures such as Glorvina were literary representations of underlying native political and cultural practice, the nocturnal agrarian disturbances of those who opposed English curfew law inject another dimension of political reality into generic convention, one which begins to associate Irish nationalism and resistance with the creatures of night and the supernatural world. The social contract between the Irish Gothic writer and their reader is destabilized both by the strength of the inherited genres which are set to sustain the boundaries of the Gothic but end up overwhelming them, and also because the repressed are only too evidently continuing to return in fact as well as fiction. As the nineteenth century progresses, the mythological forces at work in transforming Irish nationalism into a dominant position derive in no small part from the political defeat of the Gothic text by its subject, and the reverse colonization of Gothic tropes that followed. From being imprisoned in the Big House, Irish Gothic developed to a point where it sallied out from the Castle of Heroes.

In *Melmoth the Wanderer* (1820), the hero (not the wanderer), John Melmoth, returns from Trinity College, Dublin to inherit the Big House in Co. Wicklow (where Michael Dwyer held out against Crown forces for some years after 1798) from his uncle, who is clearly depicted as a grasping usurper, from whom his native Irish servants steal with impunity. Melmoth occasionally translates their Hibernian English for the reader, but at other times he does not seem to understand it, or fails to see the implications in his literal translations from the Gaelic: gestures of internal alienation indicative of the relative impenetrability of the hearth speech of the locus and its private world. Melmoth is in Ireland but not of it, himself a wanderer and stranger, like the supernatural forebear he is to meet. As the narrative progresses and 'the Wanderer' appears, although the tales he tells are of the displaced Gothic world of Continental Catholicism, the horrors he narrates suggest events closer to home: so the famous cannibalistic vignette, where the lovers immured in the monastery turn from turtle-doves into predator and food parallels the tale of the grandfather 'sucking' the 'vital blood' of his granddaughter told by Biddy Brannigan as the book begins. As in William Carleton's 'Wildgoose Lodge' (1830) or Elizabeth Bowen's *The Last September* (1927), the Big House is under prolonged siege from alien forces: alien forces which are also native, insofar as they are the representatives of the Anglo–Irish and the misery of their system of landlordism.[28]

The language question was often close at hand in Irish Gothic writing, and so one might expect it to be at least equally so in Wales, for after all by 1820, as Niall Ó Ciosán notes, some 3,000 works had been printed in Welsh 'compared to less than 200 in Irish Gaelic . . . all the more striking when it was borne in mind that the population of Wales in 1800 was perhaps a tenth of the population of Ireland'.[29] This can, however, be a misleading statistic for at least three reasons: first, Welsh was a vehicle of British Protestant culture to an extent never possible in Irish Gaelic; secondly, Welsh was bound up with national identity in Wales to an extent Gaelic never was in

Ireland; and third, as a consequence of this, the native use of English was also – and that more readily because of English's ubiquity – invoked in the language politics of Irish Gothic. Welsh society – whether or not its 'Non-comformist religious fervour' ensured that the repressed stayed repressed as Sion Eirian argues – was arguably not nearly so conducive to the native Gothic as a form as were the other countries of the British Isles.[30]

Nonetheless, Welsh Gothic writing does make some significant use of national Gothic tropes familiar from elsewhere. Richard Llwyd's *Beaumaris Bay*, published in 1800, contains an appendix which offers 'An Account of the Battle of Beaumaris in 1648 and the Taking of the Castle', thus placing the final defeat of Charles I's cause in a Welsh location and casting the Stuarts – as in Scottish and Irish Gothic – as the exemplars of an old cause, a path not taken, a past defeated. The western mountains of Wales are seen as home to 'a remnant of' Britain, its ancient part. Beaumaris, on Ynys Môn, is close to the traditional island of the Druids, and here superstition's 'wizard spell' (3) can still be recalled by the poet. The ruined priory of the Catholic past calls to mind the faded grandeur of old Wales, now 'the damp abode / Of slimy snails, the spider, and the toad' (4), but the poem does not adopt this as a defeated patriot space, as might happen in an Irish context, but instead offers a divided view, for 'O'er ages past the Muse looks back with pain / Marauding chieftains and their murdering train' (5): the past is lost, but its loss is also the loss of brutal feudalism ('the Muse here shudders at the Feudal plan' (25)) and all its vices: 'when law and justice bent the knee to power' (7). Although these were days when 'the patriot host . . . drove th' invading Saxon from the coast' (9), the poem implies that the cost was too high in terms of social backwardness and instability. At best here, Gothic's displaced time offers a divided view. Though Edward's castle 'Records a sigh, a murder, or a groan' in 'every stone' (14), the oppression of the Plantagenets seems less a matter of national struggle than the general barbaric unpleasantness of the times that are no more. The alleged murder of the bards by Edward – surely critical to Llwyd given his own bardic self-identification – may be blunted as a critique through being partly presented in a manner mediated by a quotation from Gray's poem, 'The Bard' (1757) (15).[31] Likewise the memorialized dead such as 'St Meugan' are not just giants of yester-year, but foolish primitives 'Who blindly thought that Pain's inflictive Rod / Would lead the lonely Hermit to his God' (19–20). This language serves to compromise allusions in the footnotes and text to English atrocities and the fallen heroes and fading history of Wales. Much was wrong with this displaced past: one would not want it back. In this sense there is no politics of nostalgia in *Beaumaris Bay*: there are too many things to fear in the darkness to long for the rising of the moon.

If Irish Gothic sometimes only seems to displace space and time in its unearthing of the neighbourly and autochthonous, and Scottish Gothic offers a past lost but longed for under the sign of sentiment, in other contexts a most positive Enlightenment value, *Beaumaris Bay* displaces that loss sufficiently beyond the horizon of civility and decency to compromise any longing that might still be felt. Although less clearly delineated, a similar unease with the national past can be seen in texts such as Anna Maria Bennett's *Ellen, Countess of Castle Howel* (1794), where the 'continuation of ancient tradition' is possible only through compromise, while the bloody past memorialized by its architecture is part of a Celtic sublime, but one without threat, lodged drearily in the 'brown mountains of North Wales'. Ultimately, the past is 'seen as untenable'. In *Castle Howel*, Wales can be a place of ruin or mountain that haunts English modernity, but it does not thereby challenge it.[32]

Scottish Gothic sometimes presents a milder version of Irish writing in its strategies and concerns. The tropes and generic convention which set resistance at a distance and confine its potential are more successful in domesticating the insurgency of locality against core, place against universal, Gothic against Enlightened: but frequently they resort to historical distance to enable them to be sure of victory, because Scottish Gothic remains strongly localist, and is not often spatially displaced. The combination of the power of the stadialist historiographical model and the natural anaesthetic of temporal distance were added to the weight of Gothic narrative furniture, often in order to ensure that it was the more securely arranged. Where writers sought to challenge this model, they often undermined the chronology in some way: so James Hogg offers a *locus amoenus* of traditional culture which appears to be displaced by history, but in reality challenges the very tool of narrative distancing adopted, by offering (as Ian Duncan has argued) a 'synchronic' rather than a 'diachronic' history: an 'upright corpse'.[33]

The displacement of time in Hogg's fiction can either provide an alternative political and cultural narrative or one which relativizes stadial claims, or both. In *The Private Memoirs and Confessions of a Justified Sinner* (1824), the Enlightenment narrator provides the standard 'auto-exotic' narrative with manifest unreliability and a conspicuous failure to actually 'edit' the fanatical tale which follows, which is contemporary with the events it describes. The whole narrative, however, is also set within an implicit framing narrative, whereby the seduction of Robert by Gil-Martin (the Devil) runs parallel to the political momentum for Union between England and Scotland in 1704–6. Gil-Martin begins this process by appearing to Wringhim on Lady Day, 25 March 1704: the day of Our Lady on which Robert the Bruce, who delivered Scotland, was crowned is the day on which Presbyterian

Scotland is seduced by Satan. Hogg's 'national tale' doesn't posit the Gothic dimensions of his story as titillating reminders of autochthonous identity, but rather as perversions of that identity. The positive figures of the book who speak Scots – for language politics and the privacy of the native are very much part of *Confessions* – have little time either for Wringhim or Gil-Martin.

The Three Perils of Man (1821) offers a different version of this approach, where natural spirits and the native supernatural inhabitants of the landscape represent authentic Scottish identity, but black magic and overt demonology are associated with the corruptions of power. Hogg's propensity for doubleness: double narratives, doubled characters, doubled possibilities, history as the contemporary, the author as character, develops here a 'double Gothic'. Faced with the challenge of how to valorize the supernatural Gothic as a mode of particularist being and localized revenance in the face of the universal claims of Enlightenment thought and the single language of the metropolis, Hogg develops a distinctive approach. The connotations of evil, darkness, cruelty and perversion with which Gothic so often trammelled the right of return for the repressed posed problems for Scottish Gothic, written in a culture where discomfort and dissatisfaction with aspects of Scotland's relationship to the British state was far more common than outright opposition. In *Three Perils* not only does the narrator challenge the distancing of the historical novel genre borrowed from Scott but the wizardry of Michael Scott the warlock (another version of Scott himself) is at odds with the lived life of the familiar Scottish supernatural:

> The land was the abode of the genii of the woods, the rocks and the rivers; and of this the inhabitants were well aware . . . They knew that their green and solitary glens were the nightly haunts of the fairies . . . The mermaid sung her sweet and alluring strains by the shore of the mountain lake, and the kelpie sat moping and dripping by his frightsome pool, or the boiling cauldron at the foot of the cataract . . . these were the natural residenters in the wilds of the woodland, the aboriginal inhabitants of the country . . . but ever since Master Michael Scott came from the colleges abroad to reside at the castle of Aikwood, the nature of demonology in the forest glades was altogether changed . . .[34]

By portraying Michael Scott's magic as a form of artistry, one designed to reward the best story-teller and condemn the worst to be eaten in the tense competition which forms the heart of the novel, Hogg associates the subject of the Gothic novel with the narrative art that sets boundaries for the terms on which the repressed is permitted to return: hence perhaps the medieval setting of the novel. The bad connotations of the supernatural are a function of the limits placed on its role by narrative: text and subject are as one and the conventional Gothic corrupts the supernatural by presenting it as art, unnatural, while the 'true' supernatural is a function of the magical but 'natural' qualities of a place and its inhabitants, accepted on their own terms. So in *The Brownie of Bodsbeck* (1818) the narrative which makes the fugitive Covenanters supernatural does so either to protect them or to repress them: the 'traditional community' displaced by history appears to be supernatural, but is in fact 'the site of "nature"'.[35]

National Gothic in the context of Scotland, Ireland, and to an extent Wales is such a site of nature, and is often an attempt to establish the spirit of place and resist the arts of displacement which confine, corral and patronize the irrational alterity of rejected political, religious, dynastic and cultural realms. If it can only express this to a wider audience through the adoption of Gothic tropes it does so, but in a manner which renders them more contemporary and more autochthonous, and in the Irish case provides a reverse takeover of national discourse through the normalization of Gothic themes. Scottish, Irish and Welsh Gothic can never be altogether comfortable with Henry Tilney's definitive displacement of Gothic from modernity, and their 'Northanger Abbeys' are sites of lasting contestation, not transient maleficence overcome in a chapter by comedy. If the Gothic writing of Wales is more ambivalent, more blunted and more in uncertain negotiation with Enlightenment stadialism than offering the locational alterity to universal value of its Irish and Scottish counterparts, it still seems just as uncomfortable as they with a Gothic unserious enough to be dismissed as titillation. It too is a national Gothic, if one compromised and compromising with what Sarah Prescott identifies as 'contributionism', in which 'Welsh traditions are important only in relation to what they can offer England'.[36] In still presenting a distinctive voice in English however, it negotiates rather than capitulates. There were – to use Elizabeth Edwards's term – numerous 'fault lines' between Welsh and British history and culture, but they were not always stark enough to find representation in the chiaroscuro suitable for Irish or Scottish Gothic.[37] Welsh Gothic saw no return of the repressed, but neither did it witness their disappearance.

Notes

[1] Rictor Norton, 'Introduction', in *idem* (ed.), *Gothic Readings: The First Wave, 1764–1840* (London, 2000), p. ix; Anthony Smith and William Hughes, 'Introduction', in *eidem* (eds), *Empire and the Gothic* (Basingstoke, 2003), pp. 1, 2.
[2] David Punter, cited in Dani Cavallaro, *The Gothic Vision* (London, 2002), p. 11 (see also pp. 29, 30, 61).

[3]   See Murray Pittock, 'What is a National Culture ?', *Litteraria Pragensia*, 19, no. 38 (2010), 30–47.

[4]   See Jarlath Killeen, 'Irish Gothic: A Theoretical Introduction', *Irish Journal of Gothic and Horror Studies*, 1 (2006); Luke Gibbons, *Gaelic Gothic* (Galway, 2004), and *idem*, 'Romantic Ireland: 1750–1845', in James Chandler (ed.), *The Cambridge History of Romanticism* (Cambridge, 2009), pp. 182–203 (186 ff).

[5]   Murray Pittock, 'Scott and the British Tourist', in Gerard Carruthers and Alan Rawes (eds.), *English Romanticism and the Celtic World* (Cambridge, 2003), pp. 151–66; Anne H. Stevens, *British Historical Fiction before Scott* (Basingstoke, 2010), pp. 78–80.

[6]   Fred Botting, *Gothic* (London, 1996), pp. 1, 5.

[7]   Markman Ellis, *The History of Gothic Fiction* (Edinburgh, 2000), pp. 10, 34, 38, 57–9.

[8]   Gibbons, *Gaelic Gothic*, p. 20.

[9]   See Michael Charlesworth, 'The Jacobite Gothic', in *idem* (ed.), *The Gothic Revival 1720–1870: Literary Sources and Documents. Volume I: Blood and Ghosts* (Mountfield, 2002).

[10] Maria Purves, *The Gothic and Catholicism* (Cardiff, 2009), pp. 1, 79, 93, 101–2.

[11] Michael Gamer, *Romanticism and the Gothic* (Cambridge, 2000), pp. 1, 4, 30.

[12] Cavallaro, *Gothic Vision*, p. vii; Toni Wein, *British Identities, Heroic Nationalisms, and the Gothic Novel, 1764–1824* (Basingstoke, 2002), p. 7; Ellis, *The History of Gothic Fiction*, p. 52; Norton, 'Introduction', p. vii.

[13] Kathryn White, 'Introduction', in Matthew Lewis, *The Monk* (London, 2009), p. 8.

[14] Cavallaro, *Gothic Vision*, p. 7, for the transmutation of 'northern' to 'southern' qualities in Gothic.

[15] Murray Pittock, 'Slavery as a Political Metaphor in Scotland and Ireland in the Age of Burns', in Sharon Alker, Leith Davis and Holly Faith Nelson (eds.), *Robert Burns in Transatlantic Culture* (Aldershot, 2012), pp. 19–30.

[16] Jacqueline Howard, *Reading Gothic Fiction: a Bakhtinian Approach* (Oxford: Clarendon Press, 1994), 2.

[17] Stiofán Ó Cadhla, *Civilizing Ireland* (Dublin, 2007), pp. 74, 113.

[18] Kathryn Barush, '"Ancient Footprints Everywhere": The Ashmolean's "Britain and Italy" Gallery', *British Association for Romantic Studies Bulletin & Review*, 37 (2010), 15; Jane Austen, *Northanger Abbey*, ed. Anne H. Ehrenpreis (London, 1985), p. 199.

[19] Ann Radcliffe, *The Italian* (London, 1824), p. 89.

[20] Peter Walmsley, 'The Melancholy Briton: Enlightenment Sources of the Gothic', in Marian Wallace (ed.), *Enlightening Romanticism, Romancing the Enlightenment: British Novels from 1750 to 1832* (Aldershot, 2009), p. 39; see also Tara Ghoshal Wallace, 'Reading the Metropole', pp. 131–41, in ibid.

[21] Joep Leerssen, *Remembrance and Imagination* (Cork, 1996), p. 35 ff.

[22] Claire Connolly, 'Wakes and the Death of the Irish Past', unpublished paper, Romantic Historiography conference, University College, Dublin, 23 July 2010.

23 Ibid.; Nigel Leask, review of David Collings, *Monstrous Society*, *British Association for Romantic Studies Bulletin & Review*, 37, 21; Ellis, *The History of Gothic Fiction*, p. 93; H. G. Schenk, *The Mind of the European Romantics*, with a preface by Isaiah Berlin (Oxford, 1979), p. 12.

24 Clifford Siskin, 'What Romanticism did to History', unpublished paper, Romantic Historiography conference, University College, Dublin, 22 July 2010.

25 Murray Pittock, *Scottish and Irish Romanticism* (Oxford, 2008).

26 John Keegan Casey, 'The Rising of the Moon', *The Field Day Anthology of Irish Writing*, II, ed. Seamus Deane (Derry, 1991), p. 110.

27 Vera Kreilkamp, 'Fiction and Empire: The Irish Novel', in Kevin Kenny (ed.), *Ireland and the British Empire* (Oxford, 2004), p. 164.

28 Charles Robert Maturin, *Melmoth the Wanderer*, ed. Douglas Grant (London, 1968), pp. 11, 212.

29 Niall Ó Ciosán, *Print and Popular Culture in Ireland, 1750–1850* (Basingstoke, 1997), p. 163.

30 Sion Eirian, 'Welsh Gothic', in Marie Mulvey-Roberts (ed.), *The Handbook of the Gothic* (2nd edn., Basingstoke, 2009), p. 324.

31 Richard Llwyd, *Beaumaris Bay, a Poem* (London, 1800). Page references are to this edition. The reference to Gray could be read in a more complex fashion than that of a suppressive accepted Anglicized reference: see Sarah Prescott, *Eighteenth-Century Writing from Wales: Bards and Britons* (Cardiff, 2008), pp. 70–82.

32 Anna Maria Bennett, *Ellen, Countess of Castle Howel* (London, 1794); Prescott, *Eighteenth-Century Writing from Wales*, pp. 139, 140–1, 145. See also Andrew Davies, '"The Gothic Novel in Wales" Revisited: A Preliminary Survey of the Wales-Related Romantic Fiction at Cardiff University', *Cardiff Corvey: Reading the Romantic Text* 2 (1998), at *http://www.cardiff.ac.uk/encap/journals/corvey/articles/cc02_n01.html*.

33 Ian Duncan, 'The Upright Corpse: Hogg, National Literature and The Uncanny', *Studies in Hogg and His World*, 5 (1994), 29–54.

34 James Hogg, *The Three Perils of Man*, ed. Douglas Gifford (Edinburgh, 1996), pp. 375–6.

35 Duncan, 'The Upright Corpse', 29, 31.

36 Prescott, *Eighteenth-Century Writing from Wales*, p. 71.

37 Elizabeth Edwards, 'Iniquity, Terror and Survival: Welsh Gothic, 1789–1804', *Journal of Eighteenth-Century Studies*, 35, no. 1 (2012), 119–33. I am very grateful to Elizabeth for having let me see a draft of this article.

Terror, treason and tourism: the French in Pembrokeshire 1797

HYWEL M. DAVIES

The French landing in Pembrokeshire has been variously interpreted as an almost legendary event or as a comic episode, 'a mixture of French farce and Welsh flannel'.[1] Why the French were in Pembrokeshire in February 1797 was unclear from the outset. Was it actually an invasion? It was referred to initially as 'the descent on the coast of Wales',[2] and was officially declared not to count as an invasion.[3] London-based politicians were anxious to play down its significance in order to restore political and financial confidence. To the Welsh people concerned, however, it was a most terrible and momentous event. This chapter will draw on testimonies from Welsh-language texts such as ballads and local remembrances of the landing, as well as English and French sources.

It was the travel writer James Baker who first called the landing an invasion. The invasion attracted the 'banter of strangers', those English tourists who discovered Wales and other picturesque parts of Britain in their droves in the 1790s.[4] The tourists wrote about Wales from without, looking in. The earliest published account of the invasion both in terms of text and visual representation came from James Baker's *Picturesque Guide through Wales and the Marches*. Number 30 of the *Picturesque Guide* was published in 1797 as his *Brief Narrative of the French Invasion . . . and of their Surrender to the Welch Provincial Troops*. The author stated that, 'in compliance with requests, he hath caused a few hundred of the plates to be struck off for non-subscribers'.[5] For James Baker, the French Invasion demonstrated the loyalty of the people in this picturesque part of Britain and also helped him to sell more guides. There is no evidence that Baker was an eye-witness to the events of February 1797, even though he is possibly depicted in one of the prints. But according to the Welsh Baptist historian of Britain, Titus Lewis, writing in 1810, the invasion caused 'dychryn mawr trwy'r holl gymydogaethau' (great fear throughout all the vicinities).[6] The terror extended across south Wales. As Iolo eloquently put it:

> Breeches, peticoats, shirts, shifts, blankets, sheets (for some received the news in bed) have been most wofully defiled in south Wales lately on hearing that a thimble-full of French men landed on our coast. I hope that you will have the goodness to compassionate our unfortunate wash-women.[7]

The original intention of the expedition was undoubtedly to strike fear into the hearts and minds of the enemy. In support of the main French expedition to Ireland, Hoche decided to send a small, subsidiary force to England, 'to execute a coup de main on Bristol' – not so much to fight in any conventional military sense (indeed engagement with regular forces was to be avoided), but to devastate and to terrify and thus prevent the sending of reinforcements to Ireland.[8] The leader of the force was the Irish-American William Tate.[9] Tate's original instructions were to sail to the west coast of England, attack and burn Bristol, land one thousand or so of his men, 'if possible, in or near Cardigan Bay', and then head for Chester and Liverpool.[10] Admiral Castagnier's instructions were then to sail to Dublin Bay to prevent any ships leaving. Although in February 1797 it proved impossible to carry out the instructions to the letter, the landing off Cardigan Bay was no accident, but part of the original plan.[11]

One of the reasons why the authorities in London discredited the force was its composition: they were convicts, detritus from French gaols which had been 'vomited' on the coast of Wales for no other purpose than to be captured.[12] The presence of convicts was a deliberate, terrorist feature of the general strategy of *chouannerie* drawn up by Carnot.[13] There was nothing in this composition which, with the right leadership, would have prevented it from achieving its terrible purpose. What was a mystery then and continues to be so now is why this force left Brest long after the Bantry Bay failure had been well and truly established.[14] This strange landing baffled Whitehall. The Duke of York called it a 'predatory incursion' intended to destroy the towns on the coast of Pembrokeshire and possibly liberate the French prisoners of war held in Pembroke castle.[15] The timing of the expedition and the motivation of some of the troops is open to question, but the quality and experience of slightly less than half of the force that landed in Pembroke-shire was impressive and perfectly capable of wreaking havoc. Lord Cawdor claimed a few months after the invasion that 'about 600 of them were as fine and as fit for service as any that were ever employed in this country'.[16] In the first edition of the *History of the Real and Threatened Invasions of England*,

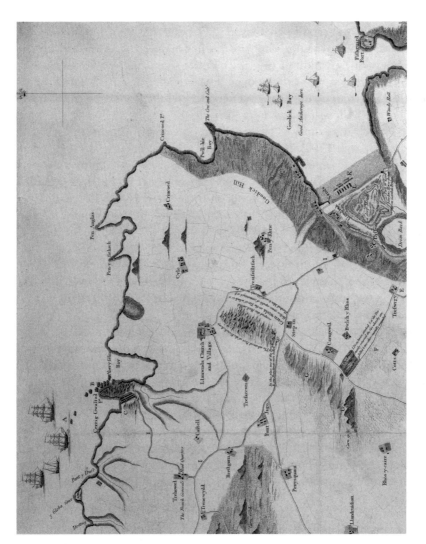

Figure 9. Detail from 'A Plan of Fishguard Bay' by Thomas Propert, 1798.

the French descent on Wales was explained simply as the disposal of convicts 'surrendering themselves prisoners of war'.[17] The second edition a year later offered a more hesitant conclusion. Why were there five or six hundred 'as fine men as were ever established' amongst the party, equipped with seventy cart-loads of powder and ball, if the purpose was to dispose of them as delinquents?[18] A persuasive analysis in the *Critical Review* of 1798 concluded that it was more probable that the French wanted to demonstrate the feasibility of an 'invasion of England', in the face of her powerful marine, and to test the temper of the people. The French ministry flattered them-selves that the troops would have been joined on their landing by considerable numbers of the 'lower classes of the people'.[19]

The French invasion was packaged for consumption from the start. As early as 20 March 1797, the first dedicated commemorative/souvenir map of the landing was published.[20] On 11 February 1798 Thomas Propert published his map together with four London dealers. This map provided an eye-witness account of the events on these three days in February 1797 and a guide to the landmarks.[21] Other souvenirs of the event were also acquired. A Frenchman fell over the west side of the precipice on landing, and died there. A reverend gentleman went down, when it was safe to do so, and cut off one of his fingers, 'meaning to keep it as a memorial of the French invasion'. Visitors to the French encampment at Trehowel, a tourist hot spot, later 'took bone after bone and joint after joint, till there was no remnant left of the unfortunate man'.[22]

The French managed to land their troops and equipment on the rocky headland of Carreg Wastad at night. There was loss of life, and a loss of crucial ordnance, but the actual landing of the troops was a military feat and a mark of their potential. They set the grass and gorse on fire to give them light.[23] The news of their landing and the surprise set off a *grand peur*. In Cardiganshire the cobbler John Davies, Ystrad, wrote in his journal of the 'great noise about the French landing in Pembrokeshire'.[24] The in-habitants of the Pen-caer peninsula fled, the yeomen farmers driving their animals before them. There is Welsh-language testimony, a local and authentic remembrance written by a contemporary in his old age, which conveys the alarm:

> Ymdaenodd y newydd dychrynllyd trwy yr holl wlad, fel tan gwyllt yn difa sofl; ac yr oedd trigolion Abergwaun yn ffoi ac yn cludo gyda hwy bob peth o werth ag a allent ddwyn ymaith.[25]

> (The terrible news extended throughout the country, like a wild fire burning up stubble, and the inhabitants of Fishguard fled taking everything of value that they could carry away.)

The Frenchmen were half-starved; of the few provisions they had some had been lost in their ascent. They set about pillaging all the houses and farms in the vicinity, as Propert's map put it, 'west of Manorowen and Goodwick Hill'. Some of the food was eaten half-raw, and even a week after the surrender seventy-five men were too sick to leave Fishguard.[26] There was serious plundering, and in the aftermath £1,311 16s. 10d. was paid in compensation.[27] The French had no tents. All the window-frames at Trehowel were removed and used as fuel for their camp-fires. It was not just a matter of scavenging; there were fatalities, casualties and atrocities. They killed at least two Welsh peasants who refused to surrender their livestock, and raped Mary Williams of Trelem. As the Welsh-language account described it:

Ni adawodd y lladron unrhyw dy, na mawr na bychan, trwy yr holl ardal heb ei chwilio, a chymeryd ymaith yr hyn a allent ei ddwyn, gan ddryllio y celfi, a chyflawni pob dyhirdra perthynol i'r gelfyddyd uffernol o ryfela.[28]

(The thieves did not leave any house, large or small, in the whole vicinity without searching it and taking away what they could carry, smashing the furniture and performing all kinds of wickedness associated with the hellish art of warfare.)

There were French fatalities too. The local people had no firearms and complained about their lack of weapons, but they were able to improvise with scythes and pitchforks. As Philip Dafydd's ballad put it:

A'r holl wlad i gyd yn codi
Â'u hen arfau gyda'i gily',
A'u pladuriau, a'u ffyn ddwybig,
A'r crymanau, i gymeryd.

(And the whole country rising up
together, with their ancient arms,
and their scythes and their pitchforks
and the reaping hooks, to seize the enemy.)[29]

The French banditti (*lladron* in the Welsh accounts) roamed across the Pencaer peninsula on the Thursday, looting communion plate from Llanwnda church. And there were even bigger prizes available to them; had they but known it, the town of Fishguard was at their mercy. The defence of Fishguard and its vicinity was in the hands of Thomas Knox, whose influential father, William Knox, owned the Llanstinan mansion four miles from the town. Thomas Knox heard of the landing whilst at a social function, and decided, unwisely in retrospect, to fall back towards Haverfordwest on Thursday morning, leaving Fishguard entirely at Tate's mercy.

By 5 p.m. Lord Cawdor's forces from Haverfordwest had arrived within a mile of Fishguard. Shots were exchanged around the farm-house at Manor-owen. The next few hours were to prove crucial. Cawdor's plan was to advance towards the French position on Garngelli down the Trefwrgi Lane (E on Propert's map). The French were in waiting, under the command of the capable Irishman Barry St Leger (hand-picked by Tate), who would have ambushed them between the high hedges had Cawdor not decided, with darkness falling, to withdraw to Fishguard. By so doing he avoided the massacre of what would have been a 'death-trap lane'.[30] What became a fiasco could have been a bloodbath.

The mood of the local people now changed, and they were the ones making the noise. There was a beating of drums and firing of cannon at Fish-guard.[31] The change in the temper of the people on the Pen-caer peninsula coincided with the worsening position of Tate and his troops. At around the same time as Barry St Leger was waiting to spring an ambush on the Trefwrgi Lane, Tate was signalling the departure of the ships. This was pre-planned. These ships were some of the most modern in the French fleet, and included two of the latest and largest frigates of the French navy and the only two of their type: *La Vengeance* and *La Résistance*. *La Résistance* was making her maiden voyage.[32] It is noteworthy how these ships dominate the pictures of James Baker. They were instruments of warfare and of escape and their departure must have undermined the morale of the French troops who were not aware of the larger strategic mission. They now had no escape route and were left to cope by their own devices, demoralized, hungry, and threatened by a hostile population.

Tate was not equal to the task. He had difficulties in imposing and main-taining military discipline and in curtailing unruly elements within his force. The strength of the local resistance surprised him and he was also receiving counsel from his officers that he should surrender. That Thursday night he sent a delegation, under a flag of truce, into Fishguard to negotiate surrender. Tate had come to terrorize, and he was not prepared to confront the military in pitched battle. His declaration of conditional surrender (dated the fifth year of the Republic in true Revolutionary terms) implied that 'the circum-stances' of the landing rendered it 'unnecessary to attempt any military operations'.[33] Tate's terms were rejected and Cawdor gave an ultimatum of unconditional surrender by 10 a.m. the next day; otherwise, Cawdor bluffed, superior forces would attack Tate. Tate accepted the ultimatum. On Friday 24 February at 2 p.m., with drums beating but without their banners, the French marched down to Goodwick beach where they stacked their weapons.

Tate and his officers were ordered to remain at Trehowel and it was here that Cawdor received his surrender and his sword. But there remains some uncertainty about the reasons for the surrender and its timing.

Local correspondents claimed that the French put down their arms when they were approached by 400 women dressed in red flannel that they mistook for a regiment of soldiers. This narrative does not appear in the earliest published account by James Baker, nor does it appear in the accounts of Cawdor, the Duke of Rutland or Knox. No mention is made of the role of the women in the Welsh ballads. The author of the 'Adgofion' also dismisses it; Tate had signed the surrender the night before, and the troops left their camp the next day without their banner, before sight of any women in their red flannels.[34] It was an early narrative nonetheless, arising from anti-French propaganda, popular hostility and aggression towards the French as well as the circumstances of surrender. It was a theme which was taken up by the later tourists and travel writers and is now the dominant strand in the popular memory of the Fishguard invasion, linked inextricably to its heroine, the Amazon-cobbler Jemima Nicholas.

Jemima Nicholas was a real person, but the story that the surrender of the French was brought about by a regiment of women under her leadership was a Victorian invention or embellishment.[35] There were undoubtedly individual acts of heroism. As early as 23 February, the day after the landing, Colonel Knox had learnt the true number of the enemy from a prisoner brought in by 'some of the country people'.[36] Some of the rustically armed peasants stood a respectful distance away, but what is remarkable is the degree of interaction between the French invaders and the local Welsh inhabitants, and this is revealed by the accounts submitted to the treason trial of the local Dissenters who were alleged to have assisted the French.[37]

The recently discovered Ann Knight correspondence contains the earliest evidence that local women actively helped to bring about the surrender of the French. In a letter written at Haverfordwest on 28 February, just four days after the surrender, Knight states that:

the english or rather Welsh got together all the women and children with the red flannels over their shoulders and placed them in such a position that the french could only see their heads and they thought it was a large army of men and one of our officers spoke to their general and told him we they [sic] had ten thousand men under arms and gave him his choise either to come to an engagement directly or surrender.[38]

Cawdor's bluff to Tate concerning 'the superiority of the force under my command, which is hourly increasing' was made in his correspondence with Tate, and this correspondence appeared in print as early as 27 February.[39]

The surrender of so many French troops would have been an anxious occasion, and the presence of a large crowd would have been useful to quell any thoughts that the enemy might have had of resisting surrender as they assembled in impressive military order, fully armed, on Goodwick sands. It is unlikely that there was any degree of orchestration by the crowd at Fishguard to act out any military or semi-military ploy to aid the authorities.[40] The presence of women in the crowd, along the cliffs surrounding Goodwick sands, dressed in their traditional costumes probably gave rise to the legend.[41] Stories spread after the surrender and after the publication of the letters announcing the bluff, explaining how Cawdor had deceived the French. What is remarkable is how quickly the story became regarded as fact. It was successful because it was such a humiliating insult to the defeated and hated French. The French soldiers knew of the story and used it in their evidence to traduce those who had ridiculed them in the first place. Iolo Morganwg, in the passage already quoted about the effect of the landing on the collective bowels of south Wales, went on to say, as early as 7 March 1797, that 'the old women of Pembrokeshire had secured the damned Republicans, as it seems we are requested to call them'.[42]

Theophilus Jones, writing in 1798, reflected almost wearily on how wide-spread the story of the women and their red cloaks was: 'how much the colour and the garment contributed, on the occasion just alluded to, to strike the enemy with consternation, is too well known to be mentioned'.[43] Theophilus Jones stood up for the role of Welsh men in the conflict in his critique of Welsh tours; the labouring men of Pembrokeshire, he contended, were 'mostly thick set, short men, from five feet two to five feet six, muscular, bony, brave, determined and resolute: (as the French desperadoes who lately landed on their coast can attest)'.[44]

The references to the martial role of the Welsh women could also be indirect criticism of the role of the Welsh men in the militia and their English officers as well as being a complete and mocking reduction of the martial standing and masculinity of the French. The caricature of the plump, jolly, but distinctly non-martial Fishguard Fencible (see Frontispiece) that appeared very shortly after the events in March 1797 contains text which mocks both the French and the 'Welch Poys':

Py St. DAVID they took da Womens red cloaks for soldiers and look'd as pale as the Tiffel himself – let em come – whose afraid – WELCH POYS – reaping hooks – toasted cheese-creen Leaks and Little FISHGUARD for ever![45]

The early tours do not mention the story of the women and red cloaks, but do refer to general popular aggression against the common enemy, in which even the women played their part. Henry Skrine, for example, wrote in 1798:

> Crowds thronged together on the first rumour of the French invasion; peasants unused to military discipline, ranged themselves under the standard of Lord Cawdor, and even the women of Pembrokeshire contributed to dismay the enemy.[46]

Female aggression was a feature of a potentially atrocious anti-French blood-lust, prevalent amongst both men and women, which the military found difficult to control. George III was informed of 'innumerable numbers of colliers, peasantry, farmers, laborers, *in short neither age nor sex*, restrained anyone from all the exertions they were able to make to meet and attack the invaders' (my emphasis).[47] Thomas Mante commented that the 'Welsh peasantry flew to arms and attacked the enemy before any troops could be assembled'.[48] According to *The Times* the magistrates were fearful of the fury of the country-people against the French 'as they felt so indignant at such a rabble insulting their coasts'.[49] The incidents of resistance to the French soldiers came from the rustically armed country-people (the armed sailors of Solva being the exception); because of Tate's surrender, the militia did not have to engage with their French adversaries in actual combat. The 'mopping up' operation was done by the local people in marauding parties across the Pen-caer peninsula bringing in the French scavengers who had plundered all the houses within six miles of the sea.[50]

The tourist accounts were attracted to this theme of popular aggression; one noted the difficulty of restraining 'the impetuosity of the mountaineers who fell upon the French without order indeed but with irresistible fury'.[51] The Duke of Rutland in his tour, written a few months after the event, commented that there were 'several instances of Frenchmen being saved by some of the English officers, when on the point of sinking under the fury of the peasantry'.[52] English officers had to intervene to save a Frenchman from the fury of his Welsh assailant but 'had a difficulty even then to save him, as neither of them could speak one syllable of English'.[53] A poem by Edward Charles mentions the French trembling in fear of the Welsh mowing them down with their sickles,[54] and the popular (non-gender specific) fury observed in the tourist accounts is also in evidence in the violent language of the ballads, such as this one published in 1799:

> A chwedyn cododd pawb o'r wlad
> Fel cewri cedyrn ar eu tra'd;
> Yr hen a'r ieuainc yn gytûn
> Am ladd a llarpio'r bleiddiaid blin.

(And then everyone in the country arose
upon their feet like powerful giants;
the old and the young in agreement
wishing to kill and devour the vicious wolves.)[55]

When the French troops laid down their arms on Goodwick sands, sentinels were put in charge to guard the avenues to the beach 'in case the mob should attempt to rush in'.[56] The safety of the French as prisoners of war was also a major security concern; as one tourist put it, 'when they were brought in as prisoners, the Military had great difficulty to prevent their putting them to death'.[57]

There is some evidence that the English gentry in charge were almost as concerned about the prospect of an armed Welsh peasantry as they were about the French troops. General Rooke instructed Knox on 1 March to search for the 3,000 stands of arms that had been landed by the French to ensure that they should not fall into the hands of the country-people as was rumoured.[58] And the ballad by Philip Dafydd mentions that weapons did actually fall into local hands:

Yn lle ein lladd ni bob gradd
Trwy ymladd a'n hymlid
Nhwy i garchar gadd eu cyrchyd
A ni gael drylliau'r rhai dychrynllyd.

(Rather than killing us of all ranks
by fighting and chasing us,
they were taken to gaol
and we had the rifles of the terrible ones.)[59]

Rutland was unsure of the loyalty of the armed 'country people' in the militia. The peasants, on the other hand, were brave and heroic but even some of these were 'disaffected', and these were, he explained, 'those all around the place where the enemy landed. They are chiefly Anabaptists and some men were afterwards taken up for having communicated with the enemy.'[60] He states later in his journal that 'Fishguard is one of the most disloyal places in Wales. The inhabitants are chiefly Anabaptists and the meeting houses swarm.'[61]

Contrary to the official accounts, it was believed locally that not everyone had behaved loyally, and that a few were guilty of treason for colluding with the French. When the dust had settled, questions were asked which revealed the tensions and divisions in Pembrokeshire and Carmarthenshire. Had the

French been encouraged to land in Pembrokeshire by some local people who had plotted treason? There was a search for scapegoats and prosecutions ensued. The prosecutions were initiated locally, not from London. This was an example of the State at work on a local level. Magistrates were convinced that primary responsibility for maintaining order rested with them rather than with a remote Home Office. They had a strong sense of their territorial jurisdiction and a suspicion of the tendency of central power to encroach upon and to curtail the independence of local authorities.[62] Two ordained Baptist ministers were amongst the suspects. It was rumoured far and wide that Henry Davies of Llangloffan had stood on a rock to instruct the French how to land.[63]

Two men were arrested and released as soon as they proved they were not Dissenters, whilst two men who were both well-known Dissenters were sent for trial and held in close confinement in the dungeons of Haverfordwest castle. Thomas John of Summerton in Little Newcastle, a farmer and Baptist preacher, and Samuel Griffith of Pointz Castle, a yeoman farmer and Independent, both men of status within their communities, were charged with aiding and comforting the enemy and urging them not to surrender.[64] The Duke of Portland visited these 'state criminals' as he called them: 'one of them (a Nonconformist) seemed as desperate and determined a villain as was ever seen'.[65] The French prisoners of war on the other hand were 'all uncommonly fine men and were dressed in their uniforms . . . they had all of them excellent voices and sung in quite a polished method'.[66]

The trial took place at Haverfordwest on 7 September 1797. The record of the trial is missing, but what is extant is the remarkable *Cwyn y Cystuddiedig a Griddfanau y Carcharorion Dieuog*, a diatribe in defence of the accused which was published anonymously for obvious reasons.[67] The author was the radical Baptist William Richards, a minister at King's Lynn in Norfolk who was originally from the Haverfordwest area. Richards used to spend entire summers with his relatives in Pembrokeshire and was wired into the local Dissenting network.[68] He published in both English and Welsh, and was a complex and prickly character. As a closed communion Baptist he would not take communion with anyone who was not baptized as an adult by total immersion; he was opposed to any form of clerisy and allegorization of Scriptures, and detested all religious enthusiasm, particularly Methodism. He was also a lexicographer, and his translation of Burke's infamous 'swinish multitude' was 'y fochaidd werin'.[69]

The accused were arrested on the evidence of French prisoners. It was claimed that Thomas John had told the French that half the local force were women in red flannels, and that many of the local people would join the French.[70] Richards argued that John and Griffith had been arrested because they were Dissenters and that the intention was to condemn all Dissenters through them and thereby open the door to persecution in general. He believed that the victimization of the Baptists in particular was a consequence of the fear that they had become too numerous in north Pembrokeshire. The success of the Baptist denomination in Pembrokeshire was one of the themes of Richards's correspondence with fellow-Baptists in the United States.[71] It was in order to curtail the increase in preachers, Richards claimed, that John had been arrested. There is no doubt that Cawdor distrusted the Baptists and questioned their reliability, and Colonel Colby of Ffynone loathed the 'anabaptists'. However, Richards reserved his disdain not for the local gentry but for the Methodists. He devoted four pages of the *Cwyn* to attack them. It was an intimate and personal attack because the Methodist behaviour against the Dissenters was portrayed as a betrayal. He focused on the ballad written by Philip Dafydd, a Methodist preacher from Newcastle Emlyn, which had denounced the accused for colluding with the French and 'bargaining with beggars'.[72] Richards claimed that this accusation was completely baseless and emanated from 'ysbryd a chrefydd yr hen Gain' (the spirit and religion of old Cain). Apparently, the local gentry hinted that if he should ever publish his Welsh defence in English 'they would not answer for the consequence'.[73] But the French witnesses subsequently changed their testimony en bloc, and neither Thomas John nor any of his thirty-five defence witnesses were called to give evidence. A disappointed judge had no alternative but to find the defendants innocent, which he did through gritted teeth.

The landing of the French in Pembrokeshire reflected the ambivalence of Welsh identity in a British state at war. In the eyes of the authorities the response to the French invaders demonstrated loyalty and unity, but on the other hand fears about the supposed unreliability of the few showed that loyalty could not be assumed and that there were disunities beneath the surface. The historian Richard Fenton, writing in 1811 and with local knowledge, regretted the invidious attempts that had been made to 'tarnish the luster of this event'.[74] Fenton was writing for a British market, and portrayed the accused as 'ignorant fanatics' whose minds had been poisoned by the corresponding societies in the capital; he wondered how these men could have communicated with 'foreigners in an unknown tongue, who scarcely knew the patois of their own'.[75]

The sudden surrender of the French seemed to the Methodists in particular to be a miracle, an act of divine intervention and a deliverance from evil. Richard Fenton recounted a meeting with a prominent Welsh Methodist – most likely David Jones of Llangan, whose home was in Manorowen near Fishguard – who gave him a 'very different account of the French descent on this coast'.[76] The victory was not due to the local forces but to Divine Providence which had issued the French with 'the fiat – hitherto shalt thou go, and no further'.[77] He gave Fenton a poem he had privately printed which referred to the French tyrants soiling this 'ancient British ground' and paying the cost 'where oft of yore, the Saxon and Dane had bled before . . .'[78]

The Welsh-language ballads stress the providential dimension and the requirement to give thanks to God, and focus not on the tyranny of the French but on their lack of grace. Whether this was a result of their atheism or their Catholicism is not specified, but what is stressed is their intention to land in Ireland and kill all the Protestants.[79] The great deliverance had been achieved 'trwy law Duw a Lord Cawdor' (through the hand of God and Lord Cawdor).[80]

In Philip Dafydd's ballad God's presence permeates the terrible events of the three days, and the French atrocities are ascribed to their paganism:

> Sarnu'n bwyd a rhwygo'n dillad,
> Dechreu treisio'n ddigon anllad;
> Llosgi'n Biblau, lle mae bywyd,
> Wnae'r paganiaid melldigedig.
>
> (they ruined our food and tore our clothes,
> started to rape very wantonly;
> the cursed pagans
> burnt our Bibles, where life is.)[81]

Cawdor and his men were regarded as instruments in the hands of God, and the death of Welsh boys, the rape of Welsh girls and the destruction of little children were to be avoided by direct appeal to God. If the Welsh maintained their allegiance to God there would be peace eternal, gospel success and no heresy – 'egwyddorion afiach Priestley' (the unhealthy principles of Priestley).[82]

The political and cultural idiom which accommodated the Welsh to the politics of British patriotism was the wide-spread notion that they were the 'ancient Britons'. The period 1797 to 1800, it has been claimed, was a defining moment in what Britain was to be.[83] The Fishguard invasion demonstrated the brave on-the-spot patriotism of the Welsh in repelling the French foe, and enabled the well-used identity of the Welsh as ancient Britons to be connected with a particular military campaign.[84] Judge Hardinge at the Grand Jury in Cardiff linked the spirit of the ancient Britons with the prompt repulsion of the 'Enemy in Pembrokeshire'.[85] The association of the landing in Pembrokeshire with the martial spirit of the ancient Britons was official and loyalist propaganda, the counterpoint to the discourse that depicted women performing the martial duties of the men.

This martial spirit did not necessarily translate into a patriotism in defence of the nation. The metropolitan language of patriotism often had at least as much to do with safeguarding the benevolent social, political and cultural hegemony of the empire's Anglicized élite as it did with encouraging wider popular participation either in England or in the Celtic fringe.[86] The rhetoric of the Welsh as 'ancient Britons' recognized that the Welsh were the heroic and masculine descendants of the first Britons, but would they defend the realm as modern and true Britons? An undated handbill, produced after the Fishguard invasion, appeals directly to the Welsh to take up arms alongside those from other parts of Britain and to do as government officials instructed. By so doing they would prove by their present actions that they were the true descendants of the ancient Britons:

> Y mae gwaed yr hen frython yn gweithio drwy wythnau Prydain oll; un deyrnas ydym yn awr, ag un bobl.[87]

> (The blood of the ancient Briton pulsates through the veins of the whole of Britain; we are now one kingdom, and one people.)

This Welsh-language handbill, and another produced by Walter Davies (Gwallter Mechain), encouraging the Welsh to take up arms to fight for Britain as their ancestors had done, did not mention the landing in Pembroke-shire at all,[88] and neither did the English-language poem, *The Horrors of Invasion*, which was published in Wrexham in 1804, addressed to 'the People of Great Britain' and 'all Welshmen in particular'.[89]

The composition of the French force, the uncertain purpose of the exped-ition, the rapid and unconditional surrender and the circumstances of that surrender made it difficult to present the events of February 1797 at the time as 'an invasion', or as a military success. The early narrative of the women and their red cloaks detracted from the achievement as well as belittling the French enemy. The anti-French response of the Welsh peasantry did not lend itself to simple political analysis. The French invaders surrendered, they were not defeated. The Welsh peasants did not fight as volunteers – and even the volunteers were not loyalists in the sense of being actively opposed to democratic and republican societies, rather than merely supporting con-stitutional propriety and the established order.[90] The Welsh peasants were defending themselves, their families and their property against a hostile, foreign and pagan/papist foe, invariably described as *lladron* (thieves) in the Welsh-language accounts. Theirs was a contingent, spontaneous, local response; not motivated by patriotism or by loyalty to Britain, even though the protection of property and the integrity of the family was an essential concern of the loyalist movement in the early 1790s.

There were far more significant and strategic military and naval victories to be celebrated to inspire patriotism and the British cause than the events in Wales in February 1797. Gillray's caricature 'The Table's Turned' of March 1797 has Pitt in the claws of Devil Fox in the left pane, with the Devil saying; 'Ha Traitor – there's the French landed in Wales! What d' ye think of that, Traitor'. In the right pane, Pitt confounds the old Devil with news of the defeat of the Spanish fleet at Cape St Vincent.

But uncertainty and anxiety remained in Wales: would the Welsh fight outside their local communities on behalf of the British state? Linda Colley has argued that a higher proportion of Welshmen and Scots attached themselves to volunteer corps than did Englishmen.[91] However, after 1798 the initiative for volunteering passed from local landlords to Parliament, and it appears that Welsh landlords did not give these measures their full backing.[92] At the start of the nineteenth century, remote, rural, monoglot Welsh-speaking north and central Wales, lacking the military tradition of the Scots, remained 'the parts of Britain most resistant to control from the centre'.[93]

The data is incomplete and its interpretation has been selective. Figures in the Welsh press suggest higher numbers as do the studies of local historians in the area.[94] To see the military impact of the Welsh after 1798, we must look not to Wales but to Ireland. Of the thirteen militia regiments in Ireland raised from England and Wales, six were Welsh. These were from all parts of Wales: Glamorgan in the south-east, Carmarthenshire and Pembrokeshire in the south-west, Montgomeryshire in mid Wales, and Denbighshire and Merionethshire in the north.[95] A Fencible cavalry regiment from Merionethshire and Denbighshire and the border counties fought ferociously and savagely under the command of Sir Watkin Williams Wynn in Ireland. These were the Ancient British Fencible Cavalry, known as 'the bloody Britons'. They had their own song, sung to the tune of the 'Vicar of Bray':

> Hibernia's blood stain'd rebels dread
> A Welshman's resolution
> When France on Pembroke's Plains did flee
> She met her just reward, Sir
> And Cambrian courage still shall be
> A free-born Briton's guard, Sir.[96]

The Ancient British Fencibles was a notoriously cruel regiment even in the bloody context of the civil war that was the Irish rebellion of 1798.[97] They were 'the terror of the rebels', reducing the country around Newry into

submission by a series of atrocities and running amok at Newtownmount-
kennedy in April and Ballymore-Eustace and Dunlavin in west Wicklow
in May, where they perpetrated massacres and summary executions.[98] These
were the men said to have used the fat from the burnt body of the rebel
leader Father Murphy to grease their boots.[99] They paid for their brutality
by being massacred in turn by the rebels at Ballyellis.[100] The Ancient Britons
in Ireland were instruments of terror on behalf of the British state. This
identification, in terms of the military collective memory and tradition, was
first made manifest in Pembrokeshire in February 1797 when the Ancient
Britons defeated the French, the enemy of the British state.

When Britain faced Napoleon in 1803–4 and there was a serious invasion
fear, the example of the French invasion of Pembrokeshire in 1797 could
be employed usefully for propaganda purposes, albeit in a limited fashion,
to illustrate by actual experience, focusing on the atrocities of the French
against women in particular. In *An Address to the People of the United Kingdom
of Great Britain and Ireland*, there was an annex on 'Specimens of French
Ferocity and Brutality in Wales' which detailed the rape of a woman in
childbed and her seventy year old mother, in front of the husband who was
bound. This text also mentioned the role of the women in their red cloaks
effecting the surrender of the French, thus women are represented both as
heroines and victims, and the French men are both mocked for their cowardice and stupidity and reviled for their animal behaviour. This handbill and the
incident described was translated faithfully into Welsh, *Cyfarch i Bobl Prydain
Fawr* and 'Ymddygiad creulon anifeilaidd y Ffrangcod yng Nghymru'.[101]

The sites of the landing and the French HQ at Trehowel became hot
spots for tourists from all parts of Britain, and Mr Mortimer of Trehowel
was noted for his hospitality to visitors and related many 'entertaining and
interesting anecdotes'.[102] There is nothing implausible in the story of the
French lady aristocrat who visited the camp at Pen-caer at the time of peace
following the Treaty of Amiens and purchased one of the red shawls to take
home to France to ridicule the military.[103] It was around the time of the
1803–4 invasion scare that the story of the women was revived and refreshed
by giving it wider currency. Lady Francesca Boscawen, the widow of Admiral
Edward Boscawen, prominent in fashionable and artistic society, wrote in
1803: 'if we should have a French visit it will surely find an English welcome;
and even our women employed (as I knew they were when the enemy
landed in Wales)'.[104] From 1803 onwards the story becomes a standard feature
of tours to Pembrokeshire.[105]

The actors in what has been called the greatest event in Pembrokeshire's
modern history were drawn from all parts of Britain, including Scotland and
Ireland, and the wider Atlantic World, and the event had international

resonances. The French *chef de brigade* was an American from South Carolina of Irish birth. The hero of the hour was Baron Cawdor of Castlemartin, otherwise known as John Pryse Campbell (Squire Campbell), scion of the Campbell clan, who held land in both Wales and the north of Scotland.[106] He sat as MP for Nairnshire from April 1777 until May 1780, and in 1808 he became mayor of Carmarthen. Thomas Knox's father, William Knox of Llanstinan near Fishguard, had once been provost marshal of Georgia, was on the wrong side in the conflict over independence and was hung in effigy at Boston and Savannah.[107] The Welsh themselves were heterogeneous, the most obvious linguistic division being the Landsker between the Welsh speakers of north Pembrokeshire and the English speakers of the south. *Can Newydd am y Waredigaeth Fawr* refers to the actors by where they were from and by their occupation, and the sense of neighbourhood is strong: the soldiers of Fishguard, the men of Trefdraeth, the sailors from the Haven, the 'rough, black colliers' from the hills of Preseli.[108] The men of St David's were noted for their particular bravery.[109] There were a number of Irish in the French force, and the link with Ireland is significant. Wolfe Tone was impressed by the impact of 1,200 convicts in Wales, and in a French memorandum written in October 1797 he wondered what impact fifteen to thirty thousand men would have on a country 'très mécontent, et . . . deux doigts d'une insurrection ouverte et générale' (very discontented, and . . . on the verge of an open and general insurrection).[110] He had Ireland not Wales in mind.

Back in France, the French themselves did not dignify the campaign with the term invasion. The type of unsavoury subversive practices associated with Carnot's vendetta against Britain for fostering royalist civil war in the Vendée and Quiberon Bay were no longer acceptable. The French wanted a military defeat of Britain not a piratical campaign by desperadoes. Carnot's reputation was a direct casualty and he was finally removed in the coup d'état of Fructidor in September 1797.[111]

The French landing in Fishguard was used by the forces of the State in Britain who were in charge of the defence to stress the loyalty of the 'ancient Britons'. The loyalty of the Welsh peasantry was an immediate theme of the official correspondence between Lord Milford and the Home Office. It was also a theme taken up by loyalist apologists with Welsh connections, such as Richard Watson, the bishop of Llandaff. In 1798 Watson wrote in his *Address to the People of Great Britain* that the French would not find any support if they invaded Great Britain:

They have already made a trial; the event of it should lower their confidence; the Welsh, of all denominations, rushed upon their Gallic enemies, with the impetuosity of ancient Britons; they discomfited them in a moment, they covered them with shame and led them into captivity.[112]

From this Welsh particular, Watson was able to move directly to a statement of general popular loyalty for Britain as a whole:

> The common people in this fortunate island, enjoy more liberty, more consequence, more comfort of every kind, than the common people of any other country . . . they will never erect the tree of liberty.[113]

The Fishguard landing was used effectively within Wales by the Welsh Methodists to counter the allegations of disloyalty that were being made by English churchmen and tourists. High-Churchmen denounced Methodists as Jacobins, and their enthusiasm was seen as a greater threat to the Church than Dissent.[114] In 1798 one of the Welsh Methodist leaders, Thomas Jones, published *Gair yn ei Amser*: a principled, popular, public positioning on Methodism, Wales and the political order. The pamphlet denounced the French and their principles, declaring loyalty to the king and the constitution. *Gair yn ei Amser* was translated into English as *A Word In Season*. The English version was necessary to demonstrate the loyalty of the Welsh Methodists to English commentators whose touristic accounts continued to insist that the Welsh Methodists were 'instruments of Jacobinism' and secret disseminators of the works of Tom Paine in translation.[115] Fishguard was used in the argument as a practical and recent example of Welsh loyalty.[116]

The disposition of the local people in response to the landing of the French is still a matter of debate. One commentator concludes that the people of Fishguard and Pen-caer acted as 'British patriots', whilst another argues that the evidence of collusion between some local people and the invaders was strong and that their loyalty was never really put to the test.[117] But Wales was not Ireland. An eye-witness noticed amidst the French arms collected at Haverfordwest 'some flags with the Tree of liberty painted on them'.[118] This was the flag which James Baker mentioned being flown by the French from Carnwnda, 'as if they possessed the false opinion that political disputes had divided the country in their favour, a part of which would flock to their standard'.[119] At the end of his account, it is the British flag that dominates over an empty Fishguard fort.

Notes

1 Roland Quinault, 'The French Invasion of Pembrokeshire in 1797: A Bicentennial Assessment', *WHR*, 19, no. 4 (1999), 618.
2 'News of descent in Wales' was how William Windham noted the event in his diary; Mrs H. Baring (ed.), *The Diary of the Right Hon William Windham 1784 to 1810* (London, 1866), p. 353. In the first edition of Charles Knight, *A History of All the Real and Threatened Invasions of England* (London, 1797), a work which documented the frequency of foreign incursions onto British soil and how the foreign invaders had been consistently beaten back, the incident is described as 'the descent on the coast of Wales' (p. 67).
3 Col. Thomas Knox was later accused of cowardice because he did not attack the enemy as soon as they had landed, a charge he denied. He demanded that his case be heard at court martial. This request was rejected by the Duke of York because 'a volunteer corps are not subject to martial laws, except during the existence of an actual invasion'. Thomas Knox, *Some account of the proceedings that took place on the landing of the French near Fishguard, in Pembrokeshire on the 22nd February 1797* (London, 1800), p. 61.
4 James Baker, *A Brief Narrative of the French Invasion, near Fishguard Bay: Including a perfect description of that part of the coast of Pembrokeshire, on which was effected the Landing of the French Forces, on the 22nd of February, 1797, and of their Surrender to the Welch Provincial Troops, headed by Lord Cawdor* (Worcester, 1797). H. M. Davies, 'Wales in English Travel-Writing, 1791–1798: The Welsh Critique of Theophilus Jones', *WHR*, 23, no. 3 (2007), 65–93.
5 Baker, *A Brief Narrative of the French Invasion*, printed wrappers.
6 Titus Lewis, *Hanes Wladol a Chrefyddol Prydain Fawr* (Carmarthen, 1810), p. 610.
7 *CIM*, II, p. 19, Iolo Morganwg to William Owen Pughe, 7 March 1797.
8 For Hoche's instructions to Tate, translated by Wolfe Tone, see D. Salmon, 'The French Invasion of Pembrokeshire in 1797', *West Wales Historical Records*, 14 (1929), 136–9.
9 For Tate see John D. Ahlstrom, 'Captain and Chef de Brigade William Tate: South Carolina Adventurer', *The South Carolina Historical Magazine*, 88, no. 4 (1987), pp. 183–91.
10 Instructions for Colonel Tate, in *Report of the Committee of the House of Commons, in consequence of the several motions relative to the treatment of prisoners of war. Including the whole of the examinations taken before the Committee, the correspondence relative to the exchange of prisoners; the instructions of Colonel Tate* (London, 1798), p. 127.
11 The best account of the political purpose of the expedition, as well as its precise composition, is still Marianne Elliott, *Partners in Revolution: The United Irishmen and France* (Yale, 1982), pp. 113–18, 134.
12 Editorial, *The Times*, 1 March 1797.
13 'Following the example of the buccaneers in the West Indies, they should know how to carry death and despair into the ranks of their enemies'; 'A portion of the troops can be made up of convicts and galley slaves – such of them as may be found to possess the physical and moral qualities requisite in the men of this

expedition', Carnot, *Instructions pour l'Etablissement d'une Chouannerie en Angleterre*, 'Carnot's Plan for Invading England', *Fraser's Magazine*, new series, 15 (1877), 201–2.

[14] Elliott, *Partners in Revolution*, p. 117.

[15] A. Aspinall (ed.), *The Later Correspondence of George III* (5 vols., Cambridge, 1963), II, pp. 543–4, the Duke of York to Lieutenant-General Rooke, 25 February 1797.

[16] John, Duke of Rutland, *Journal of a Tour through North and South Wales, the Isle of Man* (London, 1805), p. 133.

[17] Knight, *A History of All the Real and Threatened Invasions of England*, p. 67.

[18] C. Stuart, *A History of All the Real and Threatened Invasions of England* (2nd edn., Windsor, 1798), p. 202.

[19] *Critical Review*, 24 (1798), 252–3.

[20] Quinault, 'The French Invasion of Pembrokeshire', 637.

[21] Ibid.

[22] H. L. Ap Gwilym, *An Authentic Account of the Invasion by French troops on Carreg Gwastad Point, near Fishguard 1797* (Haverfordwest, 1842), p. 31.

[23] Ibid., pp. 2–3.

[24] NLW 12350A, Diary of John Davies, Ystrad, 1796–9.

[25] Anon., 'Adgofion Tiriad y Ffrancod yn Swydd Benfro', *Y Traethodydd*, XII (1856), 364–5.

[26] Lieut-Gen. Rooke to the Duke of Portland, 3 March 1797, cited in Salmon, 'The French Invasion of Pembrokeshire', 167; Bill Fowler, *The French Invasion at Fishguard* ([Haverfordwest?], 1997), p. 26.

[27] John Mortimer, the owner of the farm at Trehowell where Tate had his short-lived HQ, claimed and was given £133 10s. 6d. in compensation: H. Mathias to Lord Milford, 24 April 1797, cited in Salmon, 'The French Invasion of Pembrokeshire', 170. £1,311 16s. 10d. was the sum mentioned in *The Times*, 27 July 1799, 'for expences, etc, incurred, and compensations for losses sustained by sundry persons, when the French landed in Wales'.

[28] 'Adgofion Tiriad y Ffrancod', 367.

[29] Text and translation from Ffion Mair Jones, *Welsh Ballads of the French Revolution 1793–1815* (Cardiff, 2012), pp. 206–7.

[30] Bill Fowler, '"The invasion was halted . . . The power struggle was just beginning"', *Pembrokeshire Life* (July 1996), 35.

[31] 'Adgofion Tiriad y Ffrancod', 367.

[32] Bill Fowler, 'Who Sails in the Sunset?', *Pembrokeshire Life* (April 1996), 7.

[33] Tate's letter, addressed and dated 'Cardigan Bay, 5th of Ventose, 5th year of the Republic', and Cawdor's reply, addressed and dated 'Fishguard, Feb. 23 1797', appeared in the *London Gazette Extraordinary* on 27 February, in *The Times* on 28 February and in James Baker's first published account in 1797: Baker, *A Brief Narrative of the French Invasion*, pp. 7–8.

[34] 'Adgofion Tiriad y Ffrancod', 375.

[35] The parish record of Mathry has the baptism date of a Jemima Nicholas as 2 March 1755. There is no reason to doubt therefore that Jemima was a contemporary to

the events. See *http://news.bbc.co.uk/1/hi/wales/south_west/4874226.stm*. But there is no evidence that Jemima or any other woman or man tricked the French troops into surrendering by arranging for the local women to dress a certain way.

36 Knox, *Some account of the proceedings*, p. 13.

37 The *London Gazette Extraordinary* for 26 February has a letter from Lord Milford to the Home Office, which claimed that 'many thousands' of the local gentlemen and peasantry attacked the enemy armed with pikes and scythes before the arrival of the troops. There is exaggeration at work here but the Welsh-language accounts endorse official reports and also refer to a local willingness to engage with the enemy.

38 The Knight correspondence is discussed in Richard Rose, 'The French at Fishguard: Fact, Fiction and Folklore', *THSC*, new series, 9 (2003), 74–105.

39 Cawdor's letter, addressed and dated Fishguard, 23 February 1797, see note 33 above.

40 The author of the 'Adgofion' gives vivid eye-witness detail conveying the tension of the surrender amongst the onlookers. They did not understand the meaning of the military movements or the beating of the drums, nor did they appreciate the symbolism of the absent flag: 'Adgofion Triad y Ffrancod', 370.

41 See The New Sheridan Club: Lectures, at *http://www.newsheridanclub.co.uk/essays. htm* for the letter from the Revd Arthur Hill Richardson, dated 20 January 1841.

42 See note 7 above.

43 'Cymro', 'Cursory Remarks on Welsh tours or travels', *Cambrian Register*, II (1799), 441.

44 Ibid., 440.

45 The caricature (reproduced in E. H. Stuart Jones, *The Last Invasion of Britain* (Cardiff, 1950), p. 97) is a familiar image but scant attention has been paid to the text. See frontispiece.

46 Henry Skrine, *Two successive tours through the whole of Wales, with several of the adjacent English counties* (London, 1798), p. 271.

47 Aspinall (ed.), *The Later Correspondence of George III*, II, p. 545, Duke of Portland to the king, 26 February 1797.

48 Thomas Mante, *The Naval and Military History of the Wars of England* (8 vols., London, 1807), VIII, p. 147.

49 Editorial, *The Times*, 4 March 1797.

50 Extract of a letter from Haverfordwest, dated 24 February, *The Times*, 28 February 1797.

51 C. Cruttwell, *A Tour through the whole island of Great Britain* (6 vols., London, 1801), III, p. 208.

52 Duke of Rutland, *Journal*, pp. 128–9.

53 Ibid., p. 129.

54 BL Add 14959, Edward Charles, 'Hanes Llu o Filwyr Ffraingc a ddaeth i fewn i Ddeheudir Cymru AD 1797'.

55 Text and translation from Jones, *Welsh Ballads of the French Revolution*, pp. 234–5.

56 Duke of Rutland, *Journal*, p. 184.

57 NLW 1340C, p. 100, 'Mr M.', 'A Tour to South Wales etc 1801'.

58 Knox, *Some account of the proceedings*, p. 28.
59 Text and translation from Jones, *Welsh Ballads of the French Revolution*, pp. 214–15.
60 Duke of Rutland, *Journal*, p. 129.
61 Ibid., p. 183.
62 D. Eastwood, 'Amplifying the Province of the Legislature: The Flow of Information and the English State in the Early Nineteenth Century', *Historical Research*, 62 (1989), 279–80.
63 D. Davies, *The Influence of the French Revolution on Welsh Life and Literature* (Carmarthen, 1926), p. 235.
64 Francis Jones, 'Disaffection and Dissent in Pembrokeshire', in *idem*, *The Francis Jones Treasury of Historic Pembrokeshire* (Brawdy, 1998), pp. 100–2.
65 Bill Fowler and Richard Davies, 'The Story of Nonconformist Thomas John . . . Almost a Martyr', *Pembrokeshire Life* (December 1995), 44.
66 Fowler, *The French Invasion at Fishguard*, p. 24.
67 [William Richards], *Cwyn y Cystuddiedig, a Griddfanau y Carcharorion Dieuog: neu, ychydig o hanes dyoddefiadau diweddar THOMAS JOHN a SAMUEL GRIFFITHS* . . . (Caerfyrddin, 1798).
68 For William Richards, see R. T. Jenkins, 'William Richards o Lynn', *Trafodion Cymdeithas Hanes Bedyddwyr Cymru* (1930), 17–68. For the Baptist involvement and the treason trial, see D. Carl Williams, 'Ein Treftadaeth Fedyddiedig: De-Orllewin Penfro', *Trafodion Cymdeithas Hanes Bedyddwyr Cymru* (1998), 11–15.
69 William Richards, *Geiriadur Saesneg a Chymraeg. An English and Welsh Dictionary* (Carmarthen, 1798).
70 D. Salmon, 'A Sequel to the French Invasion of Pembrokeshire', *Y Cymmrodor*, 43 (1932), 64.
71 See H. M. Davies, *Transatlantic Brethren: Samuel Jones and his Friends, Baptists in Wales, Pennsylvania and Beyond* (Bethlehem, 1985), p. 204.
72 See Jones, *Welsh Ballads of the French Revolution*, pp. 208–9.
73 Mrs Irving H. McKesson Collection (Jones section), Historical Society of Pennsylvania, William Richards to Samuel Jones, 19 March 1798.
74 Richard Fenton, *A Historical Tour through Pembrokeshire* (London, 1811), p. 14.
75 Ibid.
76 A Barrister [Fenton], *A Tour in quest of Genealogy* (London, 1811), pp. 32–6.
77 Ibid., p. 32.
78 Ibid., p. 35.
79 Jones, *Welsh Ballads of the French Revolution*, pp. 234–7.
80 Ibid., pp. 158–9.
81 Text and translation from ibid., pp. 204–5.
82 Ibid., pp. 214–15.
83 A. Murdoch, *British History 1660–1832: National Identity and Local Culture* (London, 1998), p. 147.
84 See, for example, the toast of Lord Romney to the Friends of the Marine Society, *The Times*, 3 March 1797.
85 H. M. Thomas (ed.), *The Diaries of John Bird of Cardiff* (Cardiff, 1987), pp. 97–8, entry for 29 March 1797.

[86] Eliga H. Gould, 'American Independence and Britain's Counter-Revolution', *Past and Present*, 154 (1997), 129.

[87] NLW 13232E (Mysevin 12), William Owen [-Pughe] Miscellanea, 'At y Cymry'.

[88] NLW 1752A, *Annerch at y Cymry*. On Walter Davies, see Geraint H. Jenkins, 'The "Rural Voltaire" and the "French madcaps"', in this volume.

[89] Robert Holland Price, *The Horrors of Invasion: A Poem. Addressed to the People of Great Britain, in general, and to the Chirk Hundred Volunteers, and all Welshmen in particular. Dedicated by permission, to the Right Honourable Lady Eleanor Butler and Miss Ponsonby* (2nd edn., Wrexham, 1804).

[90] A. Gee, *The British Volunteer Movement 1794–1814* (Oxford, 2003), p. 267.

[91] Linda Colley, *Britons: Forging the Nation 1707–1837* (Yale, 1992), p. 293.

[92] Ibid., p. 294.

[93] Ibid., p. 295.

[94] See D. Russell Davies, *Hope and Heartbreak: A Social History of Wales and the Welsh 1776–1871* (Cardiff, 2005), p. 135; Bryn Owen, *The History of the Welsh Militia and Volunteer Corps 1757–1908. Volume 1: Anglesey and Caernarfonshire* (Caernarfon, 1989); Hugh J. Owen, *Merioneth Volunteers and Local Militia during the Napoleonic Wars, 1795–1816* (Dolgellau, 1934).

[95] Bryn Owen, *The History of the Welsh Militia and Volunteer Corps 1757–1908. Volume 2: The Glamorgan Regiments of Militia* (Caernarfon, 1990), p. 40.

[96] NLW 11558C, Mr E. Alfred Jones, London, notebook.

[97] For the Ancient British Fencibles in the country around Newry, see A. T. Q. Stewart, *The Summer Soldiers: The 1798 Rebellion in Antrim and Down* (Belfast, 1995), p. 37; in Wexford, see D. Keogh and N. Furlong, *The Mighty Wave: The 1798 Rebellion in Wexford* (Dublin, 1998), pp. 21, 124, 129, 159; in Kildare, see Liam Chambers, *Rebellion in Kildare 1790–1803* (Dublin, 1998), pp. 73–5; and in Wicklow – their main theatre of operations and violence – see Ruan O'Donnell, *The Rebellion in Wicklow, 1798* (Dublin, 1998).

[98] 'The terror of the rebels' is a quotation from the Irish politician John Beresford: *The Journal and Correspondence of William Lord Auckland* (4 vols., London, 1861), IV, p. 442, John Beresford to Lord Auckland, 1 June 1798. See Myles V. Ronan (ed.), *Insurgent Wicklow 1798* (Dublin, 1948), chapter 2, for atrocities, as well as O'Donnell, *The Rebellion in Wicklow*.

[99] Watkin Williams Wynn dismissed this allegation as a calumny: see the *Salopian Journal*, 9 December 1801.

[100] For a contemporary account of Ballyellis, see George Taylor, *An historical account of the rise, progress and suppression, of the rebellion in the county of Wexford, in the year 1798* (Dublin, 1800), pp. 212–14.

[101] *Cyfarch i Bobl Prydain Fawr ar fygythion y Ffrangcod i ruthro i'w gwlad; wedi ei gyfieithu o'r Saesneg gan y Parchedig Edward Davies rector Llanarmon, Dyffryn Ceiriog* (Llundain, 1804), p. 15.

[102] Cliff, of Worcester, *The Cambrian Directory, or, cursory sketches of the Welsh territories* (1800), p. 56.

[103] 'Adgofion Tiriad y Ffrancod', 375; Ap Gwilym, *An Authentic Account of the Invasion*, p. 42.

104 C. Aspinall-Oglander (ed.), *Admiral's Widow: Being the Life and Letters of the Hon Mrs Edward Boscawen from 1761 to 1805* (London, 1942), p. 196, Fanny Boscawen to her cousin, 24 May 1803.

105 See, for example, B. H. Malkin, *The Scenery, Antiquities and Biography of South Wales* (2nd edn., 2 vols., London, 1807), II, pp. 240–1.

106 See *ODNB*.

107 Ibid.

108 Jones, *Welsh Ballads of the French Revolution*, pp. 158–9.

109 See, for example, 'Adgofion Tiriad y Ffrancod', 367–8.

110 T. W. Moody, R. B. McDowell and C. J. Woods (eds.), *The Writings of Theobald Wolfe Tone, 1763–1798* (3 vols., Oxford, 1998–2007), III, p. 169.

111 M. Elliott, 'French Subversion in Britain in the French Revolution', in Colin Jones (ed.), *Britain and Revolutionary France: Conflict, Subversion and Propaganda* (Exeter, 1983), pp. 45–6.

112 Richard Watson, *An Address to the People of Great Britain* (London, 1798), pp. 19–20.

113 Ibid., p. 20.

114 D. Hempton, *Methodism and Politics in British Society 1750–1850* (London, 1984), pp. 57, 78.

115 Letter from W. M. B., Denbigh, 17 August 1799; the response of Thomas Charles, 19 November 1799, in D. E. Jenkins, *The Life of the Rev. Thomas Charles of Bala* (3 vols., Denbigh, 1908), II, pp. 362–6. These letters were published originally in the *Gentleman's Magazine*, 69, part 2 (1799), 741, and ibid., 70, part 1 (1800), 46–7.

116 Thomas Jones, *A Word in Season; or, a few plain admonitions and exhortations on the present state of public affairs . . . Addressed to the inhabitants of Wales; and translated from the Welsh language, by the author* (Holywell, 1798), p. 13.

117 Quinault, 'The French Invasion of Pembrokeshire', 641; J. C. G. Thomas, *Britain's Last Invasion: Fishguard 1797* (Stroud, 2007), p. 16.

118 John Mends, letter dated 27 February 1797, cited in Salmon, 'The French Invasion of Pembrokeshire', 156.

119 Baker, *A Brief Narrative of the French Invasion*, p. 6.

The voices of war: poetry from Wales 1794–1804

ELIZABETH EDWARDS

> Hark! from the wasted plains afar,
> Resounds the sullen voice of war;
> Remorseless ruin stalks abroad,
> Led on by arrogance and fraud;
> With craving famine in the rear,
> And wretchedness and sad despair.
> But see the teeming foe appears,
> With hostile pomp and glittering spears;
> See av'rice hide his golden god
> Beneath some unfrequented sod;
> Ill-boding jealousy o'erspreads,
> And every man his neighbour dreads.
> Why do I stare? – What do I feel?[1]

War has long been claimed as the defining feature of writings from the 1790s and beyond, 'a turbulent period at whose center lies the longest experience of warfare – twenty-two years – in modern history'.[2] New kinds and conceptions of warfare emerged in these years, among them the idea of 'total war',[3] and war seeped into the literature of this period in correspondingly totalizing ways in literally thousands of poems written from every possible perspective.[4] Mary Favret has recently argued that war became inseparable from the daily experiences of those who lived through these years, horribly melded into ordinary lives as 'the barely registered substance of [the] everyday'.[5] Life during wartime appears atomized and paranoid, hallmarked by incomprehension in the poem quoted above, in just one of the many views of war from the period 1794–1804.

War is everywhere in these years and yet, perhaps not surprisingly, the problem of how the meanings of war were produced, quite how writing war *works*, in the Romantic period has become almost endlessly debatable. Simon Bainbridge has suggested that '[i]t is through imagining war in poetry, and insisting on the public's imagining of war, that the poet can bring the war home to the reading public'.[6] Mary Favret on the other hand has discussed the readers and writers of this period, among them William Cowper and Samuel Taylor Coleridge, who emphasize the very failure of literature to bring war home in this way. In Cowper's *The Task* (1785), Favret points out, war loses its force somewhere between the battlefield and the reader's fireside: 'The sound of war / Has lost its terrors 'ere it reaches me, / Grieves but alarms me not.'[7] The reader is left, she observes, anxiously gazing onto a blurred scene of war that seems both emphatically distant and intimately present.[8]

Also blurred but just as important in this passage from Cowper is a sense of place. At this point in *The Task* the 'here' of the poem, shuttered away at home, is mainly figured as somewhere that is not 'there', not 'war'. But this sort of indistinctness about place raises questions. Should we picture a scene in Cowper's Buckinghamshire, or at some unnamed or unknown location? Does place matter? Are all wartime firesides essentially the same? Writing war has not yet been much subject to regional perspectives, but this chapter will show that Anglophone Welsh poetry of the period also asks whether writing about war brings it closer or confirms its distance. In a poem published at the turn of 1794, the stonemason-poet Edward Williams (Iolo Morganwg) closes the door on a bitter gale and similarly contemplates war in front of a blazing hearth. 'Winter Incidents' had a particularly long and complicated composition history,[9] but the Revolutionary War, just completing its first year when the poem appeared, provides one context for the speaker's willingness to welcome into his cottage an imagined emigrant Frenchman suffering the devastations of wartime:

> A stranger in the fangs of grief,
> Where no kind hand affords relief;
> He, though *contending cannons* roar,
> Shall open find my friendly door;
> And, spite of all that *Kings* command,
> Find in my cot his *native land*,
> My peaceful cot, secluded far
> From Hell-born rage of ruthless war.[10]

No specific location is mentioned in this poem and yet Iolo's sense of the seclusion of the cottage, its ability to signal or confer some form of identity, calls attention to place just as does Cowper's juxtaposition of fireside (here) and front line (there).

'Winter Incidents' points the way to the little-known subject of the response in Wales to the Revolutionary and Napoleonic wars. How were these wars imagined, experienced and described by Welsh writers? Was war poetry from Wales a 'paper shield' insulating the public from the wars, or a 'paper bullet' piercing life at home with accounts of their horrors?[11] This chapter explores the creation of a body of war poetry from Wales written in English in the period 1794–1804, before looking in more detail at two writers, Iolo Morganwg, the Glamorganshire 'Bard of Liberty', and Richard Llwyd, the 'Bard of Snowdon'. Iolo and Llwyd were directly contemporary Welsh-speaking writers and manuscript hunters, one from south Wales, the other from the north, who were deeply interested in the history and literature of Wales, who knew each other but almost never mention each another: two writers with different claims to be seen as the period's pre-eminent labouring-class Welsh poet. For all the contrasts in their poetry, the work of both writers is shaped by the complex legacies of Welsh history and by the experience of 'a world lost to war'.[12]

Wales has long been linked with a pacifist tradition, stemming from Nonconformity and developing through nineteenth-century cultural nationalism and twentieth-century political nationalism.[13] Yet Wales has also been the site of many brutal power struggles, and its landscapes are permanently marked by the remnants of colonial conquest. The subject of the past is crucial in measuring the distance, or closeness, of war in Welsh writing of this period since Welsh history fills poetry written in Wales after the French Revolution. History is of course not necessarily a post-Revolutionary subject. Wales experienced a cultural revival for much of the eighteenth century, and efforts to recover Welsh history and literature in the 1790s are part of an ongoing process. However, I want to suggest that the onset of violence in the early 1790s, particularly in France, brought new meanings to the depictions of war, death, heroism, suffering and grief found in the early Welsh poetry that had only recently been rediscovered.[14]

English and Welsh poets writing in the 1790s share a common wartime vocabulary, their work full of the worst imaginable forms of injury and mutilation. The following lines from a fast-day hymn published in the *Cambridge Intelligencer* in May 1794, are typically brutal: 'Her Rivers bleed like mighty Veins; / Her Towers are Ashes, Graves her plains; / Slaughter her groaning Vallies fills, / And reeking Carnage melts her Hills.'[15] In this period, however, poems from Wales often focus violent, bloody language on *past* conflicts rather than present ones. Their depictions of carnage and slaughter may be read as metaphorical of the Continental war that repeatedly animates the poetry of this period. For example, 'The Banks of the Menai', an ode published in 1792 by David Thomas (Dafydd Ddu Eryri), juxtaposes the bloodstained plains of the past with a modern scene of writing in Wales. In this poem Thomas sets the 'mystic toil' of ancient Welsh bards in the context of the 'philosophic blaze' of the post-Revolutionary world, calling on Welsh writers to emulate the 'nervous' and 'brave' verses of early bards, and to take their places in a long line of Welsh poets.

Unlike Iolo, Thomas was largely a conservative figure who cautiously welcomed the ideas of the French Revolution: 'Each bosom warm in freedom's cause, / And yet obedient to the laws'.[16] The poem, however, was publicly performed on Primrose Hill on 22 September 1792, shortly after the exceptionally violent phase of the Revolution known as the 'September Massacres'. The bloody excesses of recent events in France were well known in Britain by this point in September.[17] 'The French are every day bringing more and deeper disgraces upon their noble cause, by the cruel, intemperate, mean, and dreadful ferocity of their conduct', wrote Anna Seward on 4 September 1792, '[t]hey may sluice life away in rivers of blood, but it will be to no purpose respecting the restoration of monarchy in France.'[18] It is difficult not to see contemporary referents in Thomas's vision of the Welsh shore-line 'stain'd with human gore', in a poem recited in London in the shadow of French Revolutionary violence. And perhaps the massacres in Paris also account for the guarded nature of Thomas's tribute to the Revolution. Moments such as this seem to be touching points, where the French Revolution meets Welsh scenes that no longer speak only of their own history but also figure the developing situation abroad.

English and Welsh poets writing in the early to mid-1790s took a shared language of horror and devastation in strikingly different directions. Two examples published more or less simultaneously will illustrate the closeness and the contrasts between poems with different national (Welsh and English) horizons. The Bristol poet Ann Yearsley luridly depicted the spirit of Anarchy spurring on the figure of Death to ever more depraved acts of violence in a sonnet published in the *Universal Magazine* in 1796:

> Why sleep amid the carnage? – Rise!
> Bring up my wolves of war, my pointed spears.
> Daggers yet reeking, banners fill'd with sighs,
> And paint your cheeks with gore, and lave your locks in tears.[19]

In the same year, Thomas Ryder's poem on the 1158 battle of Tal-y-foel on Anglesey appeared in the *Cambrian Register.*

Pre-eminence and rank were o'er
Dismay and ruin ran before
While conflict steam'd the field with gush of human gore.

Carnage gnash'd at carnage dire,
The warring banners gleam'd with fire
And round the front of Moelfre, shook in ire.[20]

Thomas Pennant had earlier emphasized the way in which Wales, and especially north Wales, was a stained landscape, a blood-soaked nation, in successive volumes of Welsh tours (1778–84).[21] However, in the context of 1796, the language of Ryder's poem suggests that his depiction of an ancient battle is being inflected by contemporary violence: a vision of the present that is displaced or sublimated by the past. The graphic quality of Ryder's description, and particularly the sense of égalité suggested by the end of 'Pre-eminence and rank', signals that this poem has been shaped by the French Revolution even as it claims to be describing long-ended conflicts on Anglesey.

Mary Favret has recently argued that in eighteenth-century Britain '[w]ar on home turf happened back then; it was history. If it occurred now, it occurred beyond the reach of eyes and ears, somewhere else, over there.'[22] It is not unusual to dramatize the present by turning to history for parallels in this period, and the list of poets and novelists doing so in England and Wales would be an exceptionally long one. But Anglophone Welsh writing of the period 1794–1804 is perhaps more than usually preoccupied with history; it can be seen as though a whole national poetry becomes possessed by the past. Turning to history in this way does not make war any less distant, any less 'somewhere else', but it does bring war home, writes war back onto Wales, in a way that may be interpreted as distinctively Welsh. War poems written in Wales in this period treat the contemporary scene only indirectly, through glances of present-day war filtered or refracted through Welsh history. The result is that is it becomes difficult to separate out historical and contemporary war, and so what Favret calls the 'British nation's understanding of war' does not necessarily work in the same way for Wales in this period. Welsh poetry is often very graphic, lingering on bloodied plains, but what distinguishes this body of work from poems by English writers – like the Ryder poem compared with the contemporaneous Yearsley poem to which it is clearly related – is its handling of history, which in Welsh poetry often comes directly from older sources: the medieval and first-millennium texts writers quoted, alluded to, translated or embroidered their own poems onto.

And yet not all writers in Wales illustrating the horrors of war, or war as it affects life at home, foregrounded national difference through history in

their efforts to spell out the physical and emotional desolations brought
about by the war. These writers, among them Hester Piozzi and Joseph
Hucks, emphasized instead the way in which war had brought unparalleled
misery and devastation to Wales. Bidding farewell to the year 1794 in her
diary, Hester Piozzi reflected that 'so many Calamitous Events, so many
violent Deaths, so many Innocents slaughter'd by the Executioner – such a
Number of Lives lost by Plague in America & the West Indies – were
certainly never crouded [sic] till now into so short a Space of Time'.[23] In a
poem written in Denbigh, north Wales, on 31 December 1794, Piozzi
imagined future historians deliberately by-passing the horrors of this year:

> So deep in Guilt, so stained with Gore
> Is seventeen hundred Ninety four,
>
> . . .
>
> Those who peruse Historic Lore
> Will skip the page at Ninety four.[24]

Joseph Hucks prefaced his account of his travels through Wales in the summer
of 1794 with a reminder of the wider contemporary context, 'a time so
peculiarly alarming to the affairs of this country, that every hour comes
attended with some fresh calamity: when reason and justice are suffering in
the conflict of nations: when rapine and oppression are desolating the fairest
regions of Europe'.[25] By the time Hucks reached Holywell in north-east
Wales, however, the unrelenting calamity of 1794 seemed to him to have
much more local significance. Holywell's busy cotton trade had been torn
apart by the war, Hucks noted, and scenes of misery and injury had replaced
ones of thriving industry:

> The town and neighbourhood . . . abound with numbers of poor women and
> children, who are half starving, while their husbands, fathers, and brothers, are
> gloriously signalizing themselves in the service of their country; and if by chance
> the ruthless sword of war should spare the man's life, and send him to his long-
> wished for home, with the trifling loss of a leg or an arm, he will at least have
> the consolation of reflecting that he might have lost them both; and should his
> starving family, in the bitterness of want, by chance reproach him for his incapacity
> to relieve them, he will no doubt silence their murmurs, and turn their sorrow
> into joy, by reminding them, that it was in the glorious cause of their king and
> country that they suffered.[26]

Hucks's account begins to suggest the grimly plentiful supply of ideas and
images in Wales for writers who wished to depict the desolating effects of
war. However foreign or distant it may have seemed, the war fell hard on

Wales. Life there became extremely difficult from 1793–4 onwards when hunger and distress took hold; famine-level food shortages particularly characterized the mid-1790s and the period around the turn of the century. Rioting became an increasingly frequent occurrence in the war years as communities resisted rising food prices, enclosure of common land, and attempts to recruit local people into the military, or articulated their desire to mend political wrongs.[27]

Little attempt has yet been made to map conditions in Wales onto the poetry composed in this period, yet war shaped both Welsh- and English-language poetry written in Wales in the 1790s. War supplied the theme for the poetry prize in the 1795 Gwyneddigion eisteddfod – previous themes included 'Liberty' (1790) and 'The Massacre of the Welsh Bards' (1792), and the shift from these to 'War' suggests a change in the subject matter that most preoccupied poets by the mid-1790s.[28] The widespread nature of disturbances throughout Wales in 1795 gave this year 'the atmosphere of a year of revolution',[29] perhaps nowhere more so than in the particularly un-settled region of north-east Wales. Unlike other parts of Wales, poetry had an additional presence in the north through the *Chester Chronicle*, the border newspaper that served the region in the absence of any newspaper published in Wales before the nineteenth century.[30] The radical-sympathizing *Chronicle* regularly published a wide variety of local (north Wales and Cheshire) verse alongside poems copied from broadsides or London newspapers such as the *Morning Post*. In this way the *Chester Chronicle* played a double role in the culture of Anglophone poetry in north Wales, providing a forum for locally written verses and a route by which English poetry – much of it very recent, very topical and by leading writers – could travel throughout the region.

The *Chronicle* was edited by a known Jacobin sympathizer, William Cowdroy,[31] and the paper channelled a significant volume of poetry express-ing oppositional perspectives. Poets appearing in the pages of the *Chronicle* in the 1790s include William Cowper (several times), Mary Robinson (several times, including 'January, 1795' around a fortnight after it first appeared in the *Morning Post*), Charlotte Smith ('The Forest Boy'), Helen Maria Williams (poems, and extracts from *Letters from France*), Coleridge, Southey, Thelwall and Peter Pindar.[32] In March 1794, the *Chronicle* published the unsigned poem 'The Horrors of War' by one or both of the United Irishmen Thomas Russell and William Sampson,[33] and in March 1795, Robert Merry's 'The Wounded Soldier' – perhaps one of the period's most memorable depictions of the wreckage of war in human form.[34] These examples illustrate the sort of poetry that the *Chronicle* was circulating in North Wales in the 1790s: poetry that was, as a result, more readily available and better known in North Wales than it otherwise may have been.

Documents from riots or trials record the physical hardship and political frustration felt by many Welsh people in the 1790s, but poetry written in Wales during the war years captures something of the emotional suffering that also characterized life in this period. 'For the Chester Chronicle', anonymous verses pleading for peace written in Denbigh in August 1795, figures the horrors of war as the fighting on the Continent – on 'Gallia's plains'. But this poem also describes scenes of devastation that are much more local, much closer to home, and yet that are no less the consequences of war:

> [Want's] pallid mien, and ghastly form,
> Have sought our northern shore;
> For here the herdsmen droops forlorn,
> Here starves the humble poor.
>
> For want of bread the infant cries;
> The father hangs his head,
> The mother fills the air with sighs
> And wou'd her child were dead!
>
> Rather than see its infant form
> Become a prey to thee.
> "I'd hurl it headlong to the storm,
> And die in misery!"
>
> Such, haughty War, thy poignant woes,
> To thee such scenes belong,
> The painful Muse wou'd thee disclose
> In simple artless song.[35]

Nothing of distant history here, this is a poem of social protest suggesting that life in north Wales ('our northen shore' – Denbigh is near the coast), a scene of starvation and despair as elsewhere in Britain in 1795, looks like this as a direct result of war. The poem echoes themes generally found in the period but which appear specifically, too, in poems earlier published by the *Chester Chronicle*, such as 'The Horrors of War' or 'The Wounded Soldier'. By the point at which 'For the Chester Chronicle' was written, the war had become an everyday experience of destitution and misery, woven into the English-language verse of mid-1790s north Wales.

1794, Hester Piozzi's year of horrors, also became a watershed in Welsh writing in English when Iolo Morganwg finally published *Poems, Lyric and Pastoral*, the collection he had been working on for many years. Published in January 1794, *Poems* was Iolo's attempt to establish himself as a Welsh labouring-class poet in London, but the collection made disappointingly little impact in the world of English-language poetry. The lengthy composition history of the collection was part of the problem: parts of the text were first developed in the 1770s and 1780s, but *Poems* was published in literary and political circumstances that Iolo could not possibly have anticipated. Although he revised the collection right up until publication, it feels uneven as a result, mixing references to 1780s contexts (such as the American Wars) with the unfinished ones, in train, of the early to mid-1790s.

The subject of war casts various shadows over *Poems, Lyric and Pastoral*. In 'Address to the Inhabitants of Wales' Iolo places war within a specifically Welsh framework, exhorting the Welsh to emigrate to America in search of religious and political liberties.[36] The poem is ostensibly set in the seventeenth century, where the events of the Civil War account for the flight of Welsh people to begin new lives in America, but Iolo also highlights the religious and cultural persecution (such as intolerance of Dissent, or English efforts to eradicate the Welsh language) that defines them as 'Britain's injur'd race' (II, p. 68). At the same time, however, his sense of Wales as a 'Much injur'd' land suffering the burdens of wartime and longing for peace – 'A guiltless land involv'd in grief, / Your country mourns, and craves relief, / With noblest claim to peace' (II, p. 50) – equally fits the context of 1793–4. So, too, does the depiction of famine – the 'famish'd lips' and 'feeble babes' – which anticipates the portrait of distress sent from Denbigh the following year. Finally Iolo may also be voicing the widely held belief that the hunger which blighted Wales through the 1790s was being exacerbated by exports ('filching') of local produce:[37]

> The bread our industry supplied,
> Is to the famish'd lips denied,
> Though feeble babes complain;
> This bids thy soul, fond parent, bleed,
> Thy scanty stores are all decreed
> The filching Proctor's gain (II, p. 52).

Iolo wrote at turns as a London radical and as a Welsh bard in *Poems*, so war means different things at different points in his writing, even within the same collection, while the fusion of these two perspectives is a unique feature of his work. Writing as a London radical, Iolo fiercely criticizes the king and his ministers for continuing the war with Revolutionary France, and his poems in this vein have much in common with those by radical writers such as Thomas Spence or Robert Thom[p]son. In character as a Welsh bard,

Iolo becomes (somewhat implausibly) a herald of peace, guardian of all liberal and democratic ideals – a version of the bard that conveniently ignores its fundamentally warlike qualities. Much of Iolo's anti-war writing attacks the British government, an institution that he felt was thoroughly vicious and self-seeking: its indulgence in 'Wars, vain and imaginary honour, covet-ousness, Pride, luxury, and all vices' could be taken as proof of its corruption and self-interest.[38] Here Iolo shares much ground with contemporary oppos-itional commentators such as Vicesimus Knox and Joseph Fawcett, whose works he listed among books he owned.[39]

Yet just as often Iolo's war writings also figure a recurring fantasy of peace imagined as rural retirement and pastoral idyll – a tranquil and prosperous world of fidelity, fertility, good books and good conversation, all of which may be found in a poem such as 'The Happy Farmer', which offers a po-lemical account of the arts of peace versus 'detestable war'. 'Solitude' reprises the pacifist rural retirement of 'Winter Incidents', adding a bard figure whose distress on hearing of wartime atrocities forms the crux of the poem:

> [The bard] hears, with sorrow, from afar,
> The madden'd world's eternal war;
> Sees where the blameless heart is broke
> By dire Oppression's galling yoke;
> Where *Kings*, that *fiends incarnate* reign,
> With human carnage load the plain . . . (I, p. 144 –
>
> original emphasis).

'Solitude' is dated 1789 in *Poems* but it may well have been subsequently revised since it anticipates later verses that develop a radical-pacifist perspective, such as 'Ode on Converting a Sword into a Pruning Hook' (discussed below). In the long dialogue poem 'The Horrors of War' Iolo explicitly contrasts an idealized scene of rural peace with the public, masculinized brutality of 'the terrors of war' – among them death, blood, pride, ambition and victory:

> See thousands, unheeded, in misery mourn;
> War's fell desolation extends,
> O'erwhelming the land like a hurricane wide:
> . . .
> The warrior at soul is a demon complete (II, p. 140).

This poem ranks among the most intense of Iolo's anti-war writings, not least in its footnotes:

War and conquest are generally speaking, the *aim* and *ambition* of monarchs in all ages; to them the slaughtering of 40 or 50,000 subjects, whose family are thereby reduced to misery and ruin, is a thing of no moment, though this answers no other end but that of gratifying the pride, resentment, or avarice, of a very few individuals (II, p. 143 – original emphasis).

War is, he goes on to claim, a sign of the '*unchristianized*' nature of such rulers and their supporters, arguing that no truly civilized nation would permit the actions described in the footnote above. The argument develops through imagery of '*swords . . . beat into ploughshares*, and *spears into pruning-hooks*' that also underpins ones of Iolo's best-known poems, 'Ode on Converting a Sword into a Pruning Hook'.

Iolo's 'Pruning Hook' ode is stridently pacifist and egalitarian, anti-Church and anti-monarchical, taking its title and epigraph from the Book of Isaiah and borrowing Isaiah's sense of a nation in crisis. Much of the poem is chaotic and hyperbolic, but there is also a strongly performative element to its depiction of grotesque violence, which attempts to create a sense of war, or to imagine being at the centre of war:

> I saw the *Victor's* dreadful day,
> He, through the world, in regal robe,
> Tore to renown his gory way;
> With carnage *zon'd* th' affrighted globe:
> Whilst from huge towns involved in shame
> The *Monster* claim'd immortal fame,
> What lamentable shrieks arose,
> In all th' excess of direst woes!
> Loud was the *Sycophant's* applauding voice:
> Together throng'd the sceptered band,
> Hymn'd by the *Fiends* of ev'ry land . . . (II, pp. 163–4 –
> original emphasis).

Kings are monsters and ministers are fiends here, but the second half of the poem turns on the idea that the oppression and devastation described above will be destroyed by divine power. The poem concludes with a series of visions of peace:

> Thou, *strength of Kings*, with aching breast,
> I raise to Thee the mournful strain;
> Thou shalt no more this earth molest,
> Or quench in blood thy thirst again.
> . . .

> Detesting now the craft of Kings,
> Man from his hand the weapon flings;
> Hides it in whelming deeps afar,
> And learns no more the skill of war . . . (II, pp. 165–7 –
> original emphasis).

Iolo's 'Pruning Hook' poem expresses a form of pacifism more commonly seen as a nineteenth-century attitude in Wales, defined by an antipathy towards war founded on religious principles.[40] The poem's imagery could, however, work in reverse in the period, as it does in Robert Holland Price's pamphlet-length poem in praise of war, *The Horrors of Invasion* (2nd edn., 1804), which quotes the Book of Joel (rather than Isaiah) for its epigraph: 'Prepare War . . . Beat your plough-share into swords, and your pruning hooks into spears: let the weak say I am strong'. Addressing the Chirk volunteers and dedicated to the Ladies of Llangollen, Holland Price's poem is a loyalist call to arms filtered through a series of quotations from ancient Welsh literature which develops a specifically Welsh wartime identity that is distinct from, but very much part of, a larger British identity. Early Welsh literature provides the key to this duality: Holland Price uses it polemically to affirm the historical depth of the heroism of Welsh national character, which seemed so necessary during the 1803–4 invasion scare.

The related but reversed epigraphs of these two poems illustrate the dual tradition of pacifism and militarism that colours Welsh national identity.[41] Holland Price gives pride of place to the warlike bard, the herald of war rather than peace, which Iolo tried so hard to erase in his representations of Bardism, and the contrast emerges again in the two poets' different responses to the early Welsh bard Aneirin. For Holland Price, this sixth-century warrior-poet perfectly combines the muse with 'martial ardour', but Aneirin presents a much more complicated set of possibilities for Iolo, and another facet of his war writing comes into view in the ode he adapted extremely freely from the series of heroic elegies known as *Y Gododdin*. Positioned early in volume two of *Poems*, 'Ode; Imitated from the Gododin of Aneurin' puts the subject of war literally and symbolically at the centre of the collection. The poem begins with an account of a battle fought to avenge the death of a female warrior (a significant alteration from Aneirin's original, in which women barely feature at all):

> We on thy blood-stain'd beauty gaze,
> Whilst thy great soul ascends the sky,
> We whet the blade, we grasp the lance;
> Bid War's indignant rage advance . . . (II, p. 14).

This poem vividly pictures the bloodied plains of deep history, standing in for present-day landscapes of war. But it is also possible to read Iolo's 'Gododdin' as a poem that contemplates the difficulty of writing about war.

The ode markedly shifts in mood half-way through, following a graphic account of the battlefield that has obvious parallels in contemporary English verses such as the 1794 'Hymn' quoted earlier: 'The Saxons fall, we view their mingled blood / Stream down the rugged brink, and swell the crimson flood' (I, p. 16). At this point, Iolo depicts the surviving warriors, first collapsed in exhaustion and then awakening to the scene of horror around them:

> From toils of death we sought repose,
> Sleep chain'd us to th' unfeeling dead
> Till, wrapp'd in gloom, chill morn arose,
> And rous'd us from the gory bed;
> O'er *Cattraeth's* field we wander far;
> Trace, anxious trace, the track of war;
> Shroud in cold earth our honour'd slain;
> Lost in the astonishment of life,
> We view the dreadful scene of strife,
> The slaughter'd legions heap the plain (II, p. 16 –
> > original emphasis).

A sense of loss and bewilderment fills these lines: the sudden slowing of the poem conveys the appalling sense of awe that accompanies the aftermath of the battle, and which is key to explaining the poem as a whole. Through phrases such as 'Trace, anxious, trace the track of war', for instance, Iolo seems to be struggling with the subject of war poetry, as though tracing and tracking war through the act of writing, or testing the notion of writing war.

Throughout the ode Iolo implicitly contrasts sound and speech (and by extension poetry) and dumbness and silence, weighing the sounds of war against the silence of peace. The language of his war poetry is often abrasive and clashing, full of alliteration and hard cadences, conveying the 'sullen voice of war' in works such as the 'Gododdin' and 'Pruning Hook' odes. It is only when Iolo's 'Gododdin' surveys the post-battle silence that it seems to falter (but beautifully so – 'Trace, anxious trace, the track of war'), or to be momentarily suspended, or to grasp a sense of the 'Lost'. The 'Trace' phrase is compressed and slightly ambiguous, but it also arguably sounds Welsh, perhaps an example of *cynghanedd* (Welsh poetic alliteration) shifted into English verse.

Building on this sense of uncertainty and disorientation, the second half of the poem introduces a bard figure who appears increasingly helpless in the face of the horrors of war. Iolo continues to link peace with dumbness, smoothing away the noises of war with the silence after the massacre:

> Thou, sprung from dire necessity,
> Dumb Peace, the desart [*sic*] yields to thee;
> Owns now thy melancholy sway;
> Loud sounds the trump, and loud again, –
> What trump can raise th' unheeding slain? (II, p. 18).

A similar concession to silence occurs at the end of the poem, where a young woman – another of Iolo's inventions relative to the original – mourns the loss of her warrior lover:

> Struck dumb with grief, yon beauteous fair,
> Beside her clay-cold lover weeps;
> Sweet maid! Thy sighs are spent in air,
> On Death's eternal bed he sleeps.
> He wakes no more to bless thy charms,
> To glad thy soul with circling arms,
>   . . .
> Thy Bard's pierc'd heart sore feels thy rankling grief,
> Can mingle tears with thine, but what can yield relief? (II, p. 19).

These closing words portray the bard's powerlessness in the face of the desolation of war, but they equally suggest the limitations of the ode itself, which ends on a undecided note, withholding the power of poetry to resolve, explain or console. 'What can yield relief?' Iolo asks, through the character of the bard – surely not the poem, the vehicle for injury, slaughter and mourning of epic proportions? '[H]igh song' (II, p. 14) and dumb peace set in direct opposition in this poem, the 'Gododdin' ode figures poetry as somehow part of the problem of war rather than the solution to it.

Iolo's 'Gododdin' reflects on ancient war in an age of current war, through the lens of an early Welsh poem, but it offers no contemporary sense of place or time. By contrast Richard Llwyd widely used Welsh settings with a present-day twist in the poetry he wrote in the period 1794–1804, especially the collection he published in 1804, *Poems, Tales, Odes, Sonnets, Translations from the British*. Virtually unknown today, Llwyd achieved some success with his long topographical poem *Beaumaris Bay* (1800), which transformed him from a sometime domestic servant and aspiring poet to the 'Bard of Snowdon', a well-known provincial poet.[42] Llwyd is not an overtly topical writer but his 1804 *Poems* contains numerous moments that directly and indirectly refer to contemporary contexts: telescopic moments that invite readers to look through the text to something very different, though barely acknowledged, beyond the poem.

Although Llwyd rarely explicitly addresses war in his writing, his poems produce a general impression that war (historical or contemporary) is never very far away. 'Owen of Llangoed', a sort of Welsh lyrical ballad in four parts dating from 1803–4, offers a contemporary view of war that is very clearly rooted in Anglesey. 'Owen' is the tale of a monoglot Welsh-speaking shepherd boy who travels to Liverpool to begin a seafaring career, inspired by thoughts of life beyond his small island. Before long, however, he is captured by a press-gang and thrown into war against the French. Filled with a 'patriot blaze' as the poem puts it, Owen fights heroically for the British cause, witnessing 'seas of blood' in battle, before returning home to Anglesey (probably during the Peace of Amiens),[43] where he drops down dead on hearing from a passing stranger that both his parents have died just days earlier.

'Owen of Llangoed' belongs among a body of verse composed in this period on the theme of the returning war veteran, also an important motif within the Welsh ballad tradition. Llwyd was an admirer of Robert Burns, and a poem such as Burns's 'The Returning Soldier' may have suggested the plot, though Burns's poem imagines a much more positive outcome for the home-coming veteran. The bleak conclusion of Llwyd's poem suggests that other works published in the 1790s featuring dead or injured soldiers, and communities suffering wartime bereavement or poverty, also left their mark on 'Owen of Llangoed' – poems such as Wordsworth's 'Old Man Travelling' or Southey's 'The Sailor's Mother', for instance, whose plots involve sailors who have been fatally injured in the war and whose parents are desperately trying to reach them in hospitals on the south coast. In some ways, the narrative of Llwyd's poem seems more benign than Wordsworth and Southey's near-contemporary verses on dying sailors and grieving parents – at least Owen returns to Anglesey apparently physically unharmed by his wartime experiences. But there is of course a twist in the crisis of the poem's conclusion. At its close, the poem is precisely about what happens when war comes home. 'Owen of Llangoed' describes the utterly unsustainable meeting-point between home and war in a way that recalls but refigures the catastrophic ending of Robert Merry's 'The Wounded Soldier' (1795), in which the soldier's lover instantly falls down dead on witnessing the 'horid [*sic*] guise' of his injuries.

The final lines of Merry's devastatingly polemical poem express a desire that the tale may prick the conscience of 'the self-call'd great' and 'shew the

Poor, how hard's the lot of those, / Who shed their Blood, for Ministers of State.'[44] Llwyd's verses make no such claim and yet the domestic tragedy of 'Owen of Llangoed' also figures the hardships brought on the poor by war, in a remote region of Wales. The poem suggests that the horrors of war, the seas of blood, witnessed by Owen are nothing to the news of his parents' death, while Owen's own death seems unreal, narratively forced, in the context of the rest of the poem – jolting and artificial. But perhaps this is the point. War and life on Anglesey never overlap in the narrative of 'Owen of Llangoed' and yet the devastations of war and a domestic, private or personal form of loss and grief seem brought so close together in this poem as to suggest a vital relationship between them. The private lives of Anglesey's Welsh-speaking people are, we sense, transformed through Owen's wanderlust and forced enlistment, through his absence and experiences at sea. Owen's sudden, overdetermined death illustrates the depth of his attachment to his family and to life on Anglesey – impossibly peaceful, sociable and harmonious in this poem. But more broadly it also signals the ways in which that life has been damaged or violated by the war taking place beyond its horizons.

The area across the water from Anglesey, especially Caernarfon, was suffering serious food shortages and unrest in the period 1800–1, or the period in which much of 'Owen of Llangoed' appears to be set.[45] It is no coincidence that Llwyd used the figure of Owen the shepherd-sailor to bring the war into the context of Anglesey at just this moment: there is a contemporary backdrop of real distress and desperation to Llwyd's domestic melodrama. The death that marks the end of the poem is caused not by the sight of a disfigured soldier, as in Merry's poem, but by a sense that a whole community and way of life has been fractured by a far-off war. The collection of examples in this essay suggests the range of Welsh poetic responses to war in the decade between 1794 and 1804. Taken together, they chorus distinctively Welsh but disparate voices: Iolo Morganwg's universalist political protests bring English radical anti-war sentiments into a Welsh bardic scene; ephemeral newspaper verses set the consequences of the war in particular regional contexts; Richard Llwyd outlines, in ironic and bitter detail, the impact of the war on Welsh-speaking communities. War rarely seems distant in these poems – rarely (if ever) mediated by newspapers or reports from afar. Instead the shocks of war ripple through people and places in the form of historical memory (often understood, we may sense, in terms of continuity with the present) and contemporary suffering, differently felt and differently interpreted in their Welsh contexts.

Notes

1 'J. C. Foregate-Street [Chester]', 'A few Thoughts upon the Horrors of Invasion', *Chester Chronicle*, 24 March 1797.

2 Stuart Curran, 'Introduction', in *idem* (ed.), *The Cambridge Companion to Romantic Literature* (Cambridge, 1993), p. xiii.

3 Alan Forrest, Karen Hagemann and Jane Rendall, 'Nations in Arms, People at War: Analysing War Experiences and Perceptions', in *eidem* (eds.), *Soldiers, Citizens and Civilians: Experiences and Perceptions of the Revolutionary and Napoleonic Wars, 1790–1820* (Basingstoke, 2009), pp. 1–22, at p. 1.

4 Betty T. Bennett discovered upwards of 3,000 war poems from the Revolutionary and Napoleonic years while researching her 1976 anthology of British war poetry. See 'Introduction', in Betty T. Bennett (ed.), *British War Poetry in the Age of Romanticism, 1793–1815* (New York, 1976), available online at *http://romantic. arhu.umd.edu/editions/warpoetry*, ed. Orianne Smith.

5 Mary Favret, *War at a Distance: Romanticism and the Making of Modern Wartime* (New Jersey, 2009), p. 9.

6 Simon Bainbridge, *British Poetry and the Revolutionary and Napoleonic Wars: Visions of Conflict* (Oxford, 2003), p. 55.

7 William Cowper, *The Task and Selected Other Poems*, ed. James Sambrook (London, 1994), Book IV, lines 100–2.

8 Favret, *War at a Distance*, pp. 23–4. The result is, Favret suggests, an 'affective, un-joined, inarticulate response to battles fought afar' (p. 24).

9 For a detailed account of this process, see Mary-Ann Constantine, '"This Wilder-nessed Business of Publication": The Making of *Poems, Lyric and Pastoral* (1794)', in Geraint H. Jenkins (ed.), *A Rattleskull Genius: The Many Faces of Iolo Morganwg* (Cardiff, 2005), pp. 123–45.

10 Edward Williams (Iolo Morganwg), 'Winter Incidents', *Poems, Lyric and Pastoral* (2 vols., London, 1794), I, pp. 126–7 (original emphasis). All further references by volume and page number to this edition, included in the text.

11 For war writing as a paper shield, see Mary Favret, 'Coming Home: The Public Spaces of Romantic War', *Studies in Romanticism*, 33, no. 4 (1994), 539–48, at 539. For the paper bullet counter-view, see Bainbridge, *British Poetry*, p. 31.

12 Mary Favret, 'Everyday War', *English Literary History*, 72 (2005), 605–33, at 617.

13 Matthew Cragoe and Chris Williams, 'Introduction', in *eidem* (eds.), *Wales and War: Society, Politics and Religion in the Nineteenth and Twentieth Centuries* (Cardiff, 2007), p. 1.

14 Landmark new editions of early Welsh literature began to appear from 1789 onwards. *Barddoniaeth Dafydd ab Gwilym* (London, 1789) reprinted the fourteenth-century poetry of Dafydd ap Gwilym, while *The Heroic Elegies and Other Pieces of Llywarç Hen* (London, 1792) provided the text, with an English translation, of a ninth-century Welsh story cycle. They were followed by *The Myvyrian Archaiology of Wales* (London, 1801–7), three volumes of Welsh medieval poetry and prose (some of which was forged by Iolo Morganwg). See Mary-Ann Constantine,

'Welsh Literary History and the Making of "The Myvyrian Archaiology of Wales"', in Dirk Van Hulle and Joep Leerssen (eds.), *Editing the Nation's Memory: Textual Scholarship and Nation-Building in Nineteenth-Century Europe* (Amsterdam, 2008), pp. 109–28.

[15] Anon., 'Hymn', *Cambridge Intelligencer*, 15 March 1794, at *http://romantic.arhu.umd.edu/editions/warpoetry/1794/1794_8.html*. The hymn was earlier sung at a fast-day meeting in Sheffield on 28 February 1794 – see *A Serious Lecture, for the Fast Day* (Sheffield, 1794), p. 19. These verses were also translated into Welsh by (among others) the Unitarian radical Tomos Glyn Cothi (I am grateful to Marion Löffler for this point).

[16] David Thomas (Dafydd Ddu Eryri), 'The Banks of the Menai', *The Monthly Register of Literature* (2 vols., London, 1793), II, pp. 17–18.

[17] Ian Haywood notes that *The Times* reported on the massacres throughout the second half of August and into September. *Bloody Romanticism: Spectacular Violence and the Politics of Representation* (Basingstoke, 2006), p. 70.

[18] Archibald Constable (ed.), *Letters of Anna Seward: Written Between the Years 1784 and 1807* (6 vols., Edinburgh, 1811), IV, p. 40, Anna Seward to the Revd T. S. Whalley, 4 September 1792.

[19] Ann Yearsley, 'Anarchy: A Sonnet', at *http://www.rc.umd.edu/editions/warpoetry/1796/1796_7.html*.

[20] Thomas Ryder, 'The Same in Verse [the 1158 battle of Tal-y-foel]', *Cambrian Register*, I (1796), 409–10.

[21] Shawna Lichtenwalner, *Claiming Cambria: Invoking the Welsh in the Romantic Era* (Newark, 2008), p. 162.

[22] Favret, *War at a Distance*, p. 10.

[23] Hester Piozzi, *Thraliana: The Diary of Mrs. Hester Lynch Thrale (later Mrs Piozzi) 1776–1809*, ed. Katherine C. Balderston (2 vols., Oxford, 1942), II, p. 905. Thomas Spence's *Pig's Meat*, III (1795), includes another farewell poem for the year that paints the horrors of 1794 in similar terms: a 'long – long year of massacre . . . stain'd with foulest crimes . . . Thy reign a register of blood' (61).

[24] Piozzi, *Thraliana*, p. 906.

[25] Joseph Hucks, *A Pedestrian Tour through North Wales. In a Series of Letters* (London, 1795), p. 3.

[26] Ibid., p. 52.

[27] David J. V. Jones, *Before Rebecca: Popular Protests in Wales, 1793–1835* (Cardiff, 1973), extensively documents distress and disturbances in Wales in this period.

[28] *CIM*, I, p. 765, David Thomas (Dafydd Ddu Eryri) to Iolo Morganwg, 4 July 1795. Similarly in 1804 the theme would be 'Invasion', reflecting the invasion crisis after the resumption of hostilities with France.

[29] Jones, *Before Rebecca*, p. 20.

[30] Published in Chester, the *Chester Chronicle* was (with its Tory counterpart the *Chester Courant*) the newspaper for north Wales. Articles, advertisements and even poetry in Welsh catered for the *Chronicle*'s north Wales readership, which extended as far as Machynlleth. See Marion Löffler, *Welsh Responses to the French Revolution:*

Press and Public Discourse 1789–1802 (Cardiff, 2012) for a full account of the *Chronicle*'s distribution network and contents.

31 Ibid., p. 142.

32 See *Chester Chronicle*, 13 February 1795, for Robinson's 'January, 1795', and 18 August 1797 for Smith's 'The Forest Boy'.

33 See ibid., 14 March 1794, for Russell and/or Sampson's 'The Horrors of War', which was probably copied from the *Morning Post* for 1 March 1794. It may be attributed to Russell and/or Sampson through its similarity – long sections of the two texts are identical – to passages of Russell and Sampson's *Review of the Lion of Old England* (1794), which was serialized in the radical Belfast newspaper the *Northern Star* in the autumn of 1793. See James Quinn, *Soul on Fire: A Life of Thomas Russell* (Dublin, 2002), pp. 106–15.

34 See *Chester Chronicle*, 27 March 1795, for Merry's 'The Wounded Soldier'.

35 Anon., 'For the Chester Chronicle', in ibid., 21 August 1795.

36 See Gwyn A. Williams, *Madoc: The Making of a Myth* (Oxford, 1987), and Caroline Franklin, 'The Welsh American Dream: Iolo Morganwg, Robert Southey and the Madoc Legend', in Gerard Carruthers and Alan Rawes (eds.), *English Romanticism and the Celtic World* (Cambridge, 2003), pp. 69–84, for in-depth discussions of the subject of Welsh emigration in the 1790s.

37 Jones, *Before Rebecca*, pp. 16–25.

38 NLW 13123B, f. 69.

39 NLW 13136A gives three inventories Iolo made of his books. A list dated 20 May 1794 includes 'Knoxes Essays', while another from January 1802 includes 'Art of Warr a Poem' – Fawcett's *The Art of War* (1795).

40 John S. Ellis, 'A Pacific People – A Martial Race: Pacifism, Militarism and Welsh National Identity', in Cragoe and Williams (eds.), *Wales and War*, pp. 15–37, discusses the development of this position in the nineteenth century.

41 Ibid.

42 Llwyd regularly published verses (sometimes anonymously) in the *Chester Chronicle* in the 1780s and 1790s but the ambitious *Beaumaris Bay* was his first book-length publication. It is to Llwyd what *Poems* is to Iolo – an unusual and in some ways ground-breaking debut intended to make the writer's name.

43 Owen returns home during a period in which 'Peace came down . . . Discord, *for a while, at least,* / To Death's dark caves descended' (I, p. 87 – my emphasis), suggesting the pause in the war between 1801 and 1803. For a further discussion of 'Owen of Llangoed', see the introduction to Elizabeth Edwards, *English-Language Poetry from Wales 1789–1806* (Cardiff, 2013).

44 Robert Merry, *The Wounded Soldier, A Poem* (London, 1795), p. 7.

45 Jones, *Before Rebecca*, pp. 23–5. The period 1800–1 saw serious disaffection in north-west Wales, in which troops were summoned to the area amid fears of a popular uprising. See *Correspondence, Relative to the Stationing of a Troop of the Fourth Regiment of Dragoons, in the County of Carnarvon* (2nd edn., Chester, 1801).

The Revd William Howels (1778–1832) of Cowbridge and London: the making of an anti-radical

STEPHEN K. ROBERTS

On 24 November 1832 the body of the Revd William Howels was laid to rest in the new Church of the Holy Trinity, Cloudesley Square, Islington. Several hundred mourners followed the hearse to the place of burial. Chief among them was Howels's brother, Captain Jonathan Howells, whose name was beginning to be known in south Wales for his part in suppressing the recent rising at Merthyr Tydfil.[1] The carriage of the Irish peer the first marquis of Cholmondeley followed closely behind, and the coffin was deposited in the vault donated by the rector, Mr Fell, that had originally been reserved for his own eventual interment.[2] Among those who contributed to the expansive inscription on the sealed tomb were Cholmondeley and the MP for Devonport, Sir Henry Grey.[3] Howels had been a Calvinist pulpit controversialist who had acquired a taste for controversy in Glamorgan in an age of revolution. One of London's celebrity preachers, his demise was announced by the *Cambrian* newspaper with the remark that he had done 'more to exalt the character of his countrymen in London than any other Welshman'.[4] Among those who attended his sermons and who later recalled his influence on them were figures as diverse as Cardinal Henry Manning and John Ruskin. After his death, no fewer than seven collections of his pulpit utterances were published. In biographical dictionaries, Welsh Calvinistic Methodists claimed him as one of theirs, although he proclaimed himself to be a life-long Anglican, and he found his way into the Victorian *Dictionary of National Biography*.[5] By 1877 he had posthumously acquired a doctorate, even though in life he never had any degree at all, and a *bardd gwlad* of the early twentieth century could refer to Howels as 'Cennad enwog Brenin Nef' (famous ambassador of the King of heaven) without need of further gloss to her local readers in the Vale of Glamorgan.[6] But posthumous reputation,

like fate, is fickle. Howels's stock plummeted after 1914. His entry in the
Dictionary of Welsh Biography is perfunctory, he is not mentioned at all in a
recent collection of essays on the London Welsh; the most authoritative
modern biographer of Ruskin dismisses Howels as a man of 'extraordinary
inability'; and so obscure has his name become that even the exact scholarship
enshrined in the new edition of *The Correspondence of Iolo Morganwg* fails to
identify him as the recipient of one of Iolo's letters.[7] The career and reputation
of Howels are worth re-examining for a number of reasons. He emerged
from the same milieu in the Vale of Glamorgan that helped shape Iolo
Morganwg and a range of other intellectual figures, in an age of ferment.
Despite this background, he found celebrity in the metropolis as a conservative
who espoused a variety of anti-radical causes. He published nothing but the
occasional comment in the press during his lifetime, and his modern biographer has constantly to contend with a persona for him that was crafted by
a number of admiring writers whose motives were as confessional and political
as they were biographical. This chapter seeks to identify the ingredients that
went into the making of Howels as a prominent voice in the London of
William IV on behalf of a variety of conservative, anti-radical causes; and
to examine the making of him in another sense, how a posthumous persona
of Howels was constructed by his admirers.

But first some biographical background. As modern drivers approaching
Cowbridge from the west leave the A48 down a spiralling short slip road
into the town, they pass an attractive Georgian property, Llwynhelyg. This,
when it was an unimproved farm-house, was the home of the Howels family
and where William was born in 1778. His father and earlier forebears were
farmers, having in successive generations moved in stages eastwards from
west Glamorgan.[8] His education in Cowbridge, though fractured, brought
him under the influence of a number of prominent intellectuals in the vale.
He was educated first at the private Eagle Academy in Cowbridge under
Thomas Williams, later taught as a private pupil by Dr William Williams of
the grammar school, and at fifteen went to study with John Walters, rector
of Llandough, author of *An English-Welsh Dictionary* (1770–94) and friend
and correspondent of Iolo Morganwg, arriving under Walters's care just as
the dictionary was completed. Regardless of Walters's virtues as a tutor, he
and Howels's family had a common background of associations with the
Margam estate, the Mansel Talbot family having been patrons of Walters and
landlords to the Howelses.[9] Howels went up to Wadham College, Oxford,
in 1800 and left in 1803 without taking a degree. He underwent a spiritual
conversion in Oxford through the Baptist ministry in the town, but despite
the evident significance of Old Dissent in his life at this point, Howels
remained in the Anglican Church and was ordained in 1804. He immediately

Figure 10. Portrait of William Howels by Thomas Overton, signed
by Howels. Published as frontispiece to *Sermons . . . by the Late
Rev. William Howels* (London, 1836). Signed copies of the
print were distributed to friends and relatives.

found a niche as curate of Llan-gan, near Cowbridge, where he assisted the
celebrated preacher David Jones. Jones died in 1810, and William Howels
was then left looking for a patron and advancement. Progress in the diocese
of Llandaff seemed to be blocked because of his association with Calvinistic
Methodism of the kind promoted by David Jones from within the Church
of England. In 1812 Howels moved to London, perhaps influenced by the
example of Jones, a frequent guest preacher in the metropolis, to be curate
in Blackfriars there, but again failed to secure a more substantive living.[10] In
1817, still in Anglican orders, he became the minister at Long Acre chapel
where he remained until his death in 1832.

Howels's fame rested on his fifteen years at Long Acre. There he preached
sermons that were strongly Calvinist and evangelical in tone and substance.
The evangelicalism in the Church of England at that time was marked by

an adherence to scriptural examples and citations in preaching; an emphasis on personal salvation through repentance and conversion; an abhorrence of ceremonies of any kind; a belief in predestination and the rest of the Calvinist apparatus that would have been familiar to Puritan preachers in England, Scotland and Wales of the seventeenth century. It was a strongly intellectual creed, with none of the emphasis on raw emotion, popular music and demonstrativeness that we associate with evangelicalism of the twenty-first century, or with the more demotic varieties of Methodism in Howels's own time. It was said that Howels dropped in to hear sermons at Jewin Welsh Calvinistic Methodist chapel when not preaching at Long Acre.[11] But he did not confine himself to preaching evangelical sermons. At Blackfriars collections were taken after his sermons for unexceptionable causes such as the local poor, the ward school and Sunday schools. He was also an active supporter of the Church Missionary Society, and so in a number of respects conformed to the pattern of wider social activity expected of a beneficed Anglican clergyman.[12]

In response to allegations that he was really a Methodist, Howels insisted that he was an episcopal Anglican, albeit of a Calvinist variety not dominant in the Church of England in his day. He gloried in his orthodoxy. He was critical of all new or old varieties of Christianity that emerged during his time at Long Acre to challenge his version of the orthodox. He attacked Socinians in his sermons, and when a cleric he regarded as a Socinian found a bishopric, Howels preached that 'the Devil has got the appointment of our bishops'.[13] He engaged in a bitter dispute with Edward Irving, a rival celebrity preacher who had begun to use his Church of Scotland chapel in London to promote his own distinctive Millenarian creed.[14] After the mid-1820s, from an imposing new chapel in Regent Square, and to Howels's disgust, Irving preached that the French Revolution had been one of the signs of the end of the world, and began to encourage speaking in tongues. These were the beginnings of what became known as the Irvingite or Catholic Apostolic Church, but that came after both Irving and his would-be nemesis, Howels, were both dead.[15] What above all singled out Howels among the preachers of Regency London was his anti-Catholicism. He staunchly opposed the campaign to win concessions for Roman Catholics which culminated in Catholic Emancipation in 1829. In 1822 he presented a petition to Sir Robert Peel and another one to the bishop of London on behalf of his congregation at Long Acre, deploring any concessions to Catholics.[16] Another of his petitions, on Ireland, urged Parliament to 'deprive the Roman Catholics of Ireland altogether of the elective franchise; to extinguish the Catholic Association; . . . to visit the ringleaders of agitation with condign punishment; to banish the Jesuits (now poisoning the youthful minds of the future legislators and governors of Britain) from every part of his majesty's dominions . . .'[17]

In 1827 the British Society for Promoting the Religious Principles of the Reformation was founded. At the time of writing it still exists as a registered charity and is now called the Protestant Reformation Society. It is today a somewhat shadowy body, whose members demonstrate publicly when a papal visit or any other perceived concession to Catholics is officially made, and it has historical affinities with the Orange Order.[18] Howels was an enthusiastic founder member, and Long Acre chapel was the first local association or 'auxiliary' to belong to it, with Howels as treasurer.[19] The Long Acre branch of the Reformation Society had seventy members. Howels's enthusiasm for the cause of anti-popery remained undimmed after what was to him the disaster of Catholic Emancipation in 1829. In his will of November 1832, drawn up immediately before his death, he left money to secure the election of 'Captain' Gordon to Parliament.[20] James Edward Gordon was one of the most extreme anti-Catholics to sit in the unreformed House of Commons before 1832. He was a founder of the Reformation Society and led a national No Popery crusade in 1834–6. He was of the same family as Lord George Gordon, eponymous agitator in the anti-Catholic Gordon Riots of 1780.[21] Gordon was the subject of a verse circulating round Parliament in 1832:

> If thou goest in the smoking room
> Three plagues will thee befall
> The chlorate of lime, and the 'baco-smoke
> And the captain who's worst of all
> The canting sea captain
> The lying sea captain
> The captain who's worst of all.[22]

But the view of the denizens of the smoking room was not shared by Howels, in whose reported opinion there was 'not a man in the House of Commons whose head comes up to Captain Gordon's shoulders'.[23] After Howels's death, so sensitive were his allies to the rumour that he had left a fund to elect MPs of his own anti-Catholic persuasion that a sermon was printed that repudiated it.[24]

So how do we account for Howels's progress from Pen-llin bookish lad, who had helped the Revd Walters with his dictionary, to celebrated London anti-Catholic of the 1830s? It is clear that at one time Howels had been a radical. During his time at the Eagle School, Cowbridge, he had taken the side of the Revolutionaries in France in 1789, and welcomed it as a good example for Wales, his mind being . . . impregnated with hatred towards the English, from reading Welsh history . . . I actually harangued my fellow scholars . . . on the propriety of shaking off the galling yoke of the Saxons. I told them that England was our own, and that the time was at length come when we should drive our enemies from the shores of England.[25]

In later life Howels remained acutely aware of English–Welsh tensions and differences, but by his maturity this had softened into wry humour. Addressing the London Hibernian Society, a body intent on Protestantizing Ireland, he recounted an incident in which a relative of Lord Talbot, journeying in north Wales and arrived at a swollen river, asked a by-standing labourer if it was safe to cross. The man replied in English that it was, but the horse refused to go. The traveller asked the same question in Welsh, and received the reply, 'Sir, I beg your pardon, I thought you were an Englishman. If you try to cross here, you will be drowned.'[26]

More profoundly, it is also clear that his early religious influences account for his hostility to 'Socinians', by which Howels meant anti-Trinitarians and those who played down or denied the divinity of Christ, of every denominational stripe, not just Unitarians. The Vale of Glamorgan of Howels's youth was a shifting sand of religious opinion, in which a Protestant congregation was often barely cohesive enough to merit the word 'denomination', with its connotations of settled identity. The Methodist congregation at Aberthin, a mile away from Llwynhelyg as the crow flies, seems to have been prone to unorthodox opinions. First, outbreaks of antinomianism and Sandemanianism provoked secessions from the cause there, but these were mere curtain-raisers to the controversy of 1796, which took place when Howels was a young man. Sabellianism, a 'heresy' that like Socinianism and Arianism challenged Trinitarian orthodoxy, saw the hugely influential Bible commentator Peter Williams expelled from the Methodists.[27] The Sabellians of Aberthin were driven out of the congregation amid scenes of disorder, but one of the Methodist trustees of Aberthin was Howels's mentor, David Jones of Llan-gan.[28] One of the consequences of the disturbances at Aberthin was the founding of the celebrated Independent chapel, Bethesda'r Fro, near St Athan, and we rely quite heavily on Iolo Morganwg, a first-hand witness of the Aberthin episode and a Unitarian, for our knowledge of it.[29] Rational Dissent was the common factor in these various challenges to Trinitarian orthodoxy, but the Methodists of the border vale were themselves hardly on the back foot, with crowds turning up to David Jones's monthly communion service at Llan-gan, *Sul pen mis*, and to his preaching meetings at Pen-coed.[30]

It was William Howels's task, when appointed curate to Jones, to combat not only the godlessness of the district, but also the farmers and tradesmen of the border vale who took independent, heterodox and controversialist stances on a variety of religious doctrines. In due course, Howels's territory as curate extended to St Mary Hill and Llandyfodwg, the latter parish including the hill country of modern-day Blackmill and Gilfach Goch.[31] He was evidently devoted to David Jones, to judge from Howels's encomium after Jones's death: 'My soul had a kind of existence in that man's soul; he was every thing that man could be to me. I imbibed his knowledge, and sought to catch a measure of his love to God and souls.'[32] It is against the background of these protracted controversies that Howels's acquaintance with Iolo Morganwg needs to be considered. In letter 867 of the Iolo Morganwg correspondence, Iolo writes in 1812 to enclose a copy of his Unitarian collection of hymns, *Salmau yr Eglwys yn yr Anialwch*. He takes the opportunity to blast Methodists and Evangelicals for their 'rancorous intolerance' and 'cant glaringly superstitious and fanatical', taking side-swipes at Trinitarians as he goes, before mellowing into a more conciliatory tone, recalling his 'many conversations', the wrangling 'a hundred times in conversation before' with the recipient, acknowledging the latter's ability to read Scripture 'in their original languages', recognizing too that his 'intentions', at least, were 'pure', and appealing for his concurrence in the wish that 'our religion' should 'be that of the Bible and the Bible alone'. One imagines Howels, having not long left Wales for London, receiving this parting gift with wry ambivalence, but probably also with pleasure of some kind on hearing from an old adversary whom, of course, he would first have encountered in his pupil age with John Walters.[33]

The powerful influence of David Jones explains much of Howels's outlook as he left Wales for London, driven by a failure to find a living after the death of his patron. Jones maintained his links with his curate, and though living mostly in Pembrokeshire in his last days, probably stayed occasionally with Howels on his visits to the Vale of Glamorgan.[34] Despite his early enthusiasm for the French Revolution, he was by this time doubtless as opposed to it as his mentor had been in 1797 after Jones had come very close to witnessing the landing of the French at Goodwick, an event worthy of prayers of thanksgiving for deliverance in the eyes of Jones and the Methodists; in Iolo's a comical episode.[35] The Welsh Calvinistic Methodists had no reason to admire the Revolution in France, even though it has been demonstrated conclusively that there was more to their opposition to it than their pessimism about the human condition or a simple 'Church-and-king' reflex against it, to use Iolo Morganwg's dismissive epigram.[36]

Richard Watson, bishop of Llandaff from 1782 until his death in 1816, had ordained Howels in 1804, but had from the outset marked him down as a Methodist, and did nothing to help his preferment in the Church.[37]

Perhaps it was Watson's hostility to Methodism that earned him the not easily won approval of Iolo.[38] After David Jones's death, the living of Llangan was denied him by the patron Thomas Wyndham of Dunraven, again apparently because of his Methodist leanings.[39] Howels's biographers emphasize his lack of interest in worldly possessions, but he had to live, and he was quite capable of putting himself forward for posts. For example, he wrote in 1813 to William Wilberforce, a champion of Evangelicals who had at his disposal a number of benefices, asking for his help in getting the living at St Margaret Lothbury, London, explaining frankly how the security of a parish appointment would remove his anxieties about money.[40] Only from 1817 did he finally achieve a measure of security, when he acquired the lease of Long Acre chapel. This stood at the western end of Long Acre, and was one of a number of episcopal chapels in London that harboured the difficult characters of the Church of England. Like others of its kind, Long Acre chapel was an anomaly. It was not a parish church, nor even a chapel-of-ease. It was unconsecrated, and Howels fought off criticisms of his ministry that pointed this out by adopting an essentially Nonconformist stance on the universality of God's presence.[41] His income depended entirely on the free will offerings of his congregation, and he lived, according to one source, on 'not so much as the wages of an ordinary mechanic'.[42] His situation effectively put him beyond the disciplinary reach of his bishop, however, and he was able to preach an anti-Catholic line not officially supported by the Anglican episcopate.

Clearly, Howels's career can be read as a long search for patronage which only ended in 1817, and the patrons of Long Acre were crucial in that search. Celebrity preachers were patronized by the wealthy and influential of London, and contemporary comment noted the line of expensive carriages parked in Long Acre on Sundays. Howels was highly regarded by a number of aristocratic devotees of his preaching style and content, among them Elizabeth Gordon, duchess of Gordon, a noted collector of evangelical clergy and also a collector of twenty or thirty London sermons by Howels at Gordon Castle in Scotland.[43] Others included Robert Jocelyn, third earl of Roden, Viscount and Viscountess Powerscourt, the second marquis of Cholmondeley and his wife (daughter of the sixth duke of Beaufort), Georgina, Lady Bathurst and of course Captain Gordon. It was said of Howels's congregation that 'Most came long distances, few from the immediate locality.'[44] What these upper class patrons had in common was a commitment to the Protestant Ascendancy in Ireland and a hostility towards political or religious concessions to Catholics. Most were strong Tories. They offered vigorous support to the Reformation Society and the newspaper most closely associated with it, *The Record*, which provided them with the contemporary label of 'Recordites'. Howels was thus implanted into a political and religious context far removed from that of the Vale of Glamorgan he had left in 1812. But certain continuities are visible. His first curacy in London was at St Ann Blackfriars, where the Methodist preacher from Aberthaw, Christopher Bassett, had ministered before 1778.[45] He was supported at Long Acre by the brothers Charles and the Revd Thomas Bowdler, nephews of Henrietta Maria Bowdler, who had more than once stood in the breach to rescue Iolo Morganwg from financial ruin.[46] This middle class element in the Long Acre congregation was probably dominant, and included the parents of the young John Ruskin. To judge from the names in the minutes of the Reformation Society, there was a significant Welsh element there, too. The Long Acre chapel was noted as a place 'where men of high standing in the religious and political world were accustomed to meet during the session of parliament', and thus Howels's fierce anti-radical position was bolstered by the Tory-supporting, Recordite, Reformation Society and Bible Society nexus to whom he was minister; while he in turn, from the pulpit and by pastoral support, encouraged their political interventions.[47]

Other influences in the making of Howels, or rather in the making of the written biography of Howels, were more literary. Howels's London was Dickens's London. Long Acre chapel was no more than a block away from Warren's blacking factory in which Charles Dickens famously worked as a child. Long Acre was not a fashionable address. Descriptions of it may be found in *Sketches by Boz*, in which it is the natural habitat of what Dickens calls 'shabby-genteel people'. It was a working-class district of 'brokers' and marine store shops' (a marine chandler's shop survives in the area to this day) and it was the centre of the coach-building trade. Not far from Long Acre is Seven Dials, then among the most poverty-stricken, notorious slums in the metropolis.[48] The attendance of the aristocrats at Long Acre chapel was decidedly *de haut en bas*. Nor was Howels's home address any more superior. He lived apparently throughout his time in London at Water Street, north of Blackfriars Bridge and in the shadow of the grim Bridewell prison. Commentators found his choice of residence inexplicable: it was 'a place which none but Mr Howels, or such a man as he, would ever have dreamed of singling out as his home'.[49]

The contrast between the grand patrons and their dependent pastor, ministering and living in lower-class parts of London, sets up further strange paradoxes. Though Howels was evidently a popular preacher, some said he was virtually unintelligible, as did Henry Manning on his first encounter with him. His voice was described as 'harsh . . . husky . . . greatly aggravated by a strong provincial accent and a bad enunciation'.[50] A number who listened to him commented on his voice. Manning, whose spiritual journey took him from among the rabid anti-Catholics of Long Acre to become a cardinal of the Catholic Church itself, referred to Howels as 'a crack-voiced Welshman'; another described Howels as having 'a harsh voice and a peculiar manner'.[51] The strange accent and pronunciation were of course from the Vale of Glamorgan, and the cracked voice was apparently a product of Howel's incessant smoking, a habit which, it was said, was another negative he brought with him from Wales.[52] Many asides about Howels emphasize his un-English voice, his smoking habit, his trouble understanding English mealtimes, and his sermon style, described as having 'more of the character of the Irish than the English pulpit'.[53] To London minds, evidently all Howels's more outlandish habits and traits could be ascribed to non-English origins.

Howels never published anything of substance on his own account, and fiercely resisted publication of his sermons by others while he lived.[54] But his corpse was literally barely cold when the task of fashioning his posthumous legacy began. No portrait of Howels was known to exist, but within a few hours of his death a cast was taken of his entire head, and Thomas Stothard proposed to create a life-size bust from it. Subscriptions were invited, but the project was derailed when it emerged that Howels had in fact sat for a portrait after all, by Thomas Overton. This was published as the frontispiece to the first volume of Charles Bowdler's *Sermons of the Rev. William Howels*.[55] For those who sought to capture his pulpit ministry, a prevalent metropolitan culture of extensive or even verbatim note-taking of sermons enabled the publication by different entrepreneurs soon after his death of seven editions of his prayers and sermons.[56] There were also biographical sketches, and reading these it is hard to avoid the impression that a persona was under construction of Howels as an *ingénu* or even a holy fool. Many anecdotes of Howels's 'eccentricities' have survived. There was the occasion when a number of gentlemen went to his quarters in Water Street, where they sat with Howels and his Welsh housekeeper. They went to consult the oracle on spiritual matters, but Howels said nothing but yes or no for the whole three hours of the consultation.[57] In the pulpit there were many homely but odd allusions and metaphors, which evidently commended themselves to Howels's hearers but which come across to us as peculiar in some respect or other. There was the story he told in a sermon of a good man 'persecuted by the papists' who hid in a cave and was saved from his enemies by a spider weaving a web across the mouth of a cave, which convinced his pursuers he could not be within. This was in fact no refugee from the papists, but Mohammed the prophet, as critics were quick to point out.[58] But alongside these come the remarks on his 'originality', on how 'striking' he was, on how 'profound' a theologian. From one of these commendations arises a ludicrous misreading by John Ruskin's biographer. Ruskin kept a letter written by Howels which Ruskin annotated. Ruskin writes that Howels was a man of 'extraordinary originality', which Tim Hilton has misread as 'extraordinary inability', going on to wonder why Ruskin and his parents wasted their time listening to a 'laughing-stock'.[59]

Howels's sermons and prayers were first published in a time of great ferment, in the 1830s just after the First Reform Act and in the heyday of Chartism. The causes Howels held dear struck a discordant note in a chorus of voices for emancipation and enfranchisement. Another round of the publication of his works took place between 1850 and 1854, the time of so-called 'Papal Aggression', when the Roman Catholic hierarchy was established in England, and in response broke out the most sustained burst of anti-Catholic sentiment since the Gordon Riots.[60] Howels was post-humously pushed into the breach to help defend the nation against popery. Probably all biographies of clergy are to some extent hagiographical, but the literary construct of Howels as a mix of the deeply spiritual, original and eccentric betrays the motives of the artificers of his life-story. His originality was his claim to being noticed by writers, while emphasis on his eccentricities and holy fool persona offered his biographers a way of minimizing his political commitedness and disarming him as a controversialist, so that his life could be presented as innocuous in what was in fact a deeply divisive and highly political battle against concessions to Catholics.

What is striking about the milieu in which Howels moved in London, as strongly in evidence at his funeral as during his ministry, is its self-consciously British character.[61] The aristocratic members of the Long Acre chapel were Irish, not English peers. Howels's comments on the Welsh and the English have been noted; he also professed himself devoted to the Irish and regretted he could not preach in the Irish language. He helped his friend, Charlotte Elizabeth Tonna, who wrote under her pen name, Charlotte Elizabeth, to set up sermons in Irish in London.[62] But this was Britishness through the medium of anti-Catholicism. Roden, Powerscourt and Cholmondeley all fought against any political or religious concessions to the Irish; Tonna considered her first missionary steps in London to be planted among 'the most wretchedly ignorant and bigotted of the Irish Romanists', later penning what her late Victorian biographer considered 'quite the best Orange songs that have been written'.[63] It has become clear that anti-Catholicism was not at a constant level of intensity between the Reformation and Catholic Emancipation in 1829, and indeed, the years of Howels's youth were, in British terms, a time when anti-Catholic prejudice was easing off.[64] He happened to arrive in the metropolis when defensive, Protestant Britishness was particularly vocal.

Howels moved to London from Glamorgan a decade after the Act of Union with Ireland and a couple of years before the battle of Waterloo ended twenty years of war with the French. His schoolboy response to the French Revolution, as a model to be emulated, gave way quickly enough to anti-popery by way of the Francophobia exhibited by the Calvinistic Methodists. The sluggish response in Wales to the siren call of the Reformation Society has persuaded Trystan Owain Hughes that Wales stood aloof from opposition to Catholic Emancipation and to other concessions to Catholics.[65] This is an inversion of Charles Bowdler's curious view in the 1830s that 'popery' itself 'never triumphed' in Wales.[66] Would Howels himself have believed this? In Glamorgan his main opponents had been the 'heretics' emboldened by Rational Dissent into challenging Trinitarianism, rather than Catholics. As for Bowdler, he may here have been echoing Iolo Morganwg, channelled through Henrietta Maria, his aunt. It has been demonstrated that Iolo had reasons of his own for 'writing Roman Catholicism out of his bardic narrative' and for insisting on the Protestantism of Ancient Britons; he directed more animus towards Calvinistic Methodists and Anglicans than towards Catholics.[67] The notion that Wales in the first half of the nineteenth century did not share in the anti-Catholicism of Britain as a whole has been dispelled by the findings of Paul O'Leary, the tolerance of radicals like Richard Price notwithstanding.[68] It would be facile to argue that when Howels left Cowbridge for London, he was moving from a Welsh context, in which Rational Dissent and the stirrings of the Romantic movement were dominant, to a metropolitan one where he was claimed by patriotism, fear of popery and the imperial potentialities of Great Britain. His own family personified British imperialism, after all: one of his brothers was a career soldier who fought in the Peninsular war; another died in Jamaica in 1835 after an entire career spent there as a planter.[69] From Wales Howels certainly took to London his brand of Anglican Calvinistic Methodism, his taste for controversy and the personal traits which made him a singular character in the city.

Howels's biographers have explained his theological tastes and distastes as if they were selected by him from a feast of religious ideology spread before him, but after his move to London, and certainly once he had become the minister at Long Acre, he was rather hemmed in, as an Evangelical Calvinist in the episcopal church, without a parish and dependent on a certain kind of lay patronage. What makes Howels's example distinctive is this patronage and the part it played in sustaining him. It is hard to see how in Wales he could have created an eyrie for himself as he did at Long Acre. In Wales he might have found a single patron, as his mentor Jones did at Llan-gan, but he would have been subject to episcopal discipline. If he had 'come out' as a Methodist, he would have been similarly constrained by the polity of that church. The episcopal chapels, themselves deserving further study, together with a range of wealthy and politically well-connected lay patrons and backers, gave him licence to express both his 'originality' and his 'eccentricity'. As Iolo Morganwg's letter of 1812 to Howels makes clear, the two men had moved in different directions since their many debates. In 1819 the celebrated Carmarthen eisteddfod is said to have pitted Iolo against Thomas Burgess, the monoglot English bishop of St David's: bullish Rational Dissent versus Anglicanism at bay.[70] Both the career and associations of William Howels tend to muddy rather than clarify this neat polarity. Having been denied a living, Howels had little reason to be grateful to the episcopate, but the 'Ultra-Tory' Burgess put his full weight behind the Reformation Society in 1829, one of only two bishops to be vice-presidents, and like Howels he was in active support of a range of Anglican voluntary societies.[71] But if Howels and Burgess shared an anti-Catholic, British and evangelical vision briefly, the future was to show how much of Howels's success was of its own particular time. After his death, a number of his clergy associates, such as Baptist Noel (destined in 1848 for the Baptist ministry, where his principles as well as his name seemed naturally at home) seceded from the Church of England.[72] Richard Basset, a friend of Howels, was said to be the last Calvin-istic Methodist Anglican clergyman in Wales.[73] By the 1850s the coals of anti-popery needed to be blown upon to keep them glowing, Long Acre chapel itself was demolished in 1866, and today Howels's principles are unpopular, even downright rebarbative.[74] In his pomp in London, Howels was without doubt a Tory voter, but was he really at heart a Tory? He was devoted to the constitution as it had been settled in 1688, to Calvinism and to biblicism; was hostile to popery, to popular enthusiasm in religion such as speaking in tongues and Millenarianism. In this and in the sense that people had of him that he was from a time and place other than 1820s London, he seems less a Regency Tory than a country Whig of a much earlier period, who would have rejoiced at the victories of William III in Ireland. In essence, William Howels may never have moved far from the natural loyalties of the Vale of Glamorgan farming stock whence he came.

Notes

[1]   Gwyn A. Williams, *The Merthyr Rising* (London, 1978), pp. 124, 141, 219. The brothers seem consistently to have spelled their names as given here, differently from each other. For particular help in my research on Howels, I am grateful to Cathryn Charnell-White, Mary-Ann Constantine, Ffion Mair Jones, Diane Tyler of the Ruskin Library at Lancaster University and John Wolffe. I am also grateful to the participants at the Association of Welsh Writing in English conference, Gregynog, April 2011, for discussion on a first version of this chapter.

[2]   *The Record*, 26 November 1832.

3   Charles Bowdler, *Sermons . . . by the Late Rev. William Howels* (2nd edn., 2 vols., London, 1836), II, frontispiece and p. x.

4   *Cambrian*, 29 December 1832.

5   John Morgan Jones and William Morgan, *The Calvinistic Methodist Fathers of Wales*, trans. John Aaron (2 vols., Edinburgh, 2008), translated from John Morgan Jones and William Morgan, *Y Tadau Methodistaidd* (2 vols., n.p., 1895–7), II, pp. 463–77; Joseph Evans, *Biographical Dictionary of Ministers and Preachers of the Welsh Calvinistic Methodist Body* (Caernarfon, 1907), pp. 124–7.

6   *Special Religious Services in Theatres, Halls and Mission Rooms [Report of the eighteenth winter course of these services for the people]* (London, 1877), p. 5; Mary A. Richard (Mair Tir Iarll), *Y Pren Pêr* (Caerdydd, n.d.), p. 13.

7   E. Jones (ed.), *The Welsh in London, 1500–2000* (Cardiff, 2001); Tim Hilton, *John Ruskin: The Early Years, 1819–1859* (New Haven, 1985), p. 20; *CIM*, III, pp. 107–11, Iolo Morganwg to William Howell, 23 June 1812.

8   West Glamorgan Archives Service, NAS/Gn E21/48, 56. For the essentials of Howels's biography, see *DNB* and *ODNB*, both based on Bowdler, *Sermons*, and E. Morgan, *A Brief Memoir of the late Rev. W. Howels* (London, 1854).

9   Cardiff 4.505, f. 3.

10 For Jones's London connections, see Edwin Welch (ed.), *Two Calvinistic Methodist Chapels 1743–1811* (London, 1975), pp. 60, 73, 74, 79, 81, 84.

11 Evans, *Biographical Dictionary*, p. 125.

12 For collections after services taken by Howels at Blackfriars, see Guildhall Library 4512. For Howels and the Church Missionary Society, see University of Birmingham, CMS Archive, G/AC 1/2, p. 474; G/AC 3, William Howels to Dandeson Coates, 22 April 1824; G/AC 3, opinion by E. Sugden, E. V. Sidebotham, 25 February 1833.

13 James Grant, *The Metropolitan Pulpit* (2 vols., London, 1839), I, p. 97.

14 Morgan, *A Brief Memoir*, pp. 88, 182–4.

15 For Irving, see *ODNB* and many references in Grayson Carter, *Anglican Evangelicals* (Oxford, 2001), esp. pp. 172–6, 179–82.

16 BL Add 40347, f. 46.

17 Bowdler, *Sermons*, I, pp. ciii–civ.

18 The Orange Order in Manchester is the '3rd Earl of Roden Memorial Loyal Orange Lodge No. 184': *http://www.manchesterorange.co.uk/Home*. Roden was a supporter and mourner of Howels.

19 *First Annual Report, British Society for Promoting the Religious Principles of the Reformation* (London, 1828), p. 19. John Wolffe, *The Protestant Crusade in Great Britain 1829–1860* (Oxford, 1991), p. 42, has Long Acre as the second auxiliary. Wolffe points out that differences exist between copies of the *First Annual Report* in the Bodleian Library and the BL (p. 329).

20 The National Archives, PROB 11/1809, f. 87ᵛ.

21 *ODNB*.

22 Quoted in Philip Salmon, 'Gordon, James Edward', in D. R. Fisher (ed.), *History of Parliament: The Commons, 1820–32* (7 vols., Cambridge, 2009), V, p. 307.

Chlorate of lime was thought to prevent cholera, then widespread in English and Welsh conurbations.

23   *The Record*, 26 November 1832.

24   H. Melvill, *A Sermon Preached at Long Acre* (3rd edn., London, 1832), p. 42.

25   Morgan, *A Brief Memoir*, p. 181.

26   *Leisure Hour* (March 1894), 329, quoting from *Sunday at Home*, DCCIII, 19 October 1867, 667.

27   Jones and Morgan, *The Calvinistic Methodist Fathers*, I, p. 685; Gomer M. Roberts, *Emynwyr Bethesda'r Fro* (Llandysul, 1967), pp. 21–30.

28   Roberts, *Emynwyr Bethesda'r Fro*, pp. 22, 28; R. B. Higham, *The Rev. David Jones Llan-gan, 1736–1810, and his Contribution to Welsh Calvinistic Methodism* (Lampeter, 2009), p. 76; Branwen Jarvis, 'Iolo Morganwg and the Welsh Cultural Background', in Geraint H. Jenkins (ed.), *A Rattleskull Genius: The Many Faces of Iolo Morganwg* (Cardiff, 2005), p. 41.

29   *CIM*, II, pp. 12–17, Iolo Morganwg to Theophilus Lindsey, 10 February 1797.

30   Higham, *The Rev. David Jones*, p. 83.

31   Bowdler, *Sermons*, I, p. xlix. For the godlessness of the area around Llan-gan, see J. Hughes, *Methodistiaeth Cymru* (3 vols., Wrecsam, 1851–6), III, p. 54.

32   T. C. Evans (Cadrawd), 'David Jones', *Cymru*, XXIII (1902), 18, probably quoting from *Sunday at Home*, DCCI, 5 October 1867, 629.

33   The editors of *CIM* have settled on the Revd William Howell (1740–1822) of Swansea as the recipient of this letter (which, it should be noted, is preserved as an unfinished draft). Howell was a Presbyterian and an Arian, seemingly unwilling to follow the logical drift of his denomination, rooted both in Old and Rational Dissent, into Unitarianism. Howell was evidently a spent force by 1812, and it is hard to see why Iolo should have worked himself up, as he does in this letter, if he was writing to one who was not a Calvinist but not a Unitarian either. The letter is plainly a pugnacious challenge to one with whom Iolo was used to arguing, and it is not clear how Iolo would have encountered Howell 'a hundred times before', or why the nearly blind Howell would have been in London. But the key point is in the addressing of the letter: to the 'Rev. William Howels, London', using Howels's consistent spelling of his own name. See *CIM*, III, p. 107, n. 1.

34   In May 1810 Jones stayed with the Revd Mr Howels of '*Lanvrane*', which Gomer M. Roberts thought was probably a reference to Howell Howells of Trehill. But *Llanfrynach* was the parish in which Howels's home, Llwynhelyg, stood. Gomer M. Roberts, 'David Jones, Llangan's Last Diary, 1810', *Cylchgrawn Hanes y Methodistiaid Calfinaidd*, XXXIII, no. 2 (1948), 50.

35   Idem, 'The Year 1797 in the Life of the Rev. David Jones, Llangan', *Cylchgrawn Hanes y Methodistiaid Calfinaidd*, XXIII, no. 4 (1938), 101; R. Watcyn James, 'Ymateb y Methodistiaid Calfinaidd Cymraeg i'r Chwyldro Ffrengig', *Cylchgrawn Hanes y Methodistiaid Calfinaidd*, new series, 12/13 (1988–9), 47; Mary-Ann Constantine, *The Truth against the World: Iolo Morganwg and Romantic Forgery* (Cardiff, 2007), p. 149.

36   James, 'Ymateb y Methodistiaid Calfinaidd Cymraeg', pp. 35–60.

37   Morgan, *A Brief Memoir*, p. 73.

38   *CIM*, I, pp. 646–50, Iolo Morganwg to John Walters, 21 January 1794; ibid., pp. 795–7, Iolo Morganwg to the Clergy of the Town and Neighbourhood of Cowbridge [?1796].

39   Jones and Morgan, *The Calvinistic Methodist Fathers*, II, p. 469, an account inaccurate as to dates and other details.

40   Bodleian, Wilberforce, d. 17.

41   *Special Religious Services in Theatres, Halls and Mission Rooms*, p. 5.

42   *Sunday at Home*, DCCI, 629.

43   Ibid., DCCII, 12 October 1867, 648.

44   Ibid., DCCI, 647–8.

45   Jones and Morgan, *The Calvinistic Methodist Fathers*, II, p. 189.

46   *ODNB* s.n. John Bowdler (1783–1815) and Thomas Bowdler the younger (1782–1856). Thomas Bowdler subscribed to Howels's Memorial Inscription; Charles Bowdler was his executor and first biographer.

47   Morgan, *A Brief Memoir*, p. 105.

48   Jerry White, *London in the Nineteenth Century* (London, 2007), pp. 11, 56, 175; Michael Slater (ed.), *The Dent Uniform Edition of Dickens' Journalism: Sketches by Boz and Other Early Papers, 1833–39* (London, 1996), pp. 176, 261.

49   Grant, *The Metropolitan Pulpit*, I, p. 94; *Sunday at Home*, DCCI, 630; Bowdler, *Sermons*, I, p. clvi.

50   Grant, *The Metropolitan Pulpit*, I, p. 100.

51   E. S. Purcell, *Life of Cardinal Manning* (2 vols., London, 1895), I, pp. 64, 68; F. L. Bevan, *The Peep of Day* (London, 1908), pp. 24–5.

52   Bowdler, *Sermons*, I, pp. lvii–lix.

53   William Prior Moore, *Remains of the Rev. William Howels* (Dublin, 1833), p. x.; *The Quiver*, XIX (January 1884), 32.

54   Bowdler, *Sermons*, I, pp. cxxv–cxxvii; Lancaster University, Ruskin Library, Bembridge, L41; *Sunday at Home*, DCCI, 631.

55   *The Record*, 26 November, 6 December, 10 December 1832; for Stothard, see *ODNB*; for other portraits by Overton (active 1818–38), see National Portrait Gallery Online Collection at *http://www.npg.org.uk/*.

56   In addition to Bowdler, op. cit., Moore, *Remains of the Rev. William Howels*; William Howels, *Two Sermons* (London, 1835); idem, *Sermons on the Lord's Prayer; to which is added, a Sermon on Spiritual Worship* (London, 1835); idem, *Twenty Sermons*, ed. W. Bruce (London, 1835), idem, *Fifty-Two Sermons . . . taken from notes by H. H. White* (London, 1836), idem, *Prayers of the late Rev. W. H. as delivered before and after the Sermon* (London, 1835).

57   Grant, *The Metropolitan Pulpit*, I, pp. 106–7.

58   *British Critic*, XVII (January 1835), 156.

59   Lancaster University, Ruskin Library, Bembridge, L41; Michael Wheeler, *Ruskin's God* (Cambridge, 1999), p. 4, quoting from Hilton, *John Ruskin: The Early Years*, p. 20.

60   Wolffe, *The Protestant Crusade*, p. 2. Morgan, *A Brief Memoir* (1854), pp. 293–4, makes explicit the continuing relevance of Howels to the cause of anti-Catholicism;

other products of this period were W. P. Moore, *Remains of the Rev. William Howels* (2nd ed., London, 1852), W. Bruce (ed.), *Choice Sentences* (London, 1850).

[61] For anti-Catholicism in the British context, see Linda Colley, *Britons: Forging the Nation 1707–1837* (London, 1992), pp. 324–34.

[62] Morgan, *A Brief Memoir*, p. 189; Charlotte Elizabeth, *Personal Recollections* (London, 1841), pp. 307, 336.

[63] Elizabeth, *Personal Recollections*, p. 304; D. J. O'Donoghue, 'Charlotte Elizabeth Tonna', *DNB*.

[64] Linda Colley, 'Radical Patriotism in Eighteenth-Century England', in Raphael Samuel (ed.), *Patriotism, The Making and Unmaking of British National Identity* (London, 1989), pp. 181–4; Wolffe, *The Protestant Crusade*, pp. 13–17.

[65] Trystan Owain Hughes, 'Anti-Catholicism in Wales, 1900–1960', *The Journal of Ecclesiastical History*, LIII (2002), 313.

[66] Bowdler, *Sermons*, I, pp. xlvi–xlvii.

[67] Cathryn A. Charnell-White, *Bardic Circles* (Cardiff, 2007), pp. 70–2, 172.

[68] Paul O'Leary, 'When was Anti-Catholicism? The Case of Nineteenth- and Twentieth-Century Wales', *The Journal of Ecclesiastical History*, LVI (2005), 308–25; *idem*, 'A Tolerant Nation? Anti-Catholicism in Nineteenth-Century Wales', in R. R. Davies and Geraint H. Jenkins (eds.), *From Medieval to Modern Wales: Historical Essays in Honour of Kenneth O. Morgan and Ralph A. Griffiths* (Cardiff, 2004), pp. 197–213. For an example of Price's sympathy for Catholics, see W. Bernard Peach and D. O. Thomas (eds.), *Correspondence of Richard Price* (3 vols., Durham, 1983–94), II, pp. 190–1.

[69] Jones and Morgan, *The Calvinistic Methodist Fathers*, I, p. 463; P. Wright (ed.), *Memorial Inscriptions of Jamaica* (London, 1966), p. 295.

[70] Geraint H. Jenkins, 'The Unitarian Firebrand, the Cambrian Society and the Eisteddfod', in *idem* (ed.), *Rattleskull Genius*, pp. 269–92.

[71] Wolffe, *The Protestant Crusade*, pp. 24, 37, 52.

[72] Carter, *Anglican Evangelicals*, pp. 312–55.

[73] Jarvis, 'Iolo Morganwg and the Welsh Cultural Background', p. 41.

[74] *Sunday at Home*, DCCI, 628.

Index